CW01676853

The Picturesque

The term *picturesque* once meant a radical blurring of art and life – a reordering of hierarchies of taste and of relations between the arts of architecture, painting and landscaping. Today, the idea of understanding experience through images is so ubiquitous and the technology for doing this so sophisticated, that the word picturesque is frequently used to describe aesthetic failure, trivial cultural products and naïve tastes.

In this fresh and authoritative account of the picturesque, John Macarthur presents the eighteenth-century idea in the light of its reception and affects on modern culture. The series of essays explains the theory of the picturesque thematically, drawing on its history and present issues as much as on its original formulation. Macarthur offers a major overview of the picturesque: what the concept of the 'picture' does in the picturesque and how this relates to modern theories of the image; and where visual values such as 'irregularity' become the basis of modern architectural planning.

The picturesque is a matter of cultural history, yet there is little understanding of how its concepts and techniques remain at work in contemporary culture. This is an important new account, which will make engaging reading for all those studying architecture, art history, cultural history or visual studies.

John Macarthur is Reader in Architecture at the University of Queensland, Australia, where he teaches design and the history and theory of architecture.

The Classical Tradition in Architecture

Series Editor: Caroline van Eck, *Leiden University, Netherlands*

Classical architecture not only provided a repertoire of forms and building types capable of endless transformation; it was also a cultural actor and provided cultural capital, and was used to create political and religious identities. This series provides a forum for its interdisciplinary study, from antiquity to the present day. It aims to publish first-class and groundbreaking scholarship that re-examines, reinterprets or revalues the classical tradition in the widest sense. The series will deal with classicism as a cultural phenomenon, a formal language of design, but also with its role in establishing the agenda, method and grammar of inquiry in Western history of art and architecture and recent reconsiderations of these roles.

Power and Virtue
Architecture and intellectual change in England 1660–1730
Li Shiqiao

Landscapes of Taste
The art of Humphry Repton's Red Books
André Rogger

The Picturesque
Architecture, disgust and other irregularities
John Macarthur

The Florentine Villa
Architecture History Society
Grazia Gobbi Sica

Architecture, Print Culture and the Public Sphere in Eighteenth-Century France
Richard Wittman

Festival Architecture
Edited by Sarah Bunnemaison and Christine Macy

The City Rehearsed
The architectural worlds of Hans Vredeman de Vries
Christopher Heuer

Architecture, the City, and the Public in Eighteenth-Century France
A reader
Edited by Richard Wittman

The Picturesque

Architecture, disgust and other irregularities

John Macarthur

Routledge
Taylor & Francis Group
LONDON AND NEW YORK

First published 2007
by Routledge
2 Park Square, Milton Park, Abingdon, Oxon OX14 4RN

Simultaneously published in the USA and Canada
by Routledge
711 Third Avenue, New York, NY 10017, USA

Routledge is an imprint of the Taylor & Francis Group, an informa business

Cover image: Kenneth Browne (with Priscilla Baschieri-Salvadori),
'The Quay and University, Civilia', 1971
Cover design: Ricardo Felipe

Typeset in Galliard by Keystroke, 28 High Street, Tettenhall, Wolverhampton

British Library Cataloguing in Publication Data
A catalogue record for this book is available from the British Library

Library of Congress Cataloging in Publication Data
Macarthur, John, 1958–
The picturesque : architecture, disgust and other irregularities / John Macarthur.
p. cm. — (The classical tradition in architecture)
Includes bibliographical references and index.
1. Picturesque, The, in architecture. 2. Aesthetics, Modern. I. Title.
NA209.3.M33 2007
701'.18—dc22
2007001879

ISBN10: 1–84472–141–8 (hbk)
ISBN10: 1–84472–011–X (pbk)

ISBN13: 978–1–84472–141–2 (hbk)
ISBN13: 978–1–84472–011–8 (pbk)

In memory of Natalie and Jock Macarthur

Contents

List of figures and credits

5.13 Gordon Cullen, '1915 Well Hall Estate, Eltham', *Townscape*, London: Architectural Press, 1961: page 165. By permission of RIBA Library Photographs Collection.
5.14 The Editor, 'The First Half Century', *The Architectural Review* 101 (1947): page 31. By permission of RIBA Library Photographs Collection.
5.15 & 5.16 Kenneth Browne (with Priscilla Baschieri-Salvadori), 'Swan Wharf, Civilia', fig. 64, page 66; and 'The Quay and University, Civilia' (also cover image), fig. 92, pages 90–91, in Ivor de Wolfe ed. *Civilia: The End of Sub Urban Man: A Challenge to Semidetsia*, London: Architectural Press, 1971. By permission of RIBA Library Photographs Collection.
6.1 John Vanbrugh, Blenheim Palace, Oxfordshire, design *c*.1705. Photograph © John Macarthur (1984).
6.2 Carlo Maderno, S. Susanna, Rome, 1597–1603. Photograph © John Macarthur (1994).

Illustration credits

The author and publishers gratefully acknowledge the above for permission to reproduce material in the book. Every effort has been made to contact copyright holders for the permission to reprint material in this book. The publishers would be grateful to hear from any copyright holder who is not acknowledged here and will undertake to rectify any errors or omissions in future editions of the book.

Preface and acknowledgements

One of the first lectures I heard as a university student was on the eighteenth-century gardens of Stowe, in Buckinghamshire. As I was studying architectural design at an Australian university, perhaps this should have struck me as odd, but it did not; and my experience was not uncommon. Teachers of architecture, then and now, maintain a degree of property in the cranky eighteenth-century concept of the picturesque, which is an historical curiosity for most other disciplines, including landscape architecture. This is because landscape gardens of the period provide a vivid illustration of important points of modern architectural technique and a concept of design for durational experience. Gardens show how, without a programme of uses, without the logic of building construction or even of enclosure, space can be formed by attending to what is seen from where, and in what sequence. Now, any garden – Chinese or Italian, ancient or modern – indeed, many natural landscapes and unplanned 'townscapes' are amenable to this kind of recognition and analysis. But there is usually a certain privilege given in such discussions to Stowe, Stourhead, Sherringham, to an original scene: the English garden, in which the concept of this visual and spatial understanding was first reached and its fundamental weakness was also revealed. Doubtless, this privilege given to the picturesque was typical of an education that centred on the European canon and was heavily biased towards Britain, but it also has something to do with the meaning of the picturesque for architects, and the way in which this term, to a greater extent than others from the history of gardening or architecture, raises issues about the perception of images and spaces, which are very much alive for designers today.

Christopher Hussey begins his brilliant book, *The Picturesque: Studies in a Point of View*, with an anecdote of his discovery of the concept, and my memoir above is intended to parallel his, but also to highlight some differences. In the 1920s, Hussey discovered in his grandfather's study at Scotney Castle, Kent, a copy of Sir Uvedale Price's *Essays on the Picturesque*. In doing so, he realized that what he had taken for the natural good taste of his family and class was, in fact, a particular kind of aesthetic training with which his grandfather had made the house and the landscape around him (with the help of William Sawrey Gilpin and Anthony Salvin). Hussey then set out to reveal the theory and history of what had become the hidden sub-structure of English taste in his time. By contrast, I learned the picturesque at university through texts such as Hussey's; and I did so in Australia, with a slight, self-conscious distaste for the patrimony of English culture (never having seen Kent, and reading Hussey on the beach). More significantly, I understood the picturesque through the practice of the design studio and through books such as Mitchell's *The Poetics of Gardens* and Cullen's *Townscape*, where, to all intents and purposes, the picturesque was another account of what Le Corbusier described as the ***promenade architecturale***. Equally uninterested in the history and the Englishness of the picturesque, I learnt it not as a 'point of view' but as technique and a concept of technique. In doing so, I was learning the picturesque somewhat anachronistically, as both it and the accumulation of its effects since 1800.

When I turned from the study of design to focus on history and theory, it seemed obvious to me that the picturesque was at the base of much contemporary culture, particularly intersections between the visual arts and architecture. Questions of composition in painting, I thought, could be best understood in relation to the same issue in architecture or landscape, where there was no frame. The articulation of camera and viewpoint in cinema seemed to have the same basis as the planning of buildings. I avidly read into eighteenth-century texts on the picturesque, modern aesthetic and artistic concepts such as the 'as-found' and 'appropriation'. Yet, when I tried to discuss my views with contemporaries in university departments of art history and cultural studies, my ideas were met with bemusement. Why would I choose to connect such issues around the picturesque? When I began to study the topic systematically, I was quickly overwhelmed with the particularities of the society and politics of eighteenth-century Britain, which drew the topic further and further from the purposes in architecture through which I had first understood it.

When I later had the opportunity to study in Britain, with the guidance to read the original materials and with the objects of the picturesque laid around me, I felt that I could set right an account of the eighteenth-century picturesque. My aim was not to challenge the position of Hussey (which was by then greatly substantiated by David Watkin) but to emphasize those traits of the picturesque which are relevant to architects now over the story of how the picturesque influenced the development of architecture in Britain. My research was accepted where it was important at the time, but when I began to present my ideas more widely, a realization and a difficulty arose. Cultural historians could not see, or did not accept, the architectural logic that gave my account different emphases to the existing scholarship; and architects did not see anything other than curiosity in discussing the fundaments of modern architectural technique in the idiosyncratic language of gentlemen aesthetes of the turn of the nineteenth century. Architects now, like Hussey then, are so imbued with the picturesque that it is invisible to them. They are unaware of the quite definite history of techniques and issues, particularly in the planning of buildings and towns, which bind them to the picturesque. At the same time, scholars of cultural history and visual culture have had little occasion to realize that this continuity of technique in architecture is a privileged point for understanding the system of the arts in modernity, the relation of disciplines and media, and of art to aesthetics. And so, I began this book by turning a variety of invitations to write and speak into occasions to look at the picturesque thematically and to do so drawing on its later history as much as on its original formulation. I attempted to marshal the resources of scholarship around a model of the picturesque quite like my first naïve and ruthless appropriation of the concept.

As this book has had such a long gestation I have many colleagues, friends and students at the universities of Queensland, Griffith, Cambridge and RMIT, who have helped in forming my interests, quietening my enthusiasms and showing me my errors – I thank them all. Similarly, the members of the Society of Architectural Historians, Australia and New Zealand, have been very patient and supportive in receiving perennial papers on the picturesque at their annual conferences.

In the 1980s as a young researcher I had the good fortune to be taught by some perceptive and original thinkers who directly contributed to the agenda that became this book. I'd like to acknowledge the help and inspiration of Anne Freadman, Jeffery Minson, Ian Hunter, Beverly Brown, Joseph Rykwert, Mark Cousins and Robin Evans. Brit Andresen gave the lecture about Stowe that I recall. In preparing the book I've been assisted by comments and advice on various parts of the text by: Mathew Aitchison, Greg Bamford, Donald Barry, Christopher Brisbin, Beverly Brown, Mark Dorrian, Pedro Guedes, Rosemary Hawker, Mark Hiley, Michael Hill, Mark Jarzombek, Andrew Leach, Li Shiqiao, Andrew McNamara, Antony Moulis, Shane Murray, Nicholas Ray, Charles Rice, Christoph Schnoor, Naomi Stead, William Taylor, Anthony Vidler and Andrew Wilson. In particular my ideas of Le Corbusier's planning, and the significance of Townscape, rely in part on research that Antony Moulis and Mathew Aitchison have undertaken for their PhDs under my direction. I was able to develop my ideas because of opportunities to speak and to publish and I thank the editors and referees of the journals and conference proceedings who have published preliminary versions of this work.

I was able to write the book because of the support of the Australian Research Council, whose generous Discovery Grant has relieved me of some of my teaching duties and provided other assistance from 2003 to 2006. Similarly the University of Queensland has given tangible support, which made the research and the preparation of the book possible. I've also been fortunate in the last few years to have had assiduous and sympathetic research assistants: Victoria Hamilton, Angela Hirst, Jacquie Maestracci and Anna Tweeddale who have hunted references, images and permissions. I am particularly grateful to Angela Hirst for her careful and thorough text-editing. I am also grateful for the help and advice of the series editor Caroline van Eck and Caroline Mallinder at Routledge.

My wife Rosemary Hawker knows more about this book than anyone else, having seen the ideas develop over twenty years. She asked me some of the more difficult questions at the beginning of my project, which have helped me frame my approach, and which I trust that she will agree I have now answered. I am deeply grateful for her personal and intellectual support.

1
Introduction

In modern usage Picturesque = quaint, a meaning having almost nothing in common with the eighteenth century use of the term.

(Hubert de Cronin Hastings, *The Architectural Review*, 1944[1])

Looking at the world as if it were a picture is a relatively recent activity. The practice adopted the word 'picturesque' from the language of painting in the eighteenth century, and the possibilities of pictorial vision underlie much subsequent thought on nature, landscape, buildings and urban form. Today, understanding experience through images is ubiquitous and its accompanying technology so sophisticated that the term 'picturesque', which once meant a radical blurring of art and life, is frequently used as a synonym for aesthetic failure, trivial cultural products and naïve tastes. This popular understanding is consistent with a bifurcation in academic study of the picturesque, where it is generally understood in two ways that are mildly contradictory. 'The picturesque' is said to have been of value in its time, but in its present usage, is seen as a pathological remnant. It is as if we are speaking of two concepts: an eighteenth-century picturesque theory and practice that is valued; and the historical consequences of this in popular practices and tastes that become less worthy the further they are removed from an original theory and historical circumstance.

This received impression of the picturesque is not untrue but it is simplistic. First, the theoretical aspects of the picturesque have been enormously successful in underpinning numerous tropes and strategies of modern art and architecture that have nothing to do with cloying images of rural life. Second, and more importantly, this split between a naïve and a critical picturesque, is not in the first place one of history. It already existed in eighteenth-century texts and debates: this is what gave the picturesque its critical edge. At the moment of its emergence, and faithfully since, the picturesque has provided an ever-refreshing image of a precocious aesthetics; as if 'the picturesque' were a name already prepared for those teenage moments lost in sentiment and sensation in every era, that need direction through a rigour which is equally part of the picturesque. This lapse into sentiment and its correction are the mechanisms by which the picturesque has proceeded historically. Its history is not one of a critical idea's defusion and dilution, but rather the infection of the arts with an equivocation, an instability – indeed, an anxiety – which began when the word 'picture' was given licence to attach itself so promiscuously across the arts, and across the divide of art and life.

To understand what is curious, destabilizing and productive about the picturesque would be a narrow study if it required us to stay in the eighteenth century, putting aside what the picturesque subsequently became. The picturesque and its emergence are relatively well known, even if their interpretation is much contested. The longer history of the picturesque through to its present use, has, however, rarely been studied. John Ruskin, Heinrich Wölfflin, Nikolaus Pevsner, Colin Rowe, Robert Smithson, Yve-Alain Bois and Rem Koolhaas, at various times, locate themselves in relation to this prominent but seldom visited landmark of Western culture. They develop the concept and manage its reception, frequently through denigration. This received picturesque and its later adventures interest me as much as its original, ambiguous form. The present volume proposes a new synoptic understanding of the picturesque as an ensemble of concepts and techniques and it does so drawing not only on eighteenth-century materials but also on later developments of the picturesque; on its reception and use. I aim not so much to establish the influence or genealogy of the picturesque, as to show how it has been, and remains, at work in cultural theory. The themes and issues of the book are based around what the picturesque can explain as much as they are attempts to delimit the concept. Each chapter discusses concerns of relevance today: the history of the pictorial surface, or support, in relation to building; aesthetic theories of disgust and the idea of ugly and demanding architecture; the development of the concept of architectural planning; the way that aesthetic appropriation becomes an analogue of political theory; and lastly, the way that the paradox of applying pictorial form to lived experience undoes a too easy opposition of movement and stasis.

The picturesque concept is so endemic and diffuse that everyone knows quite a lot about it, whether they realize this or not. Older ideas of the picturesque are assumed in many present attitudes towards image-rich environments, and any explicit attempt to think through the relation of pictorial form to visual experience is likely to have a useful bearing on the matter. Some background will be helpful, nevertheless, for those whose concept of the picturesque does not include a rough map of its history and major contributors; that is the role of this introduction.

A picturesque genealogy could take one a long way into the past. Most descriptions of the concept, notably that of Christopher Hussey and Pevsner, begin in the early eighteenth century in Britain, some scholars make a case for it beginning in the background treatment of Italian Renaissance painting,[2] and many note the legend that the picturesque is a European appropriation of much older Chinese landscape ideas.[3] To debate the origin of the picturesque will not, however, in my view, contribute much to our understanding of the concept as it has developed since the late eighteenth century, which is the task of this book. The picturesque of modern times is clearly the result of the substantial reorganization of existing concepts by William Gilpin, Sir Uvedale Price, Richard Payne Knight and Humphry Repton. A useful watershed date is 1795, as the first publications of the latter three theorists cluster around that date, when there was a brief public controversy over the meaning and value of the picturesque. Throughout the book, I treat the period 1780–1830 as the apotheosis of the picturesque, what happened earlier as a pre-history, and what happened after as a matter of uptake, development and impact of the concept. The texts of the 1790s themselves organize and present the earlier history and are the source for later commentators, so this simple chronology will suffice to introduce the authors and designers to whom I will later refer. The chapters that follow will bear the responsibility of showing that 1795 is a sufficiently deep historical context to the ideas discussed, and equally, that these old texts maintain some bearing on cultural issues of today.

The genesis of the picturesque

In the first decades of the eighteenth century in England, intellectual speculation about nature and the development of neo-classicism in architecture led to a new style of gardening that explicitly refused a geometrical layout. The traditional pleasure gardens of England were based on room-like cabinets of space, which tended to follow a Dutch style. The high art of gardening of the time followed seventeenth-century French royal gardener André Le Nôtre, who played geometric patterns against lines of sight to make illusions of scale and to connote philosophical ideas of space as extension. England had talented garden designers such as George London and Henry Wise, who developed a Baroque axial style, and Charles Bridgeman who, from 1713, designed the extensive garden at Stowe, which was a brilliant fusion of geometrical layout and scenic naturalistic passages. Gardening on geometric formulae involved pleaching trees and hedges to shapes that expressed the geometry of its plan. The English garden, as it was later known, had an irregular plan, and allowed the trees and plants to grow in their natural manner. The lack of any visible determination by a plan figure emphasized scene-like qualities of successive screens and atmospheric perspective, rather than linear perspectives that extend into the distance. This contrast of plan and elevation was, in fact, most clearly made in 1777 by a Frenchman, Rene Girardin,[4] the Marquis d'Ermonville. Dora Wiebenson has shown that the picturesque has been overly identified with England, and that French gardeners and writers had a major influence over the development of the idea from the mid-eighteenth century.[5] However, the over identification itself has a long history. French and German contemporaries identified the shift in style with England (or England and China), and 'Englishness' came to be contrasted with absolutism in politics as well as gardening and associated with British political liberalism. The fullest development of picturesque theory happened in Britain at the end of the century, and, although significant aspects of the idea were developed by Scots, it is still powerfully connected to Englishness because of explicit campaigns to do so in the mid-twentieth century. However 'English' they were, those gardens were thought to be a radically natural style. It is also possible to see a shift in mode of high status display 'gardens': from that of the productive horticultural garden (which is geometrical for practical reasons), to the kind of husbandry involved in keeping woods, pasture and hunting parks. The English garden innovation should not, however, be understood as a matter internal to garden history. These new gardens were popular because of the philosophical questions that they occasioned.

The intellectual issues here are those of the relation of art and nature, and what the rise of aesthetics meant for this ancient pairing. Aesthetics was a mid-century neologism of the German philosopher Alexander Gottlieb Baumgarten (1714–62), meaning 'received by the senses'. The need for this term was slightly older, in the idea that there could be an empirical account of perception prior to the feelings and thoughts that attach to perceptions. Theories of beauty before the eighteenth century, such as those of Leon Battista Alberti, assumed that the value of beauty was in concordance, or the harmony of the senses, understood as the immanence of the ideal in phenomenal experience.[6] Aligning material things according to abstract geometric shapes is a clear path to achieving this. From around 1700, and perhaps first in the thought of Anthony Ashley Cooper, the Earl of Shaftesbury (1671–1713), arose the distinction of an aesthetic sense from those of reason and morality.[7] After complex developments, the distinction was rigorously formulated at the end of the century in the philosophy of Immanuel Kant. With the rise of aesthetic discourse, beauty, rather than being a matter of perfection, became a reflection on whether the 'taste' of something pleases the eye or ear, as foods do the tongue. Only subsequently did the question of propriety in the Albertian sense arise. Aesthetics is a concept of the reception of empirical sensation; understood strictly, it cannot allow for general difference between art and nature. There can be no difference in kind between trees and painting – each appeals to the senses and is judged pleasing or not. At one level, the fact that English gardens of the early eighteenth century took their formal vocabulary from woods and meadows rather than from buildings and furnishings, is a result of the new freedom to understand art as an effect on the senses rather than the rule of a discipline. We see something of this separation of reason and taste in Sir William Temple's claim, in 1685, that the taste of the Chinese was superior to the Europeans because of the former's irregular gardens. Temple wrote that in China, 'the beauty shall be great, and strike the eye, but without any order or disposition of parts'.[8] In lacking geometrical order, Temple thought that Chinese gardens showed that they are free of prescription, and that also in China, the ability to reason was not mistaken for taste and discernment.

While Temple advised against constructing such gardens in England, others shortly afterwards did. Lord Burlington's villa at Chiswick had irregular gardens designed by the architect William Kent beginning around 1715. The poet, Alexander Pope, began construction of an irregular garden at his villa in Twickenham from 1719. By the time that Kent and Lancelot Brown remodelled the great park at Stowe in the 1730s, the irregular style was the paradigm of English gardening. As early as 1712, Joseph Addison stated the paradox of such an art that disguises itself. Describing his own garden, he writes, 'if a foreigner, who had seen nothing of our country should be conveyed to my garden at his first landing, he would look upon it as a natural wilderness'.[9] Addison thinks the fineness of distinction between garden, art and nature demonstrates the subtlety of English taste and its remaining unspoiled by the artificialities of culture. How fine could such a distinction become? And if taste has nature as its model then is art necessary to its exercise? According to Horace Walpole, Kent 'saw all nature as a garden'. This connotes great powers of mind on his part, but also shows how close the whole project of the natural garden is to tautology.[10] The question arises: need such gardens be constructed at all, or, can the cultivation of an aesthetic sense in the reception of the natural world replace art?

The term picturesque was first used to describe the aesthetical view of nature; only later is it connected to gardens, where it solved some of the conceptual problems of a 'natural garden'. The word was borrowed from the Italian *pittoresco* or the French *pittoresque*, meaning 'in the manner of painters'. It is clear, however, from the mid-eighteenth-century English usage, that this referred not to painting in general but to the painting of scenes. The word is inextricable from the rise of the genre of painting called 'landscape'. Our current use of the word landscape to mean an appreciation of the world as if it were a visual artefact is the result of the meeting of the picturesque concept with gardening.

The picturesque idea was developed and popularized by William Gilpin (1724–1804). Gilpin was a clergyman and headmaster, who learnt and later taught drawing, more as a personal accomplishment and satisfaction than to make artworks. From 1768 to 1776, Gilpin undertook tours of parts of Britain, recording his observations in prose and fine watercolour and ink wash drawings. Gilpin's manuscripts were widely circulated and admired, and after some difficulty with the illustrations, then published from 1782 onwards. What Gilpin sought in his travels was 'picturesque beauty', and his elegant descriptions of his own visual experience, and how drawing allowed one to reflect on this, were enormously influential. Gilpin's friend, William Mason, was probably the first to connect the words 'picturesque' and 'garden' in his poem *The English Garden*, which appeared in parts from 1772. At a semantic level, the attraction of the usage 'picturesque garden' is immediately clear when compared to the tautological direction in which the English garden was heading. Picturesqueness provided the remove by which gardening could be understood to be an art imitating, rather than merging with, nature. While the matter and material of the English garden could be plants and topography in forms familiar from nature, the garden would have a formal character like landscape paintings, which were already an abstraction and analysis of the visible order of the world. The picturesque is, thus, a compromise term or a space of delay and compromise. Gilpin developed his concepts from the theory of painting as debated in the French Academy, and particularly, the writing of Roger de Piles. This meant that debates of artists over the visual and rhetorical roles of painting, and the role of the system of genres of painting, were as important as the new aesthetic thinking. The picturesque is a product of this lively intersection.

The balance or compromise between art and aesthetics that the picturesque represents also lies between two of the most important thinkers of the time: Edmund Burke (1729–97) and Sir Joshua Reynolds (1723–92). Burke's *A Philosophical Enquiry into the Origins of Our Ideas of the Sublime and the Beautiful* of 1756 is one of the foundations of modern aesthetics. Burke proposes that beauty has neurological causes in the perception of certain visual forms and that the sublime (or high style of rhetoric) could similarly be explained as a relation to visual sense. He explores how affects of love arise from beauty, and fear and exhilaration from the sublime. He postulates that the sight of smooth and rounded things of small relative scale causes sensations we name as beauty, and that rough, angular and vast things excite the nerves into the sublime. Although these suppositions are perhaps the least interesting, and least argued, parts of Burke's *Enquiry*, they had immediate impact because they were taken to be directions for artistic production. This proto-psychology of perception was something of a threat to understanding art as a discipline with its own concepts.

The opposing position, which we could understand as something of a reply to Burke and Addison, is that of Reynolds. More than his admirable paintings, Reynolds' achievement lies in the establishment of the Royal Academy and his *Discourses*, delivered to it annually from 1778. Reynolds is a key figure in the history of the picturesque because, although he wrote of it little and quite dismissively, he had immense authority. Gilpin had developed the concept with the aim of gaining Reynolds' approval. Price continued to argue Gilpin's side in dialogue with Reynolds' texts after the latter's death in 1792. The *Discourses* suppose a discipline that has an intrinsic authority in its history and the operative concepts that painters use in painting. Reynolds, thus, is greatly concerned with issues of genres – or forms of painting, their appropriate subjects and handling – matters that can have no meaning in aesthetics, understood as a matter of sense. Reynolds is, at base, a Platonist, thinking that there are ideal forms and that painters can express the imminence of these forms in visual experience. He defends the idea of academies of art from the radical generalization of 'taste', however, his arguments take on some of the complexity of this opposition. Reynolds thinks that 'taste' and the purely empirical appropriation of art as pleasure are interests that confine issues of taste to the lower genres. If, however, matters proper to painting, such as genre and paint handling, are to be considered a part of the experience of art, this means that painting's history and conventions are themselves 'aesthetic' at some level. Reynolds proposes that art is a meta-taste, an inter-subjective development of judgement. We see, yet again, the crucial place of gardening in this circumstance. Arguably, the reason that gardening comes to be elevated to an art at this time is because of the role that it can play in these debates: it is an art without history or institution. It is, therefore, on one hand, a model for what painting or architecture might become under the regime of aesthetics. On the other hand, to the extent that gardening soon came to have its professors and treatises, it is a model for how the philosophical concept of aesthetics might become an art and a practice.

The picturesque was not born out of concepts and debates. Arguably, history proceeds in terms of what is seen and how it is seen, and conceptualization follows. A strong case can be made for understanding the picturesque as a new rationale and conceptual framework for aspects of the Baroque and particularly its late flourishing as Rococo. The Rococo of the late seventeenth and eighteenth centuries was already pitting visual sensory values against reason, and was playing a witty game of confusing the natural and artificial. More significant for the present inquiry, it was investigating a form language of balanced asymmetry derived from vegetal forms and the 'cartouche' frames of frescos on the complex geometry of vaulted ceilings. What Temple thought evident only in the gardens of China was already in Europe in the architectural decorations of Juste Aurèle Meissonnier and the brothers Assam and Zimmermann. The Rococo supposed that there could be an order without rule still appreciable to the eye – for instance, that an asymmetrical form could be balanced by relative intensity or sparsity of detail.

In Britain, this style did not triumph but was subsumed into an interest in medieval architecture; much of the visual values of Rococo underlie the theatrical 'Gothick' style of buildings, such as Walpole's Strawberry Hill (1748–66). The intricacy of ornament and the emphasis on surface rather than structure in early eighteenth-century Gothick parallel an interest in the asymmetry of medieval buildings, but these two aspects do not articulate until the end of the century. The other important impact of the Rococo in England is in the theory of William Hogarth. Although Hogarth's comedic history painting is quite idiosyncratic, in his *Analysis of Beauty*, he shows how much of the form vocabulary of the Rococo could be reduced to the figure of the serpentine curving 'line of beauty'. In the later eighteenth century, the neo-classicism of Lord Burlington and William Kent was triumphant. Architecture followed the theory of French writers, such as Marc-Antoine Laugier, who proposed that a columnar structure should provide an intelligible order to the appearance of building. In English gardens, however, there continued much of the formal invention of the Rococo. The sweep of drives and the serpentine form of lakes of the landscapes of Lancelot 'Capability' Brown might lack the gaiety and wit of Rococo decorative arts, but the intermediary forms by which they mimic nature without looking natural derive from Rococo. Arguably, our continued appreciation of the 'English' gardens of Kent and Brown relies on the heightened effect that neo-classical country mansions have in irregular and naturalistic settings. Not only did this play up the paired and parallel orders of nature and culture, it also allowed something of a development of the formal impulses in the dialectic of architecture, understood as grammar and as appearance, as classicism and Rococo.

Like the Rococo, the picturesque disturbed the boundaries and distinctions of existing disciplines. As John Barrell has shown, developments in literature were fundamental to developments in the picturesque.[11] In the classical doctrine of *ut pitura poesis*, poetry and painting each put a challenge to the other: the problem of painting, for most of Western history, had been how to equal poetry in the painting of 'history' or narrative; while in poetry, the genre called *ekphrasis* had the famous model of Homer's attempt to describe the artwork decorating the shield of Achilles.[12] This traditional definition of painting and poetry in the terms of their contrasting abilities was greatly refreshed by Charles Alphonse du Fresnoy's verse textbook on painting and art appreciation, *De Arte Graphica*, written in the later seventeenth century and translated into English in the early eighteenth century.[13] The pastoral poets, James Thomson and John Dyer, caused a major shift in the relationship. Rather than casting, in verse, a description of their experience of painting or sculpture, as in *ekphrasis*, they took on the model and aims of painting to describe directly their visual experience of landscape. Dyer's *Grongar Hill* and Thompson's *The Seasons* popularized an appreciation of British landscape in terms that were heavily pictorial. Oliver Goldsmith's *The Deserted Village* used the form of the elegy to describe the passing away of traditional communities, and this cemented the role of nostalgia in the description of rural scenes, which reiterates into the present. Poetry, being the most prestigious of the arts, continued to play a strong role in the formation of the picturesque. The fame of William Shenstone's picturesque garden at The Leasowes (Shropshire, from 1744) depended on his literary reputation and his friendship with Thomson. The poet, Willam Mason, who made a superior verse translation of du Fresnoy with annotations by Reynolds in 1783, wrote an influential treatise in verse, *The English Garden*.[14] Mason was a friend not only of Gilpin but also of the poet Thomas Gray, who most fully developed the genre of landscape poetry, and Gray's tours, particularly to Scotland, were at least as influential as Gilpin's. Tourism itself was a phenomenon of the picturesque, made popular by the literary mode of writing descriptions of tours, but also by the shift that was involved in turning the so-called 'grand tour' to Italy and the scenery of classical literature, into domestic tourism; the literary tourist describing not so much the marvellous and distant, but providing a fresh appropriation of the close at hand.

It is close to tautology to speak of picturesque painting, and yet painting provided more than source material for the picturesque. When the theorists of the picturesque at the end of the eighteenth century write of paintings that might help make or understand gardens and buildings, they generally write of painters of a century earlier: Claude Lorrain and Nicolas Poussin. Price was also interested in Dutch and Flemish painters of the seventeenth century, which he and his father collected, such as Meyndert Hobbema, Jacob and Solomon Rusdael, Balthasar Denner, David Teniers and Philips Wouvermanns. Their landscapes were lower in genre, generally depicting everyday life in the artist's own region in modern times rather than landscapes of the Roman Campagna idealized as the ancient world, as in Poussin and Claude. Price defines the picturesque as a term suited to this interest in the near-at-hand and ordinary. He probably learned these visual values through the paintings of Thomas Gainsborough, who had been inspired by earlier Dutch artists and was a friend of Price's father and grandfather. Gainsborough had great popular success with what he called 'fancy pictures'. These were scenes of happy indolence, where the figures were, unusually, not aristocrats but peasants. Gainsborough, thus, combined the thematic and narrative of French pastorale paintings, such as those of Watteau, with the Dutch taste for close observation of everyday life. Like Goldsmith's poem, *The Deserted Village*, the paintings are politically ambiguous and were understood to be so at the time. Are we supposed to envy the simple life of the poor? Or feel sympathy for their material poverty? Is poverty a natural, if regrettable state? Or one that calls for action to overcome it? The formal frisson of paintings and their ambiguous messages arises largely from this mixing of genres, which is fundamental to the high picturesque, but it also had real if indefinite referents in rural politics of the time.

1795

In the publication history of picturesque theory 1795 is a significant date, and it also connotes something of the political context of the picturesque. From 1793, Britain was at war with revolutionary France. In 1795, its army had been evacuated from Europe after the defeat of a coalition of *ancien régime* forces. Until 1815, the wars with France dominated the political and social environment in which picturesque theory developed. Collapse of trade during the wars led to food shortages, rapid price increases and considerable civil unrest. Crowds took over the markets in several towns and cities and distributed food at traditional prices, and there was widespread rioting.[15] The 'Poor Laws', which were systems of local taxation providing for the poor, went into crisis, becoming onerous for some rate payers while allowing others to exploit the public subsidy to drive down labourers' wages. The French Revolution had considerable support in Britain, notably from the exile, Thomas Paine, whose *Rights of Man* of 1791 argued for the liberties of the American and French revolutions. Dissident members of the British middle class inspired by Paine set up 'corresponding societies' to organize support for the reform of Parliament and for widening the franchise. E. P. Thomson argues that the organized civil unrest of 1795 was an attempted revolution, because that is how William Pitt's government saw it – they staged an effective 'counter-revolution' in 1796, holding down the countryside with troops for fear that the population would rise up and invite a French invasion.[16]

In 1795, the countryside was a very vexed issue, but the conditions that made it so, to do with land tenure and the capitalization of agriculture, go back centuries. In the eighteenth century, substantial areas of land were held in common from feudal times, and rural labourers had varying access to such 'commons' as a means of subsistence, making them semi-independent of wage labour. From Tudor times, investment in improved agriculture involved 'enclosure', which meant a landholder expunging common rights and taking exclusive ownership of land.[17] This process of enclosure rapidly increased between 1750 and 1830, when some 4,000 acts of enclosure were put through Parliament. In the 1790s, part of the role of enclosure was to limit the independence and rebelliousness of rural workers by making them dependent on waged labour. These social and political issues are more than context to the picturesque. Those people who were developing an aesthetic appreciation of the landscape of Britain were also in a state of low-level civil war with its inhabitants. Price, whose *Essay on the Picturesque* of 1794 is the core of picturesque theory, published a pamphlet in 1797 that proposed a militia of property owners to oppose rioters and French invaders. While he does not write of the latter, Price's 'improvements' at his estate, Foxley, were both scenic and agricultural, and he employed the first and most famous of the agricultural experts, Nathaniel Kent, in 1775.[18] The new art of landscape gardening is carried out by the same owners and with the same management systems as agricultural improvement. These circumstances have led numerous scholars to see the picturesque as an ideology of the agricultural reforms of the period.[19] The nostalgic aspects of picturesqueness are thus supposed to function politically by naming tradional rural practices as past, as obsolete. While this is true, it helps only a little in understanding why the concepts of the picturesque formed the way that they did. This ambiguity is particularly clear in architecture, because many architects who took up the picturesque also refer to the literature on agricultural improvement of the period. Writers on agriculture often proposed that building rural housing should be a disciplinary tool as housing tied to employment would guarantee the loyalty and commitment of rural labourers. There were great contradictions between the utilitarian vision of agriculturalists and picturesque theorists, who valued visual forms from older agricultural practices. If the painters, poets and theorists were ideologues, the agricultural reformers were social mechanics and disciplinarians in the manner of Samuel and Jeremy Bentham. That no single political imperative drives these discourses is clear enough in the architectural literature of the time in which these contradictions are overlooked and both agriculture and picturesqueness are claimed as authorization for various, and often bizarre, adventures.

Price, Knight and Repton

Sir Uvedale Price (1747–1829) and Richard Payne Knight (1751–1824) inherited neighbouring estates in Herefordshire. They were concerned with improvement and had similar taste in the picturesque. These common interests formed their friendship, but they were men of very different character and ability, as was quickly established when they published their views on the picturesque in 1794. Price's *Essay on the Picturesque* and Knight's *The Landscape: A Didactic Poem* both ridiculed the formulaic naturalism of Lancelot 'Capability' Brown, and argued the superiority of the wilder, irregular picturesque of Gilpin, as a model for landscape design. Today, Brown's landscapes are often called picturesque and these differences are overlooked, yet the concepts underlying the critique of Brown are something of a watershed. Brown had developed a formal canon (which was the aim of all classical art), but the theorists debunk this as a simplistic recipe and propose a radically empirical understanding of the visual appearance of landscape, prior to any concept of its form. Price went one step further: by choosing a line between Burke and Reynolds, he argued for 'picturesqueness' as a new aesthetical value distinct from beauty and sublimity. Humphry Repton (1752–1818) was an unsuccessful merchant but skilful watercolourist from Norwich who, in 1788, decided on a new career in the design of landscape parks. Repton met and discussed the picturesque with Price and Knight and hoped for their support. Repton's success, however, rested partly on his claim to be the successor to Brown, whose style was anathema to Price and Knight. *The Landscape* included a witty attack on Repton, whose book *Sketches and Hints on Landscape Gardening* was at the printer in 1794 but delayed because of difficulty with the pictorial plates. Repton replied to his critics in a *Letter to Uvedale Price*, which he published in 1794 defending Brown and himself.[20] When *Sketches and Hints* appeared in 1795, it also defended Brown and proposed strict limits to the application of the picturesque. *The Landscape* was written in a verse style that read at the time as witty and entertaining; however, in 1795, Knight released a second annotated edition in which he used his not inconsiderable philosophical understanding to point out the weaknesses and contradictions of Price's argument. Thus the conflict became a three-cornered one that maintained some public notoriety through 1795. In subsequent years, the three exchanged barbs as they developed their publications. In his *Observations* of 1803, Repton continued to argue against what he took to be Price's idea of 'picture-gardening'. In 1805, Knight published his *An Analytical Inquiry into the Principles of Taste*, which was aesthetic theory at a philosophical level. Knight clearly distinguished sensory experience from associations with remembered experience, and developed a theory of the imagination to explain how connoisseurship activated these associations. Neither Price nor Repton understood Knight's larger frame of argument and continued to disagree about the consequences this had for their own theories. By 1810, Price's various forays had consolidated into the definitive three-volume *Essays on the Picturesque*, in which he again distinguished his position from Knight and showed how he and Repton were, in fact, in agreement.

The posthumous reputation of the three men varies on point of view. Knight was by far the most sophisticated thinker and writer, and in accounts by philosophers such as Walter Hipple,[21] ranks above Price, with Repton a distant last. There have been thorough studies of Knight, the most apposite to his architecture and picturesque theory being the book by Andrew Ballantyne.[22] Stephen Daniels has done much to rescue the reputation of Repton and Daniels and his collaborators have studied Price and Knight's practical activity on their estates.[23] There has been no authoritative study of Price.

Knight was a radical libertarian and freethinker who opposed organized religion and centralized government. As a member of Parliament, he was a supporter of the opposition radical Whig Charles Fox, and as a member of the Society of Dilettante, he published a book tracing the remnants of ancient phallic cults in Italian Catholicism.[24] His *An Analytical Inquiry into the Principles of Taste* was built out of Burke's earlier attempt to link sensation with the passions, but did so in a sophisticated manner using the associationism of Archibald Alison.[25] The picturesque was, for Knight, part of a large argument: that feelings about art works or scenes in nature are pleasing when we are able to associate them with prior experiences. This meant that he was something of a cultural relativist, thinking, for instance, that there must be a canon of beauty among Negro people that was inaccessible to him. His ideas also left a large role for connoisseurship: the broader and richer one's cultural capital the greater pleasure was available in the viewing of art or nature, because of the depth of associations. Knight begins from fundamental considerations of visual perception: he claims this is unmediated, and is pleasing or displeasing to the nervous system before any idea of the object. From here, Knight argues that there is 'improved perception': training in the arts allows one to order and compare perceptions: that is, already known ideas of sensation are associated with objects presently causing those same sensations. Beyond this, Knight supposes that there exists a higher power of imagination, where ideas and sensations are not fused but play freely. The picturesque exists at this level, where a concrete spatio-visual experience can lead to the imagination of that experience as painting, because of the train of associations and comparisons that a connoisseur of painting would have in their mind. While it is interesting to read Knight as a sophisticated representative of his time, much of what interested him was subsumed in Romantic concepts of imagination, such as that of S. T. Coleridge, which did not have the secondary project of defending connoisseurship as the superior principle of the association of images.

Knight has one other important contribution to the picturesque that should be mentioned here. Downton Castle, his home, which he most likely designed, was probably the first building wholly conceived on an irregular or asymmetrical plan. This resulted from some quite idiosyncratic ideas of Knight's about the associations that the history of architecture offered, but in further justifying his approach in the *Analytical Inquiry*, Knight opens issues that others saw in the house itself: the scenic possibilities and potential fit to function of irregular planning.

Price was the most influential of the three authors because his thought is less abstract than Knight's, being aimed at practical questions about the laying out of grounds; and because Repton's even more practical books were highly expensive, elaborately illustrated books in small editions. While Price is rambling, repetitive and often tedious to read, he is nevertheless the more important thinker in terms of cultural history because he attempted to reconcile art, as a practice, with aesthetic theory. Price had great admiration for Reynolds, whose idealist account of art was largely at odds with the empirical trend of Price's aesthetics. While Price understood his taste to be a unified field operating the same principles over pictures and views of the countryside, he nevertheless had great respect for artists, and the knowledge and insight particular to painting. Gainsborough had been a friend of Uvedale's father Robert, who was skilled in landscape and botanical drawing and both generations collected the Dutch landscape paintings that Gainsborough had re-invented as a modern British mode. While Knight approached art as a world of finished images to be received and developed as mental associations, Price saw and wrote of the visual knowledge that artists produced in the process of making art. Most likely it is for this reason, as much as for convenience to his argument, that Price also accepted the institutionalization of art, as Reynolds, another friend of Gainsborough, was developing it at the Royal Academy.

A hierarchy of genre was crucial to Reynolds' ambitions to make painting a fine art with poetry's status. As well as the traditional *ut pitura poesis* arguments for pairing painting and poetry as equally intellectual, Reynolds wanted an internal system that reached down to the levels of decorative and strictly imitative arts, integrating them as the lower grades in a hierarchy of the painting profession. Issues of technique, and hence of the institutionalization of training, would be common, while the more noble painters would rank themselves higher as they achieved higher levels of ideation. Price pitched for the picturesque and landscape as a middle ranked genre, articulating his theory with Reynolds at some levels. Price, however, also supposed that picturesqueness was mostly experienced as something mixed with beauty, leading him to the possibilities of mixed genres. What particularly interested Price was noble artists painting mean subjects, which is quite against the intent of Reynolds; it is closer to Hogarth, and seems prescient of twentieth-century interest in hi–lo contrasts, as in Pop and Arte Povera. Interest in a high take on low scenes runs through all Price's thought; politically as well as aesthetically, he was a localist. Like Knight, he was a radical Whig member of Parliament, who kept a London house and social connections, but his interests were in rural Herefordshire and the improvement of his estate, Foxley, as a productive and scenic landscape, and as a rural society. Compared to Knight, for whom the landscapes of Herefordshire and Italy are distinguished only through their utility in assisting imagination, Price's examples of aesthetic experience are astonishingly mundane and resolutely local: the earth banks of rutted lanes, rambling old cottages in decay and gypsy camps. Price deploys a concept of disgust in his argument in a rather sensational manner, which has parallels in a number of eighteenth-century thinkers, including Burke, who valued disgust as a proof of disinterestedness. The admiration of a painting of filthy cottages showed that one's interest was in art and not the objects represented. While Price plays rhetorically with the shock of disgust, his real achievement is in ordinariness; Price's picturesque is the quotidian lived environment.

Repton was the leading practitioner of landscape design from the start of his late career in 1788 until his death in 1818. Repton never intended to contract to make landscape, only to act as a consultant. This allowed him to mix widely in genteel society, which seems to have been one of his main aims. While he was often called in to advise on modifications for large aristocratic parks such as Holkham, Bulstrode, Bowood, Woburn and Longleat, many of which Brown had designed, his major innovations were in designs for smaller grounds, for villas of the growing under middle classes. Similarly, while he advertised himself as the successor to Brown, Repton realized early that without supervising the construction of his designs, his fame would have to rely on his influence on taste and his writing. A large degree of Repton's success lay in his abilities in the relatively new medium of watercolour, in which he had an economical but charmingly fluent style. He also developed a simple gimmick, what he called a 'slide': a patch of paper on which the 'as-is' scene is painted, and which, when lifted back, shows the improved scene and the extent of the changes. Repton presented his clients with reports containing prose description, occasionally some verse, and painted scenes; he bound these in red morocco leather, making them known as 'Red Books'. These were so fashionable that Repton was sometimes commissioned by those with little or no intention of following his advice, merely to obtain a Red Book. At the end of his career, Repton claimed to have made over 400 reports.

In 1795, when he had only been in practice seven years, Repton published *Sketches and Hints on the Theory and Practice of Landscape Gardening*, which excerpted his reports to clients into a publication of his thoughts on Landscape Gardening – a term he claimed to have invented. This was an extraordinary triumph of printing at the time, and with fine hand-coloured prints of his paintings, it was very costly and in a small edition. But as printing improved and the possibility of profit from publication became clearer, Repton released two later collections in much bigger editions: *Observations* of 1803 and *Fragments* of 1816. Repton's books have been held in high esteem since their publication, but not, since his death, for their theory. The common judgement seems to be that Repton has a place in the history of ideas for his exemplification of 'the theory of the picturesque', but that this is better put by Price and Knight. Repton is usually represented as an inept thinker, casting inconsistent axioms over carelessly selected examples. Walter Hipple opines that his writings are a devastating 'mixture of pompous solemnity with servile humility'.[26] This undeniable fact has tended to obscure the relatively high level of consistency in his writings, which demonstrates an underlying theoretical framework. Similarly, Daniels has shown how Repton, practising with all the exigencies of the taste and means of his clients, has much to reveal about the social and cultural values of the picturesque, unclear in the aesthetic treatises. This is particularly the case with his concept of 'appropriation', or how visual field and sense of possession might interact with extent of real property. I describe this in my chapter 'Appropriation'.

As a landscape designer, Repton was much less formulaic than Brown and did design from points and sequences of view rather than in plan. He often worked on small designs and near cities, so he was adept at using foregrounds and changes in topography to create a degree of exclusivity and compositional unity in view. His largest influence, and here he was at one with Price, was to reintroduce formal gardens and terraces between a house and its park. The extremity of the contrast that Brown produced, with pasture sweeping up the walls of the mansion, was impractical, as Repton showed with amusing images of would-be wanderers besieged in the house by stags. The formal terraces, balustrading, flower gardens and conservatories that Repton proposed, not only gave outdoor spaces adjacent to the house the traditional pleasures of flower gardens, but also solved functional difficulties in servicing and gave him foreground elements with which to compose views from the house. Much of Repton's work we would now think of as architecture, and he worked with William Wilkins, James Wyatt, and later with Jeffry Wyattville, but his closest and most productive relationship was with John Nash from 1796 to 1800. In a joint project for Luscombe House in Devon in 1799, Nash and Repton took the template of Knight's Downton Castle and developed the first building in which it is clear that the asymmetrical plan is determined by views from the house and functional convenience in servicing. Repton apprenticed his sons, George and John, to Nash, but in 1800, he and Nash fell out badly over Nash's stealing of Repton's commission and much of the design for the Royal Pavilion at Brighton.

Repton developed a concept of 'character' that was subsequently to become very important. Repton's idea mixed landscape type and the patrimony of estates. Ancient families could have characterful but relatively small parks close to villages because this context connoted a feudal connection, while new money generally meant 'elegance', that is, Palladian mansions in extensive landscape parks. Repton thought that character could be connoted by architectural style – Gothic or Tudor being the more characterful – and this led to the possible sleight of hand by which new money could look like old through the use of feudal styles and hierarchies of building. An idea of character in building was already strong in French neoclassical architectural theory, but Repton made a major contribution to the term's success by linking it to alternative architectural styles and to the idea of character being understood contextually. The work of Repton and numerous architects of pattern books for the design of cottages and ornamental buildings explore the resource that architecture's history offered as a source book for building appearance. They pre-date by some decades, however, the strong concept of style as moral choice founded on archaeological study, that dominated the mid- and later nineteenth century. In the twentieth century, the concept of character *sans* style returned strongly as a way to understand the communicative and expressive aspects of building and the dependence of this on the context of the building in towns and cities and it was this possibility that the work of Repton and Price suggested to Nikolaus Pevsner when he and Hubert de Cronin Hastings repopularized the picturesque as 'Townscape' in the 1940s.

The techniques of character and the market for illustrated books caused a flurry of architectural publications generally known as the cottage pattern books. Between 1775 and 1840, about 100 books of architectural patterns for cottages or 'small villas' were issued. The books are part of the process by which architecture developed from a model of patronage to a modern profession and thus middle-class and workers' housing design was an obvious enough topic. However, the attempts by many architects to authorize their designs by referencing picturesque theory and agricultural reform mean that the books provide crucial insights into the valencies of the picturesque idea.

The nineteenth century

Nineteenth-century thought on architecture in Britain was a conflict between historical accounts of style and picturesque ideas of appearance. At the forefront of architectural discourse and design were archaeologically inspired historicist styles, such as the neo-Greek or the Gothic, which were often identified with the nation or a religious confession. These were, however, largely impractical and excessively expensive for the broadening range of nineteenth-century building types. In a broader view, it is apparent that the concept of building planning as strategic level organization of function and appearance, which had developed in the picturesque, underlay apparently strict stylistic exercises, such as the Gothic Houses of Parliament by Charles Barry and A. W. N. Pugin or Thomas Hamilton's super-Greek Edinburgh High School. As early as the 1830s, architects, such as Antony Salvin, who were more concerned with appearance were loosening the strictures of style and looking to precedents of hybridity such as Tudor, early Renaissance, seventeenth-century Baroque, and so on, that gave greater freedom to the designer and were more adaptable to a variety of building scale and type. By the end of the century, the 'battle of the styles' had resolved largely into a comfortable choice between two historical flavours of picturesque composition: Tudor/baronial *à la* Richard Norman Shaw or an Italianate simplified irregular classicism developed by Charles Barry. This landscape of building forms was the basis on which the Arts and Crafts movement erected the next iteration of a moral theory of building, one that was greatly coloured by the localism of Price.

In terms of theory, the important figures are John Claudius Loudon (1783–1843) and John Ruskin (1819–1900). Both propagated the picturesque, while Ruskin considerably extended its conceptual scope. Loudon was son of the Scottish Enlightenment, with its unprejudiced approach to knowledge, and was apprenticed as a nurseryman while attending Edinburgh University. In a book of 1806 on *Forming Country Residences*, he presented himself as an adept of the picturesque, proposing designs that are very close to Repton's style. He relatively quickly gave up that path, moved to England, and used his real nurseryman's skills to become an agricultural reformer, making and losing a fortune in farming with improved techniques. A mixture of ill health and Jeremy Bentham's influence turned Loudon towards a career as publisher and public educator. From the mid-1820s, Loudon and his wife Jane Webb (an early science-fiction novelist) began publishing relatively cheap mass-circulation periodicals which, consistent with their progressive Utilitarian philosophy, attempted to put knowledge of all kinds – technical and aesthetic – in the hands of the middle classes. The most successful of these were the *Gardener's Magazine* and the *Architectural Magazine*. The book versions of these journals were very successful and widely distributed in North America and Australia. Loudon was something of a techno-popularist and dismissive of the picturesque. He proposed the term 'gardenesque' to replace it, and was largely responsible for turning the nascent discipline of landscape design towards knowledge of plants, which had not been a principal interest for Brown or Repton. What interested Loudon were practical matters, for instance economical ways to build a sound cottage; how ordinary people could obtain or organize the skills to construct one; how much land was needed for a subsistence garden; and how a flush toilet could be activated by a string to the door. But Loudon employed numerous architects as contributors and illustrators, and although he was sceptical of many of their designs, his *Encyclopaedia of Cottage Architecture* of 1831 became one of the main vehicles for the dissemination of picturesque ideas and stylistic pluralism at a popular level and in the New World. With a strongly analytical turn of mind, Loudon wrote a section of the *Encyclopaedia* on architectural theory and attempted to make sense of the variety of approaches in his omnibus volume. This essay is the first sensible synopsis of picturesque architecture: Loudon clearly states the principles of functional planning and external appearance determined by internal arrangements, which were inchoate in earlier picturesque pattern books.

Ruskin published a serial essay on the picturesqueness of cottages in Loudon's *Architectural Magazine* from 1835.[27] It is largely consistent with Price's interest in abject buildings, except that Ruskin insists that for the true picturesque one has to go to France or Italy, as British cottages are too neat and tidy. Ruskin's great concern in all his thought on art and architecture is for a concept of truth that can govern both moral and aesthetic considerations. He was thus attracted to the empiricism of the picturesque, and as a skilled and trained draughtsman and painter, believed that such truths grew out of artistic practice in the observation of the natural world. The occasion of much of Ruskin's thought was the painting of J. M. W. Turner, who Ruskin and his father James collected. In 1841, Ruskin began a public defence of Turner's art against its critics, which grew to a final form of five volumes in 1860, by which time it had become a broad-ranging episodic treatise on painting and aesthetics. As a part of this project, Ruskin made a famous and devastating attack on the picturesque in the name of a higher Turnerian picturesque.[28] The argument is quite like that of Reynolds, who Ruskin read and on whom he later lectured: artists of low intellect and spirit become obsessed with verisimilitude and hence with the details of the perceivable world, while noble artists can see and state the general condition of particular circumstances.[29] What Ruskin adds to this familiar hierarchy are concepts of truth and sympathy: lower picturesque artists, by seeking out details of appearance that occasion their skills, misunderstand and misstate the relations within a scene that caused it to be. Ruskin's examples of the ignoble picturesque are scenes of poverty and starvation rendered for our pleasure thus constituting a failure of truthfulness and a lack of sympathy. In this critique, Ruskin disabled one of the main features of the eighteenth-century picturesque: the representation of mundane and disgusting objects because of their value in the delimitation of a purely visual pleasure. Since Ruskin, it has been common to see this aspect of the picturesque as naïvely cruel and heartless. Seen in another light, however, Ruskin simply ramped up the aestheticization of the world that the picturesque had proposed since Gilpin. Ruskin continued to repeat the problematic of aesthetical disgust, but with the poor of foreign countries, and thus the localism of Price becomes a placeless interest in the quotidian *per se*. Similarly, Ruskin's attack on the picturesque is symptomatic of the tendency in Romanticism as a whole to shift the locus of disgust theory from reality to art. What Ruskin thinks that we should learn from our disgust at bad art is the next iteration of what Price thought that we could learn from our disgust at the mendicant poor.

Ruskin wrote all his life on architecture, and in his monumental *Stones of Venice*, he developed several strong principles that were picturesque in origin and which became greatly influential.[30] What Ruskin called the 'changefulness' of Gothic architecture was a development of Price's and Knight's interest in architectural accretion and Loudon's ideas of architectural expression. What Ruskin added was the thought that the process by which a building changed its use and form with the changing conditions and intentions of successive builders was not merely a charming inclusion of contingency. Changefulness was a social principle as well as an aesthetic merit, and Ruskin proposed that builders (by which he meant both those commissioning as well as tradespeople) should conceive the form of building loosely and incompletely, giving space for variety of opinions and approaches. Ruskin thus continued the picturesque interest in weak form into a temporal dimension. It was for the weakness of *a priori* architectural concepts and the resultant idiosyncratic buildings that Ruskin loved the architecture of Venice, praising it on account of its unresolved hybridity of Gothic and Byzantine styles. While 'Venetian Gothic' did become an identifiable style in Britain (Waterhouse's Natural History Museum and R. R. Anderson's Scottish National Portrait Gallery are examples), Ruskin's writing encouraged a more general interest in hybrid and impure styles, which I mentioned above. The Arts and Crafts movement developed out of the thought of Ruskin and William Morris on the social and aesthetic conditions of the production of art. The encouragement of crafts, which was a major feature of arts and crafts, led to a strong focus on local traditions of making and a search for characteristic building forms, which also had precedents in the picturesque of Gilpin and Price.

The picturesque in modernism

When the German cultural theorist and architect Hermann Muthesius made British Arts and Crafts ideology a policy of the Deutsche Werkbund, formed in 1907, some aspects of the picturesque became attached to the nascent modernist architecture at a pan-European level.[31] These ideas were so widely disseminated by then that they would not have been identified as picturesque, but the modernist project – that all building become architecture, or vice versa – goes back to the eighteenth-century discovery of vernacular building, and ideas of buildings having their appearance determined by internal planning. There was another more particular link of some importance: the German modification of the term picturesque itself. The eighteenth-century British texts were largely translated at the time. Fredrich Gilly, the radical neo-classicist architect, had a translation of Price in 1798. Schiller, Gotthold Ephraim Lessing and Goethe all wrote of the qualities of *malerisch*, which literally means 'painterly' but was used as the translation of 'picturesque'. English garden and building style had been fashionable in Germany, more so than France, through the nineteenth century, but Romantic sentiments about old towns led, as in Britain, to a picturesque understanding of urban forms, the high point of which was the Viennese Camilo Sitte's *City Planning According to Artistic Principles* of 1889. This was as influential in Britain as in German-speaking countries because Raymond Unwin, one of the founders of professional town planning, republished large sections of Sitte's work for its most sophisticated conceptualizations of what was by then the dominant picturesque taste in urban form.

A perhaps more fundamental issue is the abstract sense in which German art historians developed the concept of *malerisch*. Heinrich Wölfflin (1864–1945) took this usage and made *malerisch* the principal term in his description of Roman Baroque architecture, contrasting it with the linearity of the Renaissance in 1888.[32] In 1915, in his *Principles of Art History*, Wölfflin made this comparison a general dialectic of all the arts since the Renaissance, and a certain version of the picturesque became central to concepts of form in modernism.[33] In *Principles*, Wölfflin distinguishes his abstract *malerisch* from a naïve interest in things with *malerisch* qualities, in the same way and with the same reasons that Ruskin had critiqued the picturesque, before explaining the superiority of his reformed version. The English translation renders the inferior term picturesque and the better concept 'painterly', so much of what Wölfflin wrote on the matter has been received in English as more novel than it is in fact. The larger point about this is that Wölfflin and his contemporaries, such as Alois Riegl and August Schmarsow, were inventing the concepts of space as a concretely perceptible quality, that would be fundamental to modernism in architecture.[34] Sigfried Giedion, Wölfflin's pupil, connected these concepts directly to the modernist project so that Le Corbusier's explorations of space, unfolding for a moving observer, seem the fulfilment of seventeenth-century Baroque.[35] British thinkers, some of them influenced by German concepts of art history, began thinking about the picturesque in the same way. Geoffrey Scott's *Architecture of Humanism* of 1914, with its sophisticated demolition of Ruskin's moralism, marks an end to the nineteenth century and the introduction of new concepts of spatial experience. For Scott, the Baroque was picturesque and picturesqueness was simply a condition in which space was perceived in motion rather than measured from a static point.

The first, and in many ways the best modern book on the picturesque is Hussey's *The Picturesque: Studies in a Point of View* of 1927, now sadly out of print. In a broad but elegant synopsis, Hussey treats the picturesque as a general phenomenon in culture, writing of its uptake in the various arts and including some of its social aspects. While he does not use such terms, Hussey has a clear sense of what we would now call 'visuality', an acuity to certain images and manners of seeing that are broadly formed in a culture and which also serve to identify a cultural group. Hussey's insights grew out of his larger project of researching the aristocratic country houses in which much of the picturesque had been formed and on which he published extensively in *Country Life*. To an extent, Hussey's work on country houses and his admiration for the historicist architect Edwin Lutyens meant that the picturesque has been greatly identified with English national culture and its traditions. In architecture, the most significant modern writer on the picturesque was Nikolaus Pevsner (1902–83). A German émigré to Britain, Pevsner admired Hussey's work and agreed with his account of the national basis of artistic inclinations, but Pevsner was determined to show that the picturesque was fundamental to modernism. In 1936, only three years after being forced from his academic post in Göttingen, he published *Pioneers of the Modern Movement: From William Morris to Walter Gropius*. Through the war years and into the 1950s, Pevsner and his students extended Hussey's research and published versions of this in the professional architecture journal, *The Architectural Review* (*AR*), where Pevsner was one of the editorial team. With Hubert de Cronin Hastings, the owner and fellow editor of the *AR*, Pevsner developed a new ideological vehicle, 'Townscape'. This was based on his reading of Price, Knight and Repton, and its aim was to counteract the avant-garde élitist image that modernism had in Britain at the time. The *AR*'s aim was for Townscape to be a popular modernism by exaggerating the role of the picturesque in its formation; insisting that, with picturesque principles, modern buildings could fit comfortably in historical contexts; and through simple jingoist nationalism about the Englishness of all this. The high point of Pevsner's picturesque was his Reith Lecture series on BBC radio in 1955, and subsequent book, *The Englishness of English Art*, which used a Wölfflian dialectic of flowing lines and crisp lines, imagination and observation, atmosphere and objecthood, to explain the whole of English art and architecture from perpendicular Gothic to the 1950s. The last lecture, 'Picturesque England', approaches an instruction, one that can look surprising in retrospect, because the picturesque Pevsner recommends is the high modernism of Roehampton Estate.

The reception of the picturesque

Much of the uptake of picturesque ideas in modern culture has been forgotten. If remembered, it is for the curiosity of the origins of these ideas. The scholarly literature on the picturesque has grown with a heavy emphasis on its historical emergence and cultural imbrication, but with opposing values. On one side, there is David Watkin's *The English Vision* of 1982, a comprehensive study of the picturesque in architecture and landscape, which greatly substantiates the insights of Hussey by bringing together subsequent empirical research, including much of Watkin's own. Watkin is concerned with precedence and the attribution of formal characteristics. His frame is the history of English culture and an affirmation of the values of architects and patrons who developed the picturesque. Watkin is also known for his attack on the historical determinist arguments used to justify modernism, and on Pevsner his former supervisor in particular.[36] Despite this, Watkin is also an adherent to *kunstgeographie*; thus, in his hands, the picturesque becomes more English than ever and something of a justification of the historicist tendencies in late twentieth-century architecture in Britain. In opposition to this affirmation of the picturesque and its history, we find the work of Raymond Williams, John Berger and John Barrell.[37] This approach, first in studies of literature and later in painting, is varyingly influenced by Marxism and establishes that the picturesque had a largely repressive political meaning in the eighteenth and early nineteenth centuries Britain.[38] By the late 1980s, the Marxist line was more widely accepted and the model of the picturesque typical in the humanities today is as an ideology of the English countryside and of colonialism, and the origin of modern practices of tourism. With most of the facts agreed, but such different values at stake in their interpretation, the picturesque has become a somewhat awkward gift that it is hard to know what to do with, without first having a view on British culture and history.

There has been no whole-scale renovation of the concept of the picturesque as there has on the sublime, by Jean-François Lyotard and others.[39] In the first place, this is because the picturesque is less a concept than a negotiation point in history and cultural practice. The sublime of Burke and Kant was a postulated limit to culture, which is a fairly interesting issue on many occasions, while the picturesque actually resulted in techniques, motifs and genres with their own particular histories and failings. At one level, the picturesque was, and continues to be, a grand concept of an interdisciplinary project in the arts, founded on the possibilities of aesthetics and the foundations that visual sense might give to the arts. At another level, however, the picturesque has remained an historically located crossing over of disciplines that then go their own ways. In the history of literature and painting, the picturesque is something of a transition to romanticism. It is more concerned with the external world and sensation than with the sentimental subject; it lacks that dimension in which Wordsworth or Turner could make the work of art into an immanent critique of art making and historical becoming. That same lack, however, also allows the picturesque to escape some of the noisome metaphysical pretensions that romanticism left in our concept of art.

Something of the original interdisciplinary ambitions of the picturesque remains within architecture, and thus the valency of the term in architecture is a useful way to study the concept. It is no coincidence that architects continue to be interested in the picturesque, and that most of the works dedicated to it since (Ruskin, Hussey, Pevsner, Watkin and Sidney K. Robinson) have architecture as their occasion. One might expect similar attitudes in landscape architecture and urban design, but it is here that the picturesque has been anathema, because of an on-going popular taste for cottage gardens and village-esque housing estates, which are a real threat to the intellectual status of those disciplines. There is presently something of a resurgence of interest in the picturesque, as a risky kind of platform for architectural interventions outside the discipline, in what is sometimes callled called 'landscape urbanism'. Rem Koolhaas' feigning to copyright the term has led to some more serious inquiry, with issues of *Parametro* and *L'Architecture d'Aujourd'hui* devoted to the picturesque, and scholars and architects including Iñaki Ábálos, Philippe Nys and Ákos Moravánszky have published on the history or present utility of the concept.[40] Despite its current debased popularity, its conceptual inadequacies, and its deleterious ideological functions, the picturesque has remained important in architecture and may be returning at present to one of its periodic moments of popularity. The longer standing reasons for this are perhaps best thought of as technical. The picturesque technique of planning for point of view and sequential visual experience has become a fundamental in architecture because gardens and 'townscapes' are often called on to exemplify spatial relations because in landscape, space and movement can be seen independently of function and enclosure. These present uses of picturesque ideas, largely in teaching architecture and communicating it to lay people, lie over a cultural memory among architects, the importance of which is rarely stated. This is that the possibilities of modern architecture, in its combination of functionalism and sceneography, are all dependent on asymmetrical planning techniques developed in the late eighteenth-century picturesque. Even if their beliefs about it have come osmotically through a few honorific references and hackneyed examples, and despite knowing it to be naïve and outmoded, architects still think with the picturesque. Understanding the history of its architectural uses is important for any understanding of the picturesque, but architecture is, in this, as much a mode of thought as a topic. The picturesque, like much architectural thought, is instrumental in intention but leads to speculation.

The book that follows attempts a conspectus of the picturesque by relating its formulation and its subsequent history. The book does not, however, attempt to strictly account for the commonalities and differences between eighteenth-century concepts and their subsequent development. While questions of precedence, inheritance and critique are relevant at points, the picturesque is simply too diffuse a body of concepts and techniques to have a history in any more substantial sense than the sketch offered in this introduction. The themes around which the book is organized are supposed to be relevant to present issues in architecture, but this claim to relevance and utility is also a licence to speculate and rethink the picturesque in its most general ambitions.

2
Pictures

Most accounts of the picturesque rightly emphasize the '-esque'. We might say that this suffix indicates the valency of pictures; their ability to make new attachments and to have new uses. But it would be mistaken and anachronistic not to remember that in the eighteenth century 'picture' in picturesque was not 'image' in a general, abstract sense. Pictures are also material objects, with a particular spatiality and tied to, but distinct from, painting, a discipline with its own history of concepts and techniques. The once radical idea that pictorial thinking can provide ways of making architecture and landscape is now a commonplace. By focusing on the materiality and the conventions of the picture we can understand how things came about, and also unpick some of the self-evidence of the picturesque today.

Considering the specific meaning of pictures in the eighteenth century takes us in two directions. The first direction concerns the specific kind of painting that 'picture' connotes: a relatively small panel painted on an easel and made moveable, as opposed to mural, or wall, painting. In French academic theory the *tableau*, or movable panel or easel painting, had come to replace the frescoed wall as the epitome of painting by about 1700, but the consequences of this change of medium continued to develop until the mid-twentieth century when Clement Greenberg proposed that the flatness of American field painting was an historical necessity.[1] Many aspects of the spatiality of pictures changed over this period, but what is of interest here is how pictures construct a fundamental difference between pictorial and architectural space. When the space of painting became autonomous from the space in which paintings were displayed, it became the work of painting to produce the spatiality proper to it. One of the most common errors made about the concept and practice of the picturesque is the assumption that compositional techniques, particularly the manipulation of surface and depth relations, were learned from painting and applied to landscape and building. It is anachronistic to think of the relationship in this way; pictorial composition of this sort only developed after the surface of the picture was understood as flat, delimited and spatially discrete. Pictorial composition did not precede architectural composition; they developed in parallel. The 'picture' in 'picturesque' is not a relation of image-making and visual experience common to both painting and architecture; it marks the fundamental branching of the disciplines and their concepts of media. The second direction concerns genre and the hierarchy of genres in painting prevalent at the time. In this context, the 'picture' in picturesque proposes something anterior to the pictorial, the compositional, or the relation of image to perception: that views of the ordinary agricultural countryside of England be situated between the grand themes of history painting and the meanness of Dutch genre painting. It asks: What should and should not be included in such landscapes? Who is it who looks this way? And how should this be organized socially, which is to say tastefully? While the hierarchy of painting genres is less relevant in present-day culture, the picturesque proposal for aestheticizing mundane existence has only grown in importance.

This chapter begins with an overview of the relation of painting and architecture and the meaning of the rise of the panel painting, or the picture. The work of William Gilpin is then described as the purest, simplest version of the picture-*esque* – and of what it is possible to think of as pictorial composition in the late eighteenth century. Sir Uvedale Price takes us in another direction, demonstrating that it is possible to have a theory of the picturesque that almost completely ignores what we would call pictorial composition. Price's *Essays on the Picturesque*, historically the most influential text on the picturesque, can largely be understood as being a work on issues of genre. Humphry Repton, in his theoretical reflections and especially in his disagreements with Price, shows how relatively weak concepts of composition and much stronger rules of propriety were resolved in picturesque practice.

Insisting that 'picture' is not synonymous with 'image' is not only an issue of historical accuracy. In the eighteenth century, there was no meta-concept of 'image' that provided a meeting place for concepts of pictures, spaces and the imagining of buildings and gardens. But neither is there such a master term today. Although we often use 'image' as if it fulfilled this task, this tends to confuse matters now considerably more complex than in the eighteenth century. Today, designers and artists generally deal with and distinguish between such issues as the image-ability of buildings and the increasingly important circulation of images; the spatiality of different kinds of images and proliferating image technologies; the virtual space presented in an image; and the actual spatiality of an image hung or projected. In modernism the picturesque came to be seen as an antiquated and simplistic way of thinking the fundamentals of spatio-visual experience, which had their apogee in Le Corbusier's architectural promenade. But the recent explosion of image technologies and new intersections of the space of images and architectural space challenge such a view. Herzog and de Meuron's use of modern techniques for reviving the very old idea of *sgraffito*, of images incised on a building façade, can challenge some of the self-evidence of picturesqueness as an architectural value, and thus, perhaps, give it back to us as a specific and useful concept.

Painting and pictures

The picturesque proposes that painting can ask useful questions of the visual experience of spatial arts. The term, however, arose from problems internal to painting that are not in the first place visual or spatial; they concern genre and the object that a painting is. 'Picture' is not an uncomplicated term, and its history has much to tell us, not only about the etymology of the picturesque but also about the conceptual field in which the picturesque arose. The Oxford English Dictionary shows the etymology of picturesque in the Italian *pittoresco* and the French *pittoresque*. Noting that both of these terms refer to painters, the dictionary then states: 'but in Eng. assimilated to *picture*, giving the sense "in the style of a picture".' This assimilation is not merely an error, nor is it a matter of the felicities of the different languages; it is part of a longer history during which, around 1700, at the time the word *pittoresque* was borrowed for English, the relation of painting to pictures changed drastically.

Modern ideas of composition assume that we see a picture in two ways: first, as a thing, all at once, as a plane of line and colour with a certain size and proportion, painted on a surface of canvas or timber; and second, as a space, as a represented scene, or in the case of an abstract painting, as an arrangement of marks and colour intensities. Each way of seeing – seeing surface distribution and seeing illusory depth – underlies and guarantees the other. In a landscape, for instance, a cottage in the distance and a foreground tree might each be one-third of the way in from opposite edges of the picture. Understood as marks on the surface, they balance one another; understood as representations, their relative size makes up the imagined depth. It is this kind of felicity that we typically understand as 'composition' today. There is a case, however, put most strongly by Thomas Puttfarken, that this modern idea of composition was not conceptualized until debates in the French Academy in the late seventeenth century, and that it is premised on the rise in stature of the portable panel painting or picture.[2] In the Italian Renaissance, the apogee of painting was not relocatable panels with their own internal spatiality, but whole walls and ceilings that were contrived for particular places and viewing positions. What might appear to modern eyes as the lack of a standard autonomous idea of the pictorial surface is related to the fact that, in the Renaissance, painting was not *a priori* a visual matter. As scholars such as Ernst Gombrich and Michael Baxandall have shown, the ordering principles of paintings were narratological and iconographic, and painters' visual acuity and skills served rhetorical schema.[3] Thus for conceptual and material reasons, there was no surface of painting against which to play its depths. It is often thought that the picturesque involved the application of compositional schema from paintings to buildings and landscape. In architectural history Caroline van Eck has pointed out the limits to such a thesis and shows the continued reliance on a rhetorical tradition even as the picturesque undoes Vitruvian notions of propriety in form.[4] By turning to the entwined history of architecture and the picture we can further insist that what 'composition' did exist in painting, did not long pre-date the picturesque. What was adopted was not so much the schemas by which paintings were arranged as the very possibility of visual arrangement. To understand the significance of the 'picture' in the picturesque it is necessary to sketch a longer history of pictures and painting.

Gombrich, in his essay 'The Renaissance Theory of Art and the Rise of Landscape', claims that the aesthetic values of the picturesque and the landscape painting genre arose from the contrast of figure and *campo*. The arrangement of human figures in the foreground of the painting was of prime concern to the artist, and these contrasted with the *campo*, or field, against which they were seen. The spatiality of such paintings is, then, to a large extent formulaic, and when a taste grew for realistic representations of landscape space, this was still understood as a kind of *campo*. The relation of the landscape to the figures was as much a rhetorical contrast as an attempt to place the figures in a unified space. Gombrich analyses a text by Paolo Pino of 1548, summarizing the admiration and curiosity Italians had for the high verisimilitude of Flemish painting, the way that incidental and curious rock formations, trees and old towns became suitable as a background field or *campo*. Because painting the *campo* did not include telling a story, this was not an intellectual exercise; it was purely for the pleasure of imitation and the display of skill, as *parerga* or ornaments to the main work. The *campo* is in some sense equivalent to the gilded backgrounds of medieval paintings, except that the precious material was replaced by patient skilled labour. Nevertheless, the contrast such detailed representations offered was held by Pino to deepen our understanding of the conceptual content and rhetorical skill of the painter's management of figures. Thus, Gombrich claims that Pino gives the first definition of the picturesque or *pittoresco*: the particular observation of landscape directed towards visual curiosity and pleasure, generically below narrative painting with figures, which was directed to ideation and beauty. According to Gombrich, this opposition within painting practice in the Italian Renaissance develops into the separate genres of history and landscape painting and the mutually defining oppositions of idealism and empiricism, beauty and picturesqueness.

Gombrich shows that the concept of the picturesque begins its history already caught between being a mode of visual empiricism and a genre of painting predefined by its subject matter. The term has its next development in France in the late seventeenth century when Roger de Piles borrowed it for French as *pittoresque*.[5] Landscape was by then well established as a genre and de Piles argued that what had been understood as merely a matter of painting, and hence below intellection, should rather be understood as what is proper to painting and the terms in which painting is thought. Puttfarken has argued that de Piles' theory marks an epoch in the history of painting in which modern ideas of composition and the pictorial surface are first thoroughly conceptualized. Landscape and picturesqueness play a role in de Piles' thought, and the reception of de Piles' books in England by theorists, particularly Gilpin, began the picturesque in the modern sense.

De Piles began his explorations by taking the side of the *Rubénistes* in the *Querelle du coloris*, or the 'dispute on colour', about the value accorded to line and drawing, *dessin*, compared to *coloris* and painting. The argument began in the French Academy in 1672 when the painter Phillippe de Champagne attacked the paintings of Titian and lauded the works of Nicolas Poussin.[6] The *Poussinistes* championed signification and decorum over what they saw as the sensory pleasure and emotional affectations of Titian's paintings. De Piles, who took the opposing view, greatly admired Flemish and Dutch art and so used Rubens as much as Titian in his argument, hence the term *Rubéniste*. In the theory of *Poussinistes* such as Charles Le Brun, *dessin* was fundamental to the identification of figures, facial expression, pose and action, because history and grand narrative constituted a corpus of subjects proper to painting. De Piles, on the other hand, was sceptical of the system of genre, a hierarchy of subjects, and of the *Poussinistes*' claim that history painting was a kind of knowledge. He sought to understand painting in terms proper to it, visual terms such as colour and tonality that had no easy equivalents in rhetoric. While his arguments generally used high genre examples of Rubens' history paintings, his ideas about the visuality of pictures owe much to landscape, which, with only a notional story, can be given over to semblance of place and atmosphere. It is reasonable to think that much of the picturesque's visual values have proceeded from the *Rubéniste* side of the *Querelle du coloris*.[7]

De Piles developed his ideas through theoretical annotations to Charles Alphonse du Fresnoy's poem, *De Arte Graphica* of 1668, and in his own *Abrégé de la vie des peintres* (which was translated as *The Art of Painting, and the Lives of the Painters* in 1706) and his *Cours de peinture par principes* of 1708 (rendered as *Principles of Painting* in 1743).[8] De Piles' idea of 'composition' is unlike our present understanding because it includes 'wit' and 'invention' in the choice of subject and its treatment. Preceding these aspects, however, and preparing the ground on which they are perceived, is a purely visual aspect of 'composition' that he called 'disposition'. This latter answers to a modern idea of composition and an idea of painting as primarily visual art. De Piles claims that because any visible object or scene can be a subject for painting, the value of the painting must lie, not in its subject, but in matters particular to painting. A painting must effect a *coup d'œil*: that is, it must first attract the eye through a purely visual effect before any identification of subject. As he writes in the *Principles of Painting*:

> All *visible objects* enter the understanding by the faculty of *seeing*, as *musical sounds* do by *hearing*. The eyes and ears are the doors, which admit us to painting and music. The first care therefore both of the painter and the musician should be to make these entrances *free* and *agreeable*.[9]

> In *composition*, the painter ought to contrive as much as he possibly can, that the spectator may, at first sight, be struck with the character of the object.[10]

De Piles thought that this immediacy of perception could be achieved by the disposition of parts such that they present a whole in which:

> All the objects lines, colours and lights and shades of a picture, are great or small, strong or weak, only by comparison [. . .] the effect of the whole consists in a general subordination, where the darks heighten the lights, and the lights set off the darks, and where the merit of each part is founded on a mutual dependence.[11]

For de Piles, the whole surface of the painting, all its lines, colours and tones, and whatever object they represent, must be disposed to produce the whole because: ''tis not proper to leave the eye at liberty to gaze at random; because it should happen to be detained on any one side of the picture, this will frustrate the painter's intention'.[12] De Piles recognized, like earlier theorists, that there were limits to the verisimilitude of painting in representing space. Therefore, the *coup d'œil* must lie in a visual order proper to the distribution of the painted surface and preceding any recognition of spatial depth.[13] The *coup d'œil* is largely effected by what de Piles calls *clair-obscur*. This is the overall distribution of light and shade on the painting surface (de Piles' usage and meaning differs from the *chiaroscuro* that Italian painters described as the use of shade to model objects within the painting). De Piles sums up these visual aspects of painting as a requirement for the work to have *l'unité d'objet*, which is a unity of the painting as an object. Puttfarken claims great historical significance for this idea as in all previous painting theory the visual matters of the organization of the painting served the principle concern of *l'unité de sujet*, which is to say, a correct arrangement of the persons and things represented.

Puttfarken argues that de Piles' idea of *coup d'œil* is, in fact, specific to relatively small panel painting, or *tableaux*, where, unlike a large fresco on a wall or ceiling, it is possible to see the whole in one field of view. Thus, the debates as to the priority of visual or rhetorical values in painting should be seen in the light of a long history of the painting surface, and *l'unité d'objet* as a critique of fresco. In *The Principles of Painting*, de Piles tells an anecdote of a connoisseur marching through the Vatican Stanze in search of Raphael's paintings, not noticing that they surrounded him (Figure 2.1).[14] When the guide pointed out his error, the gentleman took pleasure and improvement in examining the parts of the paintings, but the whole of them had escaped him. De Piles says this mistake shows a lack of *clair-obscur*, or an overall pattern of light and shade in the paintings, but we should also understand this as a matter of the paintings' scale and position, which obliges one to look at them sequentially.

While the art of painting on small moveable panels is as old as Western art, it was assumed to be the medium of lower genres such as portraiture and still life and was identified with Northern European art. While there are doubtless many factors in the rise of the portable panel painting, not least of which is the growth of a commerce in paintings, it is also the end point of a very long history of the painting surface. Meyer Schapiro has attempted a general definition of what he calls the 'image field' and others call the 'support' of painting.[15] Schapiro describes the fully evolved image-field as having three conventions: surface, bounded image-field and frame. Historically, they emerged in this order and all three are necessary to the modern idea of the picture. Paleolithic cave painting makes clear that art existed before the convention of a smooth, flat and featureless surface. Gombrich sketches a history of the fresco that supports Schapiro's analysis, observing that the slow rise of the rectilinear field in antique painting first placed images in horizontal bands, delimiting top and bottom as earth and sky but establishing no *a priori* limit to breadth.[16] Schapiro suggests that the frame developed first as a device to direct attention to an image on the greater

Figure 2.1 Raphael (Raphaello Sanzio), *The Fire in the Borgo*, Palazzi Pontifici, Vatican, 1514.

surface of a wall, and was subsequently discovered to aid the representation of spatial depths. Giotto's frescos on the Arena chapel are a crucial point in this history because, while he gives perhaps the first thorough demonstration of the value of spatial depth in a visual naturalism, the individual scenes are arranged in the room in strips according to a narrative and iconographic programme.[17] In his *Treatise on Painting*, Leonardo da Vinci is scathing about frescos like Giotto's, which juxtapose successive scenes, making the sky of one scene the floor of another. In this complaint, we see the balance of values shifting from the narrative to the visual. It seems that there is a teleology in painting, from primitive painting that values pure figure making to modern painting that values each of Schapiro's criteria: first, a featureless ground delimited, and then that limit insisted upon by a frame that suggests depth and the possibility of spatial representation. One final point of development lies in the practicality of a frame, which, in the case of a canvas or timber panel, will make the painting robust and transportable. The frame also makes the transportability of the picture visible, and the image-field of the painting indifferent to, and conceptually detached from, the wall on which it is hung. This millennial development of a spatiality proper to pictures also draws on the basic paradox of the perception of pictures: the illusion of their space requires a perception of their flatness. The premise of the picture is that although we necessarily perceive that a picture is a flat thing in concrete space, we ignore its phenomenal spatiality in order to occupy the space constructed by the picture. Maurice Pirenne has argued that this double spatiality of the picture is a necessary condition of perception. If we did not first recognize a picture as a picture, we could not compensate for its lack of binocular visual depth and the contingencies of visual parallax.[18]

Puttfarken places de Piles in the context of this longer history of the painting surface. In *The Discovery of Pictorial Composition*, he shows that even after the delimited rectangular field becomes the normal support for painting in the Renaissance and a single spatial conception governs the contents of painting, composition in its modern sense still does not exist. This is primarily because paintings were supposed to be ordered through and by their contents. Alongside the painters of the fifteenth century, Leon Battista Alberti, founder of the theory of painting, developed an idea of painting that unified time and place, representing the story through a crucial moment rather than multiple, sequential scenes. And yet Puttfarken shows (following Michael Baxandall and others)[19] that in the Renaissance, the disposition of paintings is made on principles that are rhetorical rather than visual, and what is arranged are bodies and their relations to one another through posture and facial expressions. To this extent, 'composition' is an arrangement of elements not dependent on the pre-existing surface or space on which they are arranged. The primacy of the human body is also coded into a painter's techniques, in the opposition of figure to *campo* that Gombrich observed. Puttfarken argues that this primacy of the figure continues to underlie the use of perspective. The centralized one-point perspective, used by Renaissance painters from Mantegna to Raphael, ordered the elements of a painting, but its main role was to cast the figures forward by unifying the space of the painting and the observer. Puttfarken's overall argument is surprising and bold: it is that a modern concept of composition was invented as late as 1700 in the debates of the French academicians. It was only then that the picture became what it is today: a surface proper to painting, where the viewpoint is abstract, conventional and indifferent to the exigencies of its placement.

Of equal interest in the present inquiry is Puttfarken's synopsis of a 'pre-pictorial' painting. This is painting interdependent with building, where the alignment of the viewer to the image is contrived both in the painting and in its concrete spatial position. Before the triumph of the picture, paintings did not rigorously separate the space represented from that occupied by the viewer, and often relied on, or adjusted for, specific viewpoints so as to make the space of the painting cohere. The picturesque as it developed as a practice in gardening and architecture remains pre-pictorial in this sense. It begins with the viewer's position and field of view, and while the picturesque alludes to that *unité d'objet*, which contemporary pictorial culture was developing, it never quite achieves this. There is a common impression that the picturesque is a whimsical conceit because any attempt to make an actual view seem like a picture will be easily discovered by moving from the set viewing position. This is correct, but should be understood in its historical context: the picturesque conceit and its necessary failure to achieve the *unité d'objet* is an exercise of the then novel distinction between abstract and concrete viewpoints.

One hinge point of Puttfarken's argument is his analysis of Titian's *Madonna di Ca' Pesaro* (1519–26, oil on canvas, S. Maria Gloriosa dei Frari, Venice) (Figure 2.2). This painting has a particular role in my inquiry because both Price and Reynolds wrote of it in relation to architecture. I describe their differences on the picturesque in this chapter, and the Titian gives us something of a key to understanding architectural movement in Chapter 6; but it is also a demonstration of the problems of how the flatness of pictorial space can be a stimulus for thinking about phenomenal spatial experience.

Titian's composition seems inexplicably radical and unprecedented in cult images; in all such previous images, the point had been to have the sacred figures face the viewer and for a centric perspective to dramatize this by linking the space of the painting and that of the viewer. In Titian's grouping of the figures, as we are familiar with it from reproductions, the Virgin looks not at us, nor into our space, but across the space of the painting at the donor. Thus, the painting seems possessed of the autonomous spatiality of the *tableau*. Puttfarken makes a careful and interesting reading of the painting in its location that aims to show that aspects of the painting are specific to S. Maria Gloriosa. Titian's Virgin is enthroned in the painting in an ambiguous architectural setting that we look on obliquely, and that supports the diagonal composition of the painting. Notable are the shafts of two great columns, apparently part of a colonnade. However, because we cannot see the capitals, it is not possible to apprehend their spatial position, nor to imagine the dimensions of the space in which the figures are arrayed. Thus, it might seem that already in the early sixteenth century, Titian has invented a 'picture' in which a surface distribution of elements is related to the space within the painting, and that the painting's relation to the space of the viewer has been elided to heighten this effect. However, Puttfarken, following David Rosand,[20] claims that this is not the case: in S. Maria Gloriosa, one approaches the Pesaro Madonna at an oblique angle and looks upward at it; and from this viewpoint, the Virgin is more centred and appears to be looking over the donors and into the space of the church. According to Puttfarken, the illusion of the autonomous space is the stronger for the fact that, when viewed on the angle of approach, the columns can be seen as 'a chapel extending at right angles beyond the wall of the aisle'.[21] The photograph (shown in Figure 2.3) supports his claim, but also shows that the alignment is not the only significant factor. The space of the painting and the church are made contiguous by the fact that we generally approach the painting through framing columns very similar in their scale and base mouldings to those painted. Deborah Howard also makes the case that the painting is a development of the use of architectural settings.[22] Underpainting shows that Titian first framed the Virgin under a barrel vault, and most likely went to the final scheme in order to coordinate the appearance of the painting with the window above it. The painting is not, then, spatially autonomous and carries Puttfarken's larger point: that Titian is not a proto-modernist with a concern for painting as surface. Rather, Titian is following the general strategy of Michelangelo's paintings in which 'composition' is a matter of the arrangement of figures and the pictorial space is reduced to a minimum to thrust the figures forward into strong relief against a background. In this light, the ambiguity of Titian's apparently deep space has the same role as the shallowness of much of Michelangelo's painting.

Both Price and Reynolds had seen the Pesaro Madonna but probably knew it best from Valentin Lefèbre's etching of 1618, where, as Puttfarken points out, it faced an abstracted general frontality. In their differences over the painting they exercise the same question that Puttfarken raises. Reynolds wrote of the columns in the Pesaro Madonna: 'Titian knew very well that so much formality or regularity, as to give the appearance of being above all the tricks of art, which we call picturesque, is of itself grandeur'.[23] In other words, Reynolds has seen the columns as delineating a regular geometrical space, engaging cognition and hence showing that Titian had risen above the mere pleasingness of appearance that Reynolds thought the picturesque to be. Although Reynolds was writing in Flanders and recalling his memory of the painting, his understanding is not inconsistent with Puttfarken's idea that Titian intended the colonnade to appear to be at ninety degrees to the wall of the chapel. Price's description is almost the reverse of Reynolds. If Reynolds thought the rationality of architecture could leaven the mere sensual pleasure of painting, Price was concerned with how grand and geometric building could have something of the charm and sensual aspects of painting if viewed at an incidental angle. It is significant, then, that in Price's view the columns connote geometrical and spatial order, but *do not show it*: 'as their bases are placed on different levels, their symmetry, though not doubtful, is not obvious.'[24] Price, who was writing some thirty years after seeing the painting and most likely while examining a print, thinks that the particularities of the Titian's appearance as image, and the difference that can be established between that imaginability and architecture, suggest a way that architecture

Figure 2.2 Titian (Vecellio Tiziano), *Madonna di Ca' Pesaro*, 1519–26. © (1990) Photo SCALA, Florence.

Figure 2.3 Titian (Vecellio Tiziano), *Madonna di Ca' Pesaro*, 1519–26. In context in S. Maria Gloriosa dei Frari, Venice.

might become irregular and possess the 'movement' of painting while still being grand. If Puttfarken is correct and Titian was allowing for and making meaningful an incidental viewpoint on the painting so that it could have a spatial order, then Price and Reynolds are writing of obverse possibilities. For Reynolds, the ratio of architecture could save painting from being a mere play of semblance, while Price sees a potential for weakening the cognition of architectural form through the incidental viewpoints, partial occlusions and the visual logic of painting.

The 'picture' is not a simple and a-historical category and it proceeds the picturesque only briefly. Painting did greatly influence the formation of picturesque theory and practice but not, as is often thought, through a reduction of spatial composition to visual composition. Neither quite existed at the time, and both are dependent on the more fundamental concept of a pictorial surface. Such compositional schema in architecture actually develop out of techniques of planning, not the arrangements of elevations, as I will show in Chapter 4. However, the possibilities of separating and then articulating plan and elevation in part derive from the model painting gave of the different and intersecting spaces of the flat panel and its represented depth. It is also the case that the emergence of the picturesque contributed to the developing concept of the picture. When Gilpin and Price apply painting theory to phenomenal vision, they clarify the concept of the *unité d'objet* by abstracting it from the issue of its material support. The history of the picturesque is a continued exchange between painting and the spatial arts: the former striving to make space in images, the latter to make space imagistic and memorable. While this section has concerned largely the history of painting, my broader argument is that the concept of the picture does not arise solely from developments there. If the picturesque was an introjection of painting's concepts into architecture, it was also the end of a material conjunction. Before the hegemony of the picture, painting and architecture literally shared a common surface in fresco, and the critique of fresco is as much a matter of architectural history as that of painting.

The end of fresco

De Piles was not alone in his dislike of frescos, but a part of a culture-wide reaction against the Rococo. When Anthony Ashley Cooper, the Earl of Shaftesbury, attempted to use the new French principles in his *Second Characters* of 1713, he defined tableaux by contrast with frescos and their architectural role.[25] He also proposed a neologism – 'tablature', because he thought 'picture' an inadequate translation of the key term of the new French theory.

> by the word Tablature (for which we have yet no Name in English, besides the general one of Picture) we denote, according to the original word tabula, a Work not only distinct from a meer Portraiture, but from all those wilder sorts of painting which are in manner absolute and independent: such as the Paintings in Fresco, upon the Walls, the Ceilings, The Stair-cases, the Cupolo's, and other remarkable Places either of Churches or Palaces. [. . .] in Painting we may give the name of Tablature, when the Work is in reality 'a single Piece', comprehended in one View, and form'd according to 'one single Intelligence, Meaning or Design; which constitutes a real whole, by a mutual and necessary Relation of its Parts, the same as the members of a natural body.'[26]

When Shaftesbury complains that frescos and the 'wilder sorts of painting' are 'absolute and independent', he means that such paintings are at fault for being insufficiently connected to and conditioned by visual experience. Paintings cannot assist the mind to produce general knowledge from out of the mass of sense data if they are so self-consisting, and their arrangements based on the constraints of painting rather than the nature of sight. In this, Shaftesbury follows de Piles in his demand for a new level of unity between the idea of a painting and its appearance. Shaftesbury's list, 'Walls, the Ceilings, The Stair-cases, the Cupolo's, and other remarkable Places', shows the variety of conditions that architecture might put on painting, conditions that have nothing to do with painting. Shaftesbury makes clear that the faults of fresco are not only that they exceed the field of view and are governed by their allegorical programme, but that they are determined by the architectural surface on which they are painted – rarely flat surfaces that are inevitably proportioned and bounded in ways that are external to the composition of the work. What Shaftesbury does not mention is that frescos are also constrained by architectural concepts: they are a part of the ornament of the building. A fresco has a signifying role through its attachment to the building that is prior to any consideration of the rhetoric or iconographic content of the painting. We must not understand the rise of the picture entirely in terms of the internal development of painting, but also as the end of a concept of ornament that had linked painting and architecture and had given them a common surface.

In architecture, ornament is a concept derived from the orders of columns, their subsidiary elements and the spatial concepts attendant on their use. The orders are at once emblems of people of different gender and age, and the measure by which the building is laid out. In the theory of Renaissance humanist architecture, the proportions of the different parts of the column and its trappings are a code in which the whole fabric of the building was supposed to be implied. At the same time, their role as emblems of the virgin, the matron and the strong man signify the character of the building. Thus the dimensions of wall surfaces that constrain mural paintings are not arbitrary; the paintings mark out and celebrate already significant surface proportions that have been determined by the metric of the chosen order. This is the case in the frescoed interiors of Annibale Carracci's Galleria at the Palazzo Farnese, or Guilio Romano's Palazzo del Te, or Pietro Cortona's paintings at the Palazzo Barberini. But these famous examples are of interiors where columns are rare and the architectural order lies largely in abstract issues such as the proportions of walls. Because so few have survived the weather, we tend to forget that Renaissance painters made exterior façade murals where painting and the orders of architecture interpolated in a more lively manner. The ornamentation of façades with figurative work, often scratched into the building's render, is called *sgraffito*. Monika Schmitter has studied records of these façades and shows that painters competed with architects for the role of ornamenting the façade.[27] While painting was cheaper and therefore less noble than carved stone, it compensated for this through its superior narrative abilities; but neither spatial representation nor surface distribution could be at stake in such paintings. As Sebastiano Serlio describes: 'if you have to decorate the façade of a building with painting, what is certain is that any opening which simulates sky or landscapes will not be suitable. These things break up the building . . .'.[28] Thus painting converges on a purely figural art that slips easily into the anthropomorphism of architectural ornament.

The subsequent history of painting has led many to underestimate the ornamental role of painting, to think of ornament as only a matter of iconography. In fact, ornament in architecture has a semiotic that is not only referential. Alberti claimed that ornament was the 'principal part of building' as well as being attached and removable. At the same time, following Aristotle, he claimed that the beauty of building was that nothing could be added or taken away. This apparent contradiction is explained by a ternary semiotic, as Joseph Rykwert and Robert Tavenor have shown: the two states of ideal geometrical and phenomenal building require a point at which their juncture is intentional – the column.[29] This is consistent with what Michel Foucault calls the Renaissance doctrine of signature: an understanding of the world based on resemblance requires a guarantee that the resemblance and its discovery are intended and significant.[30] The likeness of the orders of columns to the human body was such a signature: the geometrical order of the building and its phenomenal presence are a pair, not a coincidence. To say that painting is ornament is not to trivialize it, nor to suggest its subordination to architectural concepts. In the pre-modern world, painting a building occurred subsequent to and in excess of its construction, but equally, it was an intentional act of homage to the building's significance and a demonstration of this significance. The absence of such a guarantee left the building as a simple, brute fact. Thus two aspects of mural painting tend to be overlooked by the painting historians whose work is so otherwise illuminating. First, the physicality, the size and the position of mural painting is not a matter of pure contingency nor is it only determined by pre-existing icono-spatial schema such as in the processional liturgy. Painting is also determined by the metrics of the building, the spacing of columns, the placement of windows and the like. Second, the metrics of the building reveal a lack in the empirical world, its own futility, only redeemable through ornaments such as figurative stone and painting.

The high point of architectural painting at a monumental scale is the ceiling frescos of Andrea Pozzo, the most magnificent being the allegory of *The Transmission of the Divine Spirit*, S. Ignazio, Rome 1691–4 (Figure 2.4). In this work, perspective is the armature on which painting and architecture rest. The fresco is a work of architecture, being a complete colonnade designed in plan and elevation in such detail that it could be constructed, but instead, is painted on the surface of the vault. Equally, it is a great figurative painting, in the tradition of Michelangelo, employing the metrical elements of the orders of architecture to make the spatial recession and opening of infinite space more affecting settings for the saints depicted. From the positions on the floor where we are supposed to view the painting, the illusion of space is so convincing that the issues at stake in pictures simply do not arise. There is no surface distribution that we need to reconcile with the represented depths because we do not perceive the vault as a surface. As Pirenne describes the fresco, 'from the floor, the spectator is unable to see the painted surface qua surface'.[31] Pirenne shows that although pictorial space, whether drawn, painted or photographed, is like the visual experience of real space, it is always distinct from it because we cannot but perceive the flatness of the picture. But Pirenne and also Puttfarken misstate the nature of Pozzo's illusion by not mentioning the difference between the *Transmission* fresco on the vault and Pozzo's other illusion of the interior of a dome that was never constructed, but painted on a flat surface over the crossing. The illusion of the dome is only convincing from a point on the floor marked by a marble disc and thus relies, as Pirenne says, on the distance from the eye making binocular vision almost irrelevant. But in my experience, the illusion of the *Transmission* is effective from most parts of the nave. As the effective area is so large, one can move within it, and thus the illusion itself becomes more spatial. The difference between the *Transmission* and the other more contingent illusion is that the former image is painted on the complex curved surface of the vault and crossvaults. Even though the actual recession of the vault is not the same as that of the colonnade painted on it, the vault recedes enough to trick the eye. *Trompe l'oeil* frescos such as Pozzo's show the scope for sophisticated interplay of the spaces of painting and building that the picture, with its generic and autonomous spatiality, cannot allow.

Figure 2.4 Andrea Pozzo, *The Transmission of the Divine Spirit*, 1691–4, S. Ignazio, Rome.

Karsten Harries has studied the critique of Italian illusionism implicit in the equally elaborate ceiling frescos of the Bavarians. The Bavarians thought that too great a degree of spatial illusion, and its consequence of being able to look into heaven from the floor of the church, was sacrilegious.[32] This doctrinal view makes for a different formal character, which Harries describes in a way that is inverse to de Piles' concept of the picture, not praising 'wholeness' but rather a necessary incompleteness. Johann Baptist Zimmermann's Judgement fresco in Die Wies (1753–4) lacks the kind of integrity and unity that would make it into a self-sufficient whole; it is essentially incomplete. To do justice to it one has to consider the contribution it makes to the architectural whole, the greatest achievement of the painter's brother Dominikus.[33] Contributing to this incompleteness, according to Harries, is the Bavarians' tendency to paint landscapes and architectural settings that are not coordinated with the actual building. Cosmas Damien Assam's ceilings at Weingarten (1717–18) use Pozzo's techniques of architectural projection quite directly, but the painter also included landscape scenes. As Harries writes, this seems to be an 'impossible attempt to fuse Pozzo's illusionism with traditional panel painting' but this is not Assam's aim. Rather, Harries writes: 'The illusionism of a Pozzo leaves us secure in our point of view; the impossible illusionism of the Bavarians, with its landscapes above, *calls our point of view into question*'.[34]

Harries' book is based around a particular contention that the Rococo is the last autochonous style, the last true place of formal invention in Western art; that from this point on, the aesthetic account of art makes ornament, and hence the interaction of the arts around a rhetorical programme, impossible. The Enlightenment and modern account of aesthetics, based on sensual pleasure and the autonomy of art, is wrong, claims Harries. It substitutes beauty for the sacred and thus loosens 'the bond that once had tied the aesthetic, the ontological, and the ethical function of art together'.[35] I do not support Harries contention that these matters should be tied together, but the symptoms that he finds for their disarticulation and the resulting periodization of art are useful for this inquiry. Harries suggests that the Rococo swallows something of the conflict of an aesthetical and ornamental concept of art into its own vocabulary: the plasterwork forms of rocaille and cartouche covering the interspace between fresco and architecture.

The Rococo style of light, naturalistic ornament with its 'all-over-ness' quality, was developed in France in the beginning of the eighteenth century by Pierre Lepautre and later by Nicolas Pineau, Juste-Aurèle Meissonier and Jacques de Lajoue. At times it was called a *genre pittoresque*, according to Harries, before taking its longer lasting name from the *rocaille* or shell-work decoration that characterized cabinets of curiosity and landscape grottos of the previous century.[36] In ceiling frescos, the shell-like, asymmetrical form of rocaille is particularly suitable for resolving the complex surface of vault intersections. Between the column, with its conventional figurality, and the centre of the vault, with its regular, fresco-ready surface, there are various surfaces, pendentives and intersections of crossvaults that Harries calls the 'stucco zone'. This zone is neither governed by architectural canons nor suitable for painting. In a flurry of plaster ornament, incomplete picture frames morph into sub-architectonic elements such as fanciful architraves or console brackets and then unravel into vegetal forms. As Harries points out, they are neither architectural nor pictorial. Grammatically they are ornaments, being parergonal to both building and painting, but they have no iconographical or referential structure. This stucco zone is an aestheticization of ornament, a rare moment of the overlap of contradictory accounts of art based on ornament and aesthetics.[37] For Harries, this quite astonishing historical oddity is interesting because it is prescient of twentieth-century abstract art.[38] The discovery of the unmeaningfulness of ornament led to its critique, to neo-classicism in architecture and hence to the modernism that Harries regrets.

Harries illustrates the end of the Rococo in Bavaria using a church by Balthsar Neumann.[39] The church was built as a typical Rococo shell, but for various reasons, never painted and decorated, and thus despite its complex and lively vault, seems to be already neo-classical. For Harries, this is the death rattle of the epochal tradition of ornament. He is not incorrect when he lays the fault for this demise at the feet of aesthetics and the concept of autonomous art. But we might say he has identified the historical interests that were served rather than the killer, which is the *tableau* or picture. I have used Harries' work to show something of the complexity of mural painting's imbrication with architecture that is lacking in Gombrich's and Puttfarken's accounts. They treat building's constraint on painting as if it were not also a matter of culture. Equally, we could say that Harries' account is too architectural and too much immured in the idea of the breaking up of a replete traditional culture of space and image. The *coup d'œil* of de Piles is an innovation in painting that, by itself, is a sufficient condition to end the Rococo in architecture.

In architecture, we usually think of neo-classicism as beginning with Claude Perrault and then Marc-Antoine Laugier's insistence on legibility founded on the grammatical use of the orders – a logical architecture opposed to illusion. But the arguments by painting historians for a similar chronological break have a particular significance for architecture. Discussing the end of fresco, Michael Fried quotes Shaftesbury and also Friedrich Melichoir Grimm, claiming that a critical passage by Grimm in 1756 signalled the end of the Renaissance, Baroque and Rococo, and the epoch of modern painting. Grimm writes:

> I have always disliked enormous constructions in painting and in poetry [. . .] the artist strays from his aim as often as he undertakes epic poems, painted ceilings, immense galleries, in a word, those complicated works that have throughout the ages received such injudicious praise. [. . .] Our mind cannot embrace many objects or many situations at the same time. It gets lost in that infinity of details which you believe enrich your work. It wants to be struck at first glance by a certain ensemble, without hindrance and in a strong manner.[40]

Painting's quest for an instantaneous apprehension of visual unity results in a demand for spatial self-sufficiency; it is this that ends the ornamental tradition. The advent of the picture, in the strong sense of *tableau* that I have described, was as much an event in the history of the concept of architectural space and ornament as it was for the spatiality of pictures. A Rococo church with a complex vault and non-canonical orders can, as Harries says, look neo-classical, merely through the absence of painting on its surfaces. This allows a sense of the building as an image-form, placing it on our side of the watershed of modernity. Were we to hang this church with framed pictures we might obscure an apprehension of its spatiality, its architectural image-ability, but we would not be modifying it in any serious way. So used are we to understanding our spatial relation to pictures as an abstract matter of frontality of aspect, it has little intersection with how we see buildings. We ignore the spatiality of pictures in the act of making a mental image of a space; we ignore our actual spatiality in viewing the pictures. A whole culture of spatio-visual experience is lost along with the practice and doctrines of ornament that gave architecture and painting a common task, and a common surface. But it is exactly this separation and self-sufficiency of the concept of picture that is required for a new conversation between disciplines to occur – in the picturesque.

Gilpin, the sketch and composition at large

In 1768, the clergyman and headmaster Gilpin (1724–1804), who was shortly to launch a theory of the picturesque, published his *An Essay Upon Prints: Containing Remarks Upon the Principles of Picturesque Beauty etc.*, which begins with a precise, intelligent and unacknowledged summation of de Piles.[41] De Piles himself greatly favoured prints as a means of education in art and taste, because one can lay out the works of several masters on a table and compare them.[42] Printed engravings from paintings are a significant aspect of the history of the picture, as Puttfarken shows. Prints in a portfolio or book have all values of *coup d'œil*, because of their size, because we generally treat the page of a book as spatially indifferent, reading it flat on a table or held upright in the hand, and because prints of this time lacked colour thereby elevating *clair-obscuro*. Much of what the British eighteenth-century picturesque theorists knew about the issue of painting and pictures was derived from French academic debates and theory. Du Fresnoy's poem *De Arte Graphica* was perhaps the single most important text in transmitting Italian theories of art and the content of paintings across Europe. With de Piles' annotations, it had been rendered in English as *The Art of Painting* by John Dryden in 1694. De Piles' *Abrégé de la vie des peintres* was translated as *The Art of Painting, and the Lives of the Painters* in 1706, and his *Principles of Painting* in 1743. Gilpin's friend, the poet William Mason, wrote an important statement of the principles of the recent English gardening fashions in a poem, *The English Garden* (1772–82), and in 1783 made a new verse translation of du Fresnoy in which de Pile's annotations were replaced by those of Reynolds, President of the Royal Academy.[43] Gilpin's theory of the picturesque was published in his *Three Essays* of 1792, but had been circulated as a manuscript about 1776 when Reynolds read and disagreed with it. Thus, Gilpin's précis of de Piles in *Essay Upon Prints*, published shortly before he developed his concept of the picturesque, provides us with a glimpse of what the theory of painting contributed to the picturesque.

In the *Essay Upon Prints* Gilpin writes: 'A painting, or picture, is distinguished from a print only by colouring, and the manner of execution',[44] which makes it immediately clear that paintings should be pictures and not large-scale murals. He continues: 'When we consider a print, as we do a picture, in a double light, with regard to the *whole*, and with regard to it's [sic] *parts*.' Wholeness relates to 'design, disposition, keeping, and the distribution of light'; and the parts to 'drawing, expression, grace and perspective'.[45] As with de Piles, wholeness includes the traditional matters of 'design' or invention: the choice of subject and its staging. Design, the primary aspect of wholeness, Gilpin defines as 'proper time, proper characters and proper appendages'.[46] Thus, design consists of what, today, we would not think of as primarily visual matters: genre, narrative and iconography. Gilpin follows de Piles by making the wholeness of the picture as visible object more significant than 'design'.

> By this word [disposition] is meant the art of grouping figures, and of combining the several parts of a picture. Design considers how each part, *separately taken*, concurs in producing a *whole* – a *whole* arising from the *unity of the subject*, not the *effect of the object.* For the figures in a piece may be so ordered as to tell a story in an affecting manner, which is as far as *design* goes; and yet might want that agreeable *combination*, which is necessary to please the eye. To produce such a combination is the business of *disposition.* [. . .] It is an obvious principle, that one object at a time is enough to engage either the senses or the intellect. Hence the necessity of unity, or a whole, in painting. The eye, on a complex view, must be able to comprehend the picture as one object, or it cannot be satisfied. It may be pleased indeed by feeding on the parts separately: but a picture which can please no otherwise, is as poor a production as a machine; whose springs and

wheels are finished with nicety, but are unable to act in concert, and effect the intended movement.[47]

The first phrase of the long subtitle to the *Essay Upon Prints* says that the book contains 'remarks upon the principles of picturesque beauty', but this is not quite the case. Gilpin defines '*picturesque*: a term expressive of that peculiar kind of beauty, which is agreeable in a picture'.[48] He then defines '*picturesque grace*: an agreeable form given, in a picture, to a clownish figure'.[49] These two usages mark a semantic instability that continues to today. The former is aesthetic in the narrow sense of being based on sense; the latter is conventional and assumes a hierarchy of genre with which the picturesque toys. However, despite the definitions in the preface, the word picturesque only occurs twice more in the *Essay Upon Prints* and as a simple adjective, with no discussion of its 'principles'. We are left to understand picturesque-ness as the term of approbation suited, somehow, to the 'wholeness' proper to painting. In the third edition of 1781, the title was modernized to *Essay on Prints*, and the subtitle, with its claim to describe picturesque beauty, is dropped. By this time, however, Gilpin must have begun work on his exposition of the theory of the picturesque, published in 1792 as *Three Essays on Picturesque Beauty*.

Gilpin was an accomplished draughtsman from a family much devoted to artistic practice as well as connoisseurship. William and his younger brother Sawrey, who went on to become a successful animal painter, were taught drawing by their father Captain John Gilpin, a well-respected amateur. Their family style was much influenced by Alexander Cozens, who was acquainted with the boys' tutor Dr John Brown, who taught them to draw from nature.[50] Gilpin is likely to have been the first person to use 'picturesque' as an adjective for natural, as opposed to painted, scenery, in a pamphlet he published on the gardens of Stowe in 1748. From 1768 to 1776, Gilpin undertook a number of tours of scenic parts of Britain and presented these as books of prose description and drawing. It is from this notion of touristic sight as an occasion for drawing or writing that the term picturesque became generalized into one of an aesthetic appreciation of the countryside. Gilpin's modestly expressed attempts to connect his love of art with an appreciation of the British countryside through sketching and prose are strikingly modern.

The books describing his tours were circulated in manuscript and well known in court circles before the first, *Observations, Relative Chiefly to Picturesque Beauty, Made in the Year 1772, on Several Parts of England; Particularly the Mountains, and Lakes of Cumberland, and Westmoreland*, was published in 1786.[51] Unlike other famous tourists such as Arthur Young, Gilpin is remarkably uninterested in historical, social or economic matters and rarely mentions anything of the exigencies of travel. The Tour of the Lakes describes Cumberland as if it was a scenic discovery, but Gilpin was born there. He describes the beauty of the entry to Carlisle framed by the castle and Cathedral and how quickly after this 'the town sinks into the insignificance of its invirons'.[52] He neglects to mention that his aged father lived there, his mother having died the previous year. Similarly, in the notebooks made during the journey, now held in Duke Humfrey's Library, Oxford, scant reference is made to the persons in the party, horses, inns, meals etc. Gilpin's prose and sketches are also largely free of rhetorical figures and allegories and almost purely descriptive. Without values or identifications at stake what we are left with are the disinterested judgements Gilpin makes about the merit of what he sees, some account of the feelings he has and much detailed description of the scenes and objects occasioning this. Just as in the *coup d'œil* of de Pile's painting theory, Gilpin's tours tend to imagine an action or product of vision that exists in a subject, the countryside, but that is felt first and quite independently of any identification.

There are few useful definitions of the picturesque or consideration of its principles in the books of the Tours, but many examples of the values of 'disposition' being applied to natural scenery. It must have seemed straightforward to Gilpin that while the painter might invent dispositions, the tourist could discover them by applying a discretion learnt from pictures. While Gilpin, as an artist, might have been making these choices with the prospect of picking up his pencil or pen, to him, this comportment had no strong distinction from an unskilled person practising an artistic discretion.[53]

What interests Gilpin more than the recognition that is beauty's due is the productive mismatch of the quotidian and the pictorial, which makes a role for an observer:

> In all these cases the imagination is apt to whisper, What glorious scene might be made, if these stubborn materials could yield to the judicious hands of art! – And, to say the truth, we are sometimes tempted to let the imagination loose among them. By the force of this creative power an intervening hill may be turned aside; and a distance introduced . . .[54]

Or as he puts it more systematically in the tour of the Wye valley, his practice was 'that of not merely describing; but of adapting the description of natural scenery to the principles of artificial landscape'.[55]

It seems that Gilpin was cautious about releasing his more explicit thoughts on the picturesque as a concept. According to Carl Barbier, his manuscript on picturesque beauty had been sent to Reynolds for approval as early as 1776.[56] The response cannot have been what Gilpin had hoped for and he worked further to support and exemplify his ideas. Reynolds, in his XIIIth Discourse to the Royal Academy in 1786, considered the picturesque rather dismissively. Prior to its publication in 1791, Gilpin sent the draft of his *Three Essays: On Picturesque Beauty: On picturesque Travel: And on Sketching Landscape: To Which Is Added a Poem . . .* to Reynolds and the next year published it with a letter from the academician, and his own reply. In the letter, Reynolds gently suggests that the picturesque might be more a matter of genre than of aesthetic sense and pictorial order as Gilpin proposes.[57] The picturesque, for Reynolds, is the pleasing aspect of middle and lower genres and, as it is founded on sense rather than intellect, cannot participate in the fuller sense of beauty. In this he follows an idea of the picturesque as the merely pleasing aspects of painting that (if we follow Gombrich), go back to the origins of the landscape genre in the Renaissance. Reynolds' XIIIth Discourse, his letter to Gilpin and Gilpin's reply form the basis for much of Price's much more elaborate theory, which, to a large extent, focuses on these questions of genre.[58]

In Gilpin's *Essays on Picturesque Beauty*, we can observe the three main confusions of picturesque theory, which are, for all that, the basis for its productive role in subsequent cultural history.[59] First, picturesque theory often seems to be undecided about an aesthetic account of art. It seeks to maintain the older concepts of ornament and propriety (of the kind Harries thinks died with Rococo) within a concept of aesthetics based on sense and feeling. Second (and in many ways a continuation of the previous problem), the picturesque is uncertain about whether it is aesthetics, in the sense of an explanation of feelings of pleasure or displeasure, or a theory of how to make art. Third, when it is aesthetic, the picturesque veers between objective and psychological aesthetics. Sometimes it thinks aesthetic qualities belong to the objects held to be beautiful or picturesque, and sometimes it thinks such feelings are associations in the mind occasioned by material objects.

These are complicated matters and we need a wider view to explain them properly, yet they can be grasped in Gilpin's book because they are compounded into a simpler issue, the issue we have been following in this chapter. Gilpin's text is riddled with the word 'composition', which the *Essay Upon Prints* tells us is 'synonymous with disposition'.[60] His aim is to advise the reader on how to pictorialize the world, yet the modern concept of composition is only liminally present in his advice. It is this absence of composition that carries the weight of my argument. Gilpin never gives any principles or values that would make one composition picturesque and another beautiful. When composition is bad, the print or scene is not picturesque, and vice versa. In contrast, there are, according to Gilpin, objects in the world that are picturesque – certain rocks, castles, trees and animals. Here, Gilpin is in mild contradiction because these are matters of the subject that is being represented, whereas, following de Piles, disposition is a matter of the 'object' (the representant artwork). We could strive to make Gilpin consistent by phrasing the matter so as to say that certain picturesque things entrain the composition into picturesque beauty. Still, it must have surprised any reader of the *Essay Upon Prints* when Gilpin finally comes to define the picturesque and it turns out not to be a matter of disposition, nor of composition, nor even of 'wholeness' or unity of subject, but rather of things that might make a subject for painting: 'rough' things.

'Roughness' refers to three interdependent issues. First, roughness marks an innovation in taste, as it is a critique of the 'smoothness' or mannered pretense at nature of the gardening of Lancelot Brown. But for our present topic, the second more interesting reference is to Edmund Burke's innovative text *The Sublime and Beautiful* of 1757; and third to the practice of drawing. Gilpin turned to Burke to base the picturesque in unmediated perception and to give the picturesque a connecting role in art theory. He also proposed that a definition of the picturesque would overcome the contradiction he saw between Burke's aesthetics and a practical experience of art and nature. Burke proposed that beauty was a feeling of harmony and relaxation of the optic nerves caused by a view of objects smooth and rounded.[61] Gilpin thinks Burke overly strong in finding smoothness 'the most considerable source of beauty',[62] but agrees that in real objects, 'one source of beauty arises from that species of elegance, which we call smoothness, or neatness'.[63] Gilpin's bigger problem is that:

> in picturesque representation it seems somewhat odd, yet we shall perhaps find it is equally true, that the reverse of this is the case; and that the ideas of neat and smooth, instead of being picturesque, in fact disqualify the object in which they reside, from any pretensions to picturesque beauty. – Nay further, we do not scruple to assert, that roughness forms the most essential point of difference between the beautiful and the picturesque.[64]

Gilpin's theory seems confused if we read it as aesthetic theory. He introduces a distinction between categories of aesthetic pleasure in art and nature that Burke could not support, but then, in the manner of Burke's physiology of vision, goes on to discuss 'roughness' as an objective quality of sensation. Yet the logic and significance of Gilpin's argument is clear if we look at what he was defending: a practice of drawing in pencil and pen and an appreciation of wilder landscapes such as his native Cumbria. In the terms of de Piles' art theory, Gilpin's picturesque involves a great promotion of *dessin* or drawing. This is so because, in landscape, there is no 'unity of the subject' of the kind found in history painting where the issues of narrative and identification give a task to *dessin* – the 'design' of 'proper time, proper characters and proper appendages'.[65] In landscape the pencil and hand must relate to another kind of wholeness: disposition.

Gilpin argues from cases that artists prefer a wilder expression. One might have one's hair neatly combed before sitting for a portrait, but 'leave Reynolds to himself, and he will make it picturesque: he will throw the hair dishevelled about your shoulders'.[66] In an example that became notorious, Gilpin proposes that while Palladian architecture is elegant and pleasing as a thing:

> if we introduce it in a picture, it immediately becomes a formal object, and ceases to please. Should we wish to give it picturesque beauty, we must use the mallet instead of the chisel: we must beat down one half of it, deface the other, and throw the mutilated members around in heaps.[67]

Painters, according to Gilpin, prefer cart-horses to thoroughbreds, and cattle or asses to any kind of horse. He insists that although different criteria apply to painting and reality, the two need not contradict if we have the term 'picturesque' to mark the difference. 'It is no injury to the beauty of your Arabian, if the painter think he could have given the graces more forcibly to your cart-horse'.[68]

The reason for this preference for roughness is an issue of execution: 'if the pencil be timid, or hesitating, little beauty results. The execution then only is pleasing, when the hand firm, and yet decisive, freely touches the characteristic parts of each object'.[69] Gilpin thinks that this is, in part, because a single elegant line that avoids insipidity is difficult to master. In the kind of sketching he preferred, with a series of approximated lines, the hand is less constrained by the profile of the subject, finding it easier to convey a visual form proper to pictures. Further to this, even considered independently of the task of representation, he says, 'a free bold touch is in itself pleasing'. These strokes can be called bold 'when a part is given for the whole which it cannot fail of suggesting'.[70] Looking at his drawings and his 'Essay on Sketching', it is apparent that he admires the larger, firmer strokes of the pencil or pen that contain the geometry of the hand and wrist (Figure 2.5). What Gilpin proposed was a kind of mimetic harmony between the artist's hand and rough objects, which admit to being 'rendered with spirit'.[71]

Thus far in my exposition of Gilpin, the picturesque has nothing to do with the composition of the image field as discussed earlier. The picturesque sees and evaluates the world through the craft of drawing; and we might add, through the fuller sense of mimesis, with the act of imitating being a way of 'drawing' nearer to nature. Nevertheless, for Gilpin, this technical and manual issue had consequences in composition.

> It is not however merely for the sake of his execution, that the artist values a rough object. He finds it in many other respects accommodated to his art. In the first place his

Figure 2.5 William Gilpin, *Tintern-abbey from the road*, 1782, finished drawing in pen and wash.

> composition requires it. If the history-painter threw all his draperies smooth over his figures, his groups, and combinations would be very awkward. And in landscape-painting smooth objects would produce no composition at all. In a mountain-scene what composition would arise from the corner of a smooth knoll coming forward from one side, intersected by a smooth knoll on the other; with a smooth plain perhaps in the middle, and a smooth mountain in the distance. The very idea is disgusting. Picturesque composition consists in uniting in one whole a variety of parts; and these parts can only be obtained from rough objects. If the smooth mountains and plains were broken by different objects, the composition may be good, on a supposition the great lines of it were so before.[72]

Here, composition does not require reference to the surface of the picture but rather to the relation of objects in the painting. Gilpin illustrates his example of the failure of smooth landscape with two prints. The first shows the smooth hills (Figure 2.6), and the second has hills characteristic of 'rough' scenery with trees, banks, a castle and peasants (Figure 2.7). The confused relation of depths, which for Gilpin makes the first print a failure, is clarified in the second by the quality of line and its suggestion of proximity or distance from details. This aspect of depth in a painting, which today is often called 'aerial perspective', was called 'keeping'. In the *Essay Upon Prints* Gilpin writes:

> To make a print agreeable as a whole, a just observation of those rules is necessary, which relate to design, disposition, keeping, and the distribution of light: to make it agreeable in its parts, of those which relate to drawing, expression, grace and perspective.[73]

He later defines 'keeping' thus: 'the different degrees of strength and faintness, which objects receive from nearness and distance'.[74] We can see that Gilpin's picturesque is at the opposite pole of a range that includes his 'wholeness'. Keeping, but also design, disposition and light, all aspects of composition and hence wholeness, arise from drawing and its affinity with the roughness of the world.

The next point to note about these remarkable prints is that in a modern understanding, their compositions are the same in that the surface of the image is divided and organized in the same way. Gilpin thought that their 'great lines' are the same while their compositions are different. We might agree, with Gilpin, that the lack of 'keeping' spoils the first print. But if pictorial order is the distribution of marks on the surface and its relation to represented depths, the prints only differ on this last point: each succeeds differently at representing depths. In fact, I have shown these prints to colleagues and many prefer the smooth hills. I conjecture that what they prefer is learned through modern pictures, where the surface is more apparent and the depths less 'kept'.

Gilpin's practice and ideas of drawing are further expounded in the third essay, 'On Sketching Landscape'. Here he proposes that one should draw a hasty sketch in black lead on site, to capture the characteristics of the scene, especially the 'intersections of the country' – the 'great lines' of the intersecting hills in the previous example. Later, at leisure, one should darken the pencil lines with pen and ink and use an ink wash to 'keep' the distances. This is a sketch for the memory. To convey one's ideas to others, a second, 'adorned sketch' is made on a fresh sheet. The adornment here is 'composition', achieved by the addition of a foreground.

> the first point is to fix composition. But the composition, you say, is already fixed by the original sketch. It is true: but still may admit little alterations. [. . .] We must ever

Figure 2.6 William Gilpin, Untitled (smooth hills: example of composition 1) 1792.

Figure 2.7 William Gilpin, Untitled (rough hills: example of composition 2) 1792.

recollect that nature is most defective in composition and must be a little assisted. [. . .] The foreground is a mere spot, compared to the extension of the distance: in itself it is of trivial consequence: and cannot well be called a feature of the scene. And yet tho so little essential to giving a likeness, it is more so than any other part in forming a composition.[75]

If one compares Gilpin's own sketches from memory with those 'adorned sketches' (see Figure 2.5) he and other artists and engravers prepared for publication, one can see that what Gilpin is adjusting is 'composition' in the modern sense. A tree or outcrop in the foreground will fall one-third from the left to balance a castle in the mid-ground placed one-third from the right. He is clearly intersecting the distribution of the surface and the depths of the view: the concern for 'keeping', for the maintenance of depths into the page, is a conceptualization of the prior condition of the page, or picture, as surface.

I have spent some time recounting the instability and freshness of these practices and their conceptualization to insist that there is no law of pictorial composition preceding picturesque architecture and gardening. At this time, the possibility of pictorial composition in the modern sense is emerging, but as part of the larger issue of the picture *per se*. Gilpin's picturesque is all a matter of painting and drawing; it is a quality of pictures in pictures. Although Gilpin says much about the gardens and parks he visited, and his early *Observations on Stowe* were very important, he treats them as objects of a painting practice, and invariably prefers nature to artifice. Nevertheless, Gilpin loosens the connection of the discipline of painting from pictures by presenting his own drawings and thoughts about them, not as objects for emulation by painters, but as a practice of seeing and judging the world. It is a small step from here to seeing the pictorial as a technique applicable in gardening and architecture.

The *Essay Upon Prints* and Gilpin's drawings leave no doubt that he understood de Piles, a modern concept of the picture and its value of picturesqueness. Yet, the moment he extends the term to phenomenal views, and thus loses the surface, boundedness and framing of the picture, picturesqueness regresses into those rough details of the subject suited to be pictured. When Gilpin advises on the invention of foregrounds in a sketch, or the purely mental play of moving hills for the picturesque traveller, he is proposing that one should supply surface, boundary and frame – that is, the image-field of the picture – which is still slightly novel in his time. But for Gilpin, in its roughness, this subject-less subject of landscape is already picture-esque. It would be more logical for him to have said that this was 'painterly', or suited to the pencil and brush. This etymological correction occurred in the twentieth century when translators of Heinrich Wölfflin invented the neologism to translate the German word for picturesque *malerisch*. (I discuss this development in Chapter 6.) Yet, some of the significance of the picturesque lies in the original confusion of *pittoresco* being assimilated to 'picture' rather than 'painter', and Gilpin's marrying French theory of the optical reception of paintings to his own experience of seeing landscape and making art. One way to characterize the eighteenth-century theory of the picturesque is to think of it as mistaking the new pictorial theory as a licence for something else altogether. The picturesque, in this light, can be defined negatively as everything about pictures excepting their image-field; and thus maintaining in tourism, landscape gardening and architecture an older idea of a *unité de sujet*, where space and visual order belong to the contents of the work. Just as Harries shows that the apparent abstraction of rocaille is better understood as a paradoxical aestheticization of ornament, we should be careful of anachronism when looking for modern subjective concepts of aesthetic experience in the picturesque. This is its outcome, but the picturesque begins as an equally paradoxical aestheticization of painting craft and genre.

Price, Reynolds and genre

Price's *Essay on the Picturesque* of 1794 can be understood as the not altogether comfortable marriage of two propositions about the picturesque that had been circulating through the eighteenth century. First, that the picturesque was not a mode of beauty but an alternative and complementary term of aesthetic approbation. Second, that a study of pictures was not only training in visual sensibility but could be a direct guide to the design of particular gardens and buildings. Price's ideas are a development of the earlier ideas of Whately, Mason and especially Gilpin. Price elaborated his first highly successful *Essay on the Picturesque* with several more in which his position is restated more or less digressively until the definitive set of his *Essays on the Picturesque* was published in 1810. One of the more interesting aspects of Price's work, his writings on taste and disgust, are discussed in the next chapter. Here, his book is introduced for another reason: I will show how it can be understood as an attempt to reconcile the picturesque and an aesthetic concept of art with painting as an art discipline, particularly the institution of the hierarchy of genres. For eighteenth-century thinkers such as Price, the major issue in connecting pictures to architecture and gardens was not the technical armature of composition, which as we have seen was only emerging at this time, but rather a matter anterior to any concept of the organization of paintings – the ranking of their subjects and themes, and of the grades of merit of painters.[76]

The importance of genre is plain in Reynolds' letter responding to the manuscript of Gilpin's *Essays*, which was published with the book. Reynolds, after expressing some interest in Gilpin's text, rejected its central premise by proposing an alternative meaning for the term. He asks:

> whether the epithet *picturesque* is not applicable to the excellences of the inferior schools, rather than to the higher. The works of Michael Angelo, Raphael &c. appear to me to have nothing of it; whereas Reubens, and the Venetian painters may almost be said to have nothing else.
>
> Perhaps *picturesque* is somewhat synonymous to the word *taste*; which we should think improperly applied to Homer, or Milton, but very well to Pope or Prior. I suspect that the application of these words are to excellences of an inferior order; and which are incompatible with the grand style.[77]

Reynolds was following a tradition of grading kinds of painting or genres in terms of their nobility. André Félibien had made a hierarchy of genre one of the fundaments of neoclassicism in the debates in the French academy in the 1660s.[78] In the first place, this nobility is of the subject painted. Its acme is 'history painting': scenes from the bible or the classics, and, somewhat controversially in Reynolds' time, modern scenes of human achievement or tragedy. Below history painting was portraiture and landscape, in varying precedence, and last, what is confusingly called genre painting, which took as its subject the so-called 'still-life' of foods and flowers, but also scenes of everyday life. Reynolds' version of this traditional hierarchy is in fact simpler, having one big step between what he called the 'grand style' and ornamental painting intended for sensuous pleasure. What is grand about the grand style is its being governed by liberal ideas and not by mechanical issues of technique or attempts at sensual pleasing. Reynolds then splits history painting to make this clear, and he claims that some painters of history topics should be classed as ornamental:

> TINTORET, Paul Veronese, and others of the Venetian school, seem to have painted with no other purpose than to be admired for their skill and expertness in the mechanism of painting, and to make a parade of that art, which as I before observed, the higher stile requires its followers to conceal.[79]

He did not rank the lower genres explicitly, but considered the merits of the artist in incorporating or alluding to aspects of the grand style in their humbler topoi.[80] The hierarchy of genres was also a hierarchy of artists, the grand style requiring the greater genius, although no degree of excellence in the lower 'departments' of painting (Reynolds does not use the word genre) could equal achievement of the grand style.

The principle behind this hierarchy is a thoroughgoing idealism. Reynolds thinks that 'the beauty of which we are in quest is general and intellectual, it is an idea which subsists only in the mind; the sight never beheld it, nor the hand expressed it'.[81] The grand style is superior; it is the highest level of generalization of which art is capable. The inferior genres are so because they are based on particular observation. Reynolds was so much an idealist that he was a cultural relativist about the experience of beauty. Against Burke's attempt at an objective description of beauty, Reynolds argues that Negro peoples would have different 'species' of beauty, equally valid as those held by Europeans. Reynolds' thought, while Platonist on the whole, is also influenced by the epistemology of John Locke, who held that the mind functions to sort, order and judge sense impressions into increasing levels of abstraction and generality.[82] At one level, then, Reynolds is an empiricist, thinking that an artist's achievements come from successive close observations of nature and their distillation into ideas. This process constitutes the excellences of which the lower genres are capable. But Reynolds also gives art an inter-subjective dimension where his idealism returns. The individual artist 'dies without imparting' great truths and ideas, and it is only 'by a succession of art' that the grand style is possible.[83] Thus Reynolds' Discourses require the study of art, of collective knowledge, over and above a study of nature. This is the meaning of his suggestion that the picturesque is a matter of 'taste', or merely empirical observation and subjective judgement. The grand style is, by contrast, a sum of empirical observations greater than any one life. Artists possessed of genius grasp these great ideas and further progress them by subsuming their observation of the world to artistic ideation.

Reynolds' politely worded rejection of Gilpin is, then, quite sweeping. The picturesque is either a meaningless adjective subsumed within the genre system, or contradictory to it, and thus to be rejected. Reynolds is rejecting the idea that aesthetic experience (in the sense of sensuous experience and judgements based merely on this) could be a common basis for assessing art and nature. For Reynolds the point of understanding nature is to understand divine providence, not nature's appearance. The means to move from the observation of appearances to such ideas is through great art of the most general themes. The aesthetic question, that of the basis for our pleasure at both art and nature, does not arise. Beauty is ideation, is art, and nature (here, the question of how we process our lived experience) is a litmus test of the issue that actually concerns him: how to judge art and encourage its progress.[84]

Price's *Essay*[85] shows a detailed and thorough reading of Reynolds, of the Discourses, Reynolds' notes to Mason's edition of du Fresnoy, and (as he mentions, Gilpin's letter to Reynolds[86]), most likely Reynolds' reply. This is reason to think that it is Reynolds' rejection of the picturesque that provides the problematic Price sets out to address with his later *Essays*. It is more usual to see Price's theory of the picturesque in relation to Burke, and his splitting of the category of aesthetic feeling into the beautiful and the sublime. It is true that this is a major trajectory in Price, but we should also understand Price's proposal as framed by a larger project to reconcile aesthetic thinking with the pre-existing paradigm of sense, feeling and judgement – that is, art. Indeed, in the tensions Price identifies and seeks to overcome, we witness the beginnings of the war between aesthetics and art, continuing to this day.[87]

Price is in complete sympathy with Gilpin's visual sensibilities that arise from sketching. Uvedale's father, Robert, was an accomplished amateur artist who drew from nature, and his grandfather, Uvedale Tomkyns Price, was a friend and patron of Gainsborough. The Prices collected Dutch landscape painting of the kind that inspired de Piles and Gainsborough, and Uvedale refers to these frequently in his *Essays*.[88] Where Price builds substantially on Gilpin is in following Reynolds explicitly with his proposal to use 'picturesque' as a term of approbation for this lower genre of painting. Picturesque is then no longer, as Gilpin thought, a generalization about the quality of pictures, whether of pictorial composition or execution. In Price, the picturesque is a theory of taste and in particular of how paintings, painters and their ranks of nobility can be a matrix that aids aesthetic judgement in the improvement of country estates. Where Price differs from Reynolds and indeed, from most prior art theory, is in supposing that the spectator's preferences and the quality of their judgement cannot be inferred from the nobility of the picture or artist. Reynolds (in terms that will interest us in the next chapter 'Disgust') thought that artists of genius could enoble low subjects.

> What was said of Virgil, that he threw even the dung about the ground with an air of dignity, may be applied to Titian; whatever he touched, however naturally mean, and habitually familiar, by a kind of magick he invested with grandeur and importance.[89]

Price makes this exception into a rule and generalizes it to viewers as well as painters. Price proposes a high taste for low genre pictures, founding the picturesque on the lower genres but nevertheless elevating it to a general category of aesthetic feeling. To rationalize this, he draws on the most controversial aspect of Gilpin's and Burke's theories: the idea that the appreciation of pictures of low subjects does not necessarily imply a love of those things in life. Reconciling the alternative forms of this approbation as picturesque or beautiful, with the differentiation of art and life, leads Price to elaborate a somewhat nasty theory of disgust, which is the topic of the next chapter. Here we are concerned with the importance of genre and, again, the relative weakness of concepts of composition.

Price's weak, toadying, but none the less radical argument with Reynolds takes up much of Chapter VI.[90] He begins by discussing his concept of the picturesque in relation to Burke's ideas of perceptual physiology and psychology. Having shown, to his own satisfaction, that picturesque roughness affects the eye differently to the smoothness that Burke thought the cause of beauty, Price proceeds to discuss the 'roughness' of many famous paintings and Reynolds' opinion of their merit. By the end of the examples, Price's own graded system has appeared from a cloud of inference and he states: 'each style of painting corresponds with the characteristic marks of the grand, the beautiful and the picturesque'.[91] Price is matching the aesthetic terms against painting hierarchies. Price's 'grand' is a conflation of Reynolds' 'grand style' with Burke's sublime. Reynolds' elevation of ideas over sensual pleasure in colour and ornament Price took as evidence that the grand style is not beautiful. He has either misunderstood or wilfully ignored the idealist concept of beauty in Reynolds and replaced it with Burkean empiricism. If the grand style is not pleasing to the senses, it must therefore be sublime. In the *Essays*, Price shows no understanding of the Burkean sublime, treating the term traditionally, as an elevated rhetoric,[92] but we can see the distinction he wishes to exist when he argues that the paintings of 'Michael Angelo':

> have nothing of sensual attraction, and the same thing may be said in great measure of the other masters of his and the Roman school: their colouring, however well adapted to the character of their figures and compositions, however it may satisfy the judgement, has little to please the eye; and I should conceive that if it applied to objects divested of grandeur and dignity, the union would appear incongruous.[93]

The 'ornamental' style of the Venetians (and Rubens who followed them) has a beauty found in colour, fine graduations of tone and facial complexion, proper to that style. What Price achieved is a theory of genres, not based on a hierarchy of artistic difficulty or merit, but on the genres' grounding in differing physiological or psychological aspects of human perception. What is his aim in doing so?

Price wanted to move from a naturalist concept of genre to a conventionalist one because what interested him was the transcoding of genres, one into the other. His admiration for Shakespeare, Henry Fielding and Rembrandt shows his toleration of mixed genres, such as tragi-comedy in literary works.[94] Price followed Reynolds' argument that the higher the art the more research into particularities of surface is transcended in an apprehension of deep general ideas. This has an immediate corrolary in the artist's technique: low artists are 'high finishers' whose work is valued for the mechanics of its imitation; higher artists have their works valued not for the mechanical work of their hands but for the resonances of their mental reflections.[95] In his own pictures, Reynolds had a tendency to paint with what was later thought an affected negligence precisely to connote liberality of mind.[96] But Price goes one step further in his admiration for Rembrandt's paintings of low subjects. Rembrandt was careless of process in his genre paintings, paintings normally valued for verisimilitude; he produced 'an *idea* of detail' (my italics) and this marks him as an artist capable of painting history pictures and finishing them properly.[97]

Reynolds gives the impression that it would be inappropriate for a gentleman of taste to have any appreciation of the lower genres of art. Price clearly admires Teniers, Dow (Gerrit Dou), van Ostade, Wowermans (Philips Wouwerman), but he rarely risks praise without qualification. The great merit he claims for them is not as art, but as aid to the improver. The whole thrust of this interest in the lower genres of art becomes clear in the 'Essay on Picturesque Architecture and Building'.[98] While the sublime is no use at all in the mundane matters of estate management, and the beautiful is rarely relevant to the mansion (where decisions on improvement are required only every other generation, or so), the smaller capital works of gate-houses, decorative buildings in the park and even workers' cottages and agricultural buildings might be regular occasions for the landholder to exercise his taste. The understanding of these occasions as 'picturesque' will be sufficient, Price thinks, for the gentleman to imply that his taste is not limited to low genres but is greater for ranging freely across them all.

> All the splendid effects of architecture, and of assemblages of magnificent buildings, whether in cities, or amidst rural scenery, can only be displayed by princes, and men of princely revenues: but it is in the power of men of moderate fortunes, by slight additions and alterations to produce a very essential change in the appearance of farm buildings, cottages etc. and the grouping of them in villages and such effects, although less splendid than those of regular architecture are not less interesting. There is indeed no scene where such a variety of forms and embellishments may be introduced at so small an expense and without anything fantastic, or unnatural, as that of a village, none where the lover of painting and the lover of humanity, may find so many sources of amusement and interest.[99]

What Price thought one might learn is clear in his description of the prints of Isaack van Ostade (Figure 2.8).

> There cannot be a more thorough boor than Ostade, and it might be concluded from the monsters he has painted by way of human figures, that he never thought of form in any objects; but let anyone carefully examine . . . his pictures . . . they will see how in the insides of kitchens, he has selected every circumstance that can vary the forms, and give intricacy to their disposition. [. . .] The outsides of his cottages are no less distinguished for their variety and intricacy. Their outline against the sky, is generally

> composed of forms of unequal heights, thrown into many different degrees of perspective; the sides are varied by projecting windows and doors, by sheds supported by brackets, with flower-pots on them; by the light airy, and detached appearance of cages hung out from the wall; by porches and trellices of various constructions, often covered with vine or ivy: these, and many other picturesque objects, are so happily grouped with each other and with trees, that the bare outline would prove how much the eye may be pleased, and what skill may be shewn in the playful variety and intricacy of buildings and their appendages.[100]

His broadening of the categories of art and nature to encompass everyday surroundings, and his mention of social aims in the improving of villages, have led some to misunderstand Price's attitude as 'democratic'. This is in the double sense of progressive liberation from taste as a calculus of class; and breaking the bounds of form and content in art. As Price continues his discussion of van Ostade, it is easy to see how such an anachronistic and inverted view could arise.

> There can hardly be a stronger contrast then between a picture of Claude, and one of Ostade. [. . .] Nothing can be more directly opposite than the character of his [Claude's] and of Ostade's buildings; yet there is no slight resemblance in their manner of considering the effect of buildings in general . . . The porches and posts of the one answer those purposes as effectively as the porticos and columns of the other; projecting roofs, sheds with brackets, and rails, have the effects of cornices and balustrades: the

Figure 2.8 Isaack van Ostade, *Rest by a Cottage*, 1648.

> vulgar flower pots of Ostade take the form of urns and vases in Claude: his winding staircase, of magnificent flights of steps; it is the fable of Baucis and Philemon. Architecture is the divinity, that raises the porches of cottages and the rude posts that support them, into porticos and temples.[101]

The equivalence of Claude and Ostade on 'the effects of building in general' is not a troubling aestheticism that leads to a 'democratisation of subject matter', as the literary historian Martin Price has claimed about this passage.[102] The understanding of 'general effects' is neither a nascent architectural formalism nor an opening for architecture to take a social role in workers' housing. The fable, which is from Ovid's *Metamorphoses*, makes this clear.[103] Baucis and Philemon were poor Phrygian peasants who, after their compatriots refused, gave hospitality to travellers who were in fact Zeus and Hermes in disguise. The gods sent a storm that destroyed the region, leaving only their hosts unharmed. The cottage was changed into a temple and Baucis and Philemon to trees at its entrance. What Price is explaining is the occasion for displaying expertise and taste when treating a cottage like a temple; what is at stake here is a rising through a hierarchy – a high taste for low objects – not a levelling.

Further, note how scant is the information on the 'effects of building in general'. Apart from a few hints about broken roof-lines, we learn largely that architectural ornament could be transposed to the thatch and trellis of cottages. Just as we have established that there are no canons of pictorial composition in Gilpin, neither is there, in Price, a picturesque, architectural composition that could challenge the classical notions of disposition and ornamentation in Jacques-François Blondel or William Chambers. And yet this is precisely the outcome of architects reading Price who, in the following decade produced a manner of irregular planning and visual effect quite distinct from classicism and through this choice, opened the terrain of architectural composition. The possibility of the composition of buildings with regard to their visual appearance is present in Price, but no more than the idea that modern pictorial composition is imminent in Gilpin's recognition that the sketch makes the surface of the picture apparent. There is a strong case for seeing Price's picturesque as the advent of architectural formalism, but attending to the 'picture' in the picturesque reminds us that here, form is merely a routine in the game of genre, which only gradually becomes the 'character and composition' of nineteenth-century architecture.

I can restate these issues in more concrete terms thus: Price wishes to improve his estates in a manner consistent with his fine taste and education in art, yet his estate of Foxley, like most of England, is unlike the Golden Age landscapes of Claude Lorrain or Poussin. What is more, the affectations in the landscapes of Lancelot Brown that disgust Price and his friends result precisely in those ludicrous attempts to make England into a classical landscape. In the terms of painting, England is most like seventeenth-century Dutch and Flemish landscapes that are either wild or humble, such as those of Ruysdael, Hobbema or van Ostade, and these provide models for scenic improvement. But to appreciate such low genre paintings, and to apply to them in the exercise of one's taste, could lead to the imputation that one's taste is low or corrupted. Price wants it absolutely clear that his interest in, and use of, pictures of peasants, cottages, fields and scrubby forests does not imply a lack of appreciation of Titian, Raphael and Michelangelo. The confusion and false imputations that might arise by making low art a model for improvement are solved by the new term for approving low art and improvement. Dutch paintings are picturesque while Italian painting of the Grand Manner remains grand or beautiful. This hierarchy also articulates an issue of the relation of art to nature, and of aesthetic to moral judgement. What is beautiful in representation is also beautiful in life – that is to say, proper and desirable – while things picturesque, such as thatch in poor repair, can be praised in representation and deplored in actuality. We can appreciate immediately the door Price opens; his attempt to maintain the hierarchies of painting suggests a possible reversal. For Price or Reynolds, the highest forms of paintings, to the greatest extent, must be stitched into the fundaments of human existence. But in an aesthetic consideration, this means that they have less autonomy; that they are less purely pictures.

Breadth and connection

Price comes close to a modern concept of pictorial composition when he discusses 'breadth', which is his word for de Piles '*clair-obscur*'. But for Price, the 'connection' that this breadth effects is not only visual but also an emblem of social harmony. Breadth means that a scene forms into general areas rather than the 'broken and disjointed' form of a hill planted with poorly scattered clumps and single trees. 'In all these cases, the eye, instead of reposing on one broad, connected whole, is stopt and harassed by little disunited, discordant parts'.[104] Price, however, does not think this an issue of the general distribution of paint on canvas, but rather the 'breadth of light and shadow'. This breadth lies in the painter's power to imagine the time of day when depths can be kept by arranging a foreground in strong shadow, a distant church picked out by sunlight and so on. For Price, the main lesson of painting is to graduate the range of illumination to avoid sharp contrasts and form wholes. Landscape improvers should do the same, Price advises, by avoiding white buildings and Brown's clumpy planting. Both painter and improver are imitating the effects of twilight. 'In fact, twilight does, what an improver ought to do: it connects what was before scattered; it fills up staring, meagre vacancies; it destroys edginess; and by giving shadow as well as light to water, at once increases both its brilliancy and softness'.[105] In this, Price is completely in accord with de Piles, who was most likely his source. De Piles tells an anecdote of Titian modelling his composition on a bunch of grapes where *clair-obscur*, or light and shade, make the multitude of grapes into the unified form of a bunch:

> many Grapes, which are the parts of it, are in the Light, many in the Shadow, and the rest faintly Colour'd to make them go farther back. *Titian* once told Tintoret, *That in his greatest Works, a bunch of Grapes had been his principal Rule and his surest Guide.*[106]

Because the painter can choose the lighting, this emphasizes aspects of the painting that belong to painting rather than visual qualities of things in the view. The avoidance of white paint and red brickwork avoids the particularity of things in the view. Twilight further narrows the colour range and contrast, giving a greater connecting role for light and shadow and making an overall pattern across the picture. Richard Payne Knight makes a similar description of the quality of pictures that are picturesque, but does this with reverberations of the argument between the *Rubénistes* and *Poussinistes*.

> The great painters of the Venetian and Lombard schools; and afterwards those of the Flemish and Dutch, carried this principle of massing [of light and shadow] to a degree beyond what appears in ordinary nature; and departed from the system of strict imitation in a contrary extreme to that of their predecessors. Instead of making their lines more distinct, and keeping their tints more separate, than the visible appearance of the objects of imitation warranted, they blended and melted them together with a playful and airy kind of lightness, and a sort of loose and sketchy indistinctness not observable in

> the reality, unless under peculiar circumstances and modifications of the atmosphere; and then only in those objects and combinations of objects, which exhibit blended and broken tints, or irregular masses of light and shadow harmoniously melted into each other. Such are the objects and compositions of objects which we properly call picturesque . . .[107]

In this contrast of linearity to unbounded and merged areas of tone and colour, Knight was simplifying the famous contrast of *dessin* and *coloris*. He did so in a manner that, as Walter Hipple points out, makes his words seem prescient of Heinrich Wölfflin's much later dialectic of the linear and the painterly, which unfolds to also include clearness and unclearness.[108] This is probably because the authors have a common source in the French debates, but there are further parallels between Wölfflin and the picturesque that I will take up in Chapter 6. The passage quoted comes from a section where Knight criticizes his friend's insistence that there is a picturesque genre. Knight's definition of the picturesque in massing of light and shade and suppression of detailed delineation is, he writes, applicable to any subject:

> The boors of Ostade, the peasants of Gainsborough, and the shepherds of Berghem, are picturesque; but so likewise are the warriors of Salvator Rosa, the apostles of Raphael, and the bacchanalians of Poussin [. . .] The dirty and tattered garments, the dishevelled hair, and general wild appearance of gipsies and beggar girls are often picturesque: but the flowing ringlets, fine shawls, and robes of delicate muslin thrown into all the easy, negligent, and playful folds of antique drapery by polished grace and refined elegance, are still more so. The first, indeed, are merely picturesque; that is, they have only the painter's beauties of harmonious variety of tint, and that is disgusting; while the others have these in an equal, or even superior degree, in addition to the charms of lightness, neatness, and purity.[109]

Knight's ideas are more consistent with de Piles and with a modern concept of the visual, but Price's attempt to conserve genre and the unity of the subject of painting tells us much about the idiosyncrasies of the picturesque and why it was not modernist formalism *avant la lettre*. Price's problem is that Reynolds, to whom he is committed, is largely *Poussiniste* as far as hierarchies of genre are concerned, even if the academician's paint handling was quite expressive. Thus Price is committed both to pictorial values native to painting and to the system of genre in painting that imitates external social hierarchies. Nigel Everett has shown how Price's concept of 'connection' is as much to do with socio-political matters as painting.[110] The scattered clumps and levelled grounds that make poor composition are also the form of landscape of Lancelot Brown. For Price, the faults of these were also in the alienation of the gentry and their estates from the people. A picturesque landscape should also be one of mutual connection and dependency between ranks of society. In fact, it is not inconsistent for Price to find picturesque values in all genres *and* to have a hierarchy of genres. What Knight calls the 'merely picturesque' of disgusting things has for Price a significance not pictorial, nor social: that disgusting things please as pictures opens a way to understand art aesthetically, which is the topic of my next chapter.

Repton and the limits of the picture

Price sent a copy of his *Essay on the Picturesque* to Repton, the self-titled Landscape Gardener, who Price knew and with whom he had discussed his ideas before publication. In the meantime, Repton had been publicly mocked by Price's friend Knight and he read Price's *Essay* as an implicit attack on his practice and values. Repton then published a 'Letter to Uvedale Price Esq.' attacking Price's system of 'improving by neglect and accident'.[111] Repton claimed that Price's picturesque disallows the everyday comfort and utility associated with beauty. In doing so, he ignores Price's caveats: that the picturesque is not to be preferred to the beautiful; that empirically, they are generally mixed. Rather than seeing Repton as an unfair reader of Price, there is a case for thinking of him as motivated by an inchoate argument: Price's proposed plurality of values could not but destroy the union of taste and value – the basic ethic of his noble clients. Price's response to Repton's letter takes up 154 pages of Volume III of the *Essays* and is so tedious as to warm anyone to Repton's side. It contains only one issue relevant to our discussion of pictures: the question of high and low viewpoints.

Despite his disagreements with Price and Knight, which resulted (inconsistently) in disavowals of the term 'picturesque', Repton's design practice is the strongest case of a picturesque founded on pictorial composition. There is no doubt that Repton designed in phenomenal space using pictorial tools, and that he understood and presented the merit of his work in terms of how much a picture of the landscape improved with his alterations. His techniques are now familiar: strengthened foregrounds, framed elements within the scene such as boughs of trees, and off-centre eye-catching features in the mid or far distance. Repton, because he was a talented designer and water-colourist, demonstrated in text, paintings and on the ground, the extension of pictorial concepts that in Gilpin are almost tautological (instanced as they are in a discussion of painting) and which in Price are so vague as to be nearly irrelevant. There is an important point of agreement between Price and Repton on how the issue of the height of the horizon in a painting positions the genre of landscape painting and its relation to real property. This idea is also discussed in Chapter 5 'Appropriation', along with a fuller account of Repton's ideas and practice. Here my point is, yet again, the limits that Repton put on what he took to be the excesses of the visual aspects of the picture-esque.

A large part of Repton's *Red Book* for Attingham (1797) is given over to a refutation of Price titled 'Of Landscape Painting: The futility of Mr Price's idea "that all improvements of scenery should be derived from the Works of the great painters".' Most of this was published in *Observations* in 1803.[112] There are two pictorial demonstrations that interest us here. The first is Repton's figure II, which is a brown ink wash of a scene near the house with 'fragments of an old mill and brick arches which make a charming study for a painter, and the composition is not unlike that beautiful picture of Ruisdale's [sic] at Attingham . . .'.[113] In the background, the picture shows a segment of the neo-Greek colonnade of the house (designed by James 'Athenian' Stuart). The composition, according to Repton, leads us to a point where:

> we cannot but suppose this the fragment of some Grecian temple in ruins and not part of the modern inhabited Palace. Hence it is evident, that the mind cannot associate the ideas of elegance with neglect, or perfect repair and neatness with ruin and decay: such objects, therefore, however picturesque in themselves, are incongruous and misplaced, if near such a palace as ATTINGHAM.[114]

Hence, the ruins of the mill should be removed. Here, Repton is rejecting Price's proposition that one might mix genres; that the picturesque and the beautiful might co-exist in one scene.[115] For my present purposes, the point is a simple one. Repton, who demonstrates a better grasp than his contemporaries of the abstract concept and techniques of the pictorial, does not propose that this should be the primary ground for organizing space any more than it is the primary ground for painting. Aspects such as genre and the relations of the objects in the representation or garden, are the principal order of the picture, its 'unity of the subject', and are the necessary foundation for the purely visual composition of the picture plane.

Repton's second demonstration of the fallacies of Price's idea is more dramatic, and historically significant. Plate N:II (which is neither reproduced in *Observations* nor the Loudon edition of his works)[116] shows, in the closed position, a neat three-by-four proportioned 'landscape' with fore, mid and backgrounds, and snapped into the grid of parallel thirds by a tree and distant steeple (Figure 2.9). When the 'slide', or covering flap, is opened, what is revealed is a wide view of the proportions of one to six of which the 'landscape' had been a small part (Figure 2.10).

Repton writes of this demonstration:

> Another mistake of the admirers of Artificial landscape, is the difference in the quantity of a natural and an artificial Composition. The finest pictures of Claude De Loraine (and here again I must refer to a picture at Attingham,) seldom consist of more than one fifth of that field of vision which the eye can with ease behold without any motion of the head, viz. about twenty degrees out of ninety, and we may further add that without moving the body, our field of vision is extended to one hundred and eighty degrees.
>
> Now it is obvious that the picture of Claude already mentioned which is about four or five foot long, if it had been extended to twenty or thirty feet would not have been so pleasing a composition, because instead of a picture it would have resembled a Panorama.
>
> This I shall instance in sketch N:II which represents in miniature the view from the breakfast room, yet altho' it is by far too long for a picture, includes only half of what maybe seen . . .
>
> If we take a very small part of this view, it maybe made a pleasing picture, by supposing a tree to balance the Oak grove and form a kind of frame or foreground to the Landscape – Are we then to plant such a tree or succession of trees to divide the whole field of vision into separate landscapes? and would not such an attempt at improvement, be like putting five or six pictures of Claude into one long frame?[117]

Again, Repton's animus for Price has led him to overstate his position. In practice, he did manipulate background and foreground so that the park, apparently fortuitously, snaps into pictorial compositions from particular viewpoints. One of the reasons that Repton proposes the reintroduction of formal gardens near the house is so that they provide an ambient foreground to views onto the park. At Blaise Castle near Bristol, the broad view from the house offers two objects to view that Repton introduces: the pre-existing Castle and a Woodsman's Cottage. To focus on either of these is to mentally supply the horizontal boundaries of the 'picture', to allow one's view to be composed like a picture. Nevertheless, the obvious good sense of Repton's point remains: visual experience and pictures are not the same. Repton's demonstration supports that of Schapiro, mentioned at the beginning of the chapter: pictorial composition does not exist as a pure organization of the visual, rather, it assumes a kind of surface.

Those who think that the picturesque is concerned with making the view from a situation look strongly like a picture misunderstand not only the non-visual aspects of pictures such as genre, but also the spatio-visual aspects of the picturesque. It is not incorrect to think of

Figure 2.9 Humphry Repton, View exercise (first state), Plate NIII of the Attingham *Red Book*, 1791. © NTPL/John Hammond.

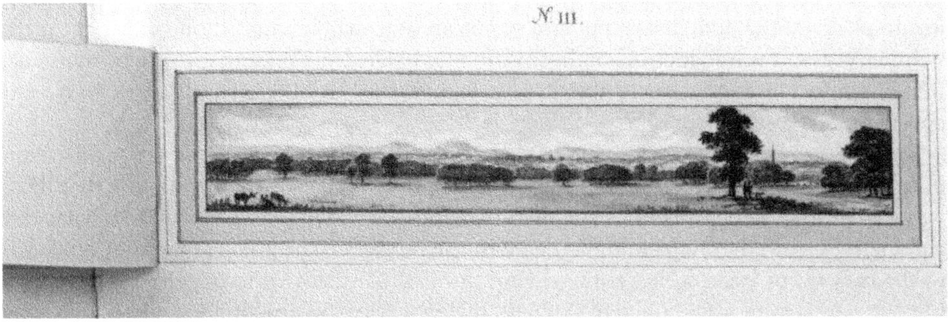

Figure 2.10 Humphry Repton, View exercise (second state), Plate NIII of the Attingham *Red Book*, 1791. © NTPL/John Hammond.

many eighteenth-century gardens as a succession of pictures, but it is wrong to think that the stilling and flattening of phenomenal visual experience was the aim. Rather the picture was, and still functions as, a prompt to spatial imagination. The picturesque had then, and continues to have, a low threshold of adequacy of pictorial composition in the modern sense. A scene need only seem to be a picture, and the compositional quality of that picture matters little for the picturesque, or at least no more so than the actual spatial coherence of a represented scene matters in a painting. The picturesque works by making a viewer strongly aware of their vision, but what they see approaches the flatness of a picture only momentarily before its actual depths unfold. The process is then repeated. In Repton's pictorial view in the Attingham *Red Book* two trees in the foreground frame an oak grove and a church spire. The 'balance' Repton produces is one in which the spire marks a vertical third and the oak grove a horizontal third of the picture plane. Repton's 'slide' produces a framing that he supposes we mentally produce in vision acculturated with pictures. This is a moment of recognition, and the enjoyment of recognizing the pictorial qualities that the view does not require us to shuffle a few paces to the side so that the spire falls exactly a third of the way into the imagined picture plane, it asks us to move on and find another picture. In the picturesque, the picture is not an invitation to become a painter, and to flatten space. Rather, like the value eighteenth-century painting theorists put on 'keeping' or maintaining a coherent representation of depth, the 'picture' of the picturesque invites us to walk into the view; to dissolve the picture in order to 'keep' its distances for one's self.

Architecture and pictures

In the picturesque, for the first time, architectural projects were considered in terms of their visual appearance. This is not as surprising as it sounds; I could weaken the claim by saying that issues of the visual appearance of buildings were, for the first time, separated from more holistic concepts of their disposition. As Puttfarken shows, while Renaissance painters were not indifferent to the appearance of their paintings, it did not occur to them to understand the visual form of the painting separately, nor to give such considerations precedence over the arrangement of the objects depicted. The 'picture', with its proposition of a visual order by which the painting could be apprehended and its contents and execution subsequently studied, is a watershed not just for painting but for architecture: first, it spelled the end of mural painting's dominance and the joint surface linking architecture and painting; second, ideas of visual form were applied from painting to architecture as Price suggested. The parallels are strong. It is not the case that architects of the Renaissance were indifferent to the appearance of their buildings, but that there would have been little sense in understanding an image of the building except as a symptom of its whole disposition, and consequent symmetry. The classical doctrine of the immanence of an ideal building within a phenomenal building also meant that there was little premium on the difference between form and appearance.

To a large extent, the argument of this chapter has proceeded by negation; its main purpose has been to correct some common assumptions. It is mistaken to suggest that there was a well-organized concept of the pictorial, and a set of techniques that architects and gardeners borrowed from painting to begin the picturesque. The import that we should give to the concept of 'picture' lies either side of this false formalist concept of the picturesque. On one side, we can place concrete technical matters. Price's instruction to architects to copy from the irregularly planned buildings of painters and to observe, as painters might, the humble accretionary buildings of rural England has two consequences. First, it causes a revolution in planning technique that is the prerequisite for nineteenth-century ideas of style and twentieth-century ideas of functional planning. This issue is examined in Chapter 4. Second, it explodes the generic difference between vernacular building and learned architecture and leads to the modern idea that architecture is a quality of consideration applicable to all building: that workers' housing could be architecture; that there can be architecture without architects, etc. On the other, abstract side, what 'picture' implies is the idea of the appearance of building, and an empirical account of the experience of building, becoming a general criterion of architecture, replacing symmetry and thus redefining the discipline at a basic level.

Understanding that there is no middle picturesque between the specificities of technique and this highly general and abstract concept of architecture as a discipline can help us avoid another error: the prevalent idea that there are forms of visuality that exist anterior to the culture and production of actual pictures and spaces. It may be that people today are trained and acculturated to understand their experience as cinematic, televisual or hyper-linked, and that Cartesian perspectivalism, the Baroque and the picturesque are historical precedents for modern ways of seeing. However, styles and modes of mental imagination, like mental images themselves, are artefacts based on the actual culture of cinema, television, the internet, buildings and pictures. There is no 'image' *per se*, growing in verisimilitude or affective power with technology.

It has been common for some time to claim that architecture is too much under the sway of images and that this lessens the importance of the palpable spatial experience of buildings. My own discussion of 'picture' in the 'picturesque' raises some of the problems with this complaint against images. While never doubting that architecture is subject to trivialization and reduction to terms other than its own, our question must be 'what images, with what spatiality?' The difference between Rococo and anti-Rococo, or in our terms, fresco and picture, is formed by the kinds of images painted. It becomes a watershed in cultural history because of the spatiality of the classes of images, and the intersection this spatiality makes with the space of building. That we can now define a concept of the 'pictorial' as a mode of relating represented depths to the picture plane understood as a surface, is the legacy not of a founding thought or abstraction, but of a project to use pictures to design spaces. Conceptualization came after technique. At the emergence of the picturesque, what we would now consider pictorial values were not clearly distinguished from physical attributes of pictures, such as the relative novelty of the picture as a transportable surface with autonomous spatiality, and from institutional aspects such as the hierarchy of genre in painting. The history of interdisciplinary moments like the picturesque is not the discovery of common foundations but a kind of introjection between disciplines, where concept becomes technique and vice versa. The consequences of this cross-pollination are numerous and discussed in other chapters of this book. They are mostly to do with matters beyond or at the edge of what can be pictured, such as: movement; the visuality of landscape (in the fuller sense that Repton describes); techniques of planning and the relation of building form and urban form; and questions of genre and the object of art, which we have begun discussing here. However, beyond correcting ideas of the eighteenth-century picturesque and opening further topics, we could now risk another kind of anachronism by assaying what it might mean to build with pictures today.

Coda: Le Corbusier and Herzog and de Meuron, or, the end of the modern picturesque

This chapter has stayed largely in the eighteenth century, but my aim is to show that understanding the picturesque's original complexity can assist in analysing later cultural developments. What the picturesque brings to modern art and architecture is described in subsequent chapters, but it will be useful to hint at this here, and also to sharpen my conclusion by putting a further historical bracket around the concept of the picture in architecture. If painting and architecture have the reciprocal relation that I have established in this chapter, then just as the distance between real and pictorial space became productive through the picturesque, would we not also expect it to close again?

Some have claimed that the modernist architect Le Corbusier and his concept of the *promenade architecturale* are the apogee of picturesque thought and technique.[118] Many would see the sense of this description even if they demur at defining Le Corbusier's approach as picturesque, as Yve-Alain Bois and Richard Etlin have done. Le Corbusier's architecture is modern; it acts not through canon or symbols or any kind of reading practice, but by gathering up the subject into an experience that is directly aesthetic. However, the techniques for doing this are picturesque; they contrive the position, view and movement of the subject. At the Maison la Roche of 1923, one's body is positioned in relation to a view composed like a picture, and yet, like a cinematic image, the edges of this picture are open to the possibility of the panning camera. The house is as much like a landscape garden as it is like cinema; there is no narrative or necessary temporal structure, and the agenda presented to the eye is never quite the route. In Chapter 4, I will examine the issues at stake in writing Le Corbusier into a history of the picturesque, and while there are difficulties, in general I agree with this received view. But here I make a brief point by remembering that Le Corbusier also painted pictures.

There is an incident in the commission and design for the Maison la Roche that will allow me to show some of the consequences of thinking of the 'picture' in the picturesque as I have in this chapter.[119] One of the major aspects of the brief for the house was a picture gallery. La Roche was a patron and collector of the Purist paintings of Fernand Léger, Le Corbusier and Amédée Ozenfant that would hang in this gallery that formed the major event of the *promenade architecturale*. However, Le Corbusier was offended by the manner in which Ozenfant and La Roche hung the space. He wrote to Ozenfant: 'The La Roche house should not take on the look of a house of a (postage-stamp) collector. I insist absolutely that certain parts of the architecture should be entirely free of paintings, so as to create a double effect of pure architecture on the one hand and pure paintings on the other.'[120] Le Corbusier designed storage so that La Roche could put away paintings that he was not presently looking at (Figure 2.11). La Roche declined to build the storage. Now, this rather strange dispute cannot be explained as rivalry between the arts in any simple sense. At a philosophical and artistic level the paintings and building were complementary and many paintings were Le Corbusier's, so why the interdiction against pictures? As La Roche put the dilemma later:

> What can I say? No doubt you have reason for complaint if the impact of your walls, of whom I have been one of the chief admirers, is ruined . . . The house, once built, was so beautiful that on seeing it I cried: 'It's almost a pity to put paintings into it!' Nevertheless I did so. How could I have done otherwise? Do I not have certain obligations with regard to my painters, of whom you yourself are one? I commissioned from you a 'frame for my collection'. You provided me with a 'poem of walls'. Which of us two is most to blame?[121]

One reason might have been that to hang a picture raises the whole problematic of ornament – the architectural need for supplementation, the potential failure of its claims to autonomy. But I think that there is also another reason. The problem with pictures for Le Corbusier is that they challenge the trajectory of architecture in becoming image, of giving haptic experience a kind of form. By an extraordinary predetermination of body position and viewpoint, the Maison la Roche has a sequential and unfolding visual field that is coordinated formally; it has images as a film has images. To an extent, the architecture needs the still space of pictures for durational lived experience to become imagistic. Rosalind Krauss has argued that Le Corbusier's design assumes a frontal view of the paintings, while the viewing of architecture is a matter of rotation. Painting becomes ideation, necessarily flat and disembodied. While architecture is the 'fruition of a lived perspective [. . .] pictorial space is that which cannot be entered or circulated through.'[122] Krauss' opposition here of frontality to incidental viewing is very much the same as that made by Reynolds, Price and Puttfarken over Titian's Pesaro Madonna. Krauss writes as if the merit of Le Corbusier is to discover this hinge between painting and architecture. However, both in relation to Le Corbusier and to the long history of this opposition Krauss underplays the antipathy, and the struggle for precedence between the visual perception of objective space, and the production of semblance out of spaces that the picturesque has been held to effect. Le Corbusier's fear is not that pictures would compete with architecture for our spatial sense, and therefore need to be seen flat on and their space idealized. It is rather that they would cover the walls, like a fresco. Le Corbusier knew that a dense hang of pictures must fail to achieve a *coup d'œil* for each picture. What would be apparent instead is the actual spatiality of the pictorial support, the shallow flat surfaces covering his surfaces with no concept to adhere them. Like a billboard in a beautiful landscape, the flatness of the pictorial support would remind us that

Figure 2.11 (top) Le Corbusier, Maison la Roche, Paris, 1923–5. View of the gallery with paintings by Le Corbusier. The gallery was partially redesigned to this form in 1928, and the table, probably by Charlotte Perriand, takes the place which would have been occupied by the controversial picture store.

Figure 2.12 (right) Herzog and de Meuron, Eberswalde Senior Technical Highschool Library, Germany 1993–6.

the house is quotidian space we wander around in, not a filmic spectacle rolling before our eyes.

In the architecture of the present, the high-art spatial choreography of Le Corbusier has come to look a little didactic, carrying overtones of instructed feeling and compelled sentiment. The consensus of taste has turned to buildings with a strong object-form, whether the 'boxes' of minimalism or the 'blobs' of various neo-expressionist architects. In this regard, the firm Herzog and de Meuron is interesting. In several projects, it combines extreme reductions of form with the application of pictures in what seems to mark the closing of the distance that Le Corbusier sought. Modernists were aware of the traditons of fresco and *sgraffito*. Fernand Léger painted panels for installation in Le Corbusier's Pavilion de l'Esprit Nouveau (1925), and in 1943 with the architects J. L. Sert and Sigfried Giedion called for a new civic iconography of kinetic sculpture, fireworks and large-scale projection and murals.[123] But until recently, the technology for applying large-scale weather-proof images has not been very successful and neither has there been the conceptual work to reconcile such explicit ornamentation with an aesthetic account of modernism. Herzog and de Meuron has worked on both fronts; their work is remarkable for its severe reduction of spatial qualities and their use of applied images. Together these moves announce a kind of end for picturesque/cinematic architecture of the Corbusian sort.

The Eberswalde Library (Germany 1993–6) is a mute box totally covered in pictures commissioned from the photographer Thomas Ruff (Figure 2.12). Ruff chose images from his archive of *Newspaper Photos*, which he had been assembling since 1981. Ruff's art practice involved rephotographing and enlarging these images so that the dot screen of the newsprint was visible, mounting them as art, then printing and exhibiting them in a salon hung not unlike the façade of the Library. In his commission for the Library, Ruff chose apparently varied images that he considered expressive of the situation of an old forestry college in the east after the reunification of Germany. These include a painting of Alexander von Humbolt, photographs of students studying, the Berlin wall being constructed, toy train sets and experimental aircraft.[124] The pictures suggest this loose thematic unity while also presenting a variety of self-consisting and unrelated spatial depths. According to Gerhard Mack, the architects conceived of this design in the tradition of *sgraffito* decoration in the traditional buildings of German towns. This *sgraffito* work was a popular uptake of the painted façades discussed earlier, in which imagery and pattern were scratched into plaster, rendered and coloured. Semper attempted to revive *sgraffito* in the nineteenth century as a consequence of his theory of architecture as dressed surface.

Ruff's image cycle is in dialogue with a building of blunt object-form where there is no sense of space being formed in a sequence of visual experience. At Eberswalde, architecture has apparently been reduced to the rationalization of use and construction, and the development of the material processes for etching images into concrete and glass. The thing is an object, a box; and it simply displaces space around it with no apparent design. In fact, this reduction of space to object foregrounds the curatorial *nous* of the architects in commissioning a neo-neo-objectivist photographer to decorate their *sachlichkeit* building. The Eberswalde Library invokes the modernist vocabulary of Mies van der Rohe and Walter Gropius, and Ruff invokes the photography of Alexander Rodchenko and August Sander, but the combination is something that would have been impossible in the 1920s. Eberswalde Library uses a grammar of the Renaissance – of the image before it was assumed to be a picture, of architecture before it was jealous of its image – but it is equally sure of its historical position after modernism.

For the same reason that Le Corbusier thought pictures were a threat to the *promenade architecturale*, the image programme of the Eberswalde Library actively negates the possibility of space being formed out of visual apperception. It is too axiomatic to see this as a matter of pictures or architecture with Le Corbusier, and pictures *and* architecture with Herzog and de Meuron. There is another level of relation. Pictures do not conflict with Maison la Roche at all levels; they are its abstract model. Le Corbusier wanted haptic experience to be fixed, to make a kind of artefact of which one can have regard, to construct a mental image on the model of actual image artefacts such as the picture, or the cinema. It is this model that the phenomenal viewing of actual pictures might disrupt. By contrast, Ruff's pictures (newspaper reportage become art on the façade of the Library) make a stiff critique of the whole idea of visual experience being formed or finalized, or having a surface proper to it, like a picture.

Of the many things to admire in the work of Herzog and de Meuron, what I like best is their anti-picturesqueness. This is not because I dislike the picturesque; on the contrary, it is because Herzog and de Meuron's clear alternative to the image/space relation cracks the cliché that the picturesque has become, returning to us something of the specificity, indeed the oddity of the picturesque, which had become so indistinguishable from the muddy consensus of architectural values. In this vein, the next chapter attempts to revive the picturesque theory of disgust.

3
Disgust

Many think of the picturesque with a tinge of disgust; and if we can avoid the feeling overwhelming thought all together, disgust can lead us a long way into the aesthetic theory of the picturesque. The things said to be picturesque are typically eighteenth-century motifs that have become clichés – china ornaments of cottages and shepherdesses; table mats with scenes of the Lakes . . . It is not difficult to find equivalences in modern life, such as television programmes about city executives downsizing to a new life in the organic communities of a rural town; or for that matter, cottage-styled suburban houses with illogically complicated roofs packed cheek by jowl in the outer suburbs. Such picturesque objects represent a too easy reconciliation of past and present, city and country, art and life; and there hangs about them a cloying whiff of *pot-pourri*, obscuring both the actuality of existence and the work that goes into authentic culture. Now, at a second order of consideration, it is obvious to those who have the sense to be disgusted at such things that the picturesque functions ideologically: that the shepherdesses were scarred with smallpox, the cottages awash with pig shit and choked with smoke; that the image of home offered by the suburban villa is thoroughly traduced when built at the densities most people can afford. Hence, disgust at picturesqueness is doubled in a disgust at those with a taste for it, who picture the world in the form of a hand-me-down wish. Those who are fond of picturesqueness offend logic, but to know this is the beginning of a fuller disgust at them, for a sensibility that exceeds their judgement, and for a facile aesthetics that leaves no space for the struggle of art. It is said that the surest kind of disgust is aroused by the taste of others. The picturesque is one term for this relation.

If this much is common sense, it has, I hope, already started to fall apart in my caricature. Today the picturesque names a taste that is trivial, sentimental and ultimately disgusting, but this is, at one level, a popularization of what earlier thinkers such as John Ruskin or Heinrich Wölfflin did in using 'picturesque' as a pejorative term. I propose that the picturesque names all parties in this contract: the sentimental and the critical aesthetic, the historical and the present picturesque; articulated in the moment of disgust. Perhaps more familiar or, more easily swallowed, is the idea that the tint of picturesque remaining in the present is here by virtue of a wider phenomenon: the visualization of culture and the exponential development of visual technologies since the eighteenth century. My claim that disgust is integral to the picturesque adds a history of affect to this history of perception. This chapter begins with a brief phenomenology of disgust, and goes on to discuss the particular utility disgust has in art and architecture. The centrality of disgust in picturesque aesthetics is not merely a matter of historical identification, of disgust at the picturesque prompting its renewal; beyond this there is a further level of picturesque disgust in the founding texts of the theory. Sir Uvedale Price's theory of the relationship between the picturesque and the beautiful also includes lengthy discussion of the ugly, deformed and disgusting. These terms rarely feature in commentary on the picturesque, and are, apparently, not known to the few modern writers on disgust. To the extent that it is useful to describe the picturesque as aesthetic theory, I contend that we are best to approach this task in the negative, through the concept of aesthetic feeling that is at the opposite pole to beauty and picturesqueness.

Disgust is not an infrequent topic in eighteenth-century aesthetic theory as it played a crucial role in turning the study of beauty from canons of form to reflection on sensory experience. The word 'disgust' was imported into English in the sixteenth century from the French *desgoust* and *degoût.* Literally it means a refusal to ingest, making it part of the wider analogy by which 'taste' became the paradigm of sensuous experience, and formed the empirical field in which eighteenth-century aestheticians sought an objective account of beauty. Commentators on the history of aesthetics tend to emphasize this issue, asking what grounds does taste give to the judgement of beauty? In such accounts, the picturesque, as merely an alternative approbation of tasty things, is somewhat beside the point. Seen, however, in the broader light of cultural practice, picturesque thinkers such as Price are, I argue, in the vanguard of contemporary thought. For Price, the issue is not whether beauty (or picturesqueness) can be known objectively; it is whether categories such as beauty, sublimity and picturesqueness can explain the relation of an individual's experience of taste to the intersubjective and social conditions by which arts, such as landscape design and architecture, are formed, and standards of excellence established for them. Price's crucial example in the discussion of the picturesque and disgust is a painting by Rembrandt, *Carcase of an Ox* (see Figure 3.6). In his discussion of meat and viscera, pictures and reality, the aesthetic and the economic meaning of things, Price opens a set of issues that modern readers of cultural theory are more likely to know through George Bataille, Jacques Derrida, Pierre Bourdieu and, more recently, William Ian Miller and Winfried Menninghaus.

Feeling and ideation

The experience of vomiting is a sensation with which we are all familiar, and it is also bound up, by powerful analogy, with the English word 'disgust', which means a reversal of eating, an anti-gustation. The idea of disgust is arguably more troubling and unpleasant than the sensation, as the mere idea of the disgusting can elicit the sensation, and collapse thought. Immediately prior to the action is the moment when we know that we will vomit – need to vomit, desire to vomit. This self-knowledge interpolates whatever piece of indigestibility we suffer into a thorough disgust at ourselves – at the reversed direction of the tube running through our bodies, making the mouth into a kind of anus.

Perhaps we could articulate a typology of disgusting objects: skin on milk, fetid slaughter waste, running sores and other substances that make us sick to think of them. It would be a mistake to think that it is merely by analogy that this actual or animal disgust extends itself upward into more etiolated regions, such as disgust at racism, at adults dressing teddy bears, or at faux Georgian houses. Since Charles Darwin, evolutionary psychologists have argued that disgust has evolved in human behaviour from animal origins to present ideational emotive life. Whether or not this is the case, what strongly characterizes the experience of disgust is that whatever the cause, material or symbolic, the feeling is the same. It would also be a mistake to think that disgust always consists in ideas driving the stomach. We can learn to be disgusted, we can govern it, we can even forget it, but still, disgust is not entirely culturally relative. Different cultures nominate different inedible animals, have a taste or not for the glutinous or acidic, eat cartilage but will not drink milk and so on; but the existence of the feeling of disgust and its peculiar relation of ideas to a set of disgust elictors is a basic part of the human creature, and of cultures.

The phenomenology that links taste and disgust is clear enough: some things we ingest give us pleasure (beyond our appetite for them); some things cause us revulsion (no matter how nutritious). Thus a process that might have begun in reason or sentiment ends in the ungovernable act of vomiting. From ancient times, the experience of disgust has been valued for its unique union of personhood. A fickle idea, culturally or personally specific – perhaps of an animal or animal part that should not be eaten – can have a somatic consequence that no amount of thinking can govern. Disgust came into its own in the eighteenth century with the rise of empirical aesthetics. Beauty became understood not as a canon of forms but through the pleasure or displeasure artworks and natural objects caused an observer, making disgust important evidence of a thing's reception. As evidence, given its strange contagion of the mental with the somatic, disgust is clearly superior to pleasure, which needs to be tested and qualified to be sure that it is not prejudiced by other than aesthetic interests.

What disgust is at a psychological level – whether it and other emotions are passions, instincts, symptoms, or facts of neurology – is beyond the scope of this inquiry. The phenomenology, indeed the semiotic, of disgust that the picturesque opens, does not require more than a recognition of the feelings I have described. There is, however, a psychology of disgust and what we are about to discuss is not inconsistent with the empirical and theoretical work of psychologist Paul Rozin and his collaborators and it is also consistent with the only theory of disgust in architecture *per se*, Mark Cousins' psychoanalytic essay 'The Ugly'.[1]

Rozin, Haidt and McCauley believe that disgust is a basic human emotion that evolved to protect the body against bad foods, but that has also come to violently reject things bad for the soul. They hold that the typical range of disgust elicitors – faeces, viscera, rotting flesh and insects – constitutes a 'core disgust' that human cultures have in common with one another and some animals. They follow Darwin who thought that the gaping mouth, a facial expression common to humans and some animals, shows that the emotion of disgust is a phylogenetic reminder of a time when we had what some animals still have: an ability to vomit at will to expel bad foods.[2] Rozin and colleagues then claim that this present reminder of our evolutionary past has expanded, psychologically and culturally, so as:

> to include other reminders of our animal nature. In addition to the animal processes of eating and excretion, disgust can be elicited by other demonstrations of our animality: sex, death, gore, and violations of the body envelope. We see this animal-origin disgust as the central concept in elaborated disgust, and suggest that fear of the animal properties of mortality and associated decay replaces the original motive of avoidance of bad taste. Further expansions of the domains of disgust, depending on the culture, may include interpersonal contamination and an association between disgust and immoral actions. At this most fully elaborated level, the disgust system may have lost both its original connections to bad taste and its intermediate value of avoiding reminders of animal origin and death. The range of disgust may expand to the point that the exemplars have in common only the fact that we want nothing to do with them. At this level, disgust becomes a powerful form of negative socialization and an abstract moral emotion.[3]

Unlike some other emotions, disgust does not well up within us but is a reaction to an exterior occurrence. For this reason, Cousins, in a study of what we have been discussing as disgust, writes instead of 'the ugly': not the human emotion, but the object that forces feelings of disgust on us. The ugly thing is either where it should not be, or it is a present absence – a hole where something should be. Cousins' is a psychoanalytical account, and explains the out-of-place-ness of the ugly in relation to Sigmund Freud's observation that we have no unconscious knowledge of our own death. Experiencing the excessive materiality of the ugly thing undoes the subject. As Cousins puts it: 'I cannot be here; the object takes all'. Ugliness reveals a contradiction: 'If I unconsciously know nothing of my death, I consciously experience it, none the less, as the approach of the punishment.'[4]

To the extent that it is useful to place disgust in the psyche (whatever the merits and explanatory powers of psychoanalysis and evolutionary psychology), Rozin and colleagues and Cousins place it with death. Disgust may be phylogenetic in the sense that we individually experience a threat response that belongs to a collective genetic past. Within the subject, understood psychoanalytically as a product of divided consciousness, disgust might be the reaction to the ugly thing that takes away the space for this fundamental division. But whatever the evolutionary origins or psychological functions of disgust, at a phenomenological level, we class disgust with other emotions such as anger, love and grief; and it is the nature of emotions to link ideas and sensations, and through the expressive aspect of emotions, for them to become communicated and social. As William Ian Miller puts it: 'I find it difficult to understand what it would mean to be disgusted and not know it'.[5] And further: 'Like all emotions, disgust is more than just a feeling. Emotions are feelings linked to ways of talking about those feelings, to social and cultural paradigms that make sense of those feelings by giving us a basis for knowing when they are properly felt and properly displayed.'[6]

It is the communication of disgust and its social existence that makes it properly a study for cultural theory. Miller's book, *The Anatomy of Disgust*, and Menninghaus' *Digust: Theory and History of a Strong Sensation*, both published in the late 1990s, are different but largely complementary attempts to theorize disgust from Western philosophy and literature.[7] At the simplest level, we can take both these books to have demonstrated that, whatever we should think of it as a feeling, disgust continues to be widely employed as cultural topos. What disgusts, how it does so, and what this means, has varied greatly in Western cultures. But the nomination of a set of disgusting things is one way in which a culture has its profile, or as Miller puts it, demonstrating what it means to be human in a particular culture: 'To feel disgust is human and humanizing. Those who have very high thresholds of disgust [. . .] we think of as belonging to somewhat different categories: proto-human like children, subhuman like the mad, or superhuman like saints'.[8] Thus, disgust is often used in discourse in a weak and analogous form. To say that a novel or a building is disgusting is often no more than a forcible statement of opinion that it, and persons who admire it, are 'outside' of culture. The force of saying 'disgust' rather than 'dislike' or 'hate' lies in its analogy to that unwilling, compulsive act – that beyond thought or reasoned reflection, a building might make us vomit.

That an idea can make one sick is crucial to the phenomenology of disgust, distinguishing it from other emotions and from the general arrangement of sense and affect. We are, perhaps, all familiar with a story of vicarious vomiting: one child vomits at the sight of another vomiting, or at the mere description of disgusting food or fearful debasement. Darwin put great significance on vomiting in response to ideas. Observing the power of ruminants and monkeys to vomit wilfully and purposefully, he hypothesized that human disgust is an evolutionary memory of a former human ability. But his evidence is more interesting for us here, as he points out:

> When vomiting results, as a reflex action, from some real cause – as from too rich food, or tainted meat, or from an emetic – it does not ensue immediately, but generally after

> a considerable interval of time. [in contrast] It is remarkable how readily and instantly retching or actual vomiting is induced in some persons by the mere idea of having partaken of any unusual food, as of an animal which is not commonly eaten; although there is nothing in such food to cause the stomach to reject it.[9]

The common experience of thoughts that make one's gorge rise, more rapidly and surely than bad food, reverses the common understanding of sensory experience as anterior to, and outside of, thought and affect.[10] That an idea can cause emotion is a more general case. The mental image of a lost loved one can cause one to tremble and cry. Tear ducts have a function – to clean and lubricate the eyes – but for them to spout streams of tears in moments of grief clearly has another cause. We understand emotions as causing bodily actions, and we identify those emotions through their expression. The uniqueness of disgust is, then, not that ideas cause a bodily reaction, but that vomiting is so supremely expressive that it fails to communicate. It does not distinguish feelings that might have caused disgust from fermentation in the gut. Vomiting has the organic function of expelling bad food, but a great variety of unpalatable thoughts – of spilling viscera, coprophilia, nests of cockroaches, and the unwanted attentions of needy lovers – come out in exactly the same way. Rozin and his collaborators attempt to make this differentiation within disgust, because, if emotions developed through evolution (as they assume) then one would expect to distinguish its original organic function from its sublimation into emotional life. They argue for a 'core disgust' at bad food and organic decay, and a second-order disgust at things that are metonymic of the body's mortality and organic finitude: 'five additional domains: sexual acts, hygiene, death, violations of the body envelope (e.g., gore, amputations, surgery), and sociomoral violations (e.g., liars, racists, and Nazis)'.[11] But if we put aside their thesis that the first set are 'core' and the latter evolutionary processes swallowed into culture, what is remarkable is the homology that disgust produces over this quite varied array of disgusting things.

Rozin and colleagues have conducted experiments showing 'that objects that look like something disgusting, but are known not to be, are often treated as disgusting. Thus, we find that many North American college students are reluctant to consume imitation dog faeces that they know is made out of chocolate fudge.'[12] This uncritical sense of disgust is not only visual; the psychologists think of it as a kind of sympathetic magic governed by a 'law of similarity' in which all things connected with the disgusting are potentially disgusting. This contamination is perhaps at the base of the role of disgust in social organization where disgust at bad manners feels the same as disgust at bad food. Contagion is undoubtedly at play in the disgust that we feel at others who eat things that disgust us: not only do they consume disgusting things; they fail to be disgusted.[13] Miller, for instance, holds that the institutions of democracy rely less on mutual respect than on disgust and equal distribution of contempt.[14]

A theory of disgust that proceeds from core bodily experience (which is also an evolutionary origin) to increasingly abstract social and symbolic disgusts has the problem of why these later, analogical disgusts feel the same, or even more pressing. Cousins has a better, or at least more general, explanation of the homology of various things held to be ugly and disgusting. Whether or not this disgust is a sickening appetite or phobic revulsion, the ugly thing is the wrong size.

> One way of clarifying the difference between the registers of beauty and ugliness is to translate them into topological entities. Broadly speaking, the beautiful object remains the same size as itself, while the ugly object becomes much larger than it is. There is an

important reason for this. All objects exist twice, both as themselves and as representations of themselves. But I have a vested interest in pretending to myself that this is not so, for if I were forced to recognize this I would have to conclude that my own existence – as myself and as my representation of myself – are different, and in certain conditions might even come apart. It is not just an idealization of the human body which is implied in the Vitruvian scheme of proportion; it is a manic insistence that an even more fundamental proportion in man is guaranteed: that he takes up only as much space as his form displaces. This phantasy depends upon a conviction about isomorphism, about the relation between objects and space. Firstly, that there will be an isomorphic relation between an object and the space it occupies. Secondly, that there will be an isomorphic relation between the outside of an object (representation) and its inside (existence). Thirdly, that this is most true when the object is a human being. For the thought of an inside being larger than its outside is one which repels human beings.[15]

Cousins' text already tells us much about the significance of ugliness and disgust for architecture, but it also provides a logic for the common observation that contamination and contagion are strong elicitors of disgust. Disgust seems to destroy not only the difference between objects but their distance. The American students' disgust at eating fake dog shit in Rozin's experiment is not simply their eyes conflicting with a reasoned assessment of contagious risk; it is a more fundamental unhinging, where, as a result of this conflict, visual similarity and spatial proximity seem too interchangeable.

Another problem that evolutionary psychology has is in explaining one of the most familiar forms of disgust described in literature and critique: disgust at an excessive sweetness that becomes cloying and insistent. How is it that things known to be good and experienced as pleasurable, sexual experiences or favourite foods for example, can lead us to overindulgence and self-loathing, disgusted at the very thing we previously desired, and what is more, which we know we will desire again? Disgust, here, might seem highly etiolated – after all, too much consumption of spun sugar rarely leads to vomiting, except in small children. But even for adults, largely in charge of their emotions, the moment to decline another slice of cake or a further embrace holds the possibility of the offer becoming insistent, smothering, a violation of one's person that arouses nausea.

Despite my emphasis on the self-demonstrating identity that disgust has in vomit, there is a tradition in thinking that disgust provides two modes by which we reach that point, and this tradition has been explored and expounded by modern theorists. Miller and Menninghaus, using largely different sources in literature and philosophy, each develop this split account of disgust. The first disgust, cognate with Rozin's 'core disgust', is the interdiction on ingesting bad substances; and the second is disgust at, or through, overindulgence of allowed substances. Both call the former 'prohibition disgust'. Miller calls the latter 'disgust of surfeit'[16] and Menninghaus 'satiation-induced disgust'.[17] Miller's division is based on a model of a bicameral mind: 'on the basis of function we can divide disgust into two distinct types. One works in the manner of Freudian reaction formation as a barrier to unconscious desire; its purpose is to prevent indulgence. The other works after the indulgence of very conscious desires; this is the disgust of surfeit.'[18]

Menninghaus takes his morphology of disgust from what he states to be the first modern phenomenological account, Aurel Kolnai's *Der Ekel* of 1929. For Kolnai, prohibitive disgust has its figure in the corpse and decomposition and it acts to warn us against decaying flesh and excrement, but also other substances believed to be unclean, such as prohibited animals or animal parts. However, the enjoyment of things not in themselves forbidden, such as the pleasures of eating or sex, have the power to turn into disgust through over-indulgence, and Menninghaus follows Kolnai in calling this satiation-induced disgust. Apart from the common response of nausea, for Kolnai, these two disgusts are linked by a relation to biological life. In a language coloured by eugenics, the figure of satiatory disgust is fecundity: the sight of 'swelling breasts, swarming broods . . .' in 'a thickening and buckling of the stream of life' as observed with vermin such as nests of rats.[19] As Menninghaus puts it, Kolnai's satiation-induced disgust is a pathological life force opposed to a normative form that is 'gestalt endowed and goal-oriented'.[20] Disgusting moral attributes such as guile or mendacity are in relation to an individual's life, or that of a people, the same as that 'life-aping, corrosive mass which usurps the place and the vigorous diversity of healthy tissue'.[21] These overlapping causalities (for those who accept them) explain the deep misogyny of disgust literature. Menninghaus traces this to ancient authors, such as Horace, directing a remarkable invective at elderly women on the double count of their being women, and so supposed objects of sexual attraction, and also old and corpse-like. Gotthold Ephraim Lessing, Kant and Karl Rosenkranz write of old women as the epitome of disgust, and Menninghaus characterizes the matter thus:

> This phantasm conventionally brings together folds and wrinkles, warts, larger than usual openings of the body (i.e., mouth and anus), foul, black teeth, sunk-in hollows instead of beautiful swellings, drooping breasts, stinking breath, revolting habits, and a proximity to both death and putrefaction'.[22]

In the figure of the witch, this disgust is confirmed by ugly appearance, taken to be the sign of an evil and rapacious nature.

Cousins' account of the ugly has a similar formal bifurcation to that which Menninghaus derives from Kolnai. For Cousins, there is little to distinguish the prohibited and the excessive; both are too big, too material, out of place and an obstacle to desire. 'Excess and lack tend in the same direction, though they take different routes.' Cousins gives the figure of the ghost to that moment when 'I am underwhelmed by the object, which takes away what I need to be'. And to the opposite of this he gives the terms 'undead' and 'the mask', for that same apprehension of 'murderous vivacity' and 'invasive contaminating life',[23] which Kolnai and Menninghaus think of as disgust at a monstrous refusal to be satisfied.

I have taken this survey of the psychology, anthropology and phenomenology of disgust as far as will be useful. Without this context the role of disgust in the picturesque might look even more peculiar and distasteful than it is. Similarly, as the picturesque is a theory of art, I have aimed merely to cover the points of the theory of disgust that bear most on a formal description of disgusting things. For this reason, Julia Kristeva's work on the role of the abject in her theory of subjectivity is beyond my remit, while the ideas of Jacques Derrida and Georges Bataille, which the reader might expect to see here, are dealt with directly in relation to picturesque theorists as the chapter proceeds.[24]

The picturesque supposes that art has uses for disgust, and this utility relies upon the common and communicable sensation of being disgusted. But in understanding this, what is at stake is not the truth of disgust, which is, after all, too easily invoked, but rather the problems of art. To cast forward briefly: picturesque disgust is defined in the eighteenth century by Richard Payne Knight as the co-existence of appetite and repulsion, and by Price as the combination of want and excess of form. Since the nineteenth century, and principally in the writings of Ruskin, the picturesque itself has disgusted, as an excessive interest in affect, which is a version of satiation-induced disgust. Each of these, as formal propositions of distortion or unformedness, is at a certain level too easily understood. Miller, Menninghaus and Cousins have a huge canon of art and literature on which to draw in what remains, at a certain level, an anthropology of disgust, with culture providing the imprint of feeling. My task is the obverse: to understand how art requires an anthropology of disgust to constitute and defend itself against the kind of aesthetics in which art is merely the stimulation of feeling. Whatever disgust is, it is an ancient truism that in art, the imitation of the disgusting cannot itself disgust. The older name for this principle is rhyparography, and since the rise of aesthetics and a sensual account of art, disgust has become one of the principle fronts on which art claims to distinguish its products from those of nature. Rozin's amusing experiment makes this point clear: his chocolate fudge faeces are imitations through which disgust travels; but art claims a special kind of imitation that haults the 'sympathetic magic' of disgust, thus distinguishing it over both nature and other kinds of imitation. Whether or not this proposition is true, asserting it has been the basis of much art in modernity. Andres Serrano's *Piss Christ* (1989) is a recent and notorious example of an artistic strategy, known since antiquity, which became a major foundation of art after the rise of aesthetics in the eighteenth century. Disgust is one way in which art shows itself to be more than sense and reflection. Disgust is also necessary to the historical continuity of art because it articulates what must otherwise remain in contradiction: an aesthetical account of art that arose in the eighteenth century, and an older account of art as a practice of imitation.

'A dirty fellow with a dirty shovel': rhyparography and the value of disgust in art

The peculiarity of feelings of disgust, and the paradoxical value that the sensation and concept make for a mimetic account of art, go back to classical times. Pliny makes an account of the painter Pyreicus (or Piraeicus), who achieved the title of Rhyparographer;[25] a term that the *Oxford English Dictionary* gives as 'a painter of mean or sordid subjects', but which has its origins in the Greek for 'painter of filth'.[26] Gotthold Ephraim Lessing was affronted by this tradition and its continuation into the 'Dutch' art of his day. He explains:

> Pyreicus, who painted barbershops, filthy workshops, asses, and kitchen herbs with all the zeal of a Dutch artist – as if such things in nature had so much charm or were so rare! – acquired the name of Rhyparographer, or the painter of filth. Indeed, the debauched rich paid their weight in gold for his paintings, as if to offset their intrinsic worthlessness by putting a fictitious value upon them.[27]

In the *Poetics*, Aristotle uses such paintings as an example when he argues that *mimesis*, or imitation, is not lying as Plato thought, but pleasurable; a kind of learning through recognition.

> There are things that we see with pain so far as they themselves are concerned but whose images, even when executed in very great detail, we view with pleasure. Such is the case, for example, with renderings of the least favored animals, or of cadavers. The cause of this is that learning is eminently pleasurable not only to philosophers but to the rest of mankind in the same way, although their share in the pleasure is restricted, because the reason they take pleasure in seeing the images is that in the process of viewing they find themselves learning, that is, reckoning what kind a given thing belongs to: 'This individual is a so-and-so.' Because if the viewers happen not to have seen such a thing

> before, the reproduction will not produce the pleasure *qua* reproduction but through its workmanship or colour or something else of that sort.[28]

For Aristotle, then, we need to recognize the disgusting, and the disgust that we would have if the object were actually present, before taking our pleasure in classing the object and in the sensation of 'colour or something else of that sort'. Someone who has 'not seen such a thing before' could not have the pleasure of recognition, but this problem would occur in any imitation. The situation of someone who does not know which animals are 'least favoured' is the stronger case: if one did not know that it was prohibited to eat dogs, then the butchery of dogs would not disgust and the viewer would lose the lesson that the pleasure had been at the imitation alone. The traditional meaning of the term *mimesis* in the visual arts is not merely imitation of appearances, but also the act of mimicking, of being like the object. There is, given the pressing, contagious aspects of disgust, a certain frisson in an artwork that brings one closer to the disgusting. The viewer must have a strong sensation beginning in disgust but ending in some more affirming arousal. The artist has the challenge of drawing the viewer close while at some other level introducing a distance that allows the artwork to be enjoyed without becoming an emetic. In the process, disgust becomes valued as an occasion for the demonstration of artistic technique.

Norman Bryson, in his discussion of 'still life', claims that this challenge has been implicit in the genre system since the *xenia* of antiquity. These were wall paintings of produce, rural and urban scenes, and were a major genre of painting, described by Philostratus and consistent with paintings found on the buildings of the Roman Campania.[29] Bryson understands these as 'rhopography', a word for still life painting received through French signifying the painting of 'petty wares', although its Greek etymology is the same as rhyparography. For Bryson, the core or necessity of still life as a genre is in its opposition to higher genres of history painting or portraiture that celebrate ideal or actual human life: 'in still life we never see the human form at all. Still life negates the whole process of constructing and asserting human beings as the primary focus of depiction. In opposing the anthropocentrism of the "higher" genres, it assaults the centrality, value and prestige of the human subject.'[30] We can add to Bryson's observation that still life subjects are not only motionless and trivial, but in their focus on foodstuffs and flowers (which signify the arts of horticulture and hospitality), they depict human needs and appetites. Paintings of geese, cheeses and other comestibles stand outside of personhood, as does excrement, as parts of the same process of our animal life and origins, which disgust us. Thus, still life is anti-anthropomorphic because it lacks the human figure but also because it depicts human alimentary processes. So the emotion of disgust has its role in art in the lower genres and in base subjects. The strongest feelings in art are often thought to lie in the sublime, taken to be a transcendence of the human into spirit or idea. This aim, however, of departing the human into abstraction is arguably only a conjecture from much more common experiences of the animal within us.

Before the modern era, the role of disgust in culture related to the politics of honour. Miller recounts Icelandic sagas in which ascendency is asserted by confining enemies for a period of three days, forcing them to soil their houses. Conversely, the stories of Saint Catherine of Sienna, who sucked the suppurating tumours of those in her care, signify disregard of her own body and the dedication of her soul to God.[31] François Rabelais claimed the title 'Rhyparographer', and his low humour is a hyperbolic kind of *momento mori* that places us insistently in our bodies and below heaven.[32] In such pre-modern works of art and literature, the people represented are disgusted, or disgusting, and so are we to the extent that we identify or not with them. Disgust establishes a hierarchy of those who impose it and are above it, and it can also work the hierarchy from below as Rabelais does by confronting the vanity of those who think themselves clean. To an extent the system of genres can be understood as an interpolation of a hierarchy in the representations onto the condition of representation.

What changed in the modern era with the invention of aesthetics was that disgust added to this direction-finding role another to do with the nature of sensation. The production and reception of artwork in pre-modern times was largely a matter of canons and norms; beauty was what is correct, precise and true. Aesthetics proposes that beauty is what pleases, and that we can know what truly pleases by reflecting on our sensory experience. This means that we can have an empirically founded knowledge of beauty: we can taste things and see if we like or dislike them. In the eighteenth century, this analogy to the taste of the mouth extended vastly to mean our reflection on any sensory experience, and our ability to judge this experience and reconcile it with the taste of others. Disgust is at the base of this extended analogy, both in the new role taste has in a critical account of sensory experience, and, as we will see, in the maintenance of pre-aesthetic systems of genre hierarchy within the new aesthetic culture.

One point where we can observe this change is in the novel idea that one can be disgusted at art works in which nothing disgusting appears. This is the case with eighteenth-century British connoisseurs' reception of Dutch and Flemish genre painting, largely of the previous century, which included 'still lives' of flowers, comestibles and also 'genre' paintings of peasants' everyday lives. In their own time and place, some of these paintings represented Rabelaisian sentiments of the low revels of the poor, some were attempts to acculturate the then novel experience of affluence, and all had moral sentiments of the *vanitas* kind. For instance, the sub-genre of 'kitchen paintings' often include scenes of the butcher's trade, but also evoke the biblical story of the prodigal son. 'Dutch' painters were famed for the high verisimilitude of their pictures, and to an extent the representation of blossoms, fowl, joints of meat, or the weatherbeaten clothes of peasants were equal challenges to the brush. British connoisseurs were uninterested in the iconography of the Low Countries painters but were fascinated by the combination of high realism and low subjects. In the first place, this was a classic interest in rhyparography, but it gradually transmuted into disgust at versimilitude as an aim in art, which is only incidental to disgusting subjects.

Edmund Burke gives a version of Aristotle when he writes: 'So it is with most of the pieces which the painters call still-life: in these a cottage, a dung hill, the meanest and most ordinary utensils of the kitchen, are capable of giving us pleasure'.[33] Burke's evocation of this problematic, however, serves a different argument. As a visual empiricist, he thought that what kept disgust out of the picture was not the virtue of art but the simple fact that painting is visual, not a full spectrum of sense. Knight makes a similar observation, but more subtly, by showing how acculturation affects vision:

> It is by a love and study of pictures that this beauty is perceived; because painting, by imitating the visible qualities only, discriminates it from the objects of the other senses with which it may be combined, and which, if productive of stronger impressions either of pleasure or disgust, will overpower it; so that a mind not habituated to such discriminations, or (as more commonly expressed) a person not possessed of a painter's eye, does not discover it till it is separated in the artist's imitation. Rembrandt, Ostade, Teniers and others of the Dutch painters, have produced the most beautiful pictures by the most exact imitations of the most ugly and disgusting objects in nature; and yet it is physically impossible that an exact imitation should exhibit qualities not existing in

> the original; but the case is, that in the originals, animal disgust and the nauseating repugnance of appetite, drown and overwhelm every milder pleasure of vision . . .[34]

Knight's short remark encapsulates much of what I have discussed thus far in this chapter. His double causes of disgust are 'animal' and 'the nauseating repugnance of appetite', consistent with the two modes of the modern commentators. Isaack van Ostade's *Pig-Killing* (Figure 3.1) is an example of what Burke or Knight might have been examining.[35] If Knight had been present, his animal disgust might well have been aroused by the carcass whole on its gallows, being neither the creature nor food product, or, by the general dirtiness of the decaying barn or cottage. And of course, these two elicitors of disgust combine with the meat's proximity to dirt and vermin, as demonstrated by the hen scratching for grubs on the earth floor. The boy, blowing up the still warm bladder, is close enough to ingesting it to cause disgust. The adults wash the pig's guts at the pump, and one man, his hands engaged, holds a bloody knife in his teeth. The 'nauseating repugnance of appetite' is a little harder to grasp. 'Repugnance' can mean contradiction as well as refusal and it is possible that Knight means that, were he there, he would desire some of the better cuts and that his own appetite for pork would, in the circumstances already described, disgust him. Arthur Schopenhauer gives an example of the 'unworthily charming' in art: 'the still-life painting of the Dutch, when they err by depicting edible objects. By their deceptive appearance these necessarily excite the appetite, and this is just a stimulation of the will which puts an end to any aesthetic contemplation of the object.'[36] It is more likely that what would disgust Knight is not his own appetite but that of the poor, which, in van Ostade's numerous paintings of pig slaughter and butchery, is demonstrated in the use of every part of the animal, particularly the offal, the head and the feet, which, in the cuisine of gentlefolk, would fall in the prohibited category.

What are the pleasures of such a painting? Some are material, such as the sensation of colour and tone. Some, perhaps, are formal, at least in the way that the long process of entropy, dragging the building into formlessness, contrasts with the strong figure of the pig, radically distorted. But the main enjoyment of such a painting must lie in its verisimilitude,

Figure 3.1 Isaack van Ostade, *Pig-Killing*, 1642.

its truth. This is first in the sense of its creation of a pictorial space into which we look, and second in the accurately observed details of people's work and lives, which can be placed into a sequence and narrative: the knife in the teeth slit the pig's throat moments before; the children will go outside to kick their new football, and so on.

The point of Burke's and Knight's observations on Dutch still life painting is that disgust has been held within the represented space. Burke's point here is a sensory one: disgust, as apprehended through smell, touch and vision, when artificially separated from the manifold of the senses, and rendered to sight alone, is not perturbing. Knight is more sophisticated, and tries to make Burke's 'sensible' beauty compatible with an intellectual and cultural approach.[37] Knight thinks (with Burke) that there is an objective quality of beauty sensed as a 'grateful medium of grateful irritation'.[38] Beauty strikes the nerves less sharply than discord, but does exercise them, unlike monotony. On this basis, Knight, in one of his amusing asides, is confident that zebra are objectively beautiful and rhinoceros are not.[39] But as for choosing preferred examples within a species, Knight thinks that this is a matter of custom and association. He largely follows Sir Joshua Reynolds in thinking that there is no objective standard for the beauty of women, and that there must be canons of Negro beauty to which he is not a party. Conversely, he supposes: 'The African black, when he first beholds an European complexion, thinks both its red and white morbid and unnatural, and of course disgusting'.[40] Knight reminds us: 'we should not forget that perception and sensation, are quite different; the one being an operation of the mind, and the other an impression on the organs . . .'.[41] The imagination comes into play in perception and hence what we perceive, as opposed to our raw sense, is subject to associations constructed in culture as a whole and by the work of artists in particular. Because he identifies art and mundane sight to be different modes of perception, Knight does not need to imagine, as Burke must, that the woman washing the pig's puddings under the pump is disgusted. Further, Knight thinks the painting's frame breaks not tactile apperception but understanding: painting is not a different relation of senses but a different relation of perception, imagination and understanding. He writes about the fantastic and decrepit buildings depicted by painters such as van Ostade, or David Teniers:

> Yet, were we to meet with such extravagant and disproportioned buildings in reality; or such monstrous combinations of human animal and vegetable forms in nature, our understandings would revolt at them, and we should turn from them with scorn and disgust: but in judging of the imitative representation of them we do not consult our understandings, but merely our senses and imaginations; and to them they are pleasing and beautiful.[42]

Whatever the model of disgust, sensualist or conventionalist, in the passages quoted, disgust in art is given a value as the thing that distinguishes and gives us self-knowledge of art and nature.

Menninghaus explains how, in German literature of the mid-eighteenth century, sensory accounts of disgust get put to work in the divisions between art and nature and art and art. Disgust properly belongs to what Moses Mendelsohn called the 'dark senses' of smell, taste and touch.[43] It is the odour of rotting meat or the feel of spongy fat that disgusts. The 'lucid senses' of sight and hearing cannot naturally provide percepts that disgust – they are matters of distance – and disgust is proximate, too proximate. Burke and Knight would agree and think that painting cannot, therefore, disgust, except by analogy. But for Mendelsohn and Johann Adolf Schlegel, this natural state of sensory disgust can be disturbed in art. Art's power is in the presentations of sensations with mixed affects; in tragedy, we can take a kind of pleasure heightened by the presentation of suffering. However, such a sensationalist theory of art relies on a firm distinction between art and nature. Disgust names the collapse of this distinction. A painting of tragic death can represent pain and sorrow without it being felt, but a painting of the same hero's evisceration might lead to the lucid sense of sight being overwhelmed by what is proper to dark senses. Disgust is the collapse of the art–nature divide experienced in kinaesthesis.

Disgust at an artwork is itself contagious, signifying not merely the failure of that particular work but the artist's misunderstanding, and by the confounding of art itself. Perhaps the best-known example of the power of this question to define art is Lessing's discussion of the Laocoön sculptor's correct understanding of the limits of sculpture. While in the poem Virgil has Laocoön screaming in agony, the sculptor turns away from too much verisimilitude. According to Lessing: 'the scream had to be softened into a sigh, not because screaming betrays an ignoble soul, but because it distorts the features in a disgusting manner'.[44] Price applies the same test to distinguishing sculpture from painting, but in his own jocular manner:

> I remember a picture of Wovermans, in which the principal objects were a dungcart just loaded; some carrion lying on the dung; a dirty fellow with a dirty shovel; the dunghill itself, and a dog, that from his attitude seemed likely to add to it. These most unsavoury materials the painter had worked up with so much skill, that the picture was viewed by every one with delight. Imagine all this in marble ever so skilfully executed, it would be detestable.[45]

What marks the threshold of disgust varies culturally of course, but this relativism itself encourages disgust, as there is nothing so sure as the disgust we feel at another's failure to be disgusted. We know that Ruskin read Price and I wonder if he had the passage I have quoted open on his desk when he wrote of Philips Wouvermans and David Teniers: 'All their life and work is the same sort of mystery to me as the mind of my dog when he rolls on carrion'.[46] Putting aside Ruskin's characteristic forcefulness, his opinion demonstrates that disgust at art can be disgust not at the depiction of appetite, but at art's appetite for depiction. Still life and genre painting disgust when the ordinariness of their subjects suggests a voracious appetite for representation that makes no distinction between proper and improper comestibles.

Disinterestedness

There is a possible argument that would subsume all our discussion thus far: that disgust is a melodramatic version of the basic aesthetical principle of disinterestedness. Kant explains disinterestedness thus: 'where the question is whether something is beautiful, we do not want to know whether we, or any one else, are, or even could be, concerned in the real existence of the thing, but rather what estimate we form of it on mere contemplation (intuition or reflection)'.[47] The authors I have cited do tend to use the epithet of 'disgusting' to insist on their disinterestedness in the objects judged. However, disinterestedness in British philosophy has a more nuanced meaning than that which Kant gives it, including a certain kind of interest, as we will discuss in the next section. Even in Kant's own texts, however, the difference between disinterestedness and disgust is not clear.

Menninghaus and Jacques Derrida both argue for the centrality of disgust in Kant's aesthetics, and in these terms, we might even understand disinterestedness as a polite or enlightened form of disgust. It would be a positive disinterest, the one point of externality that makes the abstraction of disinterestedness possible. Menninghaus states such a claim forcefully, writing: 'the foundation of modern aesthetics can be described negatively as a foundation based on prohibition of what disgusts'.[48] He has good evidence for this in Kant, who writes:

> Where fine art evidences its superiority is in the beautiful descriptions it gives of things that in nature would be ugly or displeasing. The Furies, diseases, devastations of war, can (as evils) be very beautifully described, nay even represented in pictures. One kind of ugliness alone is incapable of being represented conformably to nature with out destroying all aesthetic delight, and consequently artistic beauty, namely, that which excites ***disgust***. For, as in this strange sensation, which depends purely on the imagination, the object is represented as insisting, as it were, upon our enjoying it, while we set our face against it, the artificial representation of the object is no longer distinguishable from the nature of the object itself in our sensation, and so it cannot possibly be regarded as beautiful.[49]

Here, Kant gives a form to various ideas that we have been following. Art has the role that Burke and Knight claim for it: discriminating perception, evaluation, or imagination, from pure sense, morality or self-interest. Like Mendelsohn, Kant thinks that, in some circumstances, art's power to frame and hold disgust breaks down. Disgusting objects can, then, be defined as those that collapse the art/nature distinction; and in this way, they are a proof of aesthetics. Kant thinks that in determining an object or representation to be beautiful, one must do so with absolute indifference to whether the object actually exists. In disgust, this separation of the faculties becomes impossible, but why? On this point, Knight, with his double disgust, is able to be more Kantian. For Knight, disgust at pictures can only be the insistence on representation and pleasing. If we are disgusted at a painting of pig's intestines, it is for the same reasons that we are disgusted at a flower painting that is too pretty: the painting is too detailed, too mechanical, too much assumes a real interest in the thing, which we do not have. Knight, with his emphasis on educated imagination, tends towards the argument that G. W. F. Hegel later made: that aesthetics is based on art and the beauty of nature is adventitious.[50] For Kant, however, disgust remains the only matter of taste that is objective.

In an essay titled 'Economimesis', Derrida proposes that despite Kant's focus on the subject of aesthetic experience mimesis remains central to his thought, except that this is greatly abstracted so that it is no longer an imitation of nature by art; it is a 'flextion' or fold of nature upon itself.[51] The art of genius, with its free play of productivity, is imitation, not of the products of nature but of nature's productivity. 'We have recognized the fold of ***mimesis*** at the origin of pure productivity, a sort of gift for itself [*pour soi*] of God who makes a present of himself to himself, even prior to the re-productive or imitative structure . . .'.[52] For Derrida, the apparently coincidental importance Kant gives to disgust is the point at which the complete mirror of godly and artistic creation starts to come undone. Despite its reality, Kant cannot say what is disgusting, any more than he can name the beautiful. For Derrida then, like Menninghaus, disgust identifies aesthetics: it is 'what is excluded from it and what, proceeding from this exclusion gives it form, limit and contour'.[53] The relation of God's productivity to our own is not a simple mirror; it is a cascading hierarchy because Kant provides, as was traditional, a hierarchy of the arts that gives primacy to poetry. Making speech and the hearing of one's own voice the most irreplaceable of the senses in turn privileges the mouth and by analogy, taste, thereby giving significance to that other pure product – vomit. According to Derrida the insistent materiality and, at the same time, the indescribability of vomit describes the ambition and the limit of autonomous aesthetics. Vomit stands in the place of the worst, maintaining the system against a possible heterogeneity of 'others'.

> What is absolutely foreclosed is not vomit, but the possibility of a vicariousness of vomit, its replacement by anything else . . .[54]

> it is no longer a question here of one of those negative values, one of those harmful things that art can represent and thereby idealize. The absolute excluded [*l'exclu absolu*] does not allow itself even to be granted the status of negative pleasure or of ugliness redeemed by representation. It is unrepresentable. And at the same time it is unnameable in its singularity. If one could name it or represent it, it would begin to enter into the auto-affective circle of mastery or reappropriation. An economy would be possible. The disgusting X cannot even announce itself as a sensible object without immediately being caught up in a teleological hierarchy. It is therefore in-sensible and un-intelligible, unrepresentable and unnameable, the absolute other of the system.[55]

Menninghaus is scathing of Derrida's 'seduction' of the Third Critique, in which Derrida takes the apparently marginal passage on disgust and reveals it as the constitutive 'outside' of the text. To Menninghaus, it is plain that disgust is central to Kant and he claims that its treatment in the Third Critique could only appear marginal to those who do not know the mid-eighteenth-century German literature, particularly Lessing's and Mendelsohn's discussions, and Kant's own more explicit treatment in the earlier anthropological texts.[56] Disgust, for Kant, is a basis for positive self-knowledge and the progress of civilization. Its progressive value is that it is a firm rejection, which, unlike violence, is internalized. Menninghaus claims that at the moment it becomes obvious to understand beauty as pleasure, the whole aim of art and the proposition of an aesthetic infinity becomes an avoidance of satiety: 'an endless foreplay that turns into an endless afterplay without any excess or peak in between'.[57] According to Menninghaus, the particular value of disgust, for Kant, is that it compels us to feel the absence of the otherwise unprovable noumena of morality and freedom.[58] 'While virtually all pertinent scholarly work on Kant focuses on the duality of the sublime and the beautiful, the Kantian system is in fact distinguished by a triad – that of [quoting Kant] "feelings of the *sublime*, the *beautiful*, and the *disgusting*."'[59] Menninghaus proposes that the supplementation that aesthetics makes to Kant's system of the faculties is similarly triadic. While the sublime has something to tell us of reason, and beauty of morality, disgust, in which the gut can spasm in relation to an idea, tells us of the imagination.[60]

Although Derrida may have overlooked the explicit uses of disgust in Kant, his analysis of Kant's rhetoric in the Third Critique is not inconsistent with Menninghaus' demonstration of its systemic importance. Indeed, Derrida's reading shows what happens after Kant, when the simple positive value of disgust as self-knowledge becomes more complicated. Derrida's reading of disgust in Kant, as an ineluctable movement from a restricted to a general economy, takes its terms from his earlier analysis of Bataille, one of the principal exponents of disgust in the twentieth century.[61] Bataille's 'base materialism' is present in Kant's insistence on the material aspects of disgust, even if Kant would not understand Bataille's *nostalgie de la boue*. Menninghaus gives a brilliantly pithy sketch of the historical trajectory of disgust, which explains something of the relation of the Derrida/Bataille disgust to its eighteenth-century foundations.

> Grossly simplified, the last three centuries provide the following panorama of a discursive appropriation of disgust: the eighteenth century affirms disgust as doing a thoroughly 'right' and healthy job, propagates the cultivation of disgust as a spur to the progress of humanity and of civilization, and celebrates the codification of the aesthetic body as free from everything potentially disgusting; the nineteenth and early twentieth centuries discover both the costs of this sort of cultivation and the (forbidden) attractions of the disgusting; since the end of the twentieth century, the cultivation of disgust itself becomes brittle, and at the same time – as though the (repressive) barriers of disgust have grown more decisive than before – the terrain of the abandoned becomes, in virtually programmatic fashion, the promised land of a fiercely asserted revaluation of the disgusting in artistic, political and academic work.[62]

The picturesque's history and its rise to ubiquity can be given in much the same terms as Menninghaus gives to the history of disgust. It is in the other direction, in terms of the history and theory of disgust, that the picturesque has a contribution to make. The eighteenth-century sources are all writing on the problematic of disgust in the visual arts; however, Menninghaus' explorations of the later culture of disgust are largely literary and philosophical: Freud, Kafka, Sartre, Bataille and Kristeva. Language being what it is, these fascinating texts not only deploy disgust in the way that Menninghaus suggests in the passage above; they are also capable of being read as a continuing phenomenological and theoretical analysis of disgust. But in the visual arts disgust retains something of its simple formal character, even after Romanticism and the rise of a reflective, critical disgust. There are real differences between Bataille's descriptions of sexual abasement in his novel, *Story of the Eye*, and Hans Bellmer's photographs inspired by the novel. This is not only a difference arising from the familiar articulation of word and image; in the visual arts, disgust retains much of its eighteenth-century character. It maybe that Andy Warhol's oxidization paintings (made by urinating on metallic paint) are 'a fiercely asserted revaluation of the disgusting', but nothing in the work says so. What the work does, by evoking or not evoking disgust, by eliciting or not eliciting the approbation of 'beauty' for its swirling forms and its fine range of colour discords, is, to a remarkable degree, in continuity with eighteenth-century still life and rural genre painting.[63] Picturesque disgust does not tell us anything further of the phenomenon of disgust or its potential for aesthetic thinking. What it can show is what happens to disgust in formal terms, within art, for those who are not disgusted, but for whom disgust remains integral in the logic of the work, what gives it contours against quotidian reality.

What disgust has to tell us about the picturesque is perhaps already apparent in the discussion of genre painting and will become more so when we deal with architectural materials. The very proposition of disgusting architecture or disgust at architecture shows the necessity for understanding disgust at a formal level, beyond core disgust at ingestion. Yet, disgust at building maintains a level of insistent materiality, which is more than analogy.

Disinterestedness II: disgust in the republic of taste

Disgust is evidential of taste's limits. It identifies what is outside culture and what is beyond aesthetic feeling, thus defining aesthetics. Disgust is also evidence of the existence of the fundaments of art; that representation has the power to frame and hold disgust, to lessen or even completely transmute its affect. But to whom is this evidence displayed? What is it evidence for? In the eighteenth century, its undoubted purpose was to assist in understanding how taste was formed, to replace laws of beauty with norms; and to improve taste through self-conscious encouragement of production and patronage in the arts. For eighteenth-century aesthetes, the full meaning of taste was not just simple or pure preference, but this and its communication. Taste was the cumulative experience of many, one of the bases of the social. The understanding and refinement of individual preferences only had meaning in light of the pleasure or displeasure of others. Whether one believed taste was relative and capable of qualitative improvement, or an eternal and absolute standard obscured by the imperfections of the present state of civilization, the work of taste was facilitated by a larger sample; it progressed from the particular sensation to greater, more general truths.

This civic idea of taste is, perhaps, stranger to us now than disgust, as disgust, astonishment, shock and a general focus on affect – particularly negative affect – have been basic motifs of art and literature since Romanticism. To understand the picturesque in the eighteenth century and onwards, it is necessary to understand it through the double terms: taste and disgust. This might seem obvious, given the original analogy, but it is not so in the literature. There is a sparse literature on disgust in which taste, in the sense of displayed and socially formed aesthetic norms, is strangely avoided. While the discussion of disgust involves much disgust at social fact, relations, and the failure of others to be disgusted, it does not attempt to explain how, or whether, disgust itself could be inter-subjective. For Menninghaus and Derrida, taste is the field of individuated sensation that opens immediately from the economy of one's body to the general condition of culture. Eighteenth-century thinkers were more concerned with the empirical existence of differing standards of taste, and the social and institutional processes that attempt to force their conformity. Taste, in this sense, could be seen as merely an arcane, withered branch of the vigorous history of the idea of disgust. To dismiss taste or to leave it in the eighteenth century is no simple oversight; Menninghaus follows a not unfamiliar idea that disgust becomes internalized by art in Romanticism, and transmutes through astonishment and decadence into the shock of modernism.[64] After Romanticism, disgust that you or I might feel at the viscousness of spilled intestines tells us little about the right uses of art (as it did in the eighteenth century). Instead, disgust that we can share, that contains knowledge, is disgust at art overstraining at affect.

It is, perhaps, exactly this second-order disgust at art, or bad art, a disgust that distinguishes an aesthetic attitude, that disgusts Pierre Bourdieu. In his double attack on Kant's aesthetics and Derrida's reading of Kant, Bourdieu claims that both philosophers deny the social relations of taste, and monopolise 'the human' in aesthetic terms.[65] According to Bourdieu, Derrida's toying with the Third Critique as if it were literature merely reinforces an aristocratic idea that affect can only properly be experienced when mingled with erudition. Derrida's focus on disgust in Kant is just such an etiolated affect, which itself deserves disgust of the kind typically directed at the overstaining of romantic literature. For Bourdieu, the whole phenomenology of disgust covers a grosser principle: what disgusts Kant about imposed enjoyment, says Bourdieu, is the vulgar taste of lower classes that do not know or will not admit to the distinction of pleasure and enjoyment. Thus, the whole supposition of an aesthetic disgust collapses onto facts about the system of distinction that is 'taste'. The radical alterity of disgust is merely the taste of others.

There is, then, a strange lacuna in the literature if one wants to understand disgust historically as well as theoretically. One branch holds to Derrida's reading of Bataille, which claims that taste's limited economy cannot maintain itself against disgust's general economy; that taste is subsumed by disgust. The other branch are historians of taste, who if they treat disgust at all see it as a romantic ploy that disguises taste's systematic nature. Bourdieu has shown the effective intersection of a politics of taste intersecting with the 'real' politics of economy, institutions and civil life in modern times and this is all the more apparent in the explicit doctrines of civic humanist discourse, which is the picturesque's ideological context. Thus we need also to approach the question of disinterest from this issue of its interested-ness.

John Barrell's book, *The Political Theory of Painting*, reveals the limits of understanding the picturesque as an ideology of the rural economy of the time, limits that, in fact, Barrell's earlier works labour under. A tremendous amount of literature on the 'politics of the picturesque' assumes that painters', poets' and architects' imitations of rustic scenes manipulate the 'image' of the poor in the minds of the rich. Perhaps this is the case, but only in the last instance. What is actually at stake is political franchise – the social and imaginative formation of the governing class – and how this could be negotiated and evidenced in art. Barrell, following J. G. A. Pocock, traces the 'republic of taste', which mirrors the political republic in the tradition of civic humanism, taken up by the British from Renaissance Florence.[66] The issue is one of how much common knowledge and experience qualifies an individual to act in the interest of the nation. Art and literature are crucial in communicating these common experiences, if vicariously, but more importantly, the arts are crucial in that other aspect of taste: judgement. The ability to judge art, or more precisely, to have judgements of art that can be displayed and negotiated, was thought to require the same faculty as political judgement. According to Barrell (in an earlier work), the peregrinations of Joseph Andrews, the eponymous hero of Henry Fielding's novel, dramatize the extraordinary difficulty of the 'equal wide survey' by which an individual could understand the world in order to participate in its government.[67] Barrell thinks Reynolds' *Discourses* provide new argument for franchise in an increasingly complex society. Reynolds proposes that the ancient rhetorical role of painting, by which common knowledge of tropes of virtue is propagated, is no longer possible. Painting, however, could retain its role in civics by promoting a common perception, a self-consciously shared subjectivity of pictures that he calls 'central forms'. This includes issues of genre and the relation of subject matter to execution discussed in the previous chapter. Barrell summarizes: 'by central forms we are able to discover, not how to act in the public interest, but what our individual characters have in common; and thus the "public" is made a visible object, as is the basis of our affiliation to it'.[68] In this sense, in the eighteenth century, taste and disgust are not merely inter-subjective, an aggregation of individual preferences; nor are they merely analogous to judgements more important than art. Rather, taste is fundamental to theories of franchise and government.

This strong account of taste as the space of social accord, or at least its visibility, is familiar to governments' arts and cultural policies from well before the Royal Academy's formation through to the wonderful tautology of 'public art' today. But there are numerous reasons why Deans of Creative Industries in today's universities do not read Reynolds. The 'republic' that concerned Reynolds was an élite governing class whose historical survival was exactly the 'aristocracy' of legitimated culture that Bourdieu set out to disrobe. This, however, is a false reason to dismiss the civic humanist theory of painting. The achievement of universal franchise would logically imply that art become more important in turning the aggregate interests of members of a state into a real public, with common wealth and interest. What makes Reynolds' kind of civic humanism even stranger and less assimilable to the present is the definition of franchise as an interest in land. This makes the picturesque and landscape gardening of great interest and the relation between disgust and aesthetical disinterestedness even more complex.

The crucial term is 'disinterestedness', but in a form that pre-dates and differs from Kant's aesthetical disinterestedness. The prerequisite for true judgement in the polity is a disinterest in the particular outcome of any judgement. Such a disinterest in particulars can only be guaranteed by a true and generalized interest in the nation's totality. Hereditary landholders have an interest that enables them to judge policy disinterestedly, while those engaged in commerce do not. In the 'republic of taste', it is only those with the time and leisure, made possible by wealth, who can truly judge artworks. Those driven by the necessities of acquiring material goods, instead of understanding art as the occasion of generalizable judgements – analogues of true political judgements – are led to a taste in art that allows them to acquire, through representation, things that they really need. This way of thinking is a generalized application of the theories of the Earl of Shaftesbury who, arguably, invented the modern concept of aesthetic beauty as a consequence of his arguments against Hobbesian ethics, which he thought egotistic.[69] Shaftesbury's idea of virtue excludes any consideration of the consequences of virtuous action; we should love virtue merely in the regard of it. Shaftsbury was a classicist; he insisted on the identity of good and the beautiful, but rigorous disinterest is foundational for modern aesthetics as a separate realm of consideration.[70] A true interest in the beautiful must be without regard to its goodness, just as true religious devotion cannot be conducted in desire of heavenly reward.

Such doctrines of interested disinterest go some way to explaining the crucial position of the new art of landscape gardening in the eighteenth century: to make scenic improvements of land was to celebrate the basic currency of political franchise, which in turn allowed a display of taste that further demonstrated aptitude for government. The particular part of one's estate so treated was the park. The traditional use of parks, and the etymology of the word, was the keeping of game, the hunting of which was a principal aspect of the hospitality of a great house. The park, by definition, was not used for profit; it was land used for the gift of hospitality, but it also represented that surplus, which stood as surety for future generations of the family and for the inalienable nature of their relation to land. In Britain, the eighteenth century was also the time of an agrarian revolution, where large-scale investment in agriculture and improved techniques of drainage, pasturage, planting and stock breeding led to rapid increases in rural productivity and profitability, especially during the wars with France, which inflated the price of domestic produce. This revolution also required a rapid increase in the rate of 'enclosure': the change of land tenure from various customary rights to modern freehold, which resulted in great disruption and frequent impoverishment for rural communities. This latter point is discussed in some detail in Chapters 4 and 5, but the point here is a simpler one about 'interest'. The concept of estate 'improvement' covers both agricultural and scenic improvements, but the discourse of civic humanism and the Shaftesburian idea of disinterest require the two to be radically disconnected. Ownership of land is a natural interest, and a disinterested relationship to it is required. Therefore, scenic improvement should never be connected to the profits of agriculture, nor to a wish to increase them, but only to the inalienable capital of inherited property. In fact, Price managed scenic improvements of his estate, Foxely, alongside agricultural improvements, but entirely avoids discussing the issue.[71] This relation is clear in its contrary: critics of the picturesque, such as William Marshall, argue against separating the two; but Marshall was a utilitarian on the other side of the civics debate going back to Thomas Hobbes.[72]

Wheat fields are paradigmatic objects of disgust for eighteenth-century landscape improvers; they lack pictorial qualities because of their flatness and monotony and they stand for a relation to the land based on profit. This crucial distinction of interest and disinterest becomes more over-determined as a picturesque style of landscape park develops. William Gilpin, Price, Knight and Humphry Repton all argue, on formal grounds, for lowering the contrast between the park's artificial landscape and its surrounding countryside, and for allowing spectators to see out of the park. At the end of his career, Repton even advertised a design in which a view of a neighbouring wheat field is featured.[73] Thus, an interested love of the countryside as a whole, in its aesthetic, social and economic qualities, was to be expressed in the formal qualities of a landscape design which, while being an immediate neighbour and experientially similar to the countryside, needed to be understood as purely a matter of disinterested taste.

Meat had a peculiar importance in all of this. Parks were traditionally set up for deer hunting. By the late eighteenth century, this was less fashionable than fox hunting, which gave greater scope for horsemanship and was conducted outside the park in the agricultural countryside. While many parks were still stocked with deer, which provided scenic interest and larder items, increasingly parks were also grazed by cattle, or even sheep. This was notionally less problematic than growing wheat, which was synonymous with commerce, because disinterest could still be observed by claiming that one was improving the breeds out of scientific interest and ultimately in service of a national property in blood stock.[74] We can, however, observe this rhetoric in its failure, with Repton regularly slandering his tasteless clients for turning from landscape to butchery.

> Now not one moving object must appear
> Except the owner's bullocks, sheep, or deer,
> As if his landscape were all made to eat;
> And yet he shudders at a crop of wheat.[75]

We now have much of the context to understand the double politics of taste and disgust in the picturesque, why the design of a butcher's shop should play a role in aesthetics, and why taste and disgust do indeed articulate rather than collapse into each other.

A picturesque butcher's shop

In 1830, after publishing three portfolios of designs for cottages and ornamental buildings, Peter Frederick Robinson published *Village Architecture, or a Series of Designs* [. . .] *illustrative of the observations contained in the essay on the picturesque, by Sir Uvedale Price*, which claims to illustrate suggestions by Price on how landlords can have an economical occasion for exercising taste when upgrading agricultural infrastructure.[76] Robinson was the main figure in the invention of the Olde English style, later made fashionable by Richard Norman Shaw, with its askew combination of exaggerated vernacular features and its leavening through a touch of the then fashionable Swiss-ness. The longevity of Robinson's vision is such that, even today, it provides an emblem of the cloying sentimentality and pretence of tradition, which repels right-minded people from the picturesque. A little more historical context, however, can give a deeper tone to that feeling, because Robinson's designs were, in their time, intended to mix charm and disgust. In *Village Architecture*, having previously advised his readers on how to tastefully house an agricultural workforce, Robinson considers the need for a church, a parsonage, a school, an inn, a workhouse, a green market, a shambles and a butcher's shop. (A shambles is the place for the slaughter, evisceration and skinning of beasts, but there is no illustration of it.) Robinson says nothing about the butcher's shop in the designs' accompanying essay; he only refers to it in the caption to the green market, where he writes: 'The Plate No. 76 is introduced merely to show that some scenic effects may be produced by the simplest means, and at a trifling expense. With the same feeling the Butcher's Shop is made the subject of Plate 77'[77] (Figure 3.2).

The plate shows a gable-roofed building of two storeys. The upper level, we surmise, is the butcher's home, while the shop below opens through a trellis onto a wide shelf in the space of the street. Beside it is a gated low shed, perhaps for the shambles previously mentioned, although it would hardly have height for the gallows on which cattle were hung and skinned. The serving shelf is protected by a large awning; this also protects the door, which has upper and lower leaves to exclude dogs. The butcher leans on the closed lower door, looking down a short flight of steps with decorated newel posts, to converse with a man and child. The man carries a bulging sack. The building seems to be constructed on a plinth, suggesting a floor of earth, but one that is compacted and well drained, and there is a tall almost elegant chimney with two flues. These features and the glazed windows on the first floor show that this is not an inexpensive building. In the later edition of 1837, Robinson

Figure 3.2 Peter Frederick Robinson, 'The Butcher's Shop', 1830.

Figure 3.3 Peter Frederick Robinson, 'The Village Scene', with the butcher's shop to the far left, 1837.

included a new plate (Figure 3.3) showing a scenographic view of the village and we see the butcher's shop in the extreme left of the view, where a respectably dressed woman is talking with the butcher in the door of the shed. The plinth seems to have disappeared but we see some additional detail: decorated brackets holding the awning, bargeboards on the main roof, and an indicative leg of mutton hanging over the shelf. My attentive description risks exaggerating the level of Robinson's design intent. The butcher's shop is a whisker away from unmeaning pragmatism, perhaps no different from actual vernacular buildings, and certainly much less formed and ornamented than the other designs in the portfolio. Thus, the question arises as to what Robinson might have meant by saying that the butcher's shop was a 'design'.

The license for Robinson's exercise comes from two sources in Price: the 'Essay on Picturesque Architecture and Building' and the later 'Dialogue on the Picturesque'. In the former, Price gives what is perhaps the earliest and most influential textual statement of what, in the twentieth century, would be called Townscape.

> Those who are desirous of improving the landscapes of their place by means of buildings, ought surely to study what the great masters of landscape [painting] have done [. . .] how they sometimes softened and disguised the too manifest symmetry of regular architecture, by blending with other objects of a different but not degrading kind; and at other times ennobled meaner buildings by the help of some imposing mass that fixed upon itself the principal attention. This last method is capable of frequent application: as for instance, when a small hamlet or some farm buildings are in an interesting situation, where the person from whose place they are in view, would wish for something more attractive. It is true, that a rich person to whom the whole belonged, might pull them all down and place in their room a tower, or a temple, or some ornamental building: but, besides that there is something unpleasant, in destroying for the sake of mere ornament the marks of industry and habitation, such building of parade have too frequently a staring, unconnected, ostentatious appearance. Should he, however, choose to preserve the look of a farm or hamlet [. . .] any building of good form, rising higher than the rest amidst them, would probably answer to that purpose, and serve at once to vary and unite the whole group [. . .] There may be cases also where an improver, with great property all round, may have only a small piece of ground in such a hamlet, and be unable to purchase any more: a building of the character I mentioned, might do all that a lover of painting wish for, and give him a sort of property in the whole; and I know that manner of appropriating objects to be the source of much pleasure.[78]

In this passage, yet again, we see how Price's ideas of composition are not in the first instance visual, but involve the potential for visual arrangement that arises out of combining genres – mixing high and low. In the later text, 'The Dialogue', which recapitulates Price's argument, characters representing Price, Knight and an everyman, 'Mr Seymour', walk through such a village: 'both gay and modest from the mixture of trees among the houses; the church with its battlements, crowned the whole . . .'.[79] Price describes the 'ancient mansion', the fief of which we assume the village to be, and spends some time describing the parsonage house, and the Parson's daughter, both said to be picturesque and so providing an opportunity to discuss the relation between aesthetic value and attractions between the sexes. Price does not describe a butcher's shop in this section but introduces it in Seymour's conversation some twenty pages later: 'Now, I recollect that in coming through the village, we passed by a butcher's shop . . .'.[80]

The village church, in a faux-weathered medieval style, and the parsonage, in ghastly half-timbering, are clearly Robinson's high point in both genre and in the Village scene, but most of the designs are reflections on vernacular building as a stylistic source for architecture. The butcher's shop, by contrast, is either much more subtle, or simply dumber, and clearly included as the epitome of 'meanness', which the greater buildings act to ennoble through association. A more radical reading, however, is also possible. In Figure 3.2 the butcher's shop is depicted alone, framed in foliage, and we must presume it to be an architectural work, if one of staggering banality. But in the scenographic Village Scene included in the later edition (Figure 3.3) we see something more like Price's description: the work of architecture is the assemblage, not the building. Robinson did not need to design the butcher's shop; the architect's work was in its inclusion. It could well have been a pre-existing building, even one not able to be acquired by the improver; its value is in its contingency. It need not even have been positioned in view; simply by being there, meaning nothing, everything else makes sense. Such contingency is guaranteed, not by the design of the butcher's shop, but by its mute resilience from form, an aspect Price calls picturesque ugliness.

However, it is no coincidence that the shapeless building is a butcher's shop. The work of Price, and more so, the architects who illustrated his ideas, are intended to be ideological. Villages, such as those proposed by Robinson, built across Britain and often called model villages, were typically for estate workers. These families, the core work-force permanently employed on large estates, probably received various forms of assistance, including restricted rights of 'settlement' in a parish where wealthy landholders paid local taxes. In fact, the wealth of such landholders was largely generated, not by their own agricultural production, but by the renting of land to tenant farmers. Their farms drew on the seasonal labour of a different class of worker: scabrous day labourers starving in the mud-floored hovels of so-called 'open parishes', where settlement was not policed and rural migrations caused over-population relative to 'parish-rates' or the local tax system. The prosperous butcher's shop is, then, a happy image of reconciled England, produced for readers and builders whose wealth comes from villages quite unlike this one. The butcher's shop flourishes in Robinson's village because the workers have money, but also because they require it. They, like day labourers outside the estate, have been subsumed into the wage economy; have lost the rights of pasturage that once allowed them to raise and slaughter their own sheep or pigs. The fat leg of mutton hanging in the butcher's shop of Robinson's prosperous village is inextricably linked to contemporary pamphlets advising the mendicant poor on how to make nourishing soups from a cow's head.[81]

The butcher's shop is an ideology in the simple sense. It is a myth of an ageless georgic society and a settled paternal class system, in a time of rapid agricultural industrialization and huge shifts in the control and ownership of land. The interests served by such obfuscation are more vague. The situation of rural poverty, political unrest, and occasional open rebellion would have been well known to any reader of Robinson's *Village Architecture*, so it would hardly have confused them, nor is it likely that they had any guilt to be assuaged. For instance, Price, at the same time as he was writing of village improvements with deft additions, wrote a pamphlet entitled *Thoughts on the Defense of Property*. In this he proposes that all the property owners of Hereford, whatever their social class, should join together as a volunteer cavalry to charge down riotous mobs of the disaffected landless.[82]

The model estate villages actually constructed were effective in controlling a work-force through the disciplinary mechanism of privileged access to housing, employment and food supply. Ideology has little to do with this. Robinson's portfolio and Price's text do not so much produce an ideology, as take an existing trope of paternalism as the occasion for the novel idea of villages being 'architecture'. If the picturesque is an ideology of anything, it is of the coherence of culture. At a time of serious debates about whether architecture was exclusively a grand style, or applicable to ordinary building, Robinson was an architectural rhyparographer. Like many others, he takes Price's authority to imagine a system of genre in architecture as in painting, with lower orders based on the depiction of the everyday domestic life of the poor. But with his design for a butcher's shop, he is unique in reaching further down to match the Dutch still lifes, in which painters tried their skills in representing flayed carcasses. Lessing would say that Robinson has misunderstood architecture as a medium, taking a challenging idea from painting but not understanding that it would become disgusting if built. The mundane ordinariness of the butcher's shop titillates because it is so close to evoking disgust, in two directions. We might, were we to travel through Robinson's print, be disgusted at the scene of slaughter. The space between the killing and rendering of meat from the animal provides a whole typology of disgust in the viscous, the membranous, the spongy, the excremental. As well as the 'animal disgust' felt at these indefinite substances, and the proximity of the consumable parts of the animal to those which should be discarded, we might feel another nausea at the necessity of this – at appetite – or rather, at the idea of ungovernable appetite. Robinson's butcher's shop plays at satiation-induced disgust, at the limitless amount that the poor would eat.

The last reason behind Robinson's inclusion of the butcher's shop in his pretty village is the simplest: he is following Price quite literally. In the same volume from which Robinson quotes the village improvement idea, Price introduces his theory of disgust. This is largely concerned with the power of imitation to appropriate objects, which would disgust in life, into art, where they are picturesque. Villages being, at the time, objects of phobic disgust is the premise of *Village Architecture*. What is more, when Price, in his final essay, 'Dialogue on the Picturesque', makes a summative version of his disgust theory, he does so by comparing a painting of a slaughtered ox by Rembrandt with a visit to a butcher's shop.

Meat in Repton

It is likely that the landscape gardener and theorist, Repton, is referring to Price when, in his book *Fragments*, he describes going to some trouble to hide the view of a butcher's shop from his home in the village of Hare Street[83] (Figures 3.4 and 3.5). He writes:

> in improving places for others, I must consult their inclinations; at Harestreet, I follow my own. Others prefer still-life – I delight in movement; they prefer lawns fed by their own cattle – I love to see mankind; they derive pleasure from seeing the sheep and oxen fatten, and calculate on the produce of their beef and mutton: perhaps they might not object to the butcher's shop, which I have taken some trouble to hide, giving preference to a basket of roses.[84]

While very similar in appearance, the Hare Street's butcher's shop is the obverse of Robinson's. Robinson's architecture titillates by controlling in a scene what would in life disgust: the rapaciousness of the poor. For Repton, the butcher's shop is an index of those who profit from hunger. What is more, Repton's disgust is such that it cannot be bracketed and framed by art; the butcher's shop must be expelled from the scene or hidden by a garden structure of his devising. Repton uses the trope of the butcher's shop several times. In earlier passages, he gives as an example of poor taste a landholder who 'condescending to become his own tenant, grazier, and butcher, can have little occasion for the landscape gardener'.[85]

Figure 3.4 Humphry Repton, 'View from my own cottage, in Essex' (Hare Street, state 1) 1816. By permission of Rare Books and Special Collections, State Library of New South Wales.

Figure 3.5 Humphry Repton, 'View from my own cottage, in Essex' (Hare Street, state 2) 1816. By permission of Rare Books and Special Collections, State Library of New South Wales.

And he says that he has 'never admitted the word *ferme orneé* [ornamental farm] into my ideas of taste, any more than a butcher's shop or a pigsty, adorned with pea green and gilding.'[86] We know from Stephen Daniels' research that Repton's disgust at profiteering landlords was both general and personal. His paternalist 'Old Tory' beliefs about country life were offended by the capitalization of agriculture, but he was particularly affronted by the *nouveau riche* owner of the local estate failing to commission him and also forcing up the rents in Hare Street.[87] But, given the public controversy between Repton and Price, and

Price's publication of a very long refutation of Repton in the same volume of the *Essays* in which the butcher's shop features, there is a case for seeing Repton's butcher's shop as indicating two kinds of disgust: at profiteering landholders and at Price's aesthetics, which in Repton's view, fails through its excessive breadth to maintain separation between the two economies of taste and wealth. Put more simply, while Robinson's and Repton's villages each require a butcher's shop, Repton does not think that it adds to the picture's aesthetic quality.

The topic of the Hare Street chapter of *Fragments* is similar to the passage in Price quoted earlier: the improvement of villages, especially of circumstances where the improver does not have complete control of the land but must resort to the picturesque composition of view for the illusion of possession. Both authors call this process 'appropriation', but Repton's is a more elaborated concept and technique, which is described in detail in Chapter 5. At Hare Street it involved purchasing a small amount of extra land, which gave Repton the room to redesign his front garden to make a foreground that allowed for pictorial possession of the village. The first stage of this involved the removal of improper objects so that each element remaining in the view was appropriate to its genre. An iron-framed structure hanging baskets of roses hides the butcher's shop from the Reptons' front sitting room. Repton's visual editing also removes passing carriage traffic, a crippled beggar, and lessens the importance of an inn. Each of these is a problem because they look into Repton's garden, and appropriation demands that we chase away those figures that would want to share our view or objectify us in theirs, to a distance where they 'animate the scene'. The beggar, however, is a problematic figure to interpret. His multiple amputations may indicate that he is a veteran of the wars with France; but his radical asymmetry, having lost one each of eyes, arms and legs, is also slightly comic and links him, in a dreadful visual pun, to the legs of mutton hung in the butcher's shop.[88] The problem of the butcher's shop, as Repton states it in the text, is that of profiteering. This suggests some level of sympathy with the beggar as its victim, especially if he is a veteran, as immense profits were made from British agriculture owing to limits on trade with the Continent during the wars. But the butcher's shop surreptitiously guarantees our disgust at the beggar as an object of taste whatever our sympathies might be, were a different faculty of judgement called upon. The beggar calls for our charity and the butcher displays the joints to whet our appetites. Both pleas must be refused; they are unlicensed evocations of a relation to particular economies that threaten the unified character of the scene and the disinterest necessary to judge it. On the one hand we have objects of purely sensory or 'animal disgust': the mess of slaughter and the flies and road grime on legs of mutton; and the criminal desperation and gangrenous wounds of the beggar. These, however, are merely the basis of Repton's actual topic, which involves two further disgusts related to excessive appetite or the failure of satiation: first, disgust at someone who prefers to look at meat than roses; and second, disgust at the same preference turned to the scale of landscape, where the circuit of profit and poverty replaces beauty. Consistent with the general description of disgust in the eighteenth century, Repton's project was to make the disgusting part of the programme for a socially formed 'taste'. The idea of Gilpin, Repton, Price and others of their era – that the ordinary countryside of England could be 'landscape' and considered as an object of taste – was not self-evident, nor certain of assent. Repton thought this project, the picturesque project, was at risk in an understanding of everyday life in the country as profit-based. To maintain quotidian life in the realm of taste, its limit in the disgusting must be identified. The work of the butcher provides a whole phenomenology of 'animal' disgust, which gives dramatic force to Repton's insistence on a firm line between the landscape and the profits from animal husbandry that make it possible.

To show how intimate and yet disconnected these two disgusts are, we can look at another of Repton's commissions: a game larder built for his friend Sir Harry Featherstonhaugh at Uppark in Sussex. It sits in the carriage court, in the foreground of the view of the north façade. Decorated with trellis-work and paved with the vertebrae of deer, it is a mannered grotesque advertisement for the pleasures of the chase and the table awaiting arriving guests. In a letter to the client, Repton describes the building in a few sentences and a drawing, which shows how the building would allow an artistic framing of its subject. 'The game may be so disposed that the windows may all be left to a certain degree unencumbered, something in this way-. and then one, two, four, six or all eight compartments may be filled according as there is more or less to be displayed.'[89] Why should we recognize this object, with its well-hung corpses, as an ornament to a scene, but not the butcher's shop? In the latter, disgusting meat is bought and sold for profit; it is obviously attached to the outside of aesthetics, to the economy that makes aesthetics possible. To bring it into the 'view of taste' breaks the metaphor and causes disgust. The deer in the larder are killed in a ritual exchange between the host, who makes game accessible in a park, and the guest, who displays a skill; which, in turn, provides occasion for displaying the culinary skills of the household.

The *Carcase of an Ox*

The ideas of Price that Repton and Robinson are referring to occur in Price's 'Essay on Architecture and Buildings' and again in 'The Dialogue on the Picturesque' (first published 1801).[90] The Dialogue recapitulates his arguments as a dramatised conversation between Knight, an everyman 'Mr Seymour', and Price. In the earlier essay, Price discusses the lessons that might be learnt from lower kinds of painting. He makes the genre comparison of buildings in Claude and Ostade, which I discussed in Chapter 2, and then moves on to criteria for judging works on mean subjects. He quotes Burke on the value of the disgusting in isolating the pleasures of imitation and then compares two paintings of meat.

> I have seen a butcher's shop by Teniers, painted with a truth that struck every observer, and with an execution that claimed the admiration of every artist: I have likewise seen a picture of the same subject by Rembrant, the execution of which was at least as masterly, and the representation of the principal circumstances, though less obviously and popularly natural, equally just. The Teniers perfectly exemplified Mr. Burke's distinction; the pleasure (mixed indeed with some disgust) arose from, the mere power of imitation: in the Rembrant, such it arose from the artist's choice of such effects of light and shadow, as alone, would raise our admiration; and, likewise, from seeing those effects applied in such a manner as to soften all the crudeness of objects in themselves disgusting, without destroying their naturalness.[91]

To the argument that I have been presenting Price adds the idea that artists, or architects (as this is his topic) of genius can make low-genre works and their own nobility will shine through in their execution. Price dramatizes this argument in a manner that is complicated by being couched in terms of a debate with Knight, and by being a comparative description of phenomenal disgust and disgust within art.

In 'The Dialogue', Price edits to his own purpose extensive passages from Knight's 'A Note appended the Second Edition of *The Landscape*' (1795), which Price also reprints unedited for the sake of comparison. Despite *The Landscape*, a long verse satire and commentary, being in agreement with Price on taste in gardening, the Note abruptly makes clear what Knight would later argue at length in *An Analytical Inquiry*: he disagreed with Price on the need for a theory of the picturesque. Knight uses the word as an adjective to qualify beauty, to point out particular learned associations of natural beauty with painting. In 'The Dialogue', Price forms Knight's prose into the conversation of a character, Mr Howard. He gives himself the character Mr Hamilton, and introduces Mr Seymour. Seymour is an intelligent, right thinking gentleman who happens to be an *ingénue* in matters of painting. This puts Hamilton (Price) at leisure to anticipate Knight's arguments and to call on the common good sense of Mr Seymour for support. The friends' conversation takes place during a walk that has as its destination the picture gallery of a nearby country house. On their way, the gentlemen experience several scenes in nature contrived to provide them with comparisons to the paintings that they will later see. Central to this rhetorical structure and the argument is Rembrandt's painting of the slaughtering of an ox.

Early in their walk the aesthetes stop to admire a gypsy camp as if it were a painting, praising the tones and textures of objects that disgust Mr Seymour who, despite their attempts to persuade him, says:

> It is very possible, for example, that the old gypsey's tanned skin, the ass and his panniers, the rotten posts and thatch of the hovel, may match each other admirably; but, for the soul of me, I cannot think of them in the same light, with the fresh and tender colours in the cheeks of young men or women; with the shapes and colours of sleek and pampered horses, rich and gaily caparisoned: or with those of porticos or columns of marble, porphyry, lapis lazuli, or even common free-stone; and I can scarcely think that you do.[92]

The description of the dirty, godless, squatting, thieving gypsies is typical of the supposed faults of the dangerous classes during the period of agricultural discontent. The abstraction being asked of Seymour, therefore, is not about overcoming sympathy for the gypsies. Howard persuades Seymour that if the scene were painted, his disgust would dissipate; one cannot be disgusted at a representation.

When they get to the Gallery, all three admire a Claude and it reminds them of the view from a hilltop taken after leaving the gypsy camp. The painting enthrals Seymour: 'what a picture this would be to have in one's sitting-room! to always have before one such an image of fine weather, such a happy mixture of warmth and freshness . . .'.[93] To disarticulate Seymour's admiration for the painting from his wishing to be there, and to return him to the issues raised by the gypsy camp, the aesthetes show him a Teniers of a woman washing pigs' guts. Seymour remarks:

> if what the woman is washing and cleaning, were real tripes, guts, and garbage, the sense of smelling, and animal disgust, would prevent any pleasure I might have (if pleasure there could be) in such a sight. This certainly is merely the pleasure arising from imitation . . .[94]

And thus Price has the hundredth opportunity to repeat that such pleasures are better called picturesque than beautiful.

Of course picturesqueness is not about the disgusting, Hamilton (Price) insists, but with the disgusting we can practise certain discriminations that will be useful with proper objects. Seymour wants to know if, having learnt his lesson with this low material, he can then apply the picturesque mode of viewing to objects that he finds valuable. If gypsies and broken-down asses, why not gentlefolk and handsome horses gaily caparisoned? he asks. Price rewards his useful interlocutor, ending the gallery tour with a contemplation of a noble hunting party painted by Wouvermans. Seymour says he is 'glad to find, that what, according to my ideas, is beautiful and highly ornamented, may be expressed in painting, as well as what is so like dirt and ugliness, that it takes some practice to distinguish in what the difference consists'.[95] Disinterest is, of course, a prerequisite for judgement, but how can it be constructed and shown? Seymour's exercises with offal and the poor have not obliged him to remain in bad company; on the contrary, they have brought him to an evinced autonomy of judgement. Picturesque disgust is an *hors d'oevre* in the project of taste.

At the very centre of 'The Dialogue', the aesthetes show Seymour Rembrandt's painting of an ox carcass on a gallows. Most likely this is the painting now in Glasgow and called *Carcase of an Ox*[96] (Figure 3.6). This extraordinary painting, notionally within the Dutch genre of Kitchen Pieces, is here transposed as a crucifixion. Although a great lover of Dutch art, Price seems entirely ignorant of its iconography which followed the scriptural analysis which held that the story of the Prodigal Son foretells the Crucifixion. But the placement of this example in 'The Dialogue' shows, nevertheless, his appreciation of the unexpectedness of Rembrandt's elevation of a mean subject. Price placed the discussion of the Rembrandt between the Teniers kitchen painting of pigs' guts and Wouvermans' game piece, constructing a series: pigs, cattle and game, offal, flesh and whole creatures. The Rembrandt sits in the centre of 'The Dialogue' – in the centre of Price's argument – and, like the picturesque, acts to transcode genre hierarchies into aesthetic experiences. Seymour praises the painting's mellow and harmonious tints, saying:

Figure 3.6 Rembrandt van Rijn, *Carcase of an Ox*, late 1630s. Glasgow City Council (Museums).

> I see it is an ox hung up, and the painter's name Rembrandt; who, I conclude, is a Dutchman, though the picture is not so finished as the others. It certainly is very like the thing; and yet though it is so like, and the subject so offensive, I do not look at it with as much repugnance as I would have expected. [. . .] Now I recollect that in coming through the village, we passed by a butcher's shop, where a real ox was hung up in this manner; but neither of you stopped to examine it: on the contrary, we all got out of the way. Animal disgust, therefore, prevailed in the one case, and not in the other.[97]

Price's thought experiment begins with an idea about the senses similar to Mendelsohn's, but which he more likely knew from Burke. Price assumes that an actual butcher's shop will disgust us in its squeals and smells, in its visceral mess, and in its mess having a logic and necessity. We will not notice the colours, textures and *clair-obscur* that make meat such suitable material for the exercise of painting, and which are perfectly apparent and pleasurable in *Carcase of an Ox*. But let us consider what actually disgusts here, what might have happened at the butcher's shop, had our friends not possessed taste. When they saw the ox hung up, they might have gone in and bought steaks for supper, or queried the butcher on the price of beef. What is so offensive about that? Had they been hungry, or inquisitive as to the profits of rearing cattle in this neighbourhood, then, as a cost, disgust at the viscera of oxen would have exhausted its significations. 'The Dialogue' offers the implausible description of gentlemen crossing the road as a result of their 'animal' reaction of nausea. In their imputed disgust there is a doubling, a second unlikely disgust at someone who might not cross the road – a poor and hungry person, or perhaps a ghoulish gentleman. In the extreme oppositions of the example, we lose any possibility for knowing these gentlemen aesthetes also breed cattle.

In 'The Dialogue', life is made to imitate art. To maintain the double and separate nobilities of wealth and taste, Price constructs an experience of the butcher's shop that mirrors his understanding of the experience of Rembrandt's *Carcase of an Ox*. In fact, his characters would be as unlikely to feel disgust at the butcher's shop as they would be to praise the meat for its tones and colours. A single, unlikely exclusion of prosaic experience and practical judgement marks both descriptions: the valuing of meat. What would truly disgust is not the sight of real gore, but of Seymour losing patience with his friends' interminable debate and taking the opportunity, provided by the Rembrandt, to guess the weight of the carcass and its price at market. Then, two economies circulating in parallel would suddenly tie together. There would be no possible play of reference between the skill of distinguishing different types of objects and values in painting and the management of estates. There would be no categorical difference between meat and painting, between hunger and taste.

It is likely that Knight is satirizing Price on exactly this point when, in *An Analytical Inquiry*, he argues that even our ideas of beauty in animals are not unmediated; they are associative. He recounts that in Virgil's description of the beautiful bull that raped Europa, it possesses 'long palearia or dewlaps'

> to the real judge of horned cattle there can scarcely be a greater deformity. The case is that the poet and the painter are looking for those forms and proportions, which are best adapted to exhibit ease, elegance, and dignity of gesture and action, and pleasing varieties of light and shade; while the grazier is only calculating the quantity of eatable and nutritive flesh, which the animal, [. . .] may bring into the shambles . . .[98]

I have already imagined Seymour as a 'real judge of horned cattle', deflating the entire aesthetic realm; but we can also imagine other aesthetical accounts that differ. For a classicist like Lessing, the Rembrandt would likely disgust for its affectation, its attempt to compel affect in us, its refusal of the limits that art must have, and its knowledge of which art must form ideals.[99] Many of my contemporaries react to the painting in ways consistent with Mendelsohnn's account: the dark proximate senses of touch and smell, awoken by the woman ladling tripes and puddings of viscera into the bucket, improperly impinge upon and spoil any sensual pleasure they find in colour or tone. We can imagine both these reactions coordinating so that bodily nausea guarantees disgust at vitiated art, and Price's ideas of art and aesthetics would be seen as disgusting precisely because of his failure to be disgusted.

In fact, such a rejection based on sense would not necessarily contradict the logic of Price's proposal, which is based on an idea of painting as an art, not merely on the relation of a single painting to its subject. One could risk a little disgust at Rembrandt's *Ox* if such feelings were useful in clarifying bigger issues in the work of Rembrandt and painting. Price is disgusted with other paintings of food or whole carcasses when they are governed by an appetite for verisimilitude. The other quality for which the Rembrandt is exemplary is that it is 'not so finished as the others', meaning that the painting retains the marks of the brush and the layering of emulsions, the gestic aspect of painterliness that is a large part of Gilpin's idea of the picturesque. Roughness and variety are, of course, supposed by Price to be objective causes of picturesqueness, but here Rembrandt's lack of finish is an opening, too, for Price to make a long quotation from Reynolds damning excessive detail in painting. A hunger for detail takes away from the general and comprehensive matters with which great painters deal, and is 'worse than useless; it is mischievous, it dissipates the perception.'[100] In the larger consideration, painters obsessed with accuracy of detail and their clients' hunger for verisimilitude reduce painting from a liberal art to a mechanical trade. It is Rembrandt's negligent brushwork that shows him to be a painter capable of grand subjects – as an artist concerned with the relation of sensation and ideation in the hierarchy of genres, not an appetite for beef. Price is widening and deepening the remit of taste, drawing the line against disgust further out than Repton. But he is also going beyond the individual work, showing that taste for a single painting requires an understanding of the discipline and institutions of painting.

Sir Uvedale Price's theory of disgust

Price's aesthetics is consistent with Menninghaus' account of the history of aesthetics, with disgust rather than beauty as its central term. Not only is the word in frequent use and the feeling celebrated as a moment of judgement, the picturesque fits snugly into Menninghaus' recovery of Kant's triadic aesthetics of beauty, sublimity and disgust. If disgust is the name of a kind of aesthetic sense, then picturesqueness is an operative account of the use of this sense by artists and architects. As an operative aesthetics, the picturesque is largely concerned with the celebrated ability of art to fix the disgusting, allowing it to be converted to visual pleasure, that is, making disgusting things a source for art. One might think, with Derrida, that disgust 'does not allow itself even to be granted the status of negative pleasure or of ugliness redeemed by representation';[101] that what is representable cannot have been disgusting in the first place. And yet, this is exactly the value, the curiosity, of Price's work: his interest in architecture and gardening loses, or at least blurs, a sensual account of representation and develops a vocabulary of form based around the sensation of disgust. Picturesque cottages designed by architects do not disgust because they are representations of actual scabrous hovels. But apart from the smell, there might be very little difference in sense between an architectural representation and its subject. Price's work rides the familiar concept of rhyparography distinguishing the appropriable ugly from the disgusting, but he introduces a new typology of disgust: not of emotion or sense, which would retain its unique powers, but of formal qualities, so that disgusting objects can be understood and put to use by artists.

In Menninghaus' periodization, Price is half a step ahead of Kant, and for that matter, Knight. Price's theory is on the cusp of a Romanticism in which disgust moves from guaranteeing the idea of aesthetics to being a ploy of artworks. Price's interest is in forms of disgust that can split, each producing different articulations of an inside and outside of taste; every appropriation of disgust into representation being empowered by its own articulation of the dark senses. In Robinson's picturesque butcher's shop there is a double disgust: first, at the sight of evisceration and what this does to the organization of our senses; and then at the idea that this should be an object of taste. In each case, disgust might collapse thought into sensation, but in an articulated manner, from two directions. There is an interesting inconsistency in Derrida's statements on the Third Critique giving another context to Price's innovations. In *The Truth in Painting*, rather than making disgust absolute alterity and singularity as he does in 'Economimesis', Derrida claims that it is a parergon to the Third Critique: ornamenting and framing aesthetics; integral to it and distinct from it.[102] This is a position much closer to Price's theory of disgust, where the different kinds of 'negative pleasures redeemed by representation' are actually more interesting than the guarantee that the singularity of disgust gives to beauty. And the reason for this interest is obvious enough at a structural level: the singularity of disgust guarantees the uniqueness of beauty, but Price's aim is to bifurcate aesthetics.

Price is largely remembered for his argument that we can understand taste as a liking for the beautiful and the picturesque. Both Knight and Repton disagreed, thinking that Price meant an impossible split of aesthetic sense. But they and numerous commentators since misunderstand Price who argues that there are two qualities, generally experienced as mixed, which speak to the one aesthetic sensibility. An analysis such as Price's, which attends to the articulation of these two causes aims to show how differences in judgement between individuals do not necessarily threaten the unity and coherence of taste. Price's theory requires two terms for ugliness, to oppose beauty and picturesqueness. Just as beauty and picturesque are experienced empirically as taste, so actual disgust can be explained as the combined experience of two more precise formal categories – ugliness and deformity.

In terms of the theory he receives, we can understand Price as attempting to reconcile Burke's sensationalist aesthetics with the normative and culturalist civic humanism of Reynolds. One aspect of this reconciliation is that he takes on both their theories of disgust. For Reynolds, the identification of disgust in art is an education in judgement for the individual. To the degree that it can be communicated, if not exactly shared, disgust can be the basis of a public self-recognition in taste. Reynolds contrasts the liberal artist who articulates this civics from a degraded mechanic who is 'debauched and deceived by this fallacious mastery' of mechanical imitation, who is obsessed with the representation of appearances and with whom we should be disgusted.[103] This contrast implies that a true interest in art requires disinterest in the production of beauty, to avoid satiation and beauty's self-sickening affects. For Burke, disgust, like beauty, is a sensation. Burke thinks that beauty relaxes the nerve cords while sublimity tightens them. The aesthetical experience of art and nature, for him, has a common sensory basis on which they can be compared. Art's role is to moderate sensory experience; a painting of gladiators is merely a weaker form of the same sensations, suited to those whose stomachs are not accustomed to actual combat. Burke writes of genre painting and the ability of art to bring mean scenes – which in nature disgust – up to beauty, but he does not say how this is related to the model of the nerve cords. Perhaps scabrous hovels normally leave our sensorium utterly lax, and the art of painting is to tighten it up to the tonality of beauty. Price thinks that the power Burke accords to imitation, as a general and weakened relation to sense, can be more accurately described as the positive qualities of pictures in terms imminent to them: colouration, chiaroscuro, grouping and composition. What is more, this avoids an ontological (or at least lexical) problem: 'the term beautiful, applied to a picture without a single beautiful object in it, and with some, like those before you, very ugly and nasty, is used, if not in a licentious, at least in a very vague sense . . .'.[104] Picturesqueness, then, offers itself for use in such circumstances, and we have two alternatives with which to announce approval of things that have pleased us.

Price considers picturesqueness, as a sensation, to lie between beauty and sublimity. In its use, however, 'picturesque' is, like beauty, a term of approbation, which sublimity cannot be.[105] He holds that it is not within the power of landscape improvement to deal with the sublime; but, in any case, the sublime, while an aesthetic experience, stands outside the analogy of taste.[106] Reynolds, attacking the idea that the Grand Style of painting, which does evoke the sublime, might share in the picturesque, explains that: '*picturesque* is somewhat synonymous to the word *taste*; which we should think improperly applied to Homer, or Milton, but very well to Pope or Prior'.[107] In this, the British authors follow a similar logic to Kant's rhetorical question about the sublime: 'how can that which is apprehended as inherently contra-final be noted with an expression of approval?'[108] The absoluteness of the sublime and the disgusting might lead one to think they are reciprocal, but this would take disgust beyond the taste analogy that we are following.

Price does not explain it in this way, but the pairing of beauty and picturesqueness follows a logic, not unlike the earlier ideas of Claude Perrault (also espoused by Christopher Wren) of a distinction between objective and customary beauty.[109] Beauty is an objective and transcendent quality, while picturesqueness is a matter of culture and is constructed historically. Beauty is naturally occurring but art can share in it, which shows how human creativity is itself an imitation of divine production. In reciprocation, picturesqueness begins in artifice but leads us back to nature.

Price makes two attempts at describing the objective qualities of picturesqueness and beauty. In the first, he follows Burke on the smoothness and roundedness of beauty, but then argues against Burke's idea that the angular and rough is ugly. Instead, he follows Gilpin, defining picturesqueness in a roughness that speaks to the pencil and brush, and then he further generalizes this in his famous categories of the intricate and varied. But here Price finds himself in a contradiction: he believes that, empirically, beauty and picturesqueness are always mixed, but how would a mixture of smoothness and roughness be sensed? Although not admitting (or perhaps not aware of) this contradiction, Price develops a second account based on Burke's idea of degrees of sensory excitation. Burke thinks that sublimity is excitation of the nerves and beauty their relaxation; and Price suggests that picturesqueness leaves the nerves in their normal state. Walter Hipple ridicules Price for this, saying that it would be equivalent to no sensation. However, this is a very important moment: Price's attempt at neurology shows how crucial it is to him that picturesqueness be found in quotidian experience.[110] In our present task, the second account of degrees of stimulation is the more important and leads, finally, to Price's theory of disgust.

Price uses the disgust argument to show the necessity of splitting picturesqueness and beauty, and he is obliged to do it again to show the difference between them. Price worries about how to explain the failure of artworks and bad taste; failed picturesqueness cannot lie in too much beauty. Price decides to introduce two terms of disapprobation: deformity and ugliness (see Figure 3.7). The four terms align along a range of stimulus: deformity is too great a stimulus, picturesqueness a tolerable amount, beauty a pleasurable repose, and ugliness a kind of insipidity. The difference between deformity and ugliness better explains the difference between picturesqueness and beauty; the occasion of one's liking the sweet or the sour can be understood in a refusal of the sickly or the acrid. But then Price breaks with Burke's mechanical psychologism. According to Price, ugliness and deformity have the same visual causes as beauty and the picturesque; were we merely sensual and rational beings, we would separate the insipid and the beautiful from the deformed and the picturesque. Empirically, it might be difficult to distinguish the picturesque from the deformed. Quoting John Dryden on the proximity of wit and madness, Price says: 'thin partitions do their bounds divide'.[111] It is the faculty of judgement that allows us to approve both the beautiful and the picturesque, and to cast out the insipid and the deformed. Although Price's aesthetics has plural, indeed proliferating, terms, his project is actually a theory of the coherence of taste. The range within which taste varies, and where standards might be formed, is that analogy to the civil republic with which we earlier identified Reynolds. Artists have a remit that is slightly wider than persons of taste; they have the ability to see what ugliness and deformity can be brought to taste in representation.

Price arrays these distinctions in a linear manner in the story of a woman's face. Price imagines a fine featured woman: 'her eyes, eyebrows, hair, and complexion, are more striking and showy than delicate'.[112] Were we now to imagine a lessening of these showy features, finer graduations of skin tones, less eyebrows, and so on, we would have a more finished delicacy that we could call beautiful. Were we to continue the process until the skin lost colour, the eyebrows became transparent, the expression vapid, the face would pass through the angelic and become insipid, and, in Price's opinion, ugly. If, on the other hand, we took the fine-featured woman and gave her a dusky complexion, thickened her eyebrows, drew in moles and an arch cast to her gaze, then we would have taken off from beauty what we had given to picturesqueness. Thus (thinks Price) we can imagine a taste for picturesque women with *un certain je ne sais quoi*, as well as our angelic wives and daughters. But taste tells us not to go further and take pleasure in the deformities of preposterous eyebrows, squints and smallpox scars.[113]

Price's ideas are misogynist largely in the same way that Menninghaus observes across the disgust literature, most likely because he knew the same classic authors (such as Horace) that the German philosophers were taking up. However, for Price (and this might make his theory either kinder or more radical), old women are not the apogee of phobic disgust that they are for Kant. Old ladies provide a model of the picturesque for Price because one can admire them for their character without a sexual attraction.

> I have read, indeed, in some fairy tale, of a country, where age and wrinkles were loved and caressed, and youth and freshness deflected; but in real life, I fancy, the most picturesque old woman, however her admirer may ogle her on that account, is perfectly safe from his caresses.
>
> [and]
>
> Those who have been used to admire such picturesque ugliness in painting, will look with pleasure [. . .] at the original in nature; and we cannot think slightly of the power and advantage of that art, which makes its admirers often gaze with such delight on some ancient lady, as by the help of a little vanity might perhaps lead her to mistake the motive.[114]

Animals have a similar role in Burke's aesthetics. He supposes that beauty cannot be understood as a polite acculturation of sexual attraction because it is a social feeling, one that we have towards friends, and also animals:

> Men are carried to the sex in general, as it is the sex, and by the common law of nature; but they are attached to particulars by personal beauty. I call beauty a social quality; for where women and men, and not only they, but when other animals give us a sense of joy and pleasure in beholding them, (and there are many that do so) they inspire us with sentiments of tenderness and affection towards their persons; we like to have them near us, and we enter willingly into a kind of relation with them . . .[115]

Price's picturesque is not the community of affection that Burke felt in the presence of his pets, but a kind of amusement which is not apparent to the ancient lady who is its cause. As an example for Price's argument, the saucy gypsy girl with her thick arched eyebrows is still too close a mixture of picturesqueness and beauty; still too close to the interest that beauty supposes, whether it is social or sexual. The old lady, assumed to be neuter, is the epitome of picturesqueness; like the cottages of the poor, Price's interest in her is visual alone. All the more amusing if she should mistake this for something else, as the peasants might mistake the cause of the landlord's interest in their housing.

What truly disgusts, says Price, what is beyond the territory of art's appropriating powers, is the combination of the ugly and deformed.

> Deformity is to ugliness, what picturesqueness is to beauty; though distinct from it, and in many cases arising from opposite causes, it is often mistaken for it, often accompanies it, and greatly heightens its effect. Ugliness alone, is merely disagreeable; by the addition of deformity, it becomes hideous; by that of terror it may become sublime. All these are mixed in the
>
> Monstrum horrendum, informe, ingens, cui lumen ademptum.[116]

In this passage, Price anticipates one of the most famous anti-aesthetics of the twentieth century: Georges Bataille's concept of *informe* or formlessness. The quote is from Virgil describing the Cyclopes: 'A monster frightful, formless, immense, with sight removed.'[117] The paradox in Virgil's description of the monster's deformed body as 'formless' might well have been Bataille's inspiration for his definition of *informe.*[118] In any case, for Price, disgust emerges from a kind of inscriptive action that deformity exerts upon the blankness of the ugly. Imagine a man technically ugly in Price's terms, his face with 'no more features than an oyster'. Suppose a sculptor portrayed the head of such a man: 'should he then twist the mouth, make the nose awry, of a preposterous size, and place warts and carbuncles upon it, or wens and excrescencies on other parts of the face, he would then graft deformity upon ugliness.'[119] In the dramatized reprise of this argument in 'The Dialogue', the gentlemen pass by a man with: 'a complexion like tallow; an unmeaning, pudding face, the marks of the small-pox appearing all over it, like bits of suet through the skin of a real pudding: a nose like a potatoe; and dull, heavy, oyster-like eyes.'[120]

Price's contribution to the theory of disgust is, then, this description of its formal causes. There is not one class of disgusting things in life, there are two: ugliness and deformity. But these turn out to be merely animal disgust, which can be appropriated into art and made pleasurable. Even in art, however, the combination of the two produces disgust; its bodiliness overcomes the autonomy of art, and we feel sick at its representation in the same way we are sickened by decaying flesh. Absolute disgust, where one vomits in violent rejection of a sensation or idea – in that convulsion losing the difference between sense and idea – is a combination of ugliness and deformity; too little and too much form, monstrously combined.

While Price, at some points, describes a range of visual stimulus – from insufficient in 'ugliness' to excessive in 'deformity' – this tends to run against his argument for the distinct characters of beauty and picturesqueness, which are both in the middle. If we understand these as distinct characters, as Price wishes us to, then it would be consistent to think of the four terms not only arrayed along a range of stimulus but of that stimulus being made up of the overlapping ranges of picturesqueness and beauty. I have attempted a diagram that elucidates Price's theory (Figure 3.7). The excess of the picturesque character is an excess of form, understood through doctrines of ornament. While Price does write of twisting noses and otherwise modifying a form, many of his examples of deformation are additions to form: warts, scars, gashes, noses grown monstrous and so on. The most characteristic element of picturesque cottage architecture is, for instance, chimneys of exaggerated size. Price's concepts of form are not modern; they are still partly in the world of Alberti, where the beauty of form, while complete in itself, remains a-signifying without appropriate ornaments, such as the orders of architecture, to tell the relation of empirical form to cosmic form and the intendedness of all creation. It is this paradox of the ornament as supplement, being separable but essential, which explains Price's focus on the preposterous eyebrows, warts, wens and excrescences. Deformity concerns the bad supplement that no longer knows the propriety of attachment. Price's weakened character of beauty is named ugliness and insipidity which is more strongly put in his tag from Virgil as *informe*, or unformedness. When Bataille defines *informe* as something like spit, or a crushed spider or earthworm, he is not only evoking a familiar typology of disgust elicitors in body products and insects. Spit is formless, and the insects might well be when crushed underfoot, as Bataille proposes that the formless always is; nevertheless Price would correct him. The incomprehensible and contagious body product is *informe* but the spider, that super-figural, over-articulated malevolent form, is a necessary partner to spit in making up the conditions of a thorough disgust.

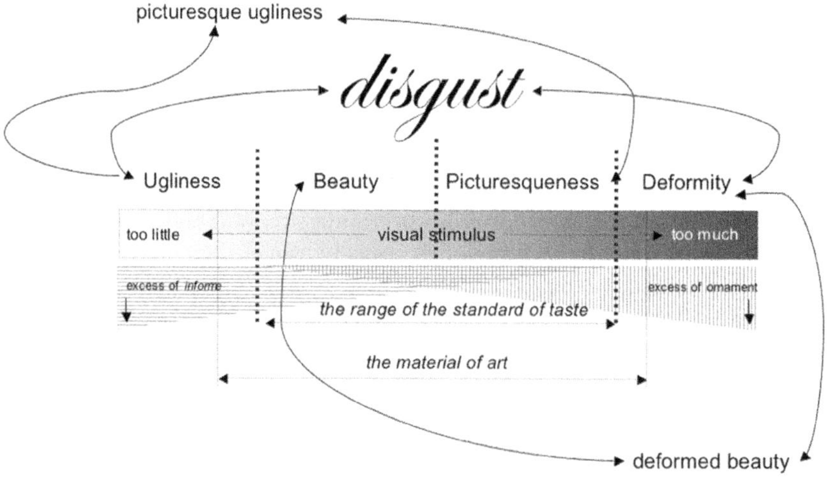

Figure 3.7 The author's diagram of Uvedale Price's theory of disgust, described in his *Essays*, 1810.

Price goes on to imagine further allegiances: picturesque ugliness and deformed beauty, taking the count up to five terms for disgust. Whereas ugliness and deformity are merely indifferently unpleasing and material for art, and while their combination is completely beyond the pale, Price is unsure what to make of ornamented cottage hovels and lightning-blasted trees. These are paradigmatic picturesque objects and yet they do not really fit his theory. Dosing the unformed cottage with the picturesqueness of exaggerated chimneys and rustic tree trunk posts ought, logically, to bring it back up to beauty. The lightning strike ought either to make the beautiful oak picturesque or deform it properly. Picturesque ugliness and deformed beauty each stand in the place of picturesqueness itself and Price is torn between including them at the cost of losing his morphology of disgust, or excluding them at the cost of losing his certainty on what disgust is. He decides that picturesque ugliness is a defused disgust; it is within the realm of taste as it shows art's productivity in raising ugly things to value. Deforming beauty must disgust, he decides, but differently. It is an aesthetic pleasure that we ought to reject, like, he says 'a gash on a living animal'. But quickly, Price re-introduces deformed beauty, with a temporal condition in the figure of the ruin. While one should never deform beauty, if that deformation has occurred then it might be enjoyed. Here, the advantage of the picturesque over the complete repair of the deformation and the return of the object to beauty is that the picturesque is 'œconomical'.[121] If one possessed a landscape scarred by a quarry, it was cheaper to convert it to picturesqueness than to beauty.[122] But the economy of picturesque improvement is not the symmetry Price would have us believe. Deformed beauty is reincorporated into taste to balance the overwhelming number of projects for improvement that have nothing to do with deformation by time. These are the ordinary unformed uglinesses of agricultural production made available to the improver's art, not because they have been located by the eye of taste, but because of an unmentionable fact: the aesthete is also the land owner. What disgusts, then, is the collapse of the aesthetic economy onto the economy as such; when talent and refinement to judge are suddenly equated with wealth to acquire; when the gentleman used to the double nobility of being born to wealth and to taste loses the space in which to deploy this ideology, as we saw at the butcher's shop.

The proliferation of Price's terms opens up a descriptive space and nomenclature for the sensuous apprehension of non-pleasing form. The picturesque is not the negative pleasure or negation of pleasure that Burke and Kant imagined with the term sublime. When Price protests that 'the sublime is beyond our contracted powers', meaning that the sublime has no utility in the making of art and architecture, he is claiming a space for an operative language of form. If empirical taste is to be the criteria of art, then form can no longer be an issue of ideals. A differentiated language of form is required that includes, in a common space, the other-than-normative, the improper, objects that are a part of the project of taste even if they are not in themselves pleasing. At its broadest level, the picturesque is a proposal for the empirical existence of form and a way of describing it other than using the transcendent expression of a trope, a proportion, an idea. Licensed by an anthropology of differing modes of becoming disgusted, the distinction of ugliness from deformity has just this role. The contradiction that 'picturesque ugliness' puts into Price's theory is, to a degree, explained by the ideological imbrication of taste in paintings of the countryside and agriculture, the productive confusion of the aesthete and the cattle breeder that we have been following. It has, however, another aspect of more than historical interest. In Rembrandt's *Carcase of an Ox*, the unformed ugliness of everyday life and appetite becomes deformed by the picturesque without being corrected into beauty, and without, counter to Price's theory, becoming disgusting. Such picturesque ugliness has no model in nature; it is a relation only possible in art. This opens a further issue: whether the distinction of art and nature exists at an empirical level, in different classes of object.

Picturesqueness and objecthood

Picturesque ugliness opens some fundamental issues about the relation of art objects to quotidian objects, both in the nature of this distinction, and the potential for art in the clash between these categories. Thus far the theory of disgust has led us to assume that what disgusts in art is the collapse of representational space, so that the disgusting thing becomes real for us, and the distinction of representation and reality is undone at some frightening, general level. But could there be, conversely, something that disgusted in art that did not in reality? Or a disgust aroused by an artwork that spread out over reality contagiously? And what of non-representational painting and architecture? What bearing does a theoretical disgust at butcher's shops have on the more typical distaste that we might feel at bad architecture?

For a strict aesthetics, based on sense and reflection on sense in the tradition of Hume, Burke and Kant, there can be no *a priori* distinction of art and nature, even if such a division is able to emerge by virtue of Kant's concept of 'aesthetic ideas'. Similarly, the ways in which art is interesting for psychoanalysis, in identification, imagination and so on, do not categorically distinguish the art object from everyday objects. For Cousins, the powers of ugliness lie in its objectification of a person; the object-ness of the thing appears excessive, expanding and oppressive, leaving no space for the subject and no difference between subjectivity and biological life. For those who hold that there is a category of the art object, either at a level of ontology or strong historically embedded convention, the monstrousness of the ugly has a further twist. Ugliness and disgust might collapse the art/nature distinction at a general level, not merely the relationship that they have in representation. A pathology of representation would not explain the continued role of ugliness in modern non-objective art, nor architecture. If one holds that there is art and that art is apparent in art objects, then the phobic disgust that arises from the object taking the subject's place has a special case: the quotidian object taking the art object's place.

Michael Fried and Theodor Adorno raise the aesthetic problems of objecthood within quite different frameworks but the same context: the end game of formalist modernism in the 1960s. Fried's essay critiquing 'literalist art' (what is generally now called minimalism) was published in 1967.[123] Since that time, the fame of 'Art and Objecthood' has been such that it has provided a matrix for progressive art practice, both of the kind Fried supported and that which he condemned. In his critique, Fried champions one kind of contemporary art – the non-representational but highly articulated and individuated sculpture of Anthony Caro – over the presentation of generic-shaped box-like objects of artists Robert Morris and Donald Judd. Fried claims minimalism was duplicitous by confronting the spectator with objects that, while being denominated as art, had the *look of not being art.* This undid the spatio-temporal nexus of painting and sculpture. Fried thinks that the concrete period of time in which art objects are perceived should not be part of the concept of the artwork. We transpose the temporal relations with spatial ones, understanding part-to-part and part-to-whole relations within the art object as spatial and independent of the order of visual inspection. Fried thinks that minimal art refuses this transposition; when inspecting it, one is aware of the duration of perception and indeed, its sequence. One looks at Carl Andre's bricks on the floor and wonders if they are art in any way beyond being named art. Time passes and nothing else arises from the work. One then becomes aware that inspecting the work *is* the work; minimalism requires the time of one's experience of it. Fried calls this theatricality – playing to an audience. In the terms of our present concern, what threatens to disgust is that art objects can no longer sit alongside quotidian objects, either all objects are art works or none are. What might be a simple category confusion, has, according to Fried, consequences for the subject quite like those described by Cousins. In his 1998 reflection on the 'Art and Objecthood' essay, Fried writes:

> My critique of the literalist address to the viewer's body was not that bodiliness as such had no place in art but rather that literalism theatricalized the body, put it endlessly on stage, made it uncanny or opaque to itself, hollowed it out, deadened its expressiveness, denied its finitude and in a sense its humanness, and so on. There is, I might have said, something vaguely *monstrous* about the body in literalism.[124]

Fried is concerned with the ethics of modes of subjectivity, and for him, the brute 'presence' of objects lacks and undoes the 'presentness' that art provides for us, to contour our subjective experience.[125]

Theodor Adorno also thinks that there is monstrosity in the object character of artwork, but for him, this is a good thing, a point of ethical subject formation; the object character of the artwork reveals the monstrosity of empirical reality.[126] Adorno thought that artists' relations to their material mirrored the dialectic of the forces and relations of production. But the mechanism of this relation between dialectics is more relevant here. Adorno thought that the material given to the artist to work, that stuff which becomes the content of the work, is actually petrified forms of earlier practice. Take, for example, the current popularity in architecture of a kind of reductive neo-modernism called 'minimalism'. The fact that this looks like canonical modernism and sometimes like minimalist art of the kind that troubled Fried is neither coincidence, nor lack of imagination, nor the return of eternal verities of form. The mute stuff on which neo-modernism works is the dead vocabulary of modernist form, a language that no longer signifies. Art forms this stuff, which is not real, into empirically existing objects. When Adorno comes to consider how these relate to objects of the world, he ends up in a very similar position to Fried.[127]

> Object in art and object in empirical reality are entirely distinct. In art the object is the work produced by art, as much containing elements of empirical reality as displacing, dissolving and reconstructing them according to the work's own law. Only through such transformation [. . .] does art give empirical reality its due, the epiphany of its shrouded essence and the merited shudder in the face of it as in the face of a monstrosity. The primacy of the object is affirmed aesthetically only in the character of art as the unconscious writing of history, as anamnesis of the vanquished, the repressed, and perhaps of what is possible. The primacy of the object, as the potential freedom from the domination of what is, manifests itself in art as its freedom from objects.[128]

Like Fried, Adorno thinks that a categorical distinction between artwork and quotidian object is required and required to be self-demonstrable. The art object is a matter of art's internal law, what he calls elsewhere its non-conceptual logic,[129] and this is like Fried's (and earlier Clement Greenberg's) concept of disciplines such as painting having a limited autonomy in their own history of problems posed and solved. What Adorno thinks we see in the artwork is not that disciplinarity; he claims that we see the primacy of the object, the empirical art object, its real presence produced out of the immateriality of the artwork. What we see, then, is what we cannot see from day to day: the actual material conditions of the world prior to their organization by us. To be art, the architectural work must pass from being an organization of space and 'material' *by us* to being an empirical object *other to us.* This exceptional empirical object, the work of art or architecture, shows the possibility of a transformed reality, and at the same time it shows the failure, thus far, of that transformation: the failed totality of social historical existence and our alienation from nature. Art shows us what we fear: that empirical reality is non-identical with us. Art deserving of the name acts momentarily to abolish that fear that has been institutionalized as culture.[130]

One of the artists to whom Fried was opposed was Robert Smithson, who took up the term picturesque. In his essay-cum-artwork 'A Tour of the Monuments of Passiac New Jersey', Smithson leaves Manhattan by bus (while reading a newspaper review of an exhibition of nineteenth-century landscape) in order to discover the rust belt town of Passiac as if he were Gilpin discovering the North.[131] Smithson refreshes the picturesque by doubling its original genre transcoding. While the subjects of his highly trained contemplation, redundant bits of the countryside, are no riskier than those of Gilpin or Price, in the meantime the picturesque itself had become something of monument. Smithson's apparently innocent reuse of it in modern circumstances has made a further precedent – the picturesque seems, in this series, a precedent for what Lucy Lippard called the disappearance of the art object, which might also be called the objectification of art practice.[132] In the visual arts, as much as architecture, the aestheticization of the everyday has come to have historiographic connotations.

In Chapter 2, 'Pictures', I argued for a degree of scepticism about the usual claim made for the picturesque as a logic of visual composition. I emphasized, instead, how much the 'picture' in 'picturesque' referred to genre and the contents of a view, and to the spatiality of the picture as a flat surface in the changing relation of art and architecture. Our work with disgust, in this chapter, has extended this argument. While there is good sense in understanding the history of art as progressing from a basis in objects to work on the subject, or, as Walter Benjamin puts it, from cult to exhibition value, this does not mean that objects become outdated by the rise of aesthetics and autonomous art.[133] Eighteenth-century systems of painting genres and ideologies of rural improvement are important, for largely historical reasons, in understanding the contextual development of the picturesque. Of more relevance in the present is the question, what happens to these aspects of art? What happens to the things in pictures, the proprieties at stake in genre systems and building types? We could say, on a general level, the eighteenth-century picturesque made a place for the object within the emerging aesthetic culture. If the objects depicted in paintings were no longer governed by rules and norms, and, in the potential interdisciplinarity of the picturesque, if artworks began to lose the self-evidence of being pictures, gardens and buildings, then an empirical account of the objecthood of art begins to unfold. While much of the history of modern art can be told as one of increasing abstraction and the imbrication of the subject's point of view, there continues another history, of art being contoured by disgust at objects.

The heartlessness of the picturesque: John Ruskin

Price's aesthetics aroused feelings of disgust from many of his contemporaries. Repton ridicules Price's work as a 'new system of improving by neglect and accident', and we have seen that the former's play on the topos of the butcher's shop is a rhetorical rebuttal, if not an actual argument. Of Price, Repton writes: 'I will not arraign your taste, or call it vitiated, but your palate certainly requires a degree of "irritation" rarely to be expected in garden scenery . . .'.[134] Despite a degree of personal animosity, this is disgust in the simple, general sense, being a refusal of Price's taste. Repton's rejection has a common ground with Price; each is arguing about the boundaries of a 'taste' in which they and all English gentlemen have property. This is not, however, the disgust that the eighteenth-century picturesque typically arouses today, which is more of the form of: 'what devilish self-interest, moral degradation, or cultural mendacity, could have led to a system where the poor and their dwellings are considered purely as scenery'? This is disgust not so much at things picturesque or disgusting, but at the operation of the picturesque as an aesthetic practice and as cultural production. Disgust at the picturesque is common today, but this is not merely a matter of historical or cultural distance between Price and ourselves. Disgust at the picturesque becomes a motif of its later history, invented by the same person most responsible for its propagation, John Ruskin, who writes:

> in a certain sense, the lower picturesque ideal is an eminently *heartless* one; the lover of it seems to go forth into the world in a temper as merciless as its rocks. All other men feel some regret at the sight of disorder and ruin. He alone delights in both; it matters not of what. Fallen cottage – desolate villa – deserted village – blasted heath – mouldering castle – to him, so that they do but show jagged angles of stone and timber, all are equally joyful. Poverty, and darkness, and guilt, bring their several contributions to his treasury of pleasant thoughts. The shattered window, opening into black and ghastly rents of wall, the foul rag or straw wisp stopping them, the dangerous roof, decrepit floor and stair, ragged misery, or wasting age of the inhabitants, – all these conduce, each in due measure, to the fullness of his satisfaction. What is it to him that the old man has passed away his seventy years in helpless darkness and untaught waste of soul? The old man has at last accomplished his destiny, and filled the corner of a sketch, where something unsightly was wanting. What is it to him that the people fester in that feverish misery in the lower quarter of the town, by the river? Nay it is much to him. What else were they made for? what could they have done better?[135]

Ruskin's disgust at the picturesque is palpable and exemplary in passages such as this. For him, the inhabitants of the picturesque scene are unconscious of their 'untaught waste of soul'. But for such distress to go unnoticed by the heartless aesthete, in search of tone and shadow, is another and parallel kind of waste: the affliction of art with a cankerous failure of sympathy. The denunciation is of the 'lower picturesque' and it is the entrée to Ruskin's discussion of J. M. W. Turner's 'noble picturesque'. To further complicate the matter of these competing picturesques, Ruskin includes a long footnote, introduced as an extract from his diary describing a 'happy walk' along the Somme. It is possible that Ruskin was attempting finding a scene to compare with a drawing by Samuel Prout, about which he later wrote.[136] The diary entry makes clear that the heartlessness he damns is a generalization of a particular experience of his own. The 'feverish misery of the lower quarter of the town' described in the body of the text is, in fact, Amiens. The decrepit buildings are the cottages of gloomy spinners and dyers. The faces of labourers, the green water and the soaking wrecks of boats match the reflexive sentences at the end of the note:

> an old flamboyant Gothic church, whose richly traceried buttresses sloped into the filthy stream; – all exquisitely picturesque and no less miserable. We delight in seeing the figures in these pushing them about the bits of blue water, in Prout's drawings; but as

> I looked to-day at the unhealthy face and melancholy mien of the man in the boat pushing his load of peats along the ditch, [. . .] I could not help feeling how many suffering persons must pay for my picturesque subject and happy walk.[137]

Ruskin explains Turner's noble correction of the picturesque in a comparison of two pictures of windmills by his hero and the 'lower' artist, Clarkson Stanfield. Ruskin assumes that we will find Stanfield's print the more attractive but that he can persuade us that Turner's is the better, not least because it refuses to be attractive for us. Turner, it seems, limits his attempts to please us by keeping his mill in a reasonably serviceable condition. Stanfield has sought and found, with evident delight, a mill packed with features of tone and line, and incidentally, so decrepit that it would doubtless be the ruin of any community who depended on it. But all this is mildly humorous, for Stanfield has changed a real poverty into an imaginary, eye-pleasing one; the conceit deserves ridicule. Stanfield tries to please even if this requires him to exaggerate; Turner refuses pleasure for the statement of general truths. Turner's sympathy has led him to a depiction of a mill that 'marks this great fact of windmill nature' by a representation of its function: an accurate delineation of parts and the inclusion of an abandoned mill-stone, which alludes to its internal mechanism.[138] Ruskin writes as if Turner has provided, rather than depicted, a serviceable mill, and while this passage of thought might seem 'sympathetic' to users of mills, it is only the first stage to Ruskin's rather darker and deeper account of Turner's sympathy:

> he feels something pensive about it. It is poor property . . . Turning around a couple of stones for the mere pulverisation of human food, is not noble work for the winds. So, also of all low human labour to which one sets human souls. [. . .] All men have felt it so this grinding at the mill, whether it be breeze or soul that is set to it.[139]

Turner's sympathy, then, is to know to be glad that he is not a manual labourer, and to have the good manners not to display his relief to those less fortunate.

Before we return to examine Ruskin's concept of sympathy and what it means for picturesque theory, note how much of eighteenth-century genre hierarchy remains in Ruskin's criticism. Price wanted the picturesque, in part, to maintain the gradient of nobility between Rembrandt and van Ostade, even when their subjects are equally low. Just as in Price's examples, the nobility of Turner is its independence from generic determination, which is exhibited in technique. Just as Rembrandt ennobled the kitchen piece by his free brushwork, Turner painted a picturesque cliché, but critically, through his powers of detailed observation. Ruskin writes that Stanfield 'pursued his career' in the picturesque, implying a salaried and hence mechanical relation to art, as opposed to Turner's free genius. What is more remarkable is that the whole structure of the chapter on the Turnerian picturesque appears as if it might have been developed from a passage in Price (which Ruskin does not acknowledge). In 'Essay on Picturesque Architecture and Building', Price approves a picture of a mill by Sebastien Bourdon over a picture of a mill at Beauvais by Francois Boucher:

> in which he [Boucher] seems to have collected together all the singularly abrupt and irregular forms that he had ever seen, in order to be superlatively picturesque; and in the same proportion that the wheels and intricate parts of the mill are less distinct in the picture of Bourdon, than they appear in the landscapes of Ruysdale or Hobbima they are more so in that of Boucher: the picture of the former, is a model of the use which

may be made of the qualities of the picturesque; that of the latter, one of the best examples I know of their abuse.[140]

The superiority of the noble picturesque artists is, in each case, their critical distance from their own mimetic faculties. By Ruskin's time, Reynolds' painterly facture, intended to mark out his other-than-mechanical artistry, was simply seen as sloppiness.[141] But Ruskin read Reynolds' theory sympathetically. There are few records of Ruskin's Oxford lectures of 1875 on Reynolds' *Discourses*, but the notes there are show a vehement continuity of the idea of a nobility of taste and a hierarchy of painting.[142] Ruskin's main disagreement with Reynolds is over his denigration of detail; Ruskin thought that the truth lay in practised observation, claiming that Reynolds would have agreed with him had he known the early Florentines rather than the mean vanity of the Dutch, who painted 'the spicula of haystacks and the hairs of donkeys'.[143] One way to understand Ruskin's contribution to the picturesque is, then, that he completes the project of Price by liberating the picturesque from still life and genre painting, and in doing so, rescues a practice of detailed observation from the stigma of mechanical technique.

The sympathy that the bad picturesque lacks can, then, be understood as a further increase in its orientation to visual inspection. Sympathy might seem in opposition to eighteenth-century concepts of disinterestedness, but it is not. In Ruskin the play of interests that guarantee disinterest is folded into the structure of art. Sympathy is an interest in the human, and humanity and its pathos is the most important aspect of Ruskin's picturesque. Ruskin accepts the categorical separation of the picturesque and the beautiful but introduces a new argument for doing so by defining the picturesque in terms of the sublime.[144] Ruskin claims that the picturesque is a *parasitical* form of sublimity.[145] The example he gives is of cottages, the roofs of which, in their decrepit and twisted shapes, might recall ranges of mountains. The equation here is a version of the opposition of nature to artifice. Art is beautiful, nature sublime, and those human works that are greatly aged and changed in use, or that result from customary unconscious practice, are half-natural. Artifice, in its unreflected picturesque state, naturally shows the pathos of human works when put against works of nature. The aesthete's experience of picturesqueness is, then, a sublimity in which the subject exceeds the object, rather than the other way around. We could conclude from Ruskin's examples that the picturesque is the human, that is, the human seen as nature rather than art. The beautiful is what humans attempt in their artefacts; it is, as it were, the human project. However, seen as objects, all human projects – architecture for instance – are *vanitas*: they are metonymic of death and the sublimity of time itself. Ruskin also calls the lower picturesque the 'surface picturesque'.[146] This surface is that of parasitic relations by which mean objects might produce visual stimuli, like noble natural objects. Ruskin supposes that these visual stimuli are so inevitably appealing and desirable that those without spiritual breadth will be seduced to look no further and will have no criteria for distinguishing mountain from cottage. On the other hand, the noble picturesque is a relation in depth. Nobility does not require one to eschew the surface relations, rather, to put this fascination 'in subordination to the inner character of the object'.[147] Turner thus knows that cottage and mountain each reward his sensorium, but he also knows that they are not the same; that the cottage is pathetic. This is his 'sympathy' and breadth of spirit.

We could put the relation of sympathy and parasitic sublimity another way by looking at Ruskin's definition of metaphor as 'the pathetic fallacy'.[148] Ruskin thinks that metaphor is a lie unnecessary to great poets, who can speak of objects and scenes directly. The pathetic fallacy of metaphorical language is that, while it is a weakness, it truly expresses the affect on the poet overcome by the thing described. Ruskin does not say that cottages are metaphoric of the sublimity of mountains, yet it is clear that the picturesque arouses feelings of pathos. We could understand the lower picturesque in a counterpart to the pathetic fallacy. The lover of the lower picturesque sees truly every detail of the cottage's shattered roof, ivy-choked chimney and damp walls, but is lying, nonetheless, through a failure to be affected by poverty and decay.

Ruskin's critique of the picturesque as parasitical sublimity was made in *Seven Lamps of Architecture* in 1849, and it is clearly derived from questions of the architectural character of cottages going back to his first published writing, 'The Poetry of Architecture' of 1837–8.[149] Further definition of the picturesque as lacking sympathy, in *Modern Painters* IV (1856), extends the scope of analysis from architecture to painting and figure painting, taking Ruskin beyond the simple material relation of cottages and mountains. In any case, it is unclear whether the geological time of the mountain's decay and weathering can be understood without the cottage, that is, without the gauge of human life.[150] In a remarkable passage in 'The Lamp of Memory', Ruskin describes the horror of imagining an alpine landscape without permanent habitations; its sublime beauties would be uncanny if it were an 'aboriginal forest of the New Continent'.[151] A scene devoid of human marks is necessarily terrible and sublime. Elsewhere, he discusses the preference of a viewer to 'choose for his subject the broken stones of a cottage rather than of a roadside bank'.[152] Roadside banks are paradigmatic picturesque objects, in Price. There is no reason that such cuttings into the earth, with their intricate and varied forms of rock, earth and roots, could not also be parasitical of the sublimity of mountains. We are, however, supposed to understand that the seeker after picturesque qualities will prefer the ruined cottage, 'to give a deeper tone to his pleasure'.[153] Ruskin's only remark is to warn that the pleasure he assumes is sought will be ignoble without authentic sympathy. In this case, 'sympathy' is Ruskin's repeating of the old axiom: there is as much joy in a life led in cottages as in palaces.

What the noble picturesque has sympathy with are sorrow and old age; explicitly human attributes, which can be extended to artefacts. Nevertheless, Ruskin insists that sorrow and age would be sublime, except that in the picturesque they are 'mingled with such familiar and common characters as prevent the object from becoming perfectly pathetic in its sorrow, or perfectly venerable in its age'.[154] This is another symptom of the genre hierarchy implicit in the picturesque, but it also leads us to further qualify 'sympathy'. The noble picturesque is the sympathetic observation of:

> *suffering*, of *poverty* or *decay*, nobly endured by unpretending strength of heart. Nor only unpretending but unconscious. If there be visible pensiveness in the building, as in a ruined abbey, it becomes, or claims to become beautiful; but the picturesqueness is in the unconscious suffering, – the look that an old labourer has, not knowing that there is anything pathetic in his grey hair, and withered arms, and sunburnt breast; . . . [Between the 'extremes' of the admitted pathos of the ruined abbey and the swept proprieties and neatness of modern England] . . . there is the unconscious confession of the facts of distress and decay, in by-words; the world's hard work being gone through all the while, and no pity asked for, nor contempt feared.[155]

At the most obvious level, human misery is being naturalized here and along with it, its causes in material poverty, which must have seemed a fact of life to Ruskin before he began to think on the systemic aspects of the maldistribution of wealth in the 1860s. Ruskin's insistence on the unconsciousness of suffering is more or less explicitly political in the terms of his day. It is clear that what would not be allowed in the noble picturesque is the knowledge of suffering on the part of the persons viewed, who might then call on the 'sympathy' of the noble viewer in a less than abstract way. In a later piece, Ruskin describes 'sympathy' as an attribute of the well-bred gentleman who is kind but reserved.[156] He argues against those who would misunderstand this reserve as a lack of sympathy. Ruskin thinks that reserve is not a failure to be generous with one's self but an acute realization of class.

> In a great many respects, it is impossible that he should be open except to men of his own kind. [. . .] By the very acuteness of his sympathy he knows how much he can give to anybody . . . and would be glad to give more if he could. [But w]hatever he said a vulgar man would misinterpret.'[157]

The poor must, thus, be unaware of their plight and the noble viewer must not speak with them. Although 'sympathy' might lead to charity at a later time, within the space of aesthetic appropriation, 'sympathy' is a relatively specialized concept of feeling, or lack of it, in art. It is an attribute of the observer, not a relation with the scene.

Ruskin's sympathy is, then, not a complete disavowal of the ghoulishness of the picturesque, but a generalization of the eighteenth-century interest in the baseness of peasant life to all human works. Ruskin's *The Stones of Venice* (1851–3) is an aesthetic idyll set in a city infamous for its descent into political and moral entropy, miasma and physical decay. His focus is St Mark's, which, to most of his contemporaries, was an ill-shapen monstrous hybrid.[158] A few years later when writing of the art of Samuel Prout, Ruskin makes clear the extension of picturesqueness that *The Stones of Venice* required, 'Before Prout to seek [the picturesque] in a city would have seemed an extravagance, to raise it to the height of a cathedral, an heresy'.[159] In fact, the idea that the picturesque might be freed from rural genre painting and applied to cities goes back to the early nineteenth century, when Repton considered this possibility and his one-time partner John Nash achieved it in the design of Regent's Street and Park. So the greater break that Ruskin makes is with Englishness. There is little ideological nationalism in Gilpin or Price; while they love their country, it is their own regions, Cumbria and Hereford, that most form their affections. Furthermore, while they identify their free taste in landscape, with a political liberalism tempered by tradition, their interest in the ordinary countryside is essentially an interest in the domestic, the familiar and the close at hand. For Ruskin to find exotic Venice picturesque is, then, a substantial development of the concept and part of the process that led to the confusion of the picturesque and the exotic in nineteenth-century popular visual culture. There is, however, another aspect of nationalism here. If today we think of the picturesque as proudly English, this is because Christopher Hussey and Nikolaus Pevsner made it so in the mid-twentieth century. For Ruskin though, and here the theme of the chapter re-emerges, picturesqueness is nothing to be proud of. While the sensibility might be English, the exercise of disgust that it involved suggests to Ruskin that picturesque objects be sought in foreign climes.

In its rhetorical finality, we might think that the argument of the 'Heartlessness of the picturesque' passage would lead on to a discussion of rural housing reform in England, an issue with which picturesque aesthetics is intimately bound up and identified. But Ruskin is not asking us to drop pencils to legislate or to repair thatch in response to his description. Ruskin's first published work, 'The Poetry of Architecture', begins with a contrast of English and French cottages: the English version is too prim and comfortable to please the eye of taste as it answers to 'a sentiment of mere complacency'; but the French cottage pleases us because of its 'impression of having once been fit for prouder inhabitants [. . .]. Every mark of dilapidation increases this feeling: while these very marks [. . .] are all delightful in themselves.'[160] Ruskin transfers all that had been familiarly said of English cottages to a more extreme, foreign picturesque. The work is that much stranger for its publication by John Claudius Loudon in his *Architectural Magazine* in 1837 and 1838. Loudon published, in 1833, his own *Encyclopaedia of Cottage Architecture*, which is firmly addressed as a remedy to the degraded misery of British cottagers; he encouraged them to emigrate to North America and Australia, where they could build their own houses. In describing Italian 'cottages', Ruskin describes aesthetic objects in words which, in England, would soon belong only to the discourse of the sanitary commissioners:

> the filthy habits of the Italian prevent him from suffering from the state to which he is reduced. The shattered roofs, the dark, confused, ragged windows, the obscure chambers, the tattered and dirty draperies, altogether present a picture, which seen too near, is sometimes revolting to the eye, always melancholy to the mind.[161]

Judged historically, there are more important aspects of Ruskin's use of the picturesque than the thread of disgust that we have been discussing. His concept of 'changefulness' in 'The Nature of Gothic' was an influential version of Price's 'variety', which valorized the new techniques of irregular planning in nineteenth-century architecture. Ruskin's early use of photography as an instrument of aesthetic inquiry contributed to that strand of photography's history, which has seen it emerge as a meta-art in the late twentieth century.[162] Most significantly, his attempt to recast the ancient semantic concept of ornament as a visual phenomenon opened building culture to an aesthetics of construction and social relations embedded in building.

However, the point of this section has been to show that Ruskin's uptake of the picturesque is consistent with what happens to disgust in Romanticism more broadly. Two further uses of disgust emerge. First, what we already see in Price's use of *Carcase of an Ox*: an affect of being disgusted, which is not entirely converted to pictorial charms but remains at work in visual pleasure. Second, like Ruskin, we can be disgusted at Price for using disgust as an artistic affectation. Menninghaus puts it this way: the actions in de Sade's novels, the lust-murder, coprophilia and so on, are not disgusting, or only in a trival sense. If we are disgusted it is at the characters' forgetting-to-be-disgusted, an elision of disgust with which we must be complicit, if we are to read on.[163] Ruskin, like other critics of Romanticism, sees fault in an art where a hunger to be affected erodes the difference between beauty, evil, horror and degradation.[164] But equally, as Romanticism changes the focus of art from the perfection of forms to the perfection of individual life, the paradigm of aesthetics shifts to a person like Ruskin, prepared to expose himself to strong feelings and to make judgements; finding beauty or picturesqueness in one crumbling village but drawing the line at a different scene of degradation on the basis of his acute sensibility.[165] In a fragmentary and incomplete text on this problem in the work of Keats and Coleridge, he tells a parable of a farmer and a poet who act differently when encountering a snake: the farmer kills it and 'proceeds in his walk – whistling. A sick and sorrowful poet, meeting the same creature, pauses – watches, follows and irritates it – takes strange pleasure in looking into its eyes, and hearing it hiss.'[166] Ruskin's general project is for a morally affirming, muscular Christian art that would have the farmer as its type. There is, however, a place for poets; the 'strange pleasure' of strong affect can be forgiven if it leads to 'Lamia' (Keats 1819), or 'Christabel' (Coleridge 1816) or perhaps the works of Ruskin.

The picturesque is the premise of Ruskin's work. His first published writing was on picturesque cottages. He read Price and Reynolds, and through the remainder of his architectural and art writing, the affects of seeing are foundational to much of his commentary. Much of the formal invention of picturesque architecture, which is the subject of the next chapter, is first conceptualized in words in Ruskin's *Seven Lamps of Architecture* and *The Stones of Venice*. Ruskin's Gothic is fundamentally an ethic of construction and experience that would have been unintelligible in the eighteenth century. Nevertheless, we can understand Ruskin's categories of 'savageness', 'changefulness' and 'grotesqueness' as combining Price's architectural 'irregularity' with ugliness and deformation, and so tuning formal descriptors to issues of aesthetical comportment. This is not to say that we can subsume all Ruskin's work to picturesque theories and principles. Rather, as a device of rhetoric, Ruskin regularly produces the picturesque as a deficiency in taste familiar to the reader, as a reminder of the necessity of his own theory. Here, the picturesque acts as an historical origin, the taste and aesthetic theory of the eighteenth century: curious, prestigious but inadequate for modern times and debased by overuse. But this same structure of inadequacy folds into Ruskin's view of individuals' taste of his own time. He writes as if the aesthetic reception of art and nature does in fact begin for all (including himself as we have seen) in a picturesque sensibility. Having been roused, this self-sickening sensibility is directed back to morality and true feeling by great artists and critics.

From savageness to Brutalism and 'The Revenge of the Picturesque'

Ruskin's ideas of labour led him to champion architecture in which manual labour was not a simple instrument but a work that occasioned the labourer's imagination. His opposition to the division of labour in design and building was at once social and aesthetic. He praised the 'savageness' of Gothic:

> gaze upon the old cathedral front, where you have smiled so often at the fantastic ignorance of the old sculptors: examine once more those ugly goblins, and formless monsters, and stern statues, anatomiless and rigid; but do not mock at them, for they are signs of the life and liberty of every workman who struck the stone . . .[167]

The nobility of work as thought leads Ruskin to strongly prefer unfinished and faulty works with spiritual ambition:

> And therefore, while in all things that we see, or do, we are to desire perfection, and strive for it, we are nevertheless not to set the meaner thing, in its narrow accomplishment, above the nobler thing, in its mighty progress; not to esteem smooth minuteness above shattered majesty; not to prefer mean victory to honourable defeat; not to lower the level of our aim, that we may the more surely enjoy the complacency of success.[168]

In Ruskin's thought, aiming for completeness is hubris; to work as if the work could be finished shows a failure to recognize our own imperfection. Buildings should visibly demonstrate their imperfection thus:

> bestowing dignity upon the acknowledgment of unworthiness. That admission of lost power and fallen nature, which the Greek or Ninevite felt to be intensely painful, and, as far as might be, altogether refused, the Christian makes daily and hourly,

> contemplating the fact of it without fear, as tending, in the end, to God's greater glory.[169]

Ruskin's religiose aesthetics came out of, and were widely influenced by, the church architecture of the time, no more so than the extremely tough buildings of William Butterfield. Butterfield, taking up from A. W. N. Pugin, pioneered a modern style, Gothic in spirit and religious sentiment but modern in materials. In particular, Butterfield used brick: traditionally a material associated with ignoble crumbling construction, but which, in the nineteenth century, had become an excellent building material through new firing processes. Brick meant, for Butterfield, ascetic comportment in building appropriate to inner-city evangelical churches. Brick also allowed a crude and vigorous decorative approach that came to be called polychromy. Butterfield followed contemporary interest in the brick Gothic of northern Italy and Southern France in which different coloured brick picked out bands and patterns in an almost childlike *horror vacui* of blank walls.[170] In churches, such as Butterfield's All Saint's Margaret Street, polychrome brickwork is set off with occasional fine stone carving, murals in encaustic tiling, and fine handicraft painting and gilding, in a hierarchy of ornamental attention from the street to the high altar. This range is also supposed to suggest, as Ruskin wrote, an inclusive attitude to ornamental offerings of all classes of skill and intellect. Butterfield's work at the time and since has been received as anti-aesthetic, as a willed refusal of taste. This impression is all the stronger for those less interested in the nuances of 'high-church' evangelical Anglican doctrine. Butterfield's Gothic, because it is not archeological, built in humble materials, and irregular or accretionary in plan, learns strongly from the picturesque, so it is not surprising that some of Price's inverted aesthetics come to be applied in describing it. John Summerson's seminal article on Butterfield of 1945 celebrates the 'glory of ugliness'; but Summerson was not the first to make this connection.

Robert Kerr, in *The English Gentleman's House* of 1864 (a book largely concerned with matters of planning, which we will return to in Chapter 4), warns any reader interested in building in Gothic against the current fashion for Ugliness.

> there has been growing up an incredible worship of the Ugly. [. . .] Chiefly on account of the preposterous practice of counterfeit with which the Classicism of the last generation of architects is so much identified [. . .] and also to some extent on account of that prevailing feebleness which came to be the ultimate destiny of their borrowed refinement, certain it is that reaction has taken the form of those qualities which are the readiest reverse of such deceptiveness and imbecility. Hence the introduction of a love for undisguised honesty in the first place, however crude, – and, in the second, for masculine simplicity, however unrefined; for unaffected construction, in other words, and unaffected form, both in their extremes; for Gothic models, therefore, because, however rough-and-ready, they are truthful and sincere, – and for the Ugly, because, however odd, it has at least not the weakness of being feminine.[171]

Kerr adds a note to this discussion in which he satirizes the earnestness of a young architect who we might take to be a pupil of Butterfield or George Edmund Street. The architect rails against the elegance required by popular taste:

> 'I don't know so much about that elegance; I rather think I should object to it. You may laugh; but I confess I like a thing to be *ugly*! I do indeed; now and then I like to see a thing downright ugly! This elegance of yours is all very well, but *I* call it *feebleness*.

> You don't see it in nature. I like a building to stand up; with a sort of – what shall I call it?; – Let us say *brusquerie* – a contempt! of fastidiousness. Well, then, there is a row of Gothic houses in ___ Street; they must suit you to admiration. – [. . .] They are built for shops, you must understand; doors narrow therefore, and deeply recessed, and up four or five steps; windows not for plate glass, or any such commonplace – strong big-boned sashes in small authentic-looking squares, – no regarding of such petty considerations as the showing of merchandize; walls of the rough and ready from bottom to top – no smile about them, but rather a frown – the intentional frown of ugliness – telling of the relentless *brusquerie* within . . .'[172]

Kerr's joke relies on our willnessness to see that an adversion to affectation can become an affectation – a studied rudeness. But his caricature shows us how close Ruskinian 'savageness' is to Price's picturesque ugliness when shorn of its ideology. Disgust cannot be a programme for art, only a tool for discriminating the appropriable from the inappropriably ugly. All Saint's Margaret Street pushes its offices to the street alignment and disguises them as the ordinary stuff of London, with nasty small windows set with 'big-boned sashes'. This is a necessary prelude to Butterfield's deformation of the church form, rendering the nave, porch, tower and lych-gate as separate components that can be packed back into the tight site like a butcher's basket. Numerous commentators contrast Butterfield's ugliness with what they take to be the pleasingness of the picturesque. In Price's more elaborate terms, this contrast would be between a pleasing mixture of the picturesque with the beautiful (where Price felt the centre of the standard of taste lay), and picturesque ugliness, which would describe Butterfield's combination of lumpishness and distortion.

While all of the nineteenth century was out of fashion in the early twentieth century, Butterfield seems to have been the hardest to swallow. In 1927, Kenneth Clarke described Butterfield as possessing a 'grasp of good building and sadistic hatred of beauty'.[173] However, the interest in Victorian architecture grew, owing much to Summerson's 1945 essay on the 'ugliness' of Butterfield's buildings.[174]

> All Butterfield's churches are to a greater or less degree ugly. And in almost all there is power and originality transcending the ugliness. I have seen churches of Butterfield's which are not strikingly ugly and in which there is only a rather sickening coarseness in all the parts. But always the Butterfield personality is there – unmistakably there.[175]

Summerson praises All Saint's Margaret Street for its 'sensuous beastliness', 'awkwardness', 'coltish negligence', 'agonies of discord' and its general 'opposition to sensibility'.[176] We can see at once links backward through Butterfield and Ruskin, to the original picturesque experiments with unpleasing architecture, and a nomenclature of form that distinguishes and articulates the want and excess of form. Summerson introduced Nikolaus Pevsner's address, 'The Picturesque and Architecture', to the RIBA in 1947, and was quite aware of Pevsner's attempts, through the late thirties and forties, to revive the picturesque as a modern idiom, one that was challenging and far from pretty. In 1944, the editor of the *Architectural Review* (*AR*) (probably working from Pevsner's notes, and rather too loosely), chastised those architects who had forgotten:

> – or never discovered – their Uvedale Price, perhaps the first man in history to reveal that an object may be 'ugly' in itself and yet in a suitable context have aesthetic possibilities. Payne Knight, it will be remembered, brought up the carcass of an ox as an

instance of a revolting object which could evoke painterly delight – could produce, that is to say, a picturesque effect.[177]

When Summerson writes of Butterfield's ugliness, he does not mention the picturesque and yet this relation is clear in the audience that Summerson is writing for: that strand of modernism that valued directness over artifice and judgement over technique. Elaine Harwood has argued persuasively that the reappraisal of Butterfield and other more gruesome Victorians by Summerson, Pevsner and Robert Furneaux Jordan, influenced the Brutalist movement. It is simple enough, at least in retrospect, to codify Brutalism's formal aspects: particularly its concern for self-finishing concrete and brick surfaces and its irregular lumpish forms, apparently determined by site or social organization – familiar picturesque matters. What Brutalism rebelled against was the idea of these aspects becoming digestible by virtue of familiarity or popularity, against architecture's status as art becoming the 'taste' of a class or time; and equally, against a taste for the brut becoming simply subsumed to the canons of institutionalized architecture. Brutalism is an instance of a recurring aspect of the picturesque, the idea of putting taste and aesthetic ideas at odds. It is felicitous that the *Companion to Aesthetics* entry on 'taste' uses Brutalism as an example of the problem of the difference between taste, as an aesthetic idea or standard, and simple preference: 'Art is a highly complex cultural phenomenon, and yet taste is not necessarily culture-bound. It is not even true that most people prefer the art of their own time and society. For example, the modern brutalist style of architecture is highly unpopular'.[178]

In 1949, the picturesque interests of the *AR* congealed into a new architectural movement, 'Townscape', based on 'the true rock of Sir Uvedale Price'.[179] Townscape was intended to be a consensual popular modernism with a fair dose of English nationalism. In fact, the major modification of mainstream modernism called for by Townscape was a modern version of Price's village picturesque: that new architecture be allowed to appropriate old buildings. Peter Reyner Banham launched 'Brutalism' as a term in 1955, in a review of the famously tough Hunstanton School by Alison and Peter Smithson. Banham was a PhD student of Pevsner, who invited him onto the editorial team of the *AR* where the review was published, and it should be seen in part as a reaction to Townscape. There were fundamental differences emerging between the two men. Banham was the intellectual convenor of a group of young artists and architects (including the Smithsons) who named themselves the Independent Group. They were determined to revive an avant-gardist posture for modernism and were deeply critical of what they saw as the *AR*'s attempt to weaken, popularize and prettify modern architecture. In retrospect, Banham described this period in architectural culture as dominated by 'The Revenge of the Picturesque' defined as the 'surrender to all that was most provincial and second-rate in British social and intellectual life'.[180]

But Banham's denunciation of the picturesque is a manoeuvre with which we are familiar from Ruskin; Brutalism is as picturesque as the *AR*'s Townscape. While Townscape emphasizes the light pleasures of a kind of fortuitous sub-beauty in the spirit of Gilpin's travels, Brutalism is an anti-aesthetic, or, rather, an aesthetic of the unpleasing. Brutalism had the same kind of sympathy for public housing as Turner had for his mill. It aimed to be aesthetically valuable but unpleasing in the same sense as *Carcase of an Ox*, to be something of a litmus test of modernist credentials.

Banham's definition of the New Brutalism in three aspects: '1. Memorability as an Image; 2. Clear exhibition of Structure; 3.Valuation of materials as found', is (apart from 'structure'), complex and obscure.[181] 'As found' we can understand in the work of visual artists such as Tapies and Dubuffet, which Banham uses to illustrate the article and which reach back to collage and dissociation techniques in Dada and Surrealism. 'Memorability as an Image' we can understand as a reference to art historian Ernst Gombrich's work on the image, which uses perceptual psychology to undo the categorical distinction between artworks and other visual artefacts. In both these aspects, Banham is saying the Smithsons' work, along with the New Brutalism he heralds, are opposed to canons of form and to any *a priori* separating of art from life and art works from quotidian objects. While the idea of avant-garde art and the reintegration of art and life are modern projects, and Gombrich's perceptual psychology has little relation to Burke's, Banham's ideas arrive on the already prepared terrain of the picturesque. In its scenographic aspects and integration with topography, in its use of rustic textured materials, and in its coherence as image rather than form, Brutalism is a picturesque development. The core of the picturesque idea, from Gilpin and earlier, is the aesthetic possibilities of the everyday world. Price's picturesque goes further, eschewing the rarity that beauty connotes and seeking aesthetic value in the mundane and ubiquitous. In both cases, disgust is valued as a test, in which the mutability and subjectivity of taste can be revealed. Dubuffet, an artist who inspired Banham and the Independent Group, explains the superiority of his art in almost eighteenth-century terms.

> I've found myself suggesting certain materials, not so much those with a 'noble' reputation like marble or exotic woods, but instead very ordinary ones with no value at all like coal, asphalt or even mud . . . in the name of what . . . does man bedeck himself with necklaces of shells and not spiders webs, with foxes furs and not their guts, in the name of what I'd like to know? Mud rubbish and dirt are man's companions all his life; shouldn't they be precious to him, and isn't one doing man a service to remind him of their beauty?[182]

Spiders and the guts of foxes are not of no value, as are pigment or mud; they are emblematic of the disgusting. Just as in Price's picturesque, in Dubuffet's works, taste is tested to its limit in disgust, before returning to the everyday ugliness of mud, rubbish and dirt.

The Smithsons' Sugden House (Figure 3.8) of 1955–6 takes up the same strategy. Sugden House is a close imitation of those aspects of suburban speculative building most offensively ugly to modernist architects. The house bears close comparison to the designs of James Malton, an eighteenth-century architect acting on Price's authority, who imitated damp- and pox-ridden vernacular cottages in 1798 (see Figures 4.9 and 4.10). In each case, only details, such as the substantial chimneys in Malton, or the unexpected symmetry in the Smithsons' fenestration, reveal that this is architecture and not expedient building. Are these details quotation marks? Subtle improvements? A kind of liminal practice of architecture? Is this a mocking appropriation of the ordinary in high artifice, or a sincere proposal of housing reform? A little of all these interpretations is justified, but the relevant point here is that architecture is impacted into the 'thingness', the objecthood, the empirical fact of building. Before the picturesque, the discipline of architecture relied, to a large extent, on the evidence of architecture's empirical existence in grand building: churches, palaces, and so on. The picturesque interest in vernacular, unselfconscious building begins a process where architecture becomes an ideation and a practice applicable to all building. Architecture from the nineteenth century abstracted into immaterial matters of archaeological authority, style as national identity, social organization and spatial empathy theory. The more this was the case, however, the more buildings became tokens and instances of an ideational architecture, the greater capacity buildings had to put a shock into thought about architecture. Just as, in

Cousins' claim, ugliness confronts the narcissism of the subject, the insistently blunt quotidian character of Brutalist building confronts architecture's claim to being applicable across the whole built environment; and shows it to be hubris.

When, in 1966, Banham wrote a retrospective account *The New Brutalism: Ethic or Aesthetic?*, he concluded that his earlier hopes for Brutalism were unfulfilled. He was affronted by the formal elegance of the Smithsons' Economist Building, which he saw as the final victory for picturesque aesthetics over faith in modernism as social and technological ethic. Banham's regrets were well founded. In the 1950s, an eschewal of rhetoric and a reduction of formal complexity towards a simplicity that was not idealist, simply lumpish, might have looked like the end of modernism's formalist classical tendency, but in fact, it was a recovery of picturesque ugliness within modernist aesthetics.

Everyday

Brutalism is popular again with progressive architects, as is, especially, the semi-anthropological strand of anti-formalism of the 1950s Independent Group. Nigel Henderson, inspired in part by his wife Judith Stephen's anthropological studies in East London, took documentary photographs of backyards, which the Smithsons referred to in designing the shed-like 'Pavilion' (Figure 3.9), a central element in the Independent Group's exhibit *Patio and Pavilion* in the Whitechapel Gallery show 'This is Tomorrow' of 1956. Quotidian reality seems somehow more objective when stilled in Henderson's photographs, and this is matched by the fine and accurate orthography of Peter Smithson's 'design' of crumpled metal sheets weighted down with discarded bicycle wheels.

There is a strong echo of this moment in the present, in a whole genre of neo-neo-objectivist photography of domestic life become raw or stark, as in the work of Nan Goldin and Richard Billingham. Similarly, the documentation of non-architectural uses of space informs the work of architects such as Atelier Bow Wow and Lacaton and Vassal. Following the peculiar manner of using 'theory' to authorize cultural developments, the works of Henri Lefebvre and Michel de Certeau are often cited, as in the issue of the journal *Daidalos* on 'The Everyday' (2000). But the focus on sociological theory in art catalogues and

Figure 3.8 Alison and Peter Smithson, Sugden House, 1955–6.

Figure 3.9 Alison and Peter Smithson, 'Pavilion' from *Patio and Pavilion* by Eduardo Paolozzi, Nigel Henderson, and Alison and Peter Smithson, from the exhibition 'This is Tomorrow', Whitechapel Gallery, London, August–September 1956.

architectural design journals should give cause for suspicion. First, because this ignores the decades of less fashionable ethnography and environmental psychological studies, called, in architecture, 'People Environment Studies', but more so because it ignores the appropriations of the quotidian that recur since the picturesque in Gothic ugliness, and Brutalism.

There are two kinds of anti-aesthetic: that which opposes the existence of aesthetics as a faculty of mind and practice of judgement; and that which admits aesthetics but rejects its foundation in sensory pleasure, normative forms and tastes. What interested the Independent Group, Art Brut, Bataille, the Situationists and all the other recently recovered anti-formalists of the post-war period is the latter not the former. Gilles Deleuze, writing of the neo-realist films of De Sica, gives an account of the critical potential of the banal. According to Deleuze, the banal is the tool by which filmmakers overcame the hegemony of the 'action image' into what Deleuze calls the pure 'optical image', or in my terms, the picturesque. This is not only close to picturesque ugliness but, because of his radical empiricism and refusal of psychological interiority, Deleuze's description reads as an echo of Price's idea that the picturesque leaves optic nerve cords just as they are, neither tightening them as in the sublime, nor relaxing them as in beauty:

> if everyday banality is so important, it is because, being subject to sensor-motor schemata which are automatic and pre-established, it is all the more liable, on the least disturbance of equilibrium between stimulus and response [. . .] suddenly to free itself from the laws of this schemata and reveal itself in a visual and sound nakedness, crudeness and brutality which make it unbearable, giving it the pace of a dream or a nightmare.[183]

The role of this chapter has been to recover the picturesque theory of disgust, because of its value to anyone interested in that emotion, but more so to explore an historical interpolation of the picturesque. Since the revival attempts of the 1940s, the picturesque has been denigrated as something that arouses facile pleasures of sense, and through an insidious cultural suasion, forces itself upon us. But this present denigration has not only forgotten the well-established motif of disavowing of picturesqueness, but also that the picturesque was from the first a theory of how the facile could become rebarbative, not failing conceptualization, but threatening conscious thought altogether. Today the picturesque arouses a satiation-induced disgust. This emphasizes its cloying sweetness, its corrosion of categories. But a reading of the history of the term reminds us of the two parts of Price's recipe for disgust: the combination of ugliness and deformity; that prohibitive disgust shadows the over-sated.

The Independent Group's *Patio and Pavilion* may look like a search for non-aesthetic culture in the quotidian, trying to find in the everyday resources for an aesthetics of the unideal. However, like Malton's designs based on the scabrous rural cottages of his time, this is a formalism liminally formed, an aesthetic of the ugly powered by the risk of disgust. Banham was correct to think that Brutalism was picturesque.

4
Irregularity

The central paradox of the picturesque is that the means to achieve picturesqueness lies not in pictures, or any kind of views, but in the plan. The picture stands upright facing us like the elevation of a building, and picturesqueness in architecture is often thought to be a concern for the appearance of buildings. In fact, the innovation of the picturesque lies in putting the issue of how the building comes into appearance before the question of what the building looks like. For pictorial qualities such as Sir Uvedale Price's 'intricacy' and 'variety' to be abstracted from painting and applied to the view of gardens and buildings, a rotation was required, and the study of pictures that Price and Richard Payne Knight recommended led architects to look into the plan.

The picturesque depends upon certain innovations in planning, and I argue that it is in these inventions that the plan itself became visible. Before the picturesque there was not so much difference between plan and elevation as kinds of drawn figures. In classical architecture, plan and elevation are alike in their shape vocabulary and strongly imbricated, making it possible to imagine an elevation on the basis of a plan and vice versa. With the picturesque, this occurs much less, and for an obvious reason: picturesque buildings have irregular or asymmetrical plans. As the plan became an instrument for seeing rather than a kind of view, its own figure and shape became less important than the relations it effected. Since then, plans and elevations have implied different branches of architectural knowledge. This separation also bears on architecture itself: the elevations of the building are seen by everyone while the plan is the specialized place for architects to condition this encounter. As Le Corbusier's aphorism has it: 'the plan is the generator', the place in which the trained architect can see what is not apparent to lay people – the conditions of the organization and structure of a building. These practical matters are not, in the first place, aspects of the picturesque. Historically, they emerged out of an architect's ability to use a plan to see what a building will be like, to test a particular viewing position and use the drawings to imagine what would be seen from there. As Nikolaus Pevsner argued as early as 1945, the empirical method of planning for view precedes, and provides, the model for a fuller development of the plan as a technique for functional analysis.[1] The picturesque is the major watershed in the history of planing. On the pre-modern side, plans were figures and emblems related to the form of the building as object. With the picturesque the plan became a means of placing a viewer, testing a design idea against perception, and then subsequently extending this empiricism of viewpoint to broader understanding of the building's function.

Picturesque building planning begins in consideration of the relation of pictures and views which I discussed in Chapter 2. Architects began to experiment with the idea of the picturesque in a genre of pattern books for the design of cottages. The pattern books took their occasion and their authority either from Price's remarks about picturesque cottages and villages, or from the disciplinary ideas of agricultural reformers, or both. As the previous chapter 'Disgust' showed, the relation of the picturesque to agriculture was a complex of political ideology, theories of judgement and affect in art, and it was this game that the picturesque architects played. The outcomes were, however, less significant as designs than as re-conceptualizations of the architectural plan, which began its passage into modernity.

There is a case for seeing the architecture of the nineteenth and twentieth centuries as a continuous development of planning techniques, underlying and relativizing the more generally accepted epoch of modernism around 1900. Le Corbusier and his architectural promenade provide a familiar case to argue these views. It has been argued that Le Corbusier's idea of architectural form based on durational experience relates to the development of cinema. Nevertheless, many scholars claim a pre-modern architectural genealogy for the promenade: variously, the Beaux Arts, the Baroque and the picturesque; and there is good reason to see all three as historically related, and also related to cinema. For different reasons and using different evidence, Peter Collins, Richard Etlin and Yve-Alain Bois all see the picturesque as the clearest precedent for Le Corbusier and modern architecture – understood as formation of spatio-visual experience in duration.[2] In such accounts, the picturesque becomes for architecture what we have already seen it become for aesthetics: a naïve prescience of modernism. This picturesque-flavoured modernism is dedicated to experience and affect over form and the internal abstract logics of art disciplines. For Bois, the picturesque is a resource for arguing against the formalist tendencies of modernism and helps explain later twentieth-century art movements such as minimalism. It is quite familiar and roughly correct to oppose the picturesque to formalism, as Bois does, but this chapter will complicate the opposition by proposing that the picturesque is also a kind of formalism.

An account of picturesque planning in the early nineteenth century shows how form and experience have a variety of possible interactions. While picturesque architects showed the power of weak form, they also showed how strong forms could act weakly: what we might call a spoiled or unideal classicism. To design picturesque cottages – to make deformation and ugliness issues of form – architects were obliged, perhaps for the first time, to develop planning as a technical space distinct from any ideal of the plan.

For buildings to appear to have the surface arrangement of pictures as well as actual spatial depths, it is the plan that must be manipulated. Thus the concept and techniques of planning come to be understood as anterior to the pictorial and its governing condition. If the picturesque begins in, and continues to foreground, an organic visual empiricism, it acts in abstractions and, historically, its most important outcome is a technique of the plan.

The architectural plan and a sketch for its history

Everyone has a degree of familiarity with maps of places and plans of buildings. Real-estate advertisements show plans in newspapers, for instance, but most people are also aware of the specialized ways of 'reading' plans that builders and architects are trained in, which allow them to use plans more fully and precisely than lay people. In this section, I consider what architects do with plans, in the first place for readers not familiar with architectural language and training, but also in the hope that the emphases in my description will make clear what is far too self-evident and implicit in architectural ideas of the plan.

The plan drawing derives from the procedure of laying out a building for construction. Lines made on site with string and timber rods to align the foundations are scaled onto a drawing representing these coordinates and dimensions. A plan is, thus, a device of measurement; in no sense is it a view. If we look down on a building that is yet to be roofed, what we see of the 'plan' is a view which recedes from us and no longer has the abstract flatness of the plan nor its utility in measurement. We might estimate, but not see, the dimensions of the rooms. Plans are not necessary for building. From the time of the ancient Romans, plans were more often drawn to describe completed buildings, or to enunciate principles of building, than to 'plan' a particular building. Most of the great medieval buildings were constructed without plans using surveying techniques and rules of proportion that enabled masons to conceive of the building as a whole while cutting stone at full scale. The drawn plan and the organizational capacity to build converged in the Renaissance because of two factors. First, Leon Battista Alberti and others attempted to redefine architecture as a liberal art, separated from the trade of building and with its own medium of drawing, *disegno*, in which architecture appears to be self-consisting, almost independently of its execution.[3] Shortly after Alberti wrote, with the printing of his book and more so with Serlio's illustrated *Treatise*, architecture was further defined through its ability to be published and distributed. Second, in the re-birth of linear perspective the difference between a view of a building and its dimensions became clear as did the possibility of imagining one on the basis of the other. Hubert Damisch claims that this relation of dimensioned drawing to view is what Filippo Brunelleschi was demonstrating with his famous perspective 'experiment'.[4] Following Brunelleschi and Alberti, the three orthographic projections of plan, elevation and section, gradually separated from the perspective view. This separation is, of course, an issue of instrumentalization; plans exist so that buildings can be built more easily and thoroughly conceived by the architect beforehand, or at a remove. But as architecture frequently serves cultures striving for the metaphysical, the instrumental nature of the plan is often thought to conceal some greater meaning. The idea of sacred geometries imminent in building links the drawing types. The geometry of a circle easily grasped in a plan is of limited significance; but the same circle apprehended in phenomenal space might be a moment of transcendence. Orthographic drawing is an instrument for building a geometry that can never be seen, as it remains shrouded by the imperfections of human sense – or so the story goes. This ambivalence in the origin of the drawing types continues today. Plans are used to imagine views (which they are not), while for many architects the *telos* of the experience of building is an enactment of patterns and geometries inconceivable outside of a plan. The experience of the user and the intention of the architect become perfectly reciprocal. Such a metaphysic of the plan, of architects as saintly interlocutors of experience, is simple self-aggrandizement. It does as much to obscure the actual history of the plan as a technical knowledge developed by architects.

The architectural plan is best explained not through its opposition to, or reciprocity with, human sight, but as a messy set of conventions within architectural culture. The plan is a horizontal section, a slice through the building; the fabric above the cut is imagined removed. There are rules and conventions for where that cut occurs, usually above the height of the windowsill and below the lintel, making fenestration clear on the plan. If fenestration is more complex than this or the floor is stepped, the section plane that makes the cut can move about to capture these salient facts. On the other hand, what is significant architecturally about a plan might happen above the section plane, in the ceiling or voids above the plan. Convention allows such features to be included in broken lines. The point of this pedantic description is to show that the geometric certainty of the plan as a projection is open to considerable judgement on the part of the architect, and that those who master the conventions and understand the abstractions are able to make the plan act as a kind of view, albeit one visible only to the trained eye. In a plan, architects see manifold aspects of the building, such as structure and services, and something of external appearance. Particular to the plan, however, are ideas of plan efficiency, legibility and fitness to site or location.

Efficiency is judged on the amount of space allocated to circulation compared to other uses, and the length of the perimeter of external walls compared to enclosed area. Trained architects can look at a plan to get a 'picture' of such matters: for instance, that a building is too mean because its compact plan shape leads to many spaces being too far from an external wall; or, conversely, that a building is too generous because its foyers, anterooms and corridors are oversized compared to the spaces dealing with the principal functions. Legibility is judged on the logic or pattern by which spatial organization is apparent from places within the building: for instance, that stairs are visible from the foyer, and that spaces for visitors to the building are easily distinguished from those for workers or residents. A legible plan means that people will not need a printed plan or signs to find their way. It is commonplace for architects to assume that extensive signage demonstrates a plan's failure, which is frequent in the complexity of an airport or hospital, where resort is made to coloured lines on the floor accompanied by signs demanding that 'out-patients follow the blue line to the orange lift', or such like. A final criterion for good architectural planning is on a building's fitness to site. The aims of such coordination might be functional: for instance, that the entry should be obvious on arrival, or, that the basement car park should give out onto the lowest point of the site to avoid ramping. The aims, on the other hand, might be ideological: urbanist typology suggests that individual buildings ought to contribute to a greater communal architecture of the city or town, and so should use planning strategies similar to those around them, or at least familiar to that culture and time. Thus, high-rise buildings, no matter how well planned, are often judged inappropriate in historic cities, not only because of their form in view, but because of their different impact at ground level, with more people, larger foyers, and less variegated aspects to their ground-floor plan. Fitness to site becomes self-evidently picturesque when the building plan is coordinated with views from the building, making exterior spaces such as courts and gardens, or distant views, relate to specific rooms, directions of sight or movement within the building.

When architects 'read' plans, efficiency, legibility and fit-to-site are, to a large degree, visible to them; they recognize in a particular plan learned patterns of successful and problematic planning. To confirm such recognitions a scale-rule, calculator and certain kinds of diacritical overdrawing might be employed. To a large extent, however, planning is 'visible' to an architect as a kind of pattern. This has always been the case and is no more interesting than the trained mental habits of any profession. What is interesting is that until about 1800, that is to say the time of the picturesque, none of the criteria of planning that I have described existed. What architects saw in plans for most of the past were patterns of geometrically shaped compartments, generally arranged axially and bounded within a simple figure. Planning was judged on matters like proportion, purity and simplicity of geometrical figures. The plan had similar epistemological status, therefore, to elevational drawings. Indeed, pre-modern plans and elevations look alike, or much more than they do in modern buildings. Much of the reason for this is construction. When buildings are made largely of load-bearing masonry walls, the plan, elevation and overall appearance of buildings are much more interdependent than in modern buildings made of long spanning materials, where the plan can be 'freed' from a determining structure. I want to insist, however, that the plan, once a description of the built object like any other projection, in modern times has become – as well as this, more importantly than this – a description of the building's relations. The picturesque is a major cause of this change, and understanding how the concept of the plan changed from one of autonomous regular figures to irregular forms visibly determined by external relations is the subject of this chapter.

Robin Evans was one of the few authors who have had much to say about the plan. In 'Figures, Doors, Passages' he argues for the differences of pre-modern planning and the resources that these might offer for thinking differently about modern architecture.[5] For Evans, Renaissance planning, which involved a matrix of rooms of indeterminate use, offered a precedent for some of the universal space and flexible servicing experiments undertaken by avant-garde architects of the 1960s. Evans sketches the rise of personal privacy in Western Europe as the driving force behind a concept of the plan that demanded 'maximum and maximally differentiated access'. He clearly regrets the loss of what he thinks of as the corporeality of architectural experience before 'planning' became an instrument for forming social relations, and recounts William and Jane Morris' move to their medieval house, Kelmscott Manor. As hosts, the Morrises were embarrassed because the building pre-dated the invention of the corridor, so bedrooms were each accessed through the other. Evans' point is that, despite its aspirations to the appearance and social life of medieval times, the couple's former home – Philip Webb's Red House of 1859 – was strikingly modern in its differentiated planning.

More detailed historical accounts, such as Patricia Waddy's *Seventeenth-Century Roman Palaces: Use and the Art of the Plan*, show that pre-modern planning was hardly the neutral libertarian space of Evans' polemic. It was highly differentiated and functioned more or less well in enabling social interaction, albeit not in the manner of modern planning. The matrix of rooms was organized into apartments, each exercising a strong hierarchy. Social organization and status were expressed through proximity to the powerful inhabitant of the apartment; to recognize adequately the different social standing of visitors might have required a series of four or six rooms. To be met by a member of the Duke's household in the vestibule was quite different to approaching the Duke in the centre of the Salon, which was different again to the Duke approaching a visitor and escorting that person through the enfilade of spaces, pointing out paintings and tapestries, before arriving at a table in a room deep in the apartment set with the best silver.[6] Studies of pre-modern interiors show how the suite and its internal hierarchy was established and adjusted through furnishing. Beds with their precious fabrics and credenza with silver were highly significant items, and their positioning made a room significant. It was not, however, the function of eating or sleeping that determined the design; it was the social hierarchy and plan depth. The plans of buildings were occasions for displaying manners and were fundamentally rhetorical, and so the thrust of Evans' contrast remains: if modern planning is concerned with efficiency acting on the building and its uses, then pre-modern planning was performative – closer to the social uses and meanings of table manners than to the organization of business. Norbert Elias has done much to show how modern ideas of personhood have grown out of feudal societies through the conduct of the body in manners of the table and personal decorum.[7] It may be that this same civilizing process is true of the development of the building plan from a rhetorical device to a productive organization. In architecture, however, this process has a distinct turning point. None of the modern criteria of planning, which I described above, are consistent with symmetry in planning. Architecture was, as a rule, symmetrical until the picturesque.

The strength of the figurative concept of the plan can be seen in the neo-classical period immediately before the picturesque. In France, the traditional concept of room 'distribution' began its articulation with 'composition', or the forming of buildings by architects such as J.-F. Blondel. Distribution and composition, however, were seen as competing demands because of the necessity of symmetry. In designing mansions on irregular city blocks, Blondel made plans that were irregular in their total figure but symmetrical in their major rooms, which opened one off the other on a central axis. Blondel achieved this by having some rooms or anterooms circular or polygonal so that the axis could shift less than ninety degrees but remain centred. Even with this expedient, however, the functions of these rooms and their servicing could be compromised. As Robin Middleton puts it:

> Symmetry was of overriding import in establishing the image of the French *hôtel*, and once again, this might often be achieved only through the neglect of comfort or even common sense. [. . .] This deeply felt need for an appearance of symmetry was a spur to the most extraordinarily ingenious feats of planning. Architects learned to dispose even the most awkwardly shaped sites so that the buildings upon them and the rooms within presented an air of the finest order and regularity.[8]

It is now quite unusual for a building to have a symmetrical plan. If a building is planned in this way, it is usually for stylistic reference or aesthetic affect. We might expect symmetry in a parliament, but not in a hospital. Most architects would think that symmetry came at a cost. For instance, a building not committed to symmetry has many more ways of sitting on its site; more options in internal room arrangement; and a greater likelihood of resolving conflicting constraints in siting and programme. Symmetry inevitably leads to a geometrical equivalence of spaces not equivalent in use, as when, either side of the central pavilion of a mansion, a wing of kitchens and servants quarters is mocked up to mirror a wing of grand rooms. Nowadays symmetry is considered an affectation constraining the rational planning of buildings, particularly their functional planning and siting. The shift from patterned matrix-like plans governed by decorum and propriety to a modern concept of the plan governed by utility and scenic experience did not happen, of course, in those terms. The older concept of planning was not broken by the new, but by a different project all together: architects tried to take lessons from painters; to imitate rural buildings, particularly humble cottages, whose 'plans' were accretions of rooms without figure.

The Truth about Cottages

The main evidence for my views on the development of the plan is the genre of books of designs for ornamental cottages of the late eighteenth and early nineteenth centuries. To understand what a cottage, and an ornamental cottage, were, involves understanding the changes in agriculture and rural life at that time. Much of this can be summed up briefly, and returns us to the previous chapter's theme: cottages were disgusting.

The cottages of rural workers in eighteenth-century Britain were dirty, crowded and inadequate in weather protection.[9] This was the case for most dwellings in the past, and is still the case for much of the world. Cottages were probably less unsanitary than most housing in cities at the time, but they were the original objects of phobic disgust at the poor as a class. Much of what would be said, by the mid-nineteenth century, of city slums was first laid out on the topic of cottages. This was because poor rural workers, often named 'cottagers', were most affected by, and most resistant to, the socio-political circumstance that changed land tenure and caused capitalization of agriculture: namely, enclosure. From the point of view of the propertied classes and their architects, cottages were vectors of disease and indicative of a raft of ancient illogical customary rights impeding the rationalization of land tenure and agriculture. Dissident cottagers were widely believed to be hoping for a French invasion, and at various times during the Napoleonic Wars, the countryside of England was in low-level rebellion. Thus, the double contagion of disease and political dissent smeared into one, shapeless emblem: the cottage, the mere sight of which was sufficient to make gentlefolk gag. In the previous chapter, we looked at Price's aesthetics of the picturesque, which puts disgust to work in a principal example: Rembrandt's painting, *Carcase of an Ox* (Figure 3.6). Peter Frederick Robinson's design for a butcher's shop in his portfolio *Village Architecture* (Figures 3.2 and 3.3), shows that what Price infers was clear to his contemporary readers: discussion of slaughter and meat – the super-figural and the ordinary, horror and appetite – provided a matrix for the aestheticization of rural life. While the motif of an escape from artifice to rural simplicity had been well known since antiquity, Price refreshed the georgic and pastoral by bringing them closer to actual cottages, where 'only a thin partition' divided picturesqueness from disgust.

This same principle of a bracketed, diffused disgust can be observed in modern popular affection for cottages. Today, the cottage is a popular image of domestic life both in Britain and in the ersatz Englands that exist on moist hills outside wealthy cities from Brisbane to Beijing. As John Betjeman puts it in introducing a guidebook on the subject: 'The great houses remain aloof and alone, but this book contains the ordinary houses – the cottages that we all dream of owning'.[10] But even tourist books marketing this myth of England typically expose the dark side of modern affections for the cottage:

> Today the loving care that many lavish on their country cottages is in their own way, an attempt to colonize, or perhaps recolonize, [such] a Golden Age, by shutting outside that other world, hedonistic, cynical and insensitive. [. . .] But, of course, the history of the cottage is really a history of the poor, the wholesale robbery of the land for enclosures, the Industrial Revolution, and the making of the British working class.[11]

In such descriptions, the cuteness of cottages is given a darker tone: the realization that what we desire was once a nexus of fear, oppression and disgust. John Woodforde's marvellous *The Truth about Cottages*, published for the Country Book Club of 1969, has sixty pages of social history preceding a spotter's guide to recognizing the types and ages of cottages in England. History only increases the affective value of the cottage, giving it that play between alterity and familiarity, that sense of the barbarousness of the past so central to the commercialization of heritage. To a degree, the historical anomalies in the present cult of cottages recasts, as a temporal difference, what already excited clients and architects in the early nineteenth century: the proximity of the picturesque cottage to its scabrous cousins. Today respectable architects are disgusted by cottage-style suburban housing, epitomized by machine-distressed bricks, plastic wood-grain doors, and those little metal straps that make plate glass look like many small panes. Architects today want to correct the cottage dweller, to encourage them away from ideology and identification towards a rational use of space and a non-auratic understanding of materials. This is, in some ways, an iteration of the eighteenth-century architects who used peasant dwellings to teach peasants how to behave and to correct the prim, downsized Palladianism of the small houses of the emerging middle class. Cottages remain a paradigm of the picturesque, not just because of their association with Englishness and the history of the concept, but also because, from an aesthetic point of view, there is not a lot of space between a prohibitory disgust at the cottage as weeping sore, and a satiatory disgust at its cloying Bo Peep sweetness.

What the actual cottages of rural labourers were like can be glimpsed in the topographic engravings of John Thomas Smith, published in his *Remarks on Rural Scenery* of 1797.

Smith claims to have prepared the views through close observation of the rural environs of London. This claim is supported by his logical and detailed representation of makeshift building construction, and the titles of the plates that give place names. We can take the cottage 'Near Mrs Teshmakers' Edmonton' (Figure 4.1) to be typical of the poorer class of cottages. Cottages generally contained one room with some partitioning for a sleeping area, while lean-to extensions accommodated livestock or firing. Stone and brick cottages were not uncommon in regions where those materials were readily available, but the majority were of cheaper construction, such as 'wattle and daub', which is mud and straw adhered to timber lathe; 'brick noggin', which is a timber frame with brick in-fill; or, as in the cottage near Mrs Teshmakers', odd timbers rammed directly into the ground, with mud to fill the gaps. Floors were earth, roofs were thatched, and for windows oiled cloth or battening were more common than glass. Smith shows a brick flue, but many reformers noted a general lack of efficient fireplaces. Such structures only offered basic shelter, and only if in good repair, which was frequently not the case. Smith preferred to draw cottages whose thatch was rotted or overgrown with plants, and whose walls and floors were damp. Most cottages would have been full of smoke from poorly flued fires and bad firing. The poorer class of cottagers would have lived with their livestock in the one 'room'. In his influential *Hints to Gentlemen of Landed Property* of 1775, Nathaniel Kent describes the plight of cottagers:

> The shattered hovels which half the poor of this kingdom are obliged to put up with, is truly affecting to a heart fraught with humanity. Those who condescend to visit these miserable tenements, can testify that neither health nor decency can be preserved in them. The weather frequently penetrates all parts of them; which must occasion illness of various kinds, particularly agues; which more frequently visit the children of cottagers than any others and early shake their constitutions. And it is shocking that a man, his wife, and half a dozen children should be obliged to lie all in one room together; and more so, that the wife should have no more private place to be brought to bed in.[12]

Kent's concern for the cottagers seems heartfelt, and so, too, his proposal to house them in sound dry cottages; but his book was also an attempt to adduce his readers' sympathy and philanthropy on the issues of managing agriculture and governing the countryside.

Before its discovery as a source of scenery, or as a public health issue, the cottage was the socio-economic unit most affected by the great increase in enclosure of common land through the eighteenth century – the cottagers were the persons most dependent on common rights. Commons were areas of land held by a parish over which rights were held by members of the parish on differing bases, but they were usually connected with ownership or tenancy of other land or cottages. The parish administered shared rights of grazing and cultivation on commons. While large enclosed pieces of land owned by a single interest had always been a form of land tenure, the end of the eighteenth century saw a vast increase in the scale of enclosure.[13] Enclosure was supposed to be accompanied by compensations for common rights subsumed, but these were frequently unjust and the process complex, as each enclosure required its own act of Parliament until 1801 when a series of general enclosure acts began to be passed, which simply standardized many of the unjust practices. It was claimed at the time that enclosure enabled a new and highly productive 'rational' agriculture: new crops, breeds and improved pastures, different rotational systems and soil management, new and heavier machinery in soil draining, ploughing, harvest and threshing. All of these improvements demanded a larger scale of agriculture in crop areas, management and investment capital. High capital investment was possible because of inflated grain prices during the wars with France, glossed with the patriotism of feeding the nation at war. Enclosing common land for agriculture increased dependence of agricultural workers on largely seasonal wages, resulting in a more tractable work-force.[14] Cyclical unemployment became part of the economic structure of improved agriculture, and this alongside the wartime shortages led to widespread rioting against grain prices and enclosures.[15]

In this situation, the cottage was crucial in two ways. First, tenancy in a cottage was often taken to give the cottager rights to common land, and therefore a means of support apart from waged labour for farmers. Most of these rights, however, were customary; they sometimes belonged to owners rather than tenants, and cottagers generally had no say in the redistribution of land under enclosure acts. Second, tenancy was connected with rights of 'settlement' under the Poor Law.[16] Each person was supposed to have settlement in a single parish and that parish took responsibility for their support in times of hardship. Funds for this support were generated from a tax on property owners in the parish, called the Poor Rates. In the eighteenth century, this support was sometimes generous, extending to clothes, nursing or the cost of funerals.[17] However, support dwindled as the numbers of workers impoverished by enclosure grew.

Settlement was also a constraint on the mobility of labourers. During the eighteenth century, an increasingly complex mechanism developed to govern how settlement could be established. These included birth, marriage, the letting of property of a certain value, forty days' residence, and in some places the building of a cottage on waste land if it could be assembled overnight with a fire smoking in the morning. Labourers could only move to another parish if given a certificate by their own parish officers admitting liability if support was required. Decreasing the Poor Rates paid by landholders for the support of the poor was a strategy for increasing the profitability of estates. It was, therefore, in the interests of 'improved' parishes, where enclosure was completed, to deny rights of settlement to the immigrant workers who had come to the parish in labour-intensive seasons, such as the harvest. The operation of stringently policed settlement along with an increasingly acute seasonal pattern of employment led, in the worst cases, to the system of closed and open parishes. A closed, improved parish had a stable, adequately employed work force with low poor rates. It would import seasonal labour from a neighbouring open parish where migrant workers would have less trouble gaining settlement but where there was high unemployment, great demand on Poor Rates and little to attract the improver. The creation of a closed parish often involved the destruction of cottages to decrease opportunities for settlement. Thomas Malthus even proposed the destruction of housing more generally to control population.[18]

Already, in the eighteenth century, there were two kinds of cottages. There were soundly built, modest and characteristic small houses, which tourist guides now call picturesque. They were built by improving landlords in reformed parishes with something of that sentiment in mind. Sound picturesque cottages were affordable because of the much larger number of the second kind of cottages, the hovels that Smith drew, and which he called picturesque on account of their neglect.[19]

Cottages – neat and neglected

The eighteenth-century discourse on agricultural reform developed from ideas about the cottage as a unit of land and labour to a concern for cottage design largely at odds with picturesque qualities. Kent's *Hints* was one of the first publications to propose that building sound cottages would not only overcome a problem, but also be productive by improving labourers through the design of their cottages (Figures 4.2 and 4.3). Apart from improving the health of workers, Kent calculates that landlords could expect a return of four per cent on the capital invested in a cottage. The main role of the cottage, however, was one of inspection: the state of the cottage demonstrated the state of the family inhabiting it. Right use of the cottage and fear of eviction, Kent writes, would inculcate right attitude:

> There are two principles which should be kept alive as much as possible in the minds of the poor; pride and shame: the former will lead them to the attainment of comfort, by honest means, and the latter will keep them from being burdensome to their neighbours.[20]

Kent's designs for even his smallest cottage of cheap 'studd work' possess a 'principal room' with stores and brick oven, and separate bedrooms for parents and children on an attic floor. Kent's ideas for the role and the equipage of a cottage were widely accepted: in the first volume of the *Communications to the Board of Agriculture* of 1797, there are five designs and much discussion of the appropriate form, rationale and management of cottages.[21] The minimum requirement was a 'kitchen, parlour and all' with a properly flued fireplace and separate bedrooms for parents and children. A separate hovel or lean-to was to be provided for animals and fuel. The cottage was carefully calculated to accommodate the family in decency without becoming a farmstead in its own right. Morality and religion required that children sleep separately from their parents. It was thought extravagant to separate boys from girls, although Robert Beeston designed a partly closed double bunk bed entered from opposite sides to extend decency to cottage children.[22] While fears of incest caused the model cottage to be larger than vernacular hovels, reformers were anxious to minimize and specify the rooms, so the dwelling would fit only the family. The concern here was partly about creating norms of familial life, but more so about making it impossible for the cottagers to take in apprentices in any independent farming attempt. Cottages were to have gardens where the wife and children could grow sufficient food to provide a safety net in times of unemployment. Gardens were carefully calculated by correspondents to the Board so as to ensure that the cottage could not be self-sufficient. This same fear that the cottagers would not be available for wage labour leads to some strange correspondence as to how cottagers could keep a cow for milk, but not breed from her.

While cow, garden and sleep arrangements provided training for cottage children, the oven defined the cottage wife. Through the eighteenth century, agricultural labour became increasingly gender specialized, and by the end of the century, the removal of women from the work-force was widely seen as a way to reduce effects of unemployment. As hardship increased, marriage rates dropped, with rural people refusing to marry without appropriate dowries. Unlicensed unions and illegitimate offspring put increasing numbers of rural poor outside the church and proper society, and, in the minds of the governing classes, under the influence of political sedition and brutish passions. The model cottage was part of a strategy to make women's labour in the home replace the dowry. In pamphlets and in good local examples, the cottage wife was advertised through her developing expertise in domestic economy, primary health care, and child rearing. While a bread oven in a cottage for one family was as unlikely as the cottagers having enough fuel to fire it, the oven symbolized much of women's newly productive interior role. The provision of a cottage was, thus, not merely a contract struck with the male worker, it was an engine to gather him up in a pattern of formal and domestic economic interdependencies.

This attempt to police and train behaviour through architecture was a widespread concern in late eighteenth-century culture, as we see in numerous designs for prisons, factories and hospitals, Jeremy Bentham's Panopticon of 1797 being the most famous.[23] Michel Foucault and Evans show, in different ways, how the Panopticon building did not actually function but, nevertheless, provided a model for diffuse techniques of social discipline that emerged through the nineteenth century in actual buildings and in methods for observing social pathologies.[24] In the history of social discipline, the cottage is a contrary case. Whether or not the architectural design of the cottage was effective in forming docile subjects, it was certainly thought to do so. The formula of the three-room minimum house, encoding relations between husband, wife and children, is taken up directly in nineteenth-century city housing reform. In 1866, Robert Kerr attacked 'the dogma of the three bedrooms', claiming that the poor preferred to live all together in a single well-appointed room, for which he provided designs.[25] Kerr was ridiculed in the Royal Institute of British Architects because the programme of the minimum house and the role of architecture in separating and classing people and behaviour was no longer open to question.[26]

Reformed cottages were unlikely to please painters. What picturesque aesthetes took to be mellow tints was damp rising in the walls. The 'connection' of cottage to landscape was foliage sprouting from its rotten thatch. From the mid-century, Thomas Gainsborough developed a genre of peopled landscapes he called 'fancy pictures'. These contain motifs of rural life in wastes and forests, including depictions of peasants apparently at leisure and in good health despite their mouldering neglected cottages. An example is the well-known *The Cottage Door*, exhibited at the Royal Academy in 1780 (Figure 4.4). Art historians have shown that social and political views underlie these pictures. Michael Rosenthal suggests that in their choice of subject – common lands, forests and wastes – the paintings participate in nostalgia and regret at the destruction of traditional rural life through enclosure, as is dramatized in Oliver Goldsmith's popular poem *The Deserted Village*. The poor in Gainsborough's fancy pictures are depicted in pleasurable and reflective idleness, poses which, in the history

Figure 4.1 John Thomas Smith, 'Near Mrs. Teshmakers' Edmonton', 1797.

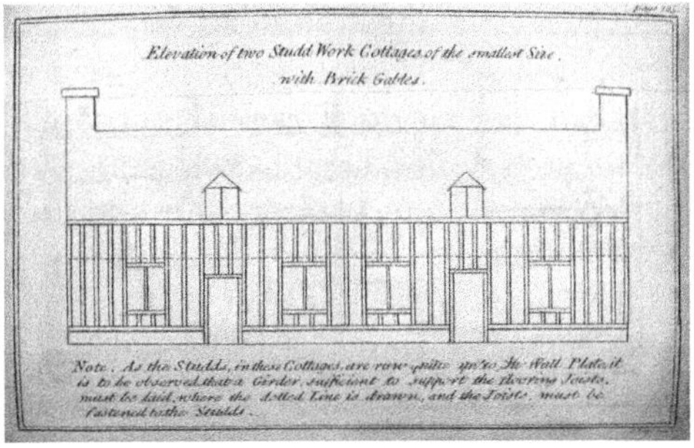

Figure 4.2 Nathaniel Kent, 'Studd work cottage' elevation, 1745. Photographed by permission of the National Library of Australia from the 1793 edition.

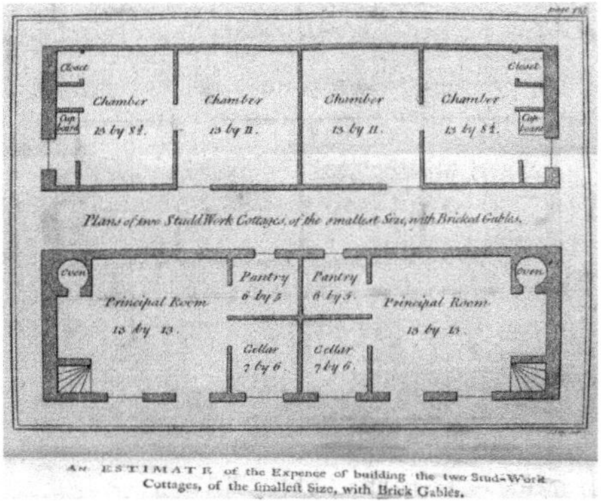

Figure 4.3 Nathaniel Kent, 'Studd work cottage' plan, 1745. Photographed by permission of the National Library of Australia from the 1793 edition.

Figure 4.4 Thomas Gainsborough, *The Cottage Door*, exhibited at the Royal Academy, 1780.

of painting, belong to modern aristocrats or the classical notion of otium, and which strongly contrast with the reformers' view that idleness in the poor was laziness. Marcia Pointon suggests that the paintings speak to a discourse on contemplative 'retirement' from the world (made popular through garden making poets Alexander Pope and William Shenstone with a history going back to Augustine and Pliny), which should be understood in a kind of dialectic with Gainsborough's society portraits and an active life in Town. That it should be peasants and not poets so depicted is, Pointon suggests, Gainsborough and his admirers taking the cottage and cottagers as contemporary remainders of a prelapsarian world; that the paintings constitute 'a serious preoccupation with the problems of how man can live a productive and virtuous life in a fallen world'.[27] John Barrell argues that Gainsborough and later painters, particularly George Moreland, depict not only the rural life under threat, but also the active resentment of this on the part of labouring people, who resisted the reforms in large numbers and so developed a consciousness of class that was to be a major factor in later British history.[28] Certainly, Price's idea of the picturesque as focused on humble subjects was greatly influenced by Gainsborough who was a friend of his grandfather.[29]

In his *Remarks on Rural Scenery* at the end of the century, Smith claims Gainsborough as his model and the originator of 'cottage scenery'.[30] What interests Smith in rural hovels is what Gainsborough helps him to see, but which he understands neither as the rhetoric of retirement nor as regret for a way of life being lost. Smith describes his etchings (see Figure 4.1) in terms that could come from the Board of Agriculture, except that for him, disgust holds the kind of potential for art we observed in the previous chapter.

> Cottage-scenery may be divided into two classes, namely the *neat* and the *neglected*.
>
> It is a maxim that in poverty, nothing will more easily, or more universally excite the attentions of benevolence, than the appearance of neatness and cleanliness: The regular, white-washed or new brick wall – the glaring red chimney-pot – the even-thatch'd roof – the equi-distant groups of sweet pea and jasmine prudishly trimmed into solid columns and cubes, stiff as a chimney, and hiding perhaps some pictoresque feature – the square border of flowers planted in exact angles and carefully preserved to deck the church-going damsel on Sundays – the oven, exhibiting a smooth unvarying surface of dead plaster, or decked only with a vine pruned into deformity – the bright yellow foot-path, straight as a line – all tend to impress an idea of frugal proprete, and will be sure to call forth the praises of the good *housewife* and the thrifty *oeconomist*: But it is nothing to the artist: As good *housewives*, or as thrifty *oeconomists* we admit that it is all very well; but we then turn from this neatness and regularity, to what *we* must esteem a far more profitable subject – the neglected fast-ruinating cottage – the patched plaster, of various tints and discolorations, which, like the garments of Otway's witch, shall
>
> 'Seem to speak variety of wretchedness'
>
> – the weather-beaten thatch, bunchy and varied with moss – the mutilated chimney top – the fissures and crevices of the inclining wall – the roof of various angles and inclinations – the tiles of different hues – the fence of bungling workmanship – the wild unrestrained vine, whose 'gadding' branches nearly deprive the chambers of their wonted light – the paper-pasted casement, with here and there a wisp of straw stuffed through a broken pane – the decayed bee-hive and the broken basket – the fragment of a chair or bench – the slatternry of tubs and dishes scattered about the door – the

> mischievous pranks of ragged children – the intrusion of pigs – and the unrepaired accidents of wind and rain – offer far greater allurements to the painter's eye, than more neat, regular or formal arrangements could possibly have done.[31]

Smith's frank and enthusiastic text makes clear what is less glaring in his well composed and quite pleasing etchings. While these have something of the charm and rustic affections of Gainsborough's paintings, Smith's engraved drawings are considerably more detailed: we find in them the pathology of the cottage that the text suggests. Under Gainsborough's brush, cottages appear almost natural objects, barely more deliberate or organized than rocks. In Smith's delineations, the building is an artefact in entropy: rags attempt to stop the cold, light fails to enter and the rutted path will set the floor awash when it rains. Smith takes the pathology of the cottage as an aesthetic agenda, adding in details that Gainsborough passes over, the piquancy of a little disgust to balance the sentimentality of his views. This is a clear example of what John Ruskin would later call 'the heartlessness of the picturesque'. Note also, how Smith's word painting of the varied wretchedness of the neglected cottage relies on the contrast that he draws with the neat cottage. From its firm foundations to its oven, neat garden, and religious observance of the cottage wife, Smith gives a thorough sketch of the reformed cottage of a 'thrifty oeconomist' such as Kent. Smith's mockery of the prim reformers, however, should not be read as a renunciation of their programme any more than we should suppose that Smith thought the neglected cottages adequate as habitations. What Smith did was to combine Gainsborough's pictorial analytic of the cottage with the agricultural reformers' analysis of it as a building. Smith's portfolio raised a possibility his readers would have known from Price: could intentionally designed, soundly built, functioning cottages have the appearance of the wretched picturesque ones?

The answer, of course, was 'yes'. Architects and clients read Price and studied prints like those by Smith, and in a few short years, from the end of the eighteenth century, the ornamental frivolous buildings built in the gardens and parks of British great houses changed from exotic samples of antiquity or China to being ornamental versions of the housing of the rural workers just outside the gates. The discovery of vernacular building as a source of architectural interest followed on the discovery of indigenous landscape, and the general change in the system of the arts caused by philosophical aesthetics and the idea of art having its own, autonomous criteria. It would, however, be difficult to overstress the conceptual and historical watershed marked by the frivolous project of architects designing cottages. In the fifteenth century, Alberti categorically distinguished architecture from building, stressing that, opposed to the mechanically determined building trades, architects should be liberal and educated.[32] For Alberti, the relation of architecture to building is like that of Latin to vernacular tongues: architecture is, above all, regulated through a conscious application of rule and precedent; it is practised as a kind of rhetorical art. What we have come to call by analogy 'vernacular' building, is, by contrast, unplanned, expedient, and unconscious of its own history, pattern or affect. Alberti's concept of the architect was gradually accepted across Europe, and during the eighteenth century became codified, first in academies of fine art, followed by professional organizations in the early nineteenth century. At the moment of its triumph, however, the concept of architecture changed its nature. From about 1800 began a process, the picturesque, in which architecture became sufficiently secure in its abstraction from building to claim to apply to all building tasks, no matter how humble. By the end of the nineteenth century, the idea emerged that architecture is the art of all building. In the latter part of the twentieth century, traditional buildings, the vernacular of non-European peoples, even the vernacular of the philistine suburbs of the West, became prized for their supposed unreflective nature, for their openness to analyses that could refresh architecture by challenging its rules and precedents.

The fashion for ornamental cottages is one symptom of a wholesale reorganization of the arts, and their detachment and subsequent re-engagement with the world across the space of a newfound autonomy. While we can interpret the idea of vernacular architecture as an episode in this general process, there is one simpler, technical issue specific to architecture. This is that the 'irregularity' of vernacular building is not only a general laxity, but also a specific lack of symmetry in the plan. For classical architects, vernacular buildings could not be said to have plans: in the sense that they were not closed completed forms, and they were not intentional in the sense that we still mean by the word 'planned'. The fashion for the picturesque led architects to use the plan drawing techniques to describe the empirically existing cottages with their shapeless, accretionary structure. The understanding that plans could take different shapes, or be shapeless, led to an another understanding: that the form, appearance and organization of the buildings are different aspects organized by the plan. In the designs, commentary and debate around the potential of 'irregularity' in architecture we see the emergence of a modern concept of the plan.

Irregularity in theory and practice

In seeking to explain that picturesqueness is the result of a building's 'irregularity', Price and Knight developed a nascent concept of architectural planning, making some rather disconnected claims about how irregularity emerged historically and the freedoms it offers to the designer. They also differed: Price finds architectural merit in vernacular building in the way that I described above, while Knight sees cottages as below any consideration of taste. Considered together, however, it is not unreasonable to follow historians, including Pevsner and Peter Collins, in seeing the criteria of modern architectural planning – function, site specificity and legibility – unfolding from these remarks on irregularity. It is, on the other hand, remarkable how absent is the discussion of any of these matters in the eighteenth-century texts, and how much the development of basic techniques of modern planning was carried out through the concepts of painting and visual appearance.

Buildings play an important role early in Price's original *Essay*, where he argues for a sensuous basis of the picturesque, one that conflicts with the theory of Edmund Burke. Price finds the causes of the picturesque in 'qualities of roughness, and of sudden variation, joined to that of irregularity'.[33] Burke had claimed that beauty has a sensuous cause in smoothness, uniformity and even variations, but Price shows that this does not explain the visual pleasure that we have and which painters reproduce in views of ruined buildings. For Price, this demonstrates the existence of a bundle of visual stimuli that are not described by Burke's definition of beauty in smoothness, nor sublimity in vastness. Hence, according to Price, the need for the term picturesque, to name the value associated with these stimuli. 'A temple or palace of Grecian architecture in its perfect entire state, and with its surface and colour smooth and even, either in painting or reality is beautiful; in ruin it is picturesque.'[34] In attributing roughness as a cause, Price follows William Gilpin's earlier insight: that our admiration for the facture of painting, the tactility of the artist's hand in the material constraint of charcoal and pigment, shows the limits of Burke's smooth beauty. In the case of the ruined temple 'weather stains, partial incrustations, mosses etc . . . [give] a degree of roughness, and a variety of tint'.[35] Price's innovation over Gilpin is to add 'irregularity' and to claim: 'among the various causes of the picturesqueness of ruins compared with entire buildings, the destruction of symmetry is by no means the least powerful'.[36]

As well as smoothness, Burke's definition of beauty emphasizes 'uniformity', which Price says is the enemy of the picturesque and is clearly unworkable as an explanation of the love of scenery, rocky outcrops, trees growing to a form braced against the wind and so on.[37] For Price, the picturesque qualities of such scenery are 'intricacy', which is a visual texture and tonality the opposite of Burke's smoothness; and 'variety', which opposes Burke's uniformity. Variety is the visual value or pleasure of which irregularity is the cause. The picturesque, by 'its intricacy, its partial concealments, it excites that active curiosity which gives play to the mind.' Interest and curiosity aroused by the picturesque differs from and ameliorates the sublime, which causes astonishment that 'chains up the faculties'.[38] Picturesqueness is 'the coquetry of nature – it makes beauty more amusing, more varied, more playful'.[39] Burke's argument that beauty has a basis in human form and sexual attraction is compatible with the ancient doctrines of classical architecture that see buildings as anthropomorphic and bilaterally symmetrical. Price was also interested in women, but suggests that Burke's pure beauty does not explain the playful naughtiness in the faces and expressions of attractive women. The French are more attuned to this nuance, Price thinks, as is evidenced in the expressions: '*une physionomie de fantaisie*, and the well-known expression *un certain je ne sais quoi*; it is also common to say of a woman – *que sans etre belle elle est piquante* – a word, by the by, that in many points answers very exactly to the picturesque.'[40] But in these titivating asides, Price is merely trying to maintain a point of articulation with Burke's authority while opposing the thrust of his main argument. Picturesqueness concerns not the inflection of regular forms, but a thorough 'irregularity'; a concept of form based not on the symmetries of the human figure but on landscape.

Price has little more to say explicitly about how irregular buildings produce the visual qualities of intricacy and variation. His descriptions of rocks and buildings are quite interchangeable. In general, picturesque building materials have texture such as rotting thatch, or tints such as weather-stained walls. These are the same visual effects as incrustations on rocks, with different causes. The irregularity of buildings is more specifically related to variety. In proper architecture, Price admires the Baroque for its broken lines, advance and retreat of forms, and the uneven distribution of ornament.[41] (This aspect of Price's thought on architecture will be addressed in Chapter 6.) It is clear, however, that in grand architecture picturesqueness is mixed with beauty or sublimity. The pure picturesque exists in only ancient castles or contemporary hovels that are asymmetrical in their plan form. Irregularity means that a building's appearance varies in its different aspects. Compared to a symmetrical building, relatively small changes in the position of the viewer generate a great variety of views. The experience of the building is less predictable. Unlike a symmetrical building, one cannot surmise from the front elevation the appearance of the side or rear elevation. This effect of varied visual experience is the only value or utility of irregular buildings that Price or Knight claim. This simple point was subsumed into architectural technique over the next few decades, but as a concept its more important development was later in John Ruskin's idea of 'changefulness', and more significantly in Heinrich Wölfflin's idea of the painterly movement of Baroque architecture. While Price and Knight have little to say about irregularity in abstract, they do discuss how such plans come to have been produced and it is these remarks that provide impetus for later architectural developments.

Knight probably had the greater role in developing the concept of irregularity, having designed and built his house, Downton Castle, on an irregular plan (Figures 4.5 and 4.6). Downton was built from 1772–8, about the time the two friends first met,[42] and the highly unusual house must have influenced the development of their diverging ideas of the picturesque before they each committed to print in 1794/5.[43] The theorists' interest in asymmetrical building, however, is not unique or unprecedented. Both Price and Knight admired John Vanbrugh, whose Castle Vanbrugh at Greenwich, built from 1717, is, perhaps, the first irregularly planned piece of architecture.[44] Vanbrugh's 'castle' began as a symmetrical building, adjusted to the topography and framed 'irregularly' by service buildings, but in the 1720s he made deliberately asymmetrical additions.[45] In 1748, Horace Walpole began constructing Strawberry Hill, his experiment in a Gothic style, on an irregular plan. Robert Adam is well known for his caprices of irregular castles in romantic landscapes, which he began drawing as a youth in the 1740s (although his Culzean Castle, begun in 1777, has a symmetrical plan). Also in the 1740s, gentleman architect Sanderson Miller built mock castle ruins of the kind that Adam drew, largely as ornamental ruins, but including an irregularly planned house styled as a castle.[46] Although Vanbrugh's work was an object of opprobrium for much of the century, Sir Joshua Reynolds was probably not too far ahead of advanced taste when, in 1786, he publicly rehabilitated Vanbrugh by connecting his architecture with the picturesque.[47] What Reynolds says in his Discourse XIII was an inspiration and also gave authority to what Price and Knight were to do.

> It may not be amiss for the Architect to take advantage *sometimes* of that to which I am sure the Painter ought always have his eyes open, I mean the use of accidents; to follow where they may lead, and to improve them, rather than to trust to a regular plan. It often happens that additions have been made to houses at various times, for use or pleasure. As such buildings depart from regularity, they now and then acquire something of scenery by this accident, which I think might not be unsuccessfully adopted by an Architect in an original plan, if it does not too much interfere with convenience. Variety and intricacy is a beauty and excellence in every other of the arts which address the imagination; why not in Architecture?[48]

The precedents for picturesque irregularity, nevertheless, are few, and often consist in the breaking or mutation of symmetrical layout, or are purely scenic in their intent. By contrast, Downton is remarkable in its thorough resiling of symmetry. Knight's and Price's widely read texts on the matter made this capricious anomaly into one of architecture's central questions.

Andrew Ballantyne shows how Knight developed the design for Downton from a close study of the site and a focus on the design of rooms.[49] Although the drawing rooms and dining rooms have a conventional axial arrangement, Knight felt free to design each as he wished. As a result, the dining room, with its dome, and the drawing room, with its engaged octagonal tower, produce an irregular perimeter to the building and a varied parapet line. Knight's licence for this strikingly modern design technique came from antiquity. He is convinced that in classical times

> the villas or country houses of the Romans were quite irregular – adapted to the situations on which they were placed and spread out in every direction, according to the wants or inclinations; the taste, wealth, or magnificence of the respective owners.[50]

Knight gives the example of Hadrian's Villa at Tivoli, which has such an open accretionary plan. We could speculate that Hadrian's vestibules to the Piazza d'Oro might well have provided the inspiration for Downton's domed apsidal dining room. Knight thinks that the symmetry of Palladian country houses, with their temple fronts, is not only incongruous in England, but the result of a failed historical understanding:

> The system of regularity, of which the moderns have been so tenacious in the plans of their country houses, was taken from the sacred, and not the domestic architecture of the ancients; from buildings, of which the forms were prescribed by religion . . .[51]

While the interiors of Downton are in an archeologically inspired classical design, it is called a castle and its irregular exterior appears to be fortified. This is not the eclecticism it might seem. Knight insists, correctly, that crenellations were a Greco-Roman invention; and further, that isolated country retreats of the ancients were not only irregular but also fortified.[52] Knight's views have not been commonly accepted, then or since, and Ballantyne shows that this has led Downton to be consistently misunderstood as an early and inept attempt at Gothic revival.[53] Beyond this little demonstration of the problems of Knight's theory of associations, there is also an issue of planning. For Knight, military architecture is another way to understand irregularity: 'the general plans of castles . . . depend entirely upon circumstances and situations; and were confined by no rules of architecture'.[54] Knight thinks such ancient fortified country houses can be studied in the buildings painted by 'Claude and the Poussins', which were built piecemeal and in such a promiscuous mix of manners and contrasting qualities of construction that they were effectively style-less. Ballantyne draws attention to some similarities between Downton and Claude's *Cephalus* and *Procris Reunited by Diana* (1645, National Gallery, London), a painting that Knight knew.[55] Thus despite his use of high-genre paintings, Knight's argument joins that of Price: the picturesque manner of architecture and gardening can eschew rules and precepts without falling into caprice because of the models and authorities found in great painting.

Knight describes the irregular plan of Downton as having the 'advantage of being capable of receiving alterations and additions in almost any direction, without any injury to its genuine and original character'.[56] Such a statement is on the cusp of meaning that rooms in an irregular plan can be interrelated more conveniently and rationally than in a symmetrical plan. However, this is ambiguous because Knight does not mention how he derived the initial plan, and the advantage of such planning is still said to be a matter of appearance, of robustness of building character. In a passage that shows how different Knight's thinking is to what we now consider picturesque planning, he writes:

> In choosing a situation for a house of this kind, which is to be a principal feature in a place, more consideration ought to be had of the views towards it, than of those fromwards it: for, consistent with comfort, which ought to be the first object in every dwelling, it very rarely happens that a perfect composition of landscape scenery can be obtained from a door or window; nor does it appear to me particularly desirable that it should be; for few persons ever look for such compositions, or pay any attention to them, while within doors.[57]

A passage from Price's 'Essay on Picturesque Architecture' is in disagreement with Knight about windows and is one step closer to modern criteria of planning: he proposes that exterior spaces and views are coordinated with those of the building – that irregularity might even be convenient.

> Now if the owner of such a spot, instead of making a regular front and sides, were to insist upon having many of the windows turned towards those points where the objects were most happily arranged, the architect would be forced into the invention of a number of picturesque forms and combinations, which otherwise might never have

Figure 4.5 Richard Payne Knight, Downton Castle. View by F. O. Morris with additions c. 1860.

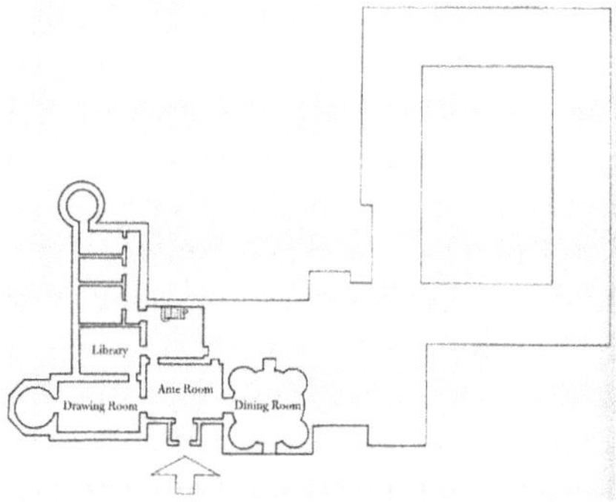

Figure 4.6 Richard Payne Knight, Downton Castle. Conjectural drawing of original plan arrangement by Andrew Ballantyne.

Figure 4.7 John Nash (with Humphry Repton), Luscombe Castle, Devon, c. 1799. View by R. Ackerman, 1828.

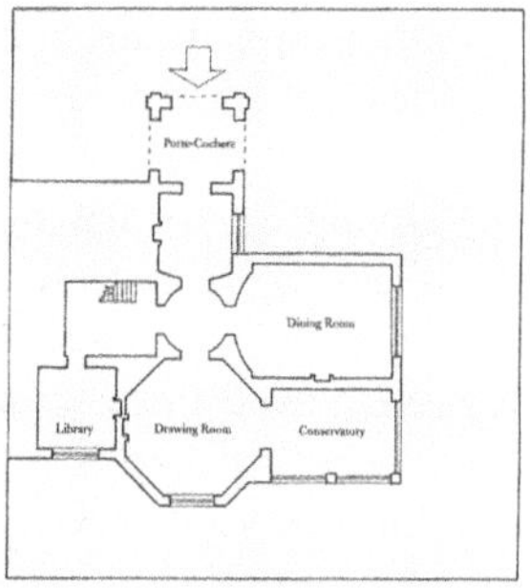

Figure 4.8 John Nash (with Humphry Repton), Luscombe Castle, Devon, plan arrangement c. 1799. Drawing by Andrew Ballantyne.

> occurred to him. . . . I am well convinced that such a disposition of the outside would suggest to an artist of genius, no less varied and picturesque effects within; and that the arrangements of the room, would oftentimes be at least as convenient as in a more uniform plan.[58]

However, it is significant that Price's causality is reversed when compared to modern understandings of a building's relation to site. For Price, visual variety is the aim of the picturesque architect; viewpoint and functional efficiency are means by which variety can be produced, not ends in themselves. However, the step by which this situation is reversed and irregularity becomes the means of coordinating interior and exterior spaces – of rationalizing the interrelation of rooms – is implicit in Knight's and Price's remarks. We should not assume that they did not also see this.

Downton had a number of important innovations in planning immediately apparent to the designers John Nash and Humphry Repton, each of whom knew Price, Knight and Downton Castle. In 1799, during their short-lived partnership, Nash designed the house and Repton the gardens of Luscombe Castle in Devon (Figures 4.7 and 4.8). Charles Hoare commissioned Repton who introduces Nash and the role of his architecture thus:

> A castle has infinitely more picturesque effect than any other stile of building. . . . My ingenious friend, Mr Nash, without losing sight of internal arrangement, disposition, or convenience, has given the house an outline which from its chaste Simplicity must always please the Eye of Taste. Its very Irregularity will give it consequence, while the offices and mere walls which in a modern building it would be essential to conceal, by partaking of the Character of the Castle, will extend its Scite, and make it an apparently considerable pile of building.[59]

Note that in the passage quoted, Repton, like Price, explains irregularity as something that requires skill if it is to be achieved without compromising internal arrangement. It is clear from the design, however, that irregularity actually enabled the internal disposition of the rooms and their relation to the landscape. Like Downton, Luscombe has its main public rooms on the ground floor and its 'offices' (service spaces, kitchens, stores and servants quarters) on the same level to the rear. The two issues of site specificity and servicing are interrelated and only possible in an irregular plan. Repton and Nash coordinated the park's design with the orientation of the drawing and dining rooms, one of which looks into a forested hill and the other down the valley to the town of Dawlish and the sea. Some years later Repton explains another project: 'the plan must be made not only to fit the spot, it ought actually to be made upon the spot, that every door and window in it may be adapted to the aspects and prospects of the situation'.[60] This remark of Repton's is confused by another discussion of climatic orientation, one that also feeds in to the issue of irregularity. Repton writes that climatic aspect and view need to be considered together because windows to the north and west will often be 'covered with wet, as to render the landscape hardly visible'. This apparently trivial point covers a more far-reaching statement on the necessity of irregular planning to climatic design: 'From hence we may conclude, that a square house, placed with its fronts duly opposite to the cardinal points, will have one good and three bad aspects'.[61]

Repton advocated ground-floor rooms where one can see the garden and then go out to it through a conservatory or the newly fashionable sash windows reaching to the floor. In the neo-Palladian mansions that Repton dislikes, major rooms are elevated and detached from the garden partly because they sit on top of a full floor (or half basement) of services. At Luscombe, the offices are at the ground level, partly visible from the garden to give the building some hierarchy in the elevation, and partly hidden by planting. Fitting service spaces into a house was one of the major challenges to architects, and once service areas exceeded what could fit in the basement, symmetrical planning became extremely difficult. In one sense, irregularity and an additive hierarchical approach to architectural form was inevitable as the social importance of country houses and the number of servants they required increased until, in the great age of country houses in the late nineteenth century, offices took up a good two-thirds of the plan.[62]

Nash went on to become the most prominent architect of his day. With the patronage of the Prince Regent, he undertook the largest remodelling of London since the Great Fire, building Regent's Street and Park on picturesque principles. He also had a large practice in country houses in the castellated picturesque manner, and with other architects such as James Wyatt, made buildings like Downton the model for nineteenth-century country houses.[63] However, while Nash's castles, and those that followed them, appear as developments of Downton, and are so at the level of their planning, they are identified with the romantic medieval nationalism that was to dominate nineteenth-century architecture in Britain, and which is slightly at odds with both Knight's ideas of castellated classicism and Price's more quotidian aesthetics. Nash also designed two sets of cottages arranged as villages that were greatly influential and have more to tell us of the picturesque than his castles. In particular, we need to look at cottages to understand why Price and Repton had so much difficulty writing about and conceptualizing the principle of irregular planning with which they were already practising.

The reason that irregularity did not reach a level of conceptualization as an architectural technique in 1800 was its associations with poverty. Paradoxically, this is also the reason that irregularity developed from visual value to planning technique. The previous section took its structure from Knight's account of grand country houses. He thinks that the fashion for rustic styles based on vernacular dwellings is a ludicrous imposture, writing that:

> to adapt the genuine style of a herdsman's hut, or a ploughman's cottage, to the dwellings of opulence and luxury, is as utterly impossible, as it is to adapt their language, dress, and manners to the refined uses of polished society.[64]

Earlier, Gilpin had been of the same mind, banning cottages from the picturesque sketch. Price, however, differs on this point, and it is his rustic picturesque that has been historically the more successful.

I earlier quoted Price on how ruination made a beautiful temple picturesque – the same passage continues with Price introducing a problem that complicates his account. Price imagines objectors who would think that admiration of ruins, and hence the picturesque, can be described more simply as a combination of Burke's two categories: the beauty of still discernable symmetry, and the sublime force of nature that ruined it. Price writes:

> But were this true, yet many buildings highly interesting to all who have united the study of art with that of nature, in which beauty and grandeur are equally out of the question; such as hovels, cottages, mills, insides of old barns, stables &c.[65]

This form of argument is typical of Price, who generalizes from higher to lower genres while maintaining their hierarchy. On this occasion, as elsewhere, Price's point is to show that his interest in the quotidian extends and broadens rather than challenges the remit of taste. More significant for the present argument is that Price finds the principle of irregular planning where it is most visible: not in vanished Roman villas but in cottages.

If, as Knight imagined, the fortified houses of the Roman Campagna developed from a core Roman villa, with the additions of fortifications in the Dark Ages and a Renaissance cortile added as civilization was re-established, then cottages show the same process in the barely discernible history of the cottage family. As the family prospered, the roofline was changed to accommodate an attic for children or extended as a lean-to to shelter a cow. With destitution, parts of the walls collapsed and thistles grew in the thatch. Exigencies meant that cottagers lacked the ability to consider their needs in relation to the life of the building. They lacked the resources to build all they needed at once, or to build in planned stages with each stage being integral to an initial plan. In the 'Dialogue on the picturesque', Price explains this point by having his characters admire the mixture of picturesqueness and beauty in an old Parsonage House, which:

> exhibited a singular mixture of neatness and irregularity. Something seemed to have been, added by each incumbent, just as a room, a staircase, or a passage was wanting: there were all kinds of projections; of roofs crossing each other in different directions.[66]

The cottage shows the same principles of an irregular architecture open to contingency even if rural happenstance lacks the grandeur and nobility of the decline and fall of Rome. Indeed, this is Price's point: Downton and the fortified villas in Claude's paintings are a mixed character of grand and picturesque; if we wish to understand the picturesque in its pure character we should resort to the cottage. While Price's admiration of the very piquant aspects of irregular rambling cottages easily avoids Knight's censure of pantomime rusticity, his interest in the aesthetic possibilities of disgust risks an opposite charge of the vitiation and perversion of taste. To the extent that Price avoids this impression, and that we do not, generally, connect his interest in cottages with his interest in flayed carcasses, this is partly because of the popularity of the paintings of rustic subjects, such as those by Gainsborough. This, however, is also because his texts are contemporaneous with interest in agricultural reform.[67] At the same time that it was being considered picturesque, the cottage was becoming an object of importance in national affairs. From both directions, it was the architecture of the cottage that was at stake.

Cottage architecture and irregularity as technique

A genre of architectural pattern books for cottage design began in the eighteenth century and continued, sporadically, into the twentieth. Between 1775, when Kent published his *Hints to Gentlemen*, and 1843, about 110 books of architectural patterns for cottages or 'small villas' were issued.[68] (See Figures 4.9 to 4.13 and 4.16 to 4.25.) The pattern books were partly a publishing phenomenon, based around the development of printing techniques by artists such as Paul Sandby, and the market for prints.[69] Aquatint, mezzotint and later lithography allowed for tonal printing which encouraged the depiction of buildings in landscape settings. The pattern books were also complicit with the early stage of the professionalization of architecture. In Britain, the first clubs and societies were organized in the decades 1790–1810, the first substantial course of lectures at the Royal Academy was that of Thomas Sandby in 1771, and the Institute of Architects was founded in 1842.[70] The pattern books were, therefore, a mode of commerce for the first cohorts of architects without aristocratic patronage, who attempted to trade their skills to an emerging middle class. For instance, in the preface to his book, John Plaw 'begs leave to inform his Friends and the Public that he furnishes Designs, and working Drawings, and will advise or attend to their execution (if required), at the usual commission. Letters post free will be duly attended to'.[71] While the history of printing technology and professionalization underly the structure of the pattern-book genre, their object was the design of small dwellings, variously called cottages, villas and retreats, required for the improvement of estates on picturesque and agricultural principles. In the descriptive texts accompanying the designs and in the essays that introduce them, architects frequently cite the picturesque theorists or the Board of Agriculture, and sometimes both, crudely wrapping together picturesque taste and the social engineering of tied housing for labourers. William Fuller Pocock puts the occasion for cottage architecture more clearly than most in his *Architectural Designs for Rustic Cottages, Picturesque Dwellings, Villas &C.* of 1807:

> [Cottages] encourage a bold and numerous peasantry . . . If a small portion of ground is attached, in cultivating which they may occupy their leisure hours, it may prevent their spending their time and money in scenes of intemperance, whereby their habits of industry are relaxed and their morals corrupted . . . [They] will become attached [to the landlord] through sentiments of gratitude; while their being able to maintain their families without parochial aid, their sentiments of honor will be preserved, their natural independence of mind remain unbroken by indigence and inactivity; and they will be in every respect more worthy members of society, and better fitted for the defense of their country when called upon. In many situations on a large estate these rustic Buildings will form pleasing and characteristic objects in the landscape. When the mind is filled with beautiful and sublime ideas from the contemplation of an extensive prospect, as the circle of vision gradually contracts, the eye dwells with peculiar delight on the clay built Cottage covered in thatch; or if emblossomed in umbrageous foliage, the roof alone be visible, this with the light and curling smoke will sufficiently enliven the scene, by pointing out a habitation.[72]

Pocock was also a proponent of the irregular Pricean style of rustic architecture, which in 1807 still had opponents, because, in this heady mixture of landscape concepts and political references, irregularity became a major issue.

In 1798, James Malton caused a controversy by publishing the first explicit apology for an irregular architecture in a book greatly inspired by Price entitled *An Essay on British Cottage Architecture: Being an Attempt to Perpetuate on Principle, That Peculiar Mode of Building Which Was Originally the Work of Chance. Supported by Fourteen Designs with their Ichnography, or Plans. . . .* The designs (Figures 4.9 and 4.10) writes Malton,

> are humbly presented as hints to those Noblemen and Gentlemen of taste, who build retreats for themselves, with desire to have them appear as cottages, or erect habitations for their peasantry or other tenants: And to the Farmer, as a guide in the construction of his dwelling.[73]

A cottage, Malton tells us, is not the 'mean habitation' given in Dr Johnson's dictionary, which is merely thatch 'sheltering only the wretched space enclosed within four mud walls'. Rather, a cottage 'may, I think, as well be the habitation of a substantial farmer or affluent gentleman, as the dwelling of the hedger or ditcher'.[74] The designs range by increment from two bedroom labourers' huts to a minor mansion with seven public rooms. There are liminal traces of reformist discourse in Malton's plea that gentlemen of cultivated taste should 'encourage a laborious peasantry' and 'take the Cottage under their protection; which unless it is speedily done, will be found to exist no where but on the canvas of the painter'.[75] Malton's concern, however, is largely for the visual character of cottage architecture.

> When mention is made of the kind of dwelling called Cottage, I figure in my imagination a small house in the country; of odd, irregular form, with various, harmonious colouring, the effect of weather, time and accident; the whole environed with smiling vedure . . . A porch at one entrance; irregular breaks in the direction of the walls; one part higher than another; various roofing materials, thatch particularly, boldly projecting; fronts partly built of walls of brick, partly brick-noggin dashed; casement window lights, are all conductive and constitute its features.[76]

Malton was a fine draughtsman and one of the first architects to use aquatint. The prints, especially those that are hand coloured, are very expressive of the varied materials he describes, and more startlingly, of weathering and minor decay. Among these more material features, on the specific issue of irregularity, Malton writes:

> I cannot agree with the author of a late publication, who, speaking of rural structures in general, observes that, 'so much is irregularity of parts a constituent of beauty, that regularity may almost be said to be deformity;' yet do I most decidedly admit that a well chosen irregularity is most pleasing; but it does not of consequence follow that all irregularity must necessarily be picturesque. To combine irregularity into picturesque, is the excellence of cottage construction . . .[77]

The irregular extremist who Malton quotes is Smith – his topographic studies of cottages in situ, which I discussed earlier, had appeared the previous year. Malton's caution has two aspects. Proposing irregularity as a principle was a radical break with all previous architectural theory, and Malton wanted to downplay this as much as possible. There is, however, a more subtle reason. Half of Malton's designs, and the majority of those in the higher social register, have symmetrical façades. They confine their irregularity to the rear of the building where roof extensions allow for service areas. This compromise on Malton's cottage principles is clearly intended for clients unable to stomach the appearance of irregularity. At the same time, it shows that Malton sees the practical advantages in irregular planning even when irregularity is no longer a visual value.

Malton's book was an affront to many of the architects of his time. Plaw was a much more successful architect than Malton, and had brought out a pattern book of whimsical pantomime cottages on symmetrical plans in 1795. In his second (equally symmetrical) book *Sketches* of 1800, Plaw blasts the new fashion of architectural irregularity:

> I beg leave to observe, the following Designs are constructed on the principles of symmetry and the correspondence of the parts; because I am aware some persons think Dwellings on a humble scale and Cottages, ought rather to be irregular in their forms, and broken in their parts, taking certain structures for examples which, in my opinion, should rather be seen as beacons of danger, warnings of bad taste. What man of genius would think of building a new house having the patchwork and bungling appearance of an old one?[78]

In 1803, the year of Malton's death of a 'brain fever', Richard Elsam published *An Essay on Rural Architecture . . . Being an Attempt, Also, to Refute, by Analogy, . . . Mr James Malton's Essay.* While agreeing that Malton's designs are picturesque, Elsam writes:

> [Peasant's cottages] . . . are not agreeable to my conception proper models of imitation for persons of fortune, who are desirous of building for themselves rural retreats, which may be styled erected to convey the idea of cottages, without being subject to the imputation of *grotesque*, or faced with some motley group of materials, as brick, wood, or plaster, or brick noggin, *dashed* to insinuate the effects of age, and the appearance of being added at different periods: all of which must rather contribute to impress the mind of the spectator with the idea of poverty rather than with a just notion of independent inhabitants.[79]

> With the greatest veneration for the antiquity of the British Cottage as the primitive invention of our peasants, I should leave them to devise their own plans as heretofore, satisfied that they are as competent to the task in all respects as their forefathers.[80]

In rejecting Malton, Elsam is hostile to both the Pricean picturesque and the Board of Agriculture's programme of cottage housing reform. His reason is two-fold. First, although Elsam admires irregularity in the placement of buildings in towns and villages, he follows tradition in thinking that architecture is anthropomorphic. Hence, individual buildings should be symmetrical.

> If a man had one eye as large as an ox, or one ear as long as an ass [etc] should we not immediately pronounce such a person deformed? the same parity of reasoning holds good with respect to regularity in detached pieces of architecture.[81]

Second, Elsam insists that peasants build their own cottages, without architectural assistance and in an irregular manner. This denies the arguments for agricultural housing reform. Elsam's argument must have been important to him because it carries him into contradiction. His 'Cluster of Four Cottages' with a shared yard and pump is typical of reformist design; it could not be imagined inhabited by gentlefolk. Elsam wants irregularity to remain a sign of not-architecture. He fears Malton's approach would lose architecture its prime role in distinguishing the cultured and wealthy from those who serve them.

In subsequent decades, the debate about irregularity became a regular motif in the introductory texts of the pattern books. Some designers chose one or other side of the argument and some assumed that the two principles were not contradictory. The degree of uncertainty was such that both Malton and Elsam changed their minds. In 1802, Malton published *Designs for Rural Retreats* (see Figure 4.25), which despite further discussion of picturesque irregularity in the essay, consists entirely of highly symmetrical designs in difficult geometries such as the triangular. While Malton's second book is of 'villas' and does not exactly contradict what he said of cottages, it is likely that he is responding to criticism of the Plaw and Elsam kind by attempting to show more conventional facility in design.

Elsam's change of mind is more complete, and interesting in relation to his career. Thirteen years after *Rural Architecture* he published *Hints for Improving the Condition of the Peasantry*, which largely contradicts his previous position, supposing as it does that architects should design irregular dwellings for rural workers. This is a sinister work, mixing ham-fisted designs with a proposed technology of social control. About the time of the publication of *Improving the Condition of the Peasantry*, Elsam was involved in the design and construction of a prison at Dover, and he later published a treatise on prison design, which shows that he had incorporated utilitarian discourse on architecture's powers to train and reform.[82] According to Elsam, a peasant is a 'humble individual' in need of 'a more characteristic style of building' and architecture could 'render him tranquil and happy'.[83] The building that does this is basically the three-room device of the Board of Agriculture, which enables morality, cleanliness and inspectability, and Elsam repeats their arguments. His innovation is to plan the cottage all on one floor because 'the character of his habitation should mingle with such an association of ideas as are likely to approximate with the occupier's humble station. The lower these buildings are therefore the better . . .'.[84] As regards irregularity, this now has an ideological function that had not occurred to Elsam in his previous book:

> the rustic cottage, supposed to be contrived by the uneducated peasant, nothing can be more characteristic or Consistent than its irregularity, it being presumed that the occupier, who is in general the builder, is unacquainted with any but the rude principles of building and therefore his humble mansion never appears so interesting as when it has the appearance of being reared in the most artless manner.[85]

The peasant in his characteristic cottage, appearing to be of his own design, seems an independent freeholder, exchanging labour in a feudal agricultural system. In fact, the labourer is part of a capitalist agriculture, defined by and dependent upon wages and the provision of tied housing from which the landlord may evict him at will. Architecture, invisible under the cloak of irregularity, can, then, perform the classification and discipline supposedly necessary to the new social order. The cottage designs themselves are exceedingly dull but elaborately illustrated, Elsam believing that his prospective clients have a right to three perspective views of each tiny building. It is fascinating to observe what difficulty Elsam has in producing an irregular plan. The buildings fall into three-bay façades with entirely gratuitous returns varying the wall surface. The excessively complicated roof structures fail to disguise the fact that the cottages are no more than variations on an orthogonal plan.

By far the most talented and inventive of the pattern-book architects is Joseph Michael Gandy, a pupil and assistant of John Soane. Gandy produced some eighty designs in two books – *Designs for Cottages* and *The Rural Architect*, of 1805 and 1806 (Figure 4.11). His stripped, elementalized classicism is uncannily prescient of early modern architecture, bearing a comparison with architects a century later such as Behrens, Tessenow, early Asplund or Mies van der Rohe. Gandy's fenestration is punched through the walls rather than articulated; the windows form a prime compositional element not only by placement but also by contrasting verticality and horizontality; there is even some fenestration set out as a horizontal strip. Roof shapes are exposed by the use of eaves with a suggestion of rafters protruding. The effect is a rustic quality, but the low roof pitches and the gable ends to the façade look classical. The buildings are drawn as sitting on a level plane – some drawings suggest this plane as a flat plinth in an undulating landscape, further emphasizing the primitive classical style that Gandy is connecting with the rustic. Gandy does not name his 'style', but it clearly fits Knight's description of a style-less classicism, except that it has no pretence of additions over time.[86]

Gandy's extraordinary disregard for rules and precedent must be largely put down to his originality and his reception of picturesque theory, but he nevertheless claims:

> The idea of the following Work was suggested by the hints thrown out in the valuable Publication issued under the direction of the Board of Agriculture. [. . . These] . . . relate chiefly to modes of construction, circumstances of distribution, and local particulars; objectives unquestionably of the first importance, and which should never be lost sight of. But the advancement of public taste requires more than this – that we should combine convenience of arrangement with elegance in the external appearance. [. . .] Artists whose business it is to study this branch of Design, are particularly called upon to lend their assistance in this National Object.[87]

This is further evidence of the direct impact of the Board's work, but it also shows that Gandy uses this discourse quite differently to Elsam. Elsam has the architect directly engaging in social problems and providing solutions in the form of designs. Gandy is happy to leave all of the 'circumstances' of 'arrangement' and 'local particulars' to the Board of Agriculture, while pointing out that a landlord must add to these considerations the skills of an architect if they are to produce a tasteful result. Gandy, in fact, is a negligent reader of the *Communications to the Board*. He seldom gives more than one bedroom to a labourer's cottage, and, with touching innocence of the Board's philosophy, in one case provides areas under cover for the cottagers' children to play on rainy days. Many of the cottages are designed as complexes with animal housing, which gives them the impression of great topicality. Gandy, however, adds and subtracts animal housing, bridges and mills to fulfil a compositional programme, paying no obvious regard to the Board's debates over the types and numbers of stock that labourers should possess.

In the 'Essay', Gandy shows awareness of the controversy over irregularity, but he does not seem to understand why this has occurred, or that it has anything to do with significations of poverty or with the National Object of cottage reform to which his work is supposedly addressed. His phrasing on the matter is laconic, but none the less historically remarkable.

Figure 4.9 James Malton, *British Cottage Architecture*, Design 5, 1798.

Figure 4.10 James Malton, *British Cottage Architecture*, Design 7, 1798.

Figure 4.11 Joseph Gandy, 'A Picturesque Cottage', 1805.

> It is a question submitted to the Public, whether Architectural Designs should in general be uniform. [. . .] Those designs which are regular may be changed into the picturesque, but taking away one wing; and the picturesque or irregular Designs will become regular by selecting a centre and repeating the parts on each side if the builder prefers such dull monotony.[88]

Malton and Elsam manage to show how an irregular plan can be consistent with an architectural idea and how a style can take on social significations, or not, as their differing ideas have it. However, their designs are often little more than a relaxed symmetry, sometimes with recalcitrant three-part compositions. Gandy is less concerned with irregularity as a concept, but greatly more adept at producing irregular plans. In Gandy's folios we find free asymmetry, symmetries that have been broken or appear incomplete, and buildings that have symmetrical outlines but irregular internal planning. While many of Gandy's designs are regular in a simple sense – not at odds with classical forms – he also has odd unclassical symmetries. One 'Overseer's Cottage' has stables and cow sheds forming wings on a triangular plan. A pair of cottages, most remarkably, is arranged on a dumb-bell-like plan with a bar of low building connecting two drums whose porches splay outwards at about 20 degrees. There is an annular building like a version of Bentham's Panopticon, and a D-shaped range of buildings similar to C. N. Ledoux's Saline de Chaux. I will consider the meaning of these strangely geometrical schemes in a later section, but here, the point is the variety of plan types and figures that Gandy presents.

The pattern books are all advertisements of architectural capacity, but where Malton and Elsam think that plan geometry is a principle to be defined before they exhibit their skills, Gandy treats planning as one more skill he can demonstrate. For instance, he proposes increasing size and room number in housing, as a reward system for labourers and to answer needs at various stages of family size. This is typical of the ideas of the period and similar to

Figure 4.12 Joseph Gandy, 'Four Cottages', 1805.

Figure 4.13 Joseph Gandy, 'Four Cottages', 1805.

the behaviourism Elsam picks up from agriculturalist discourse and prison reform. Gandy then shows how he can combine the variously sized cottages into well-composed irregular buildings of three and four habitations (Figure 4.12). His programme of size graduation does not require gathering housing together, nor does it explain why these picturesque buildings would be set in the landscape rather than in villages. The spurious social aspect of this idea becomes even clearer when Gandy shows that he can also do this 'regular'. He designs a perfectly square plan with four identical façades containing four houses of graduated size and room number (Figure 4.13). Planning constraints, whether scenic ideas of picturesque theory or the Benthamite ideas of reformers, are being treated here as occasions for a ***bravura*** performance of planning. For Gandy, there is no single irregularity opposing the canons of regular architecture; nor is there any direct corollary of irregularity in the appearance of a building. Gandy discovered that regularity and irregularity are variables within planning, specific to it, and by which we can understand the articulation of the plan with other aspects of building.

In the first decades of the nineteenth century, debating the merits of irregular planning became a regular motif of the pattern book essays and design. Proponents of irregularity include Robert Lugar, John Buonarotti Papworth, William Pocock and Edward Gyfford. Those remaining committed to regularity include Plaw, Thomas Dearn, D. Laing and Charles Busby.[89] In their designs and texts, these architects begin to discuss planning in a modern sense. For instance, Laing defends the regular against an 'ingenious artist', probably Malton, by claiming:

> the nearer the plan of a Building approaches to a Square, the greater are its Conveniences, and the Cost proportionally less. A Square . . . requires less external Walling, . . . I have endeavored to make the Building as compact as possible, whereby Convenience is produced, and Expense is saved: when the Apartments are scattered, and lie wide from

> each other, with long Passages, much Unpleasantness must be experienced, and much Expense ensue. . . .[90]

Laing's first point about compactness of the plan is a good one, and does tell of the expense of picturesque ideas as well as what becomes the general issue of plan depth. Laing, however, is a quite poor architect and falsely assumes that internal planning must be inefficient if irregular. Papworth, in justifying an irregular 'Cottage Orné' of his design, puts the matter correctly:

> Plans of this description have the advantage of losing no space by communicating passages, which too commonly increase the magnitude of buildings, and consequently the expense of them, without a corresponding benefit. The absence or spare application of passages constitutes, perhaps, one of the perfections of a plan, provided all the rooms are approachable independently of each other . . .[91]

Laing's book was published in 1800 and Papworth's in 1818. This interval marks the time taken for a modern concept of the plan to emerge from the chrysalis of irregularity. Both Price's irregularity and the room specifications from the Board of Agriculture were first seen as constraints on architecture, making it difficult to maintain a common concept of form for the appearance of the building and the distribution of its spaces. However, across this period, those who followed Price found, as Papworth states, that there were efficiencies and conveniences in irregularity that are parallel with, but distinct from, its scenic effect. Similarly, those architects, such as Elsam, who planned small buildings with the specific room designations and interrelations given by reformers, found that they had produced the irregular picturesque in any case.

Familiarity

Before continuing to discuss the forms and techniques of architectural planning in the pattern books, we need to consider another aspect of housing's social history: the bourgeois household with its reduced room number and servants, and the changed role of women. The idea that agricultural reformers could train and discipline rural labourers through house design seems an historical curiosity. As Michel Foucault and others have shown, these eighteenth-century ideas of an architecture of social discipline are better understood as diagrams and experiments for social roles and organization in the nineteenth century. Foucault shows how the idea of Bentham's Panopticon prison was a basis for disciplinary regimes that use timetables, callisthenics, legal codes and statistics. Conversely, Tony Bennett has shown that the Panopticon did become the model for new kinds of social spaces such as the exhibition and museum.[92] These are not buildings for controlling deviance but for forming the self-awareness of the emerging middle class. In Bennett's 'exhibitionary complex' just as in Walter Benjamin's analysis of retail arcades, we see the origins of the manners and mores appropriate to a new understanding of the city as something made up of public spaces. Following this general history, my point is a simple one: bread ovens and the separation of parents' and children's beds may have had little effect on the lives and behaviour of rural labourers. The same ideas were carried out large-scale in nineteenth-century urban reformed housing, but their effectivity is no clearer. This is because the planning of houses was completely changed by the growth of middle-class housing, which was only a larger and more comfortable version of what was supposed to reform the poor.

The cottage pattern books have something to tell us about this normalization of the single-family house. While most of the books address themselves to aristocratic patrons wishing to build retreats in scenic parts of their great estates, in many cases this is rhetorical ploy to flatter the architects' real clients: the middle class building houses in the suburbs – not only in Britain but also in North America and Australasia, where the books were widely distributed. Traces of this second destination for the books are found in the roles that they imagine for women.

The would-be proprietor of a cottage ornée or villa would have been intending to 'retire' – and if an aristocrat or higher gentry, from public life and office as well as the demands of extensive hospitality. The model of a 'country house' was an aristocratic one, accommodating a number of guests, their personal servants as well as one's own, spaces for large-scale formal entertainment such as balls, and kitchens and stores to service them all. Several of the pattern-book authors feel it necessary to explain what it means to retire. Robert Wetten tells us 'the modern villa in our own land is restricted to the merely necessary living and sleeping rooms'.[93] The villa and genteel cottage formula hinges on a reduction of bedrooms to those of the family alone, and a reduction of public rooms to three – typically a dining room, drawing room and library – to which could be added a breakfast room and conservatory.[94] These were the minimum requirement for ladies' morning receptions and for separating and reunifying the sexes during dining parties. The clients for such 'restricted' houses were, in general, not downsizing aristocrats, but people who could not have afforded a larger home. 'Retirement', in the first decades of the century, was a way of explaining how to use a house in the care of one's self and family, a project encompassed in the new significance that the nineteenth century gave to the word 'comfort'.[95] Pocock describes this brief for the house in a defence of his irregular genteel cottage design.

> The Cabane Ornee, or ornamented Cottage, is a building that owes its origin to the taste of the present day, and though humble in its appearance affords the necessary conveniences for persons of refined manners and habits, and is, perhaps, more calculated than any other description of building for the enjoyment of the true pleasures of domestic life, unincumbered with the forms of state and troublesome appendages. The leading feature of this style of building is to appear in every respect a dwelling calculated for comfort and convenience, without minute attention to the rules of art; every part having its uses apparent, and this appearance not in any case sacrificed to regularity.[96]

Regularity, for Pocock, means 'forms of state', which with their troublesome appendages of large servant numbers, encumber and constrain the pleasures of dwelling. The status that grand country seats of aristocrats expressed through equipage of formal hospitality was not so easily obtained by the middle classes who, in place of this, displayed the freedom to be themselves.

Pocock is not alone in thinking that irregularity can be the sign of this liberal comfort and self-formation. Malton's second book, *Designs for Villas*, begins with a long essay titled 'Reflections on the necessity and advantage of Temporary Retirement', which makes clear that while his villas are too small to entertain, this very lack constitutes another kind of advantage, particularly for women.[97] Malton wants to reassure gentlemen, thinking of building country villas, that their women will tolerate exile from the 'baubles and flattery' of town. He thinks that the female preference for reading rural poetry is a good sign of 'women, even unaided by the strong support of manly countenance, retiring from the busy world, to enjoy the calm and tranquil delights of rural nature; there to spend their time in virtue and mental acquirements.' Women need to retire to country villas because of the distortions put upon them by the town society of men. 'Men make women vain, then censure them for being so; they cripple their minds and bodies then wonder they cannot reason and contend with difficulties.'[98] The pattern books are roughly contemporaneous with the rise of the novel, and when its readership was largely female.[99] The rhetoric of retirement ought to be seen in the light of a new space of feminine sentiments, which was not disconnected from architectural planning, as Papworth points out:

> Until the formalities of earlier times, and the restraints to which females were then subjected by erroneous notions of decorum, were abandoned, the chief apartments has their stations over an elevated basement . . . but as society improved in liberal sentiment, and became more civilized, the fair sex was enabled to repossess their equal share of social freedom, and were permitted the exercise of that brilliant intellect which is their inherent property. On the instant the models of our buildings partook of a corresponding improvement . . .[100]

In this passage, and indeed for most of *Hints on Ornamental Gardening*, Papworth is paraphrasing Repton. As we saw earlier at Luscombe, Repton's idea of ground-floor rooms requires an irregular placement of offices in a highly serviced large house, but such garden-oriented rooms belong almost naturally to the small house without a service basement. Lugar connected these issues in a defence of irregularity when he wrote in his pattern book:

> To buildings of the cottage class, or cottage ornée . . . considerable indulgence should be allowed; and the fastidious should be disarmed of the severity of criticism, when the picturesque and the useful are conveniently and pleasingly united. The windows are brought down nearly level with the ground, (a striking improvement in modern architecture,) give access as well as occasional cheerfulness, to the sitting rooms.[101]

Repton wrote on and was perhaps instrumental in the introduction of modern furnishing and room usage, which he celebrated with a drawing (Figure 4.14) and one of his doggerel verses 'A Modern Living-Room':

> No more the Cedar Parlor's formal gloom
> With dullness chills, 'tis now the Living-Room;
> Where guests, to whim, or taste, or fancy true,
> Scattered in groups their different plans pursue.[102]

The 'Cedar Parlour' is a single function room elevated on the first floor, where conversation is pre-described by its setting and the furniture is arranged in the geometry of the room. Repton's living room, though apparently symmetrical, is used irregularly. Repton was one of the first and most influential designers to place furniture permanently in the centre of rooms, dividing them into territories.[103] The poem goes on to describe possible concurrent uses of political gossip, lovers' dalliance, chess, music, light reading and the study of prints. Apart from the young at heart, the modern living room gives an appropriate setting to the 'curious maid' and serious studies of 'the doctor'. The accompanying drawings show the furniture loosely arranged and the room on the ground floor opening to the garden and conservatory.[104] Repton uses the word 'living-room' self-consciously as the neologism it was at the time.[105] The proposal of a room not for a specific function but for 'living' implies a place for the whole of the self and a liberal interaction between persons in the room, free from social hierarchy. As we have seen, in the reformers' cottage the wife was to be made productive by increased differentiation and specialization of spaces, with a garden and kitchen, and bedrooms for children. The retired gentlewoman works, instead, on her own sentimental education through reading, music and the observation of nature. She can do so because of a reduction in room number and differentiation, which frees her from the role of hostess and leaves her with the intimate company of her own family and chosen friends.

Evans shows that Repton's ideas of interiors can be understood as a rejection of earlier planning strategies and techniques.[106] In the houses of the mid-century, such as Robert Adam's Keddleston, the major floor is a ring of rooms with a variety of forms and décor. The rooms are arranged to open onto one another enfilade: to progress through the circuit contrasts an experience of the overall uniformity of the symmetrical plan with the incident and variety of each room. These would have been furnished in a traditional pattern – chairs placed against the walls, matching each room's wall decoration and repeating the room's plan geometry. The circuit of rooms, elevated above a service floor, looks out to parkland that comes up directly to the house, encompassing it, and makes the view from each room a variation of the same scene, further emphasizing the plan's figure. One of Repton's main innovations in landscape design over the generation of Adam and Lancelot Brown was his insistence on a zone of flower gardens, conservatories and terraces separating house from park, providing a designed external space to which one could go out, and a varied foreground to the view from each room. The point here is not only the contrasting planning manners in large country houses. We must also remember that an architectural idea about the symmetrical plan making a figure in surrounding landscape required a relatively large number of rooms to make up the variety within the figure of the circuit. By contrast, Repton's ideas about furnishing of rooms and their arrangement into suites were entirely scale-able. By emphasizing formed visual experience, the relation of internal and external spaces, and multiple activities and territories within a room, Repton's plan required no recognizable geometric figure and could work with any suite from ten rooms to the three of the suburban villa.[107]

John Claudius Loudon recognized that the cottage villa produced a new kind of common space of domestic life across the social classes, and he writes in his pattern book: 'The great object of this work is to show how the dwellings of the whole mass of society may be equalized in point of all essential comforts, conveniences and beauties'.[108] One of the most important pattern books, Loudon's *Encyclopaedia of Cottage, Farm and Villa Architecture and Furniture*, can also be thought of as the final and definitive work on cottages. It is a massive work of some 1200 pages and 180 designs. First published in 1833, it went through expanding editions until 1846. Unlike the other pattern books, it was cheaply printed in large volumes and widely distributed. The first edition states that it was published in London, Paris, Strasburg, Edinburgh, New York, Boston, Philadelphia, Sydney and Hobart Town. The designs are intended to be suitable for anywhere, but Loudon thought them more likely to be useful in North America and Australia. Loudon exploded the cottage pattern-book genre from within by taking seriously the provision of technical advice on taste, construction and household management. Coming from a background in agricultural improvement, he had relatively little interest in the architectural discourse on style and commissioned architects to work out the appearance of the buildings. He concentrated on marrying an original theory on aesthetics of buildings to his interest in them as devices of social formation and agricultural production. Loudon's politics were quite different to the Board of Agriculture: he saw cottages as an engine, not for social differentiation, but for egalitarianism and colonialism.

Figure 4.14 Humphry Repton, 'Interiors', 1816. By permission of Rare Books and Special Collections, State Library of New South Wales.

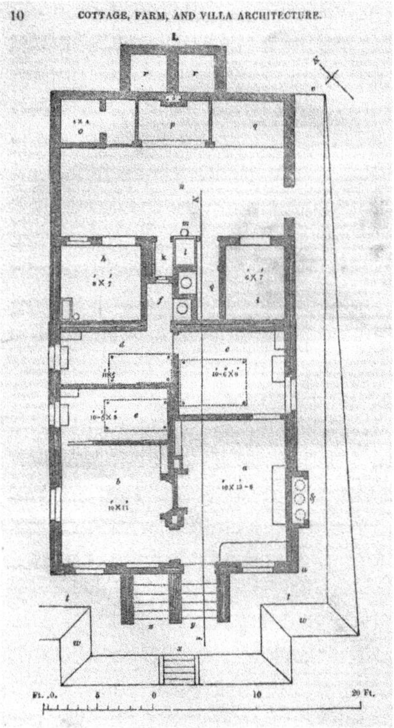

Figure 4.15 J. C. Loudon, 'Cottage', 1833.

> The designs in this book are calculated for what, in a privileged aristocracy, are called the lower and middling classes of society; but which in self-governing democracies like North America, or in newly colonized countries like Australia, constitute nearly the whole rural population. [. . .] In such dwellings every labourer ought to live, and any nobleman might live.[109]

> In countries where all the inhabitants are in possession of equal rights, every industrious individual, not living in a town, will possess a cottage and a garden; and every man who has been successful in his pursuits, and has, by them, obtained pecuniary independence, may possess a villa.[110]

Loudon discusses a generic cottage (Figure 4.15) in some detail, as the other 180 designs are supposedly adaptations of it.[111] It is an object bristling with architectural and agricultural technology: an oven in the basement heats the floors and hot water supply; the roof and grey water are collected in different cisterns; a scratching post is specified in the pig's pen; and the eaves are designed for swallows to nest so that they will hunt wasps. Of particular interest to us is Loudon's extension of the three-bedroom formula: not only does his model allow separate bedrooms for boys and girls, but the girls' room is entered through the parents' while the boys' opens off the living room. Loudon does not put any gloss on this strange arrangement, which suggests a fear of sibling incest. He instead recognizes the problem by equivocating, suggesting that another door between the children's rooms might be convenient so that the girls can go to bed without passing through the parents' rooms. Equally remarkable are the *two* water closets: an internal one for the mother and girls and one in the yard for the father and boys. Loudon feels rightly defensive about the number and expensive construction of these facilities, claiming: 'The liquid manure thus gained will be of so much value to the garden alone, independently of cleanliness and decency, to justify the expense of two closets, and both of these water closets'.[112] In this crazy – although not uncommon – preoccupation with the moral problems and agricultural power of excrement, we can get a sense of the general novelty of applying buildings to the forming of subjects.

The cottage now requires styling. Loudon's *Encyclopaedia* is profusely illustrated with hints on building style. The stylistic ideas are typical of the pattern-book genre and are generally of the rustic, Tudor or Italianate families; the latter being considered appropriately informal and inexpensive versions of the Gothic and classical. The dressing of the cottages, like their planning, was done by numerous architects with varying degrees of editorial control by Loudon, who clearly disapproves of some of them, and who thought, in any case, that architectural style was the last and least important aspect of building design. Style is nevertheless included as an occasion for developing taste, which is part of the whole moral fibre of the person. Loudon thinks that considered reflection on one's preferences will lead to an understanding of architectural principles, and knowledge of these might well foster better building design. If a good – which is to say a self-reflective, rationally developed – taste in architecture can be broadly propagated in a population, then building designs will certainly improve. From this theory of architecture based around education, Loudon draws a conclusion, somewhat startling for the period, that women should study architecture.

> The use of the present work, in improving Domestic Architecture in Britain, America and Australia, will materially depend on its rendering the reading classes architectural critics; and more especially on the influence which it has, in this respect, in improving the taste of women.[113]

It is this educative role of the book that also explains its structure: it begins with designs and proceeds to a concluding section of general principles by way of incidental remarks. This structure will

> render it more attractive to the general reader, as well as being of more immediate practical utility to persons intending to build [. . .] We also consider this mode by far the best adapted for initiating the general reader in the principles of architectural taste; and for enabling young persons, especially ladies, to educate themselves in architecture as an elegant art.[114]

Loudon's model here is gardening. He claims that British gardening's great improvement, in his lifetime, is largely due to women's increased involvement. It is not merely that women began to express preferences in garden design; they trained themselves through the close observation of natural forms in botany and watercolour painting, fitting themselves to make right judgements. It is, thus, for training the eye and hand that Loudon thinks it unavoidable that young women learn ruled drawing and study the orders of columns – which is to say – take on the traditional training of boys apprenticed to architects.

This proposition is a mark of the social progressiveness and originality of Loudon and his wife and collaborator, Jane Webb. However, in its context, this statement of affirmative action is not quite as radical as it might seem to the modern reader. First, it is a logical extension of the idea, broadly observed in the pattern books, that cottages are equipment for women's self-making. Second, what relation contemporary male readers of the *Encyclopaedia* had with architecture was equally equivocal. This is because the profession of architect was at the time rather uncertain, caught as it was between being a model for disinterested gentlemen or for tradesmen, builders and speculative investors. This is clear in the book as a whole as much as in the quoted statements. Unlike the other architect authors, Loudon is not exhibiting his talent in the hope of commissions; he is attempting to give the reader architectural skills. Loudon imagines the sophisticated amateurship of aristocracy extending to the middle classes, allowing them to make highly informed and detailed commissions of buildings. Apart from major artists conducting great public works, domestic architecture would largely exist defused through the property-owning public and in their relations with builders. In this, Loudon was prescient in part: in the villa suburbs of late nineteenth-century North America and Australasia, many families did indeed have their cottage and garden for produce, a universal equipage for domestic life, across which was splashed a light stylistic diversity. But Loudon was overly optimistic about the penetration of architectural knowledge and skill, and the economic circumstances that would allow homemakers to take command of their houses' designs. He could not, similarly, have predicted that the profession of architecture would institutionalize quite as it did and that the small house would continue as a site of experiment in architectural forms that have little or nothing to do with domestic life.

Plan-form and style

Thus far I have explained how irregular planning emerged in the picturesque and what this meant in terms of the functional specification of reformers; the view specificity of the aesthetes; the fashion for ground-floor rooms and the problems this made for service spaces; and the values of a private life of women with their families that come to be attached to a 'reduced' house. It might seem at this point that irregularity is the epitome of good planning and historical triumph of rationality over custom in architecture, but this is far from the case.

It is remarkable to a modern reader how much the rare discussion of functional planning in the first decades of the nineteenth century is made in the terms of visual appearance. Malton, for instance, sees the convenient arrangement of internal rooms as a way of disrupting regularity. 'One point, however, principally to be regarded by those, who are desirous to build picturesque rural dwellings: which is – never to *aim* at regularity, but to let the outward figure conform only to the internal conveniency'.[115] Lugar advises the irregular planner that 'the varied or broken line should arise from apparent wants, from the necessity of the case, and not for the sake of merely destroying a continued line'.[116] Loudon is more sophisticated. In a section of the *Encyclopaedia* entitled 'On the Expression of Architectural Style', he makes insightful summations of the literature we have discussed and anticipates much of what will become functional expression in twentieth-century architecture. In the section, 'Of the Expression of the End in View, in Architecture', he recommends that the volume of rooms and their use determine their fenestration. He values those parts of the plan that generate specific forms:

> turrets and projections of every kind viewed with reference to use, convey the idea of commodiousness and convenience; it being supposed that their object, in modern houses, is to supply closets and cabinets, and other minor apartments. A square house may have all these conveniences included in its cubical form; and they may have cost

> less, in building, than if they had been contained in projections: but the cubical form will give no indication of their existence to the external spectator.[117]

Loudon was also the first to explain clearly what is implicit in the work of talented irregular designers like Gandy, Papworth and Lugar: that irregularity is not simply formless, nor a kind of formlessness made legible by use. Irregularity can have its own norm – we now call this 'balanced asymmetry'. Loudon agrees with Price who thinks that symmetrical planning risks 'insipidity'; that irregular planning allows for contrast, which produces variety; and that this variety can be harmonious:

> For example, if to add some variety to the outline of a building, in which a square tower rose above a roof, a circular tower were added beside it, of the same height and general size, the effect would be discord; because the two objects, being of the same kind, of the same bulk, and at the same distance from the eye would present equal claims to attention: while, from the total difference in their forms, that attention would be divided. Let, however, the circular tower be either of the same diameter as the square one and raised only a few feet above the roof; or, let it be the same height as the square one and only a few feet in diameter, and the effect will be variety. . . .[118]

As I showed in the previous section, Loudon saw the house as a highly functional piece of equipment and understood how this might help form a way of life and a sense of self. The quotations just made show how this functional equipage might become architectural expression and a culture of forms. So it seems that we are very close, in 1833, to modern architecture. This is the case, at least, at a conceptual level. Factors the pattern-book architects identify begin the development of techniques and criteria of planning that will form the basis of modern architecture. This history, however, is occluded because the concept of planning opens mainly towards the formation of styles. Although Loudon's remarks seem prescient of modernism, they occur in a section on architectural criticism at the back of his fat *Encyclopaedia*, which is packed with drawings of buildings in a bewildering variety of fanciful styles. The many architects' contributions that illustrate the *Encyclopaedia* cause Loudon's thinking to be framed within the stylistic pluralism of nineteenth-century architecture. Price and Knight write about architecture in quite abstract terms. They certainly prefer a language of visual effects to any discussion of codified style. Their examples, however, are not obscure. Architects who turned to them quickly developed stylistic formal languages. These styles, in turn, constrain and develop planning techniques. Knight's references to buildings in the background of paintings by Claude led to the Italianate, and Price's remarks on old mansions and village houses led to the Old English/Tudor and later Queen Anne styles.

Repton's architect sons, John Adey and George Stanley, who worked for Nash, were instrumental in taking up the Pricean line of thought, of which Malton has been our principal example thus far. It is most likely that George, supervised to some extent by his employer, designed the rustic thatched cottages at Blaise Castle Hamlet (Figure 4.16) which were thought of by Humphry and Nash in 1799 but probably not designed until built, 1810–12.[119] These small irregular cottages were alms-houses gifted by Repton's client Hartford to the local village for the use of aged paupers. Some of the discourse of agricultural reform is apparent in the bread ovens and vegetable gardens with which each cottage is equipped and the communal pump onto which they look. However, Hartford was in trade and Blaise, just out of Bristol, was a grand suburban residence not an agricultural estate. The

Hamlet, consequently, is a self-conscious scenic passage within Humphry's landscape design rather than a model for housing reform. George was a talented designer – the cottages are substantial stone buildings sensibly organized on relaxed irregular plans, made more fanciful through complex roof forms and exaggerated chimneys. The houses are organized in a loose ring facing one another across a rolling green, with the rear of each house opening onto a private garden. The designs all offer the same spatial provisions, but as buildings they are greatly varied in form and features: some present gables, others hipped roofs; one offers a covered seat to the common green, another a dovecot. There is less variation of material than Malton imagined with rubble stonework and only a little weatherboard. The Hamlet was an instant critical and popular success and engravings of it are the origin of much sentimental cottage imagery in popular culture today.

John Adey Repton was less successful as an architect, but he did design a house in the style of the reign of Henry VIII in the estate of Woburn Abbey as a part of his father's commission, which is significant.[120] The building has similarities with Malton's Design 7 (see Figure 4.10), a size appropriate for a substantial farmer or manager. It has the room equipage of a villa or ornamental cottage, and its character is created through its gabled roof-form and faux half-timbered construction. Far more influential was Endsleigh Cottage, the Devon retreat of the 6th Duke of Bedford. The Reptons produced a sketch for the 'Endsleigh Cottage' in 1809, but the commision went to Sir Jeffry Wyatville, for a similar but more elaborate design built from 1810 to 1814, when Humphry was commissioned for a design of the grounds.[121] Endsleigh is a major mansion on a rambling accretionary plan, which nearly manages the conceit of appearing to be so many cottages and remnant medieval buildings stuck together. Of all the picturesque buildings actually constructed at the beginning of the nineteenth century, perhaps it is Endsleigh that most fulsomely fulfills Price's ideas. It is not only determined from the landscape but makes the kind of transcoding of cultural hierarchies which he admired. However, the size of Endsleigh in comparison to its image makes it formally difficult for modern eyes. It seems too eighteenth century, its style too obviously whimsical – a pretense intended to be discovered. The clearer demonstration of what would come are later pattern books in the Pricean mode, probably inspired by Endsleigh and perhaps also by Malton, such as those of Francis Goodwin and Robinson, whose *Village Architecture* we examined in the last chapter.[122] Robinson and Goodwin are very interested in features, particularly decorated barge boards and elaborate chimney stacks often with barley-sugar twisted chimney pots, supposedly Tudor inspired, which John Repton used at Woburn Cottage. Architecture such as this is very close to what would develop in the Old English style, and would become the base vocabulary of the Arts and Crafts movement, but it lacks an ethic of place. Robinson, for instance, having travelled in Switzerland and designed several Swiss cottages (including one that a district of London is named for), had no difficulty blending Swiss elements with his vision of rural Britain. Later architects would expect that forms and details of construction would belong to, and be authorized by, connections with particular places and their materials and crafts. But for Robinson and Goodwin, there was no ethic of style; their choice of features and forms is entirely picturesque.

Anthony Salvin carried this line of architectural thought forward. He had most likely worked for Nash, and produced a Blaise-like cottage to accompany his fanciful Gothic Mamhead Park from 1825.[123] But Salvin quickly turned from the purely pictorial values and sentimental associationism of the eighteenth-century picturesque to hybrid styles of Tudor and Jacobean, such as Harlaxton Hall (from 1831) and Scotney Castle (from 1837). This approach gave a role for authenticity within a largely free vocabulary amenable to being

Figure 4.16 John Nash (with George Repton), Cottage at Blaise Castle Hamlet, Henbury near Bristol, c. 1811.

Figure 4.17 John Buonarotti Papworth, 'A Villa' also referred to as 'Residence for an Artist', 1818.

Figure 4.18 Charles Parker, 'Residence for a small family', 1832. La Trobe Rare Books Collection, State Library of Victoria.

composed. Richard Norman Shaw was briefly apprenticed to Salvin, and later in the century we see the return of the regionalist and vernacular elements of the picturesque in Shaw's use of half-timbering, pan-tiled wall cladding and crazed chimney stacks on both grand country houses and suburban developments. More to the point of our current enquiry, Shaw was a brilliant planner, and a grand house such as Cragside (1869–85) has interior scenography almost cinematic in its determination of visual experience. This is a discussion to which we will return.

In 1802, Nash built a house, Cronkhill, in the grounds of Attingham (another of Repton's make-overs) that was irregular but clearly not rustic. Cronkhill has an arched colonnaded portico topped with classical balustrading, but this horizontal element is balanced in an asymmetrical way by a dominant tower that is round and appears as if it were the remnant of a fortification. As in vernacular building, the eaves of the roof are expressed with protruding rafters, but the whole is finished in clean render. Cronkhill was built before the publication of Knight's *Analytical Inquiry*, first published in 1805, but the tradition of a Grand Tour of Italy meant that there was already interest in the idea that Knight connected to the picturesque.[124] Lugar published a design for an 'Italian Villa' in his *Architectural Sketches* of 1805. It has a tall tower engaged with a low gable-roofed house and, like Nash, has some classical elements in a non-canonical composition.[125] Papworth has a much more sophisticated version as Plate 17 of his *Rural Residences* of 1818 shows.[126] He calls this a 'Residence for an Artist' (Figure 4.17) and in the explanatory text refers to the seventeenth-century painters. The style of the building is remarkable. The dominant tower with a belvedere is a clearer model than Nash's or Lugar's for the later Italianate houses, but the planar walls, clerestory windows, and shallow hipped roof with extending eaves are prescient of the Prairie style houses of Frank Lloyd Wright.[127] The first pattern book devoted entirely to this style is T. F. Hunt's *Architettura Campestre* of 1827, which is curious on account of Hunt's claim that the Italian is inferior to native British architecture, an inferiority which Hunt does not fail to demonstrate. A more interesting book is *On the Landscape Architecture of the Great Painters of Italy*, in which Gilbert Laing Meason, who was not an architect but a gentleman, took Knight literally, producing views of buildings from the backgrounds of particular paintings. The most successful of the Italianate pattern books is that of Charles Parker, a talented designer and illustrator, who took actual buildings in Rome and Florence as models for his *Villa Rustica* of 1832.[128] Parker's 'Residence for a small family' (Figure 4.18), developed from a lodge in the gardens of the Villa Borghese, is a charming composition of a small house with campanile, set on extensive formal terraces within a larger, wilder landscape.

For the pattern-book architects and their clients, the Italianate style offered two advantages. It was a safe picturesque for those concerned about the significations of poverty in the rustic style. Perhaps more importantly, it allowed the use of familiar and prestigious classical ornament, but in an economical mode, as accents within a picturesque whole; it did not oblige full arcades of columns with capitals and the like. For instance, Papworth's house for an artist has a little arcade of engaged pilasters with capitals at its entrance; Lugar has one halfway up his campanile; while Parker has primitive Serilian windows and balustrading. In compositions with large amounts of unadorned surface and where the other features are vernacular, such as eaves and brackets, these classical elements have the appearance of Italian medieval buildings where spoils of an ancient past have been incorporated into a humble building. For these reasons of design flexibility and relative economy, Italianate became one of the main sources for domestic architecture in the nineteenth century. Equally important, however, is that it was taken up as an academic style by Charles Barry. Barry's travels in Italy convinced him of the merits of early Renaissance architecture. In the Travellers Club of 1829–31, he made popular 'Renaissance Revival', modelled on Florentine palazzi that used compositions of cornices and architraves rather than high Renaissance (or Greek) colonnades and pediments. Barry applied these ideas to Trentham Hall, Staffordshire, 1834–42, a grand country house on an irregular picturesque plan. Trentham was the model for Prince Albert and Thomas Cubbitt's design for Osbourne House, Isle of Wight, and the royal connection gave the Italianate style enormous prestige.

Having quickly sketched the history of how Price's and Knight's ideas became distinct styles, it is also important to remember that this distinction came to mean little more than the variety that the picturesque proposed in the first place. The dissolution of style into a means of producing variety is apparent in one of the most influential sets of picturesque buildings: Nash's Park Villages (Figure 4.19). Nash rebuilt a large part of London on picturesque principles from 1811, when he obtained the commission for what would become Regent's Park and Street.[129] Urban issues are discussed in the next chapter, but the point of introducing Nash here is that, in 1823, he purchased an unpromising patch of land at the end of the Park that the new Regent's Canal ran through. On this he built a speculative housing scheme styled as Park Village East and West, made up of largely detached single dwellings in gardens looking onto the canal, as if it were a landscape feature rather than urban infrastructure. In the first proposal, Nash makes clear he wants to adapt the design of the paupers' cottages at Blaise Castle Hamlet to the middle-class housing market. By the time the Villages were constructed in 1828, however, they were a deliberate mixture of rustic cottage and Italianate villa styles. Here, style is no longer what Repton and the theorists had supposed, that is, a reflection and articulation of landscape setting; the profusion of forms that branch from the two main picturesque styles has become the space in which picturesque variety can be maintained in a suburb. The Park Villages are, perhaps, the first suburb in the modern sense; they were widely circulated in images of the London Improvements. Decimus Burton, the son of Nash's business partner and trained in Nash's office, made such suburbs the basis of his practice, starting with Calvery Estate, Tunbridge Wells, from 1828.

Figure 4.19 John Nash, Tower House, Park Village East, London, c. 1826.

When histories of architecture tell of the 'Battle of the Styles' in nineteenth-century architecture, Cottage and Italianate styles are footnotes to larger issues raised by Greek and Gothic. It is correct that the most important conceptual innovation of nineteenth-century architecture was a concept of morality in style, at first strongly associated with the Gothic. A. W. N. Pugin's bold identification of Gothic with Catholicism and a vision of the social justice of medieval society completely changed the register of architectural forms from taste and visual pleasure to right and wrong. Ruskin's more sophisticated historicism found the morality of architecture in its materiality and the role that construction gave to building workers. Pugin's and Ruskin's ethically based formalism linked the rationalist tradition of architecture into issues of social formation fundamental to modernism. If the theory of style sat largely on the side of the Gothic, its mechanism was archaeological and classical. The impact of archaeology in architecture begins with eighteenth-century attempts to confirm classical doctrines empirically, in the measurement of ruins, and reaches an apogee mid-century with Julien-David Le Roy's and then James Stuart and Nicholas Revett's folios on ancient Athenian architecture.[130] A new concept of architectural history based on evidence and stylistic classification resulted from such ventures. This mechanism was extended to Gothic with Thomas Rickman developing a nomenclature for English Gothic in 1815.[131] Picturesque architecture of the first decades of the nineteenth century seems largely irrelevant to these developments because of its basis in the discourse on taste rather than morality, and because its stylistic adventures were not greatly constrained by historical evidence. A curious design in Greek picturesque style by James Thomson can help us see the historical forces at work.

Thomson was a pupil of Papworth, who in 1826, published one of the first analyses of the visual qualities of the Parthenon.[132] Papworth concentrates on the proportions, massing and lighting of the temples. Ignoring the Erechtheion with its irregular porch and the apparent disordered siting of the temples, Papworth concludes that: 'The principles alluded to in all the foregoing observations are applicable throughout the vast field of regular architecture'.[133] However, Papworth was an adept of irregular planning, as plain in his earlier pattern books, and he might well have seen further possibilities. His essay was an introduction to a new edition of William Chambers' *Civil Architecture*, and as Chambers hated the Greeks and irregularity, Papworth's essay was already quite presumptuous. It cannot be a coincidence that Papworth's one-time pupil, Thomson, in his pattern book of 1827, conducted an experiment of irregularly planned villas in Greek style, including the remarkable 'Irregular House' (Figures 4.20 and 4.21) about which he writes:

> To the preceding observations concerning irregular buildings may be added, that they also convey the appearance of greater magnitude than they actually possess, by the successive disclosure of their features to the view. Each elevation in this design differs from the rest. The portico forms a striking object in the entrance front. A tower-like appearance is assumed on the west side. To the north a colonnade presents itself; and the east side is relieved by a rotunda. If viewed at either angle a portion of each would be seen perspectively, and create great variety of outline. The plan is also designed to produce similar effect on the interior. The breadth of the portico is immediately contrasted by a gallery-like entrance to the house, which, connected as it is with the staircase, forms a vista the whole depth of the building.[134]

Because of its combination of classical elements, Thomson's design has more of the taut and dissonant irregularity of Gandy or Gyfford than Papworth's relaxed informality. It places

Figure 4.20 James Thomson, 'Irregular House', 1827.

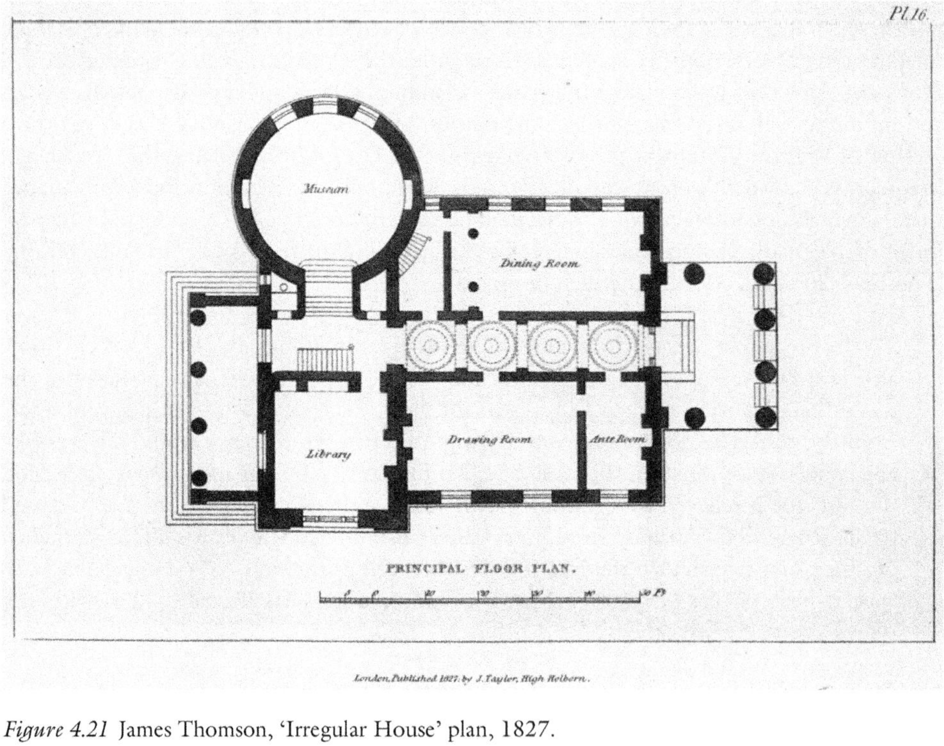

Figure 4.21 James Thomson, 'Irregular House' plan, 1827.

Figure 4.22 Robert Kerr, 'Elizabethan Style Revived', 1864.

Figure 4.23 Robert Kerr, 'Rural-Italian Style', 1864.

picturesque principles of composition directly at odds with formal principles of style, as Alexander Thomson would later do in his Glasgow churches.[135] James Thomson's work seems an historical anomaly because he was taking new archaeological knowledge back into the aesthetic manner of the early decades of the century. But the early date of the Greek picturesque of Papworth and Thomson is important because the idea is usually associated with Auguste Choisy's *History of Architecture* of 1899, one of the sources of Le Corbusier's modernism.

The stronger thread of picturesque architecture re-emerges in the latter part of the nineteenth century when the moral strictures and archaeological constraints of Gothic and Greek relax into hybrid styles such as Jacobean, Queen Anne and Italianate. These were the stylistic inheritance of the picturesque, of Nash, Robinson, Parker and the like. The reason for the success of such hybrid styles was their flexibility in planning. By mid-century Pugin had reached the view that picturesqueness should not be understood as a value or aim in design, but rather as the symptom of successful irregular planning:

> when modern architects avoid this defect of regularity, they frequently fall into one equally great with regard to irregularity; I mean, when a building is designed to be picturesque, by sticking as many ins and outs, ups and downs, about it as possible. *The picturesque effect of the ancient buildings result from ingenious methods by which the old builders overcame local and constructive difficulties.* An edifice which is arranged with the principal view of looking picturesque, is sure to resemble an artificial waterfall, or a made-up rock [. . .] all these inconsistencies have arisen from this great error – *the plans of buildings are designed to suit the elevation instead of the elevation being made subservient to the plan.*[136]

Kerr's book, *The English Gentleman's House* of 1864, is perhaps the first comprehensive book on architectural planning. It lays out clearly most of what was implicit in the pattern books, explaining the principles of plan efficiency in relation to floor area and circulation patterns. With its strong focus on service spaces and on discrete circulation for servants within a grand house, Kerr anticipates modern ideas of the plan being driven by a double determination of spatial planning and servicing strategies. If we forget for a moment that what is being organized is the bizarre social engine of the English country house, Kerr seems rigorously rational and functionalist. We can see this in his anxious and confused comments on style. Kerr thinks the choice of style is fundamentally important, but that this choice sits with the client, who ought to be confident that his architect can do any style he settles on. What is of interest to us is that Kerr explains how the different styles interact with the building's planning, which is where the true expertise of the architect lies. The Elizabethan and Rural Italian styles are Kerr's preference (Figures 4.22 and 4.23), although he describes no less than ten. Each is described in relation to the criteria of: 'Situation; Scale of building; Materials; Comparative cost; Comparative importance; Ornamental character; The use of Style internally; Influence upon the interior plan.'[137] It is the last criterion that is the most significant for Kerr, which is not surprising as three-quarters of the book concerns the functional criteria for internal planning. On the Elizabethan – after a stiff warning on the differing social forms of the nineteenth century and the foolishness of imitating Elizabethan room uses and furnishings – Kerr writes: 'The style admits of any amount of utilitarian irregularity; and this is all in favour of a convenient plan'.[138] The classical Palladian style, by contrast, is a 'manner derived directly from the antique of Italy, and adapted to modern house-building but clumsily, – graceful often, stately always, but constrained by symmetries and regularities often too heavy to bear'.[139] Kerr recommends that those with classical taste should turn, instead, to 'a rural manner of the same type as the last, but free from its restraints, and therefore, as based immediately upon modern wants, thus far both theoretically and practically perfect'.[140]

It is incorrect to understand the nineteenth-century discourse on style as having halted or slowed the relation of plan and visual experience of building, which began in the picturesque and became important in modernism. Codification of styles allowed architects to understand, at yet another level, that there are distinct planning modes and strategies determining the building envelope, suiting some styles and not others. Rural Italian, Elizabethan and Cottage styles might have had quite different associations for a lay viewer, but for an architect they had common planimetrics, and were cheaper and more functional than a Palladian design. Through the nineteenth century, planning developed into the meta-discipline of architecture: that abstract space in which everything seen, used and felt is organized.

Picturesque architecture and form

Styles became the medium in which picturesque composition developed. Through the nineteenth century, with its interest in archaeological sources and debates about the morality of styles, questions about the visual form of architecture became subsumed under other terms. For this reason, there is some sense in seeing the 1840s as the end of the story of picturesque architecture. However, twentieth-century modernist architectural theorists returned to the picturesque with gusto. This is only partly explained by their distaste for the nineteenth century and their antipathy to the discourse of styles. Nikolaus Pevsner saw the picturesque as modernism *avant la lettre*. From the 1940s for three decades Pevsner, and the journal the *Architectural Review* (*AR*), had an explicit programme to recover the picturesque as a progenitor of modernism. They thought that the Englishness of the picturesque might make modernism popular and that its impure aesthetic would better fit with existing city fabric; a process they called Townscape. I discuss their work in Chapter 5,

'Appropriation'. However, by the 1950s, neo-avant-gardists such as Peter Reyner Banham had begun attacking Pevsner and the *AR* for what they saw as a popularist betrayal of modernism. In defence, Pevsner gave a lucid account of the picturesque as a modern planning technique. He did this as early as 1947,[141] but in the article 'Twentieth Century Picturesque' of 1954, he goes a step further claiming that irregular planning is the prerequisite to functionalism and exists at a more basic historical level than questions of appearance. In answering Basil Taylor's accusation that the *AR* was promoting a Victorian Revival that could not meet the conditions of modern society, Pevsner writes:

> But the 'real determinants' of planning are exactly argument in favour of the picturesque in the twentieth century. The argument runs in my opinion something like this. If one looks at the work of the pioneers of twentieth century architecture, say as early as about 1925, Gropius' Bauhaus at Dessau or better still Le Corbusier's Stuttgart houses of 1927 and his Centrosoyus project of 1929, what are their aesthetic qualities? First those that everyone is familiar with; cubic shapes, no mouldings, large openings and so on. But in addition the free grouping of the individual buildings, a mixture of materials synthetic and natural, rough and smooth, and, beyond that, the free-planning of the whole quarter, with differentiation of levels, differentiation of vehicular traffic and pedestrian ways, with interaction between building and landscape (the tree inside the *Pavilion de Esprit Nouveau*), and between buildings of different shapes and heights. Do not these qualities define the difference between the free exercise of the imagination stimulated by the disciplines of function and technique (e.g. Wright's 'in the nature of materials') and academic rule of thumb, within whose strait-jacket architecture was confined before the modern movement set it free? And do they not show that, albeit unconsciously, the modern revolution of the early twentieth century and the picturesque revolution of a hundred years before had their fundamentals in common?[142]

If Pevsner and other modernists were merely interested in planning as a technique, then the nineteenth-century developments of irregularity (perhaps George Edmund Street or Richard Norman Shaw and later Edwin Lutyens) would have much more to say than the eighteenth-century picturesque about functionalism and the aesthetic of route-based planning. What continued to interest modern architects, however, was not so apparent under the weight of nineteenth-century ornament and the picturesque has remained of interest for that reason. The idea of relatively undecorated rambling buildings apparently determined by site or use is clear in the aesthetes' texts, and in many of the pattern books. The fact that few such buildings were constructed before the wave of historicism has kept the idea open to the imagination. The main thrust of this chapter has been the history of the plan. However, I am enough of an architect, and an adept of the picturesque, to think that one can and should make a description of the formal characteristics of picturesque architecture – putting aside, momentarily, the historical and cultural issues giving rise to irregularity.

It is not, in fact, difficult to make a caricature of picturesque buildings. These should be an open set of parts to be supplemented or reduced, as Knight suggests. They should avoid continuous wall areas, and the edges of space should be layered, framed and often open at the corners, as Price's 'recession' and variety imply. Some parts being dominant and others subsidiary, there should be a sense of directionality – of the building facing the landscape. At least, the back should be different to the front. There are some other simple tricks specific to the plan. Picturesque buildings should have long perimeters for their plan area. They should extend in one main direction, preferably across the topography, to emphasize the rise and fall of the land. There should be some points of return in the plan so that it is possible to view the exterior of the building from within. Visible roofs are good in the picturesque because their intersection and overlap with walls makes for variety. Roofs can make the plan visible as their rise and fall indicates plan depth, and so a picturesque building will have a roof plan that differs from the floor plan, generally a roof that is more complex. In fact, I think that much of picturesque architecture from 1800 to the present is simply the caricatured application of such a formula, whether in the Rural Italian style, or the regionalist modernism so prevalent in present-day Australia.

Now, a picturesque architect would say that a building cannot be designed to such a prescription, with a formal outcome in mind; that everything I describe is only picturesque if it is caused by real determinations of site and viewing positions. The strong visual empiricism of the picturesque means that any list of features, such as I have described, will be insufficiently specific. A formal description of picturesque architecture is not possible, as a description of objects in space, because it does not include sequence and duration, the concrete time of visual experience implicit in everything discussed so far. But this is not the case. Weakness, complexity and the obscuration of form have effects beyond the deteminations that they enact or fail to enact.

When Price and Knight walked about the countryside, their experience of the picturesque was not a visual experience strongly formed pictorially. As I explain in Chapter 2, a degree of framing and composed recession was in play, but to a large degree their experience was pictorial in the nominalist sense – what they saw matched the topics and hierarchies of the genres of painting; and in the purely visual sense – what they saw recalled the facture or visual texture of artists' paint handling. Their experience, however, was also formed in another way, which has little to do with pictures. A picturesque stroll forms by virtue of the sequence of what is seen; it has form in the sense that music has form in sequence and duration. A closer example is non-narrative forms of cinema. We can assume these perceptual issues are at stake in the picturesque because, although Price and Knight are not explicit about durational vision, they were writing about landscape design. The whole point of a designed landscape is to give form to the sequence, duration and variety of experience. In the next chapter, we will look more closely at how Repton worked with and wrote about such ideas, but my point here is a smaller one: picturesque writers began their theory in a critique of the landscaping style of Lancelot Brown. What they dislike about Brown's work is that it is too self-evidently formed, too visible as an object; it becomes 'the park' that one looks at, even when within it. A picturesque park should help us see as landscape painters saw, and therefore its form should not demand attention. While the picturesque is famous for the idea of forming phenomenal experience, the majority of its work lies in the simpler matter of weakening the form of the object so as to foreground subjective experience.

It is a simple equation that the picturesque proposes: weaken the form of the object to foreground the forming of phenomenal experience.

The classical ideal of symmetry is not only geometrical; it strives for an overall coordination of the whole. It also implies a kind of stillness or indifference to the time taken in attending to it. What Price thought was lack of variety in classical architecture was exactly what an architect such as Palladio sought. When walking towards Palladio's Villa Fascari, the view one sees implies every other view one will have, because much of the plan, particularly the breadth and depth of the building, but also its internal circulation, is made intelligible in the view. One does not have to be able to deduce every particular from the front elevation, but the plan must be sufficiently intelligible to provide a mental structure on which perceptions can be placed. One view gives us a concept of the building to which all of our subsequent examinations will be added, giving colour and depth of experience to an initial impression. The building that we see we are recognizing; all our viewing is at a certain level the same. Being self-aware of this produces an affect of bodily and mental stasis. For Burke, this loosening of the nerve cords causes beauty. For Price, it causes insipidity and boredom.

Price's idea that rooms should turn to face different views was intended to produce a building more like a natural object, such as a rocky outcrop. The natural form is weaker; it lacks an overall identifiable figure containing and governing its particularities. Price thought that such objects aroused the visual senses more strongly. Architects such as Nash and Soane, and some of the pattern-book architects, realized that not only the views out but the views from space to space within the building could determine its overall plan figure; that the plan could be an internal landscape. The picturesque architect attends to the direction of movement and sight like the gardener whose rule is to never let the foot travel the path of the eye.[143] Architects might reveal the foot of a stair or ramp but leave its destination unclear; or conversely, a destination such as an upper-level balcony is revealed but its access must be discovered. Spaces of varied scale open onto one another. Often these scales are illusory, constructed by contrasting light, the recession of forms and the complication of edges. Picturesque planning is based on withholding and revealing spatial information and emphasizing visual unities. Buildings are not caves any more than gardens are nature, and as in picturesque landscape gardens, there is often a privileged point in a plan where the whole organization of the building is revealed. The point of revealing this is to show that overall comprehensive knowledge was not required to use and enjoy the plan.

Some architects of a picturesque persuasion would say that planning based on a system is 'formalism', by which they mean it is false and artificial. They would say that the only test of planning is visual experience: what is seen from where and under what circumstances. The plan as a whole cannot be seen; it has no meaning as a totality. It is merely the contingent sum of what has been planned. Naturalism such as this is in the spirit of the picturesque but it lacks a critical distance and risks collapse into the kind of 'lite' phenomenology that the picturesque is often taken to be. Committed as I am to a formal description of the picturesque, I think that we should see the matter the other way around. Knowledge of the plan competes with self-conscious experience. The less we are able to understand our spatio-visual experience through the abstract coordinates of the plan, the more we are thrust back into a lived experience of the building in duration. A simple and identifiable outline figure of the plan is the biggest danger to the picturesque effect. It needs to be obscured because it allows one to gauge the building's geometry and overall dimensions; to deduce the number, position and sequence of rooms. Picturesque architecture is, in fact, close to the letter of Price: complicating, obscuring and thus weakening the outline of the plan will draw attention to the experience of the spaces in duration, *whether or not* these have been carefully planned in a picturesque scenography. The views out of the building to the landscape and to adjacent external areas, such as the terraces and formal gardens favoured by Price and Repton (and so similar to the spatial extension discovered by modernists), have another role in planning. It is not simply that the plan contorts in response to external landscape, but that in doing so, in making local unities of inside and outside, the figure of the plan outline is further reduced. The difference between the picturesque and un-picturesque is not, in the end, about the problems and limits of the concept of form, but about what is formed. Picturesque architects weaken intelligibility of the object-form of the building to form more strongly the experience of space.

Triangularity

An historical oddity allows us to continue this discussion of form, although in, perhaps, an unexpected direction. At the same time that the pattern-book architects developed irregular plans, they also began a new interest in symmetry, designing buildings with perfectly square, polygonal and circular plans. Such projects can be partly understood as classicism turning rebarbative in reaction to picturesque aformality. At the same time, we should understand these projects as a new interest in the empirical experience of symmetry. If the thoroughgoing visual empiricism of the picturesque is possible, then geometric shapes ought to have no particular power. Is it possible to have a building of strong form that does not contain and prescribe one's experience of it? This seems to be the question asked, particularly in a number of attempts at planning in a most unclassical geometry: the triangular.

I mentioned earlier that Malton's second book, *Rural Retreats*, is rigorously uniform. It seems reasonable to conclude that Malton was retreating from the controversy aroused by the irregularity of his *British Cottage Architecture*. But the symmetry that Malton exhibits in *Rural Retreats* is not a classical symmetry of repose and propriety. It is novel and rather forced as we see in designs for a dairy, a villa and a museum on triangular plans. About the villa, Malton writes:

> The construction of a dwelling on a triangular plan, does not rest as a matter of taste merely: it may be a case of necessity; aptly contriving it becomes therefore an object of important consideration. The chief obstacles in the formation are, making easy access to the various apartments, and preventing the loss of room by unavoidable corners.[144]

How could triangularity have been a necessity? What inescapable determinants can there be for a free-standing triangular building? Malton was not alone in his efforts – other pattern-book architects who tested their skills on the triangle include Elsam, Gandy, Gyfford, Lugar and Laing.[145] This fashion for the triangular probably resulted directly or indirectly from the Abbe Laugier. Marc-Antoine Laugier was the most influential architectural theorist of neo-classicism. In his *Essai sur l'architecture* of 1753 he writes:

> one might give to churches all imaginable forms; it is even good not to make them all of one plan. All geometrical figures from the triangle to the circle may serve to vary without ceasing the composition of these sort of buildings. It would be without doubt a great set-off, if in a city as Paris, there was not one church that resembled any other, if they all had something particular in the form, worthy to draw the curious attention and to entertain the minds of connoisseurs.[146]

David Watkin has shown that Soane's ideas about architecture were greatly influenced by Laugier, and around 1800, Soane built a triangular church at Tyringham.[147] He also built a triangular Arc for the Masonic Convenant in 1811, and the Soane archive contains triangular designs for pavilions, palaces and memorials. There are earlier British precedents for triangular buildings, notably Thomas Tresham's Triangular Lodge of 1596, and James Gibbs' Gothic Temple at Stowe of 1741.[148] Watkin thinks, however, that Soane's interest in the triangular was confirmed by his purchase, in 1810, of a book of drawings by John Thorpe (1564/5–1655), which contained various highly geometricized plan forms. Thorpe copied some of these directly from Jacques Androuet du Cerceau.[149] Soane's Lecture V to the Royal Academy, in 1819, refers to John Thorpe and illustrates a triangular plan enclosing a central hexagonal court.[150] While some of these earlier uses of triangular plans are symbolic of the Trinity (Tresham's certainly is), their place within a gamut of polygonal plans suggests an overarching interest in the plan as figure, whether that figure is allegorical or not. What is interesting here is Laugier's completely non-Platonic, empirical account of the visual interest of variety resulting from employment of the triangular plan.

Apart from Soane, and in some ways a more likely contemporary source for triangular designs in the pattern books, was Price's seaside retreat 'Castle House' at Aberystwyth. The only remaining evidence of the villa is a crude view in the collection of the Victoria and Albert Museum. Price had the house designed by Nash in 1797 and he wrote of the process in a letter to a friend:

> he had a mind to build me a larger house indeed, but a square bit of architecture. I told him however, that I must have, not only some of the windows but some of the rooms turned to particular points . . .[151]

Pricean theory would suggest that an irregular building would result, and it is likely that his dealings with Nash were the basis of Price's advice published in the *Essays* on how to instruct an architect in irregularity by insisting on specific room orientations. What Price neglects to mention in either the letter or the *Essays* is that the house Nash designed was not irregular, but a tri-polar star. While a 'square bit of architecture' might not have answered Price's request for view specificity, Nash had found another geometry that did.

Laing gives a slightly fuller explanation of the advantages of triangularity in his pattern book. A committed enemy of irregularity, Laing nevertheless claims to be a friend of the picturesque and writes of his triangular cottage-styled 'Villa intended to be constructed for a Lady in South Devon':

> In the arrangement of the Plan, a great variety of form is introduced, without violating convenience and economy: the diversity of outline by this combination gives an interesting appearance to the exterior, while it shews that regular buildings may produce pleasing and picturesque effects, yet may be, at the same time, perfectly symmetrical . . .[152]

Price had supposed that instructing Nash to arrange the rooms to the views would lower the sense of the building as a discrete object placed on the landscape. An irregular building resulting from Price's instructions would have had a low level of formal definition, visibly determined by the landscape. The triangular building, by contrast, would have an even higher level of formal contrivance than the square plan, being not bi- but tri-laterally symmetrical. At a certain level the triangular plan is intended to show the architects' facility. Malton can get the rooms in and still have them furnishable. Nash can follow Price's instructions but flout his intentions. Like demanding scores intended to exercise the virtuosity of a musician, triangular, circular and rigorously square plans are not intended to please in themselves so much as to occasion *bravura* performances. In a thoroughgoing aesthetic attitude to art, 'difficulty' typically undergoes such a transformation to a positive valuation as 'demanding'. With such logic, the ugliness, filth and clumsiness of vernacular cottages become conceptually equivalent to the difficulty of efficiently planning a triangular figure.[153]

The quotation from Laing makes a further factor clear: the triangular plan allows more of the building – two of the three axes – to be seen from any one viewpoint. As Laing says, it has, compared to an orthogonally planned building, a greater 'diversity of outline' – a greater number of planes and angles being visible. This is, however, hardly Price's picturesque variety, where building is determined by landscape; the triangular building is very obviously based on an *a priori* geometry. The pattern-book architect Edward Gyfford is interesting in this regard. The designs of his first book, *Elegant Cottages*, of 1806, are all regular, but a year later in *Picturesque Cottages*, he shows buildings that are triangular and cruciform alongside irregular buildings (Figure 4.24). These irregular buildings, however, like many of Gandy's, are not freely formed but are explicit clashes of geometric volumes. For instance, Gyfford has a drum building rising from a half drum, a drum joined to the side of a classically proportioned box, and a drum attached to a bar in a kind of irregular triangle.

Busby was opposed to irregular architecture because he took irregular aspects of the picturesque to be matters of visual experience and contingency of viewpoint. Regular architecture could, then, be picturesque:

> This argument [for irregularity of plan] may at first seem plausible, but it will not hold if we reflect, that in all landscapes where the building does not form a principal, the artists ought to consider then that it forms only a component part of the scenery; and that all the beautiful effects of light and shade, of colour and outline, are produced by the contrast of the regularity of the building with the picturesque variety of nature . . .[154]

Once irregularity had established that the appearance of buildings need not cohere with the form of their plans this non-relation could be repeated with geometric plans. The clashing and segmented irregular formalism of Gandy or Gyfford, asks an obvious but historically unprecedented question: can we have an account of the experience of geometric forms where cognizance of their geometry is not the aim or object of one's experience?

Malton asks this question eloquently in a perspective of the triangular museum[155] (Figure 4.25). From our position, looking at the villa across the arm of a lake, we see two of the radiating arms with their strange little domes and garlands, with the dome of the third just peeking out.[156] About this view Malton writes:

> Plate 26 is a view [. . .] so taken as best to shew its form from one station. In a view an artist is necessarily confined to a single station; and in the choice of this station his taste and judgement must be exerted to unite the most agreeable, with that, which at the same time best shews the actual form of the building.[157]

There is very little likelihood that we could fail to recognize the geometry of the building, and so it seems at first heavy handed that Malton depicts two figures in the foreground studying a plan of the building. But this is not the point, or at least not the one to take. From the view of the building, we can deduce its plan, and because of its bizarre form, we can do so with greater surety than if it were merely orthogonal. Despite this deduction we cannot see the plan's geometry except as a drawing such as that held by the figures. It is only from an incidental, mundane and phenomenal viewpoint, discovered by the judgement of the viewer, that the geometry comes into cognition, at the same time as it recedes from experience. Malton is showing us the distinction between the concept and the experience of building. Most likely, given his aim of 'elegance', concept and experience are meant to reciprocate, as in classicism. But, if this is the case, he has failed: the triangular star planned building is so strong a form that having deduced it from the view, there is little else to see. This is not the inclusive planning of classicism in which the plan is a kind of space to display and examine one's experience. Here, where architectural concept and architectural experience intersect without touching, we see the possibility of an unideal formalism that is peculiarly modern.

Le Corbusier's picturesque

The main reason that the picturesque has remained pertinent in architecture is its relationship to one of the most famous concepts of modern architectural planning: Le Corbusier's architectural promenade. The picturesque has a role to play in placing Le Corbusier historically, in terms of the state of planning knowledge at the time and his contribution to its development. Even for those uninterested in architectural history, the older picturesque materials are often used as parallel examples to explain and analyse the architectural promenade. Simplifying the picturesque and Le Corbusier to a degree is, perhaps, unavoidable when making these kinds of comparisons. There is, however, a further risk that both the picturesque and Le Corbusier become proofs that the forming of visual experience is the role of architecture, and that the plan is merely an instrument for producing visual affect. In the previous section, I suggested that phenomenal visual experience can only become architecture through a certain attention to the plan, whether to the recession and weakening of the plan figure, or to the apparently perverse strategy of exaggerating the figurative quality of the plan as we saw with the 'triangular picturesque'. This is also true of Le Corbusier: for the architectural promenade to be a lived experience, it must also be a figure.

Much of what I have characterized as the formal strategy of picturesque architecture is summed up in Le Corbusier's design for the house of Raoul la Roche of 1922. In Chapter 2, I used a disagreement between La Roche and Le Corbusier as an example of the tensions between pictorial space and the pictorialization of space that the picturesque suppose. We should now look at the house more fully. Le Corbusier first uses the concept of the architectural promenade when describing the house.

> [The house] will be then a little like an architectural promenade. You enter: the architectural spectacle offers itself successively to your view: you follow an itinerary and the perspectives develop with a great variety; we play with the afflux of light illuminating the walls or creating shadows. Window bays open views onto the exterior where you rediscover the architectural unity.[158]

In the manner of the picturesque Le Corbusier emphasizes visual experience – its variety and temporality – light making spaces recede or bringing them into prominence. The house is sensibly planned, the rooms and spaces have the relations that they need to have, but this pragmatic background is overlaid by another order: a route that leads from an arrival court, to a ground floor foyer, through a gallery of paintings, arriving at la Roche's mezzanine study. This programme is not unusual. Spatial sequences graded from public to private have been the pattern in European apartment planning for centuries. A traditional suite of rooms was also expected to provide a variety of spatial experiences, but to a large extent, this was variety founded on a known structure: that each room will open onto another like a variety of beads on a string. In a suite enfilade, each space has a distinct character and extent but the way one moves through the spaces is obvious and predictable. In the architectural promenade, this sequential structure is not so apparent, or rather, the sequence interacts with spaces and is influenced by them. In the promenade, the whole sequence is at stake in each space.

At the Maison la Roche, the entry court is formed up by the curved wall of the gallery set up on piloti and a blank wall into which the front door is let. From this point one can see

Figure 4.24 Edward Gyfford, 'Picturesque Cottage', 1807.

Figure 4.25 James Malton, 'Library', 1802.

Figure 4.26 Le Corbusier, Maison la Roche, Paris, 1923–5. View into the gallery from La Roche's study.

Figure 4.27 Le Corbusier, Villa Savoye, 1928–9, interior.

the skylight over La Roche's study through a high glass wall above the door. The curve of the galley blank wall creates the kind of interest Price calls variety, and Loudon calls, rather more clumsily, 'expression of the end in view': we assume a purpose to this curve that we will later discover. The skylight gains its role less through spatial mapping and semantics than through its visual prominence. There is a still moment in the entry court facing the closed door, with the skylight framed by the glass wall above the door. As a bright object in the background of our view, our first attention to the skylight is made through pictorial practice. The skylight also illuminates the three-storey foyer into which one enters. This space is quite disconcerting in its height and because it is not obvious where the stair, which is visible, will arrive on the next level. It arrives in the gallery, the purpose of which is now apparent, as is the logic of its shape. The bulge is caused by a ramp rising through the two-storey space of the gallery. This is curved partly to increase its length and thus decrease its steepness, but also to give changing viewpoints on the paintings hung on the opposite wall. The ramp also directs one's view upward and out of the gallery space, to strongly frame the skylight set in the ceiling of La Roche's study, which is not otherwise visible. If the door is open, we can enter the study that we now realize is perched above the foyer looking down over the entry and also into the gallery (Figure 4.26, also see Figure 2.11). It is only from this last point, that of the proprietor, that the whole sequence and its actual plan arrangement is apparent. As Le Corbusier states in the passage quoted, the 'architectural unity' has been occluded in order to foreground the 'spectacle'.

In the Maison la Roche and the later Villa Savoye (1928–9) (Figure 4.27), Le Corbusier realized a manner of architecture implicit in the picturesque: a radical visual empiricism where spatial experience is formed directly, without the support of invisible concepts. He writes:

> Man looks at the creation of architecture with his eyes which are 5 feet 6 inches from the ground. One can only deal with aims that the eye can appreciate, and intentions which take account of architectural elements.[159]

Le Corbusier's architecture is made at a point anterior to concepts of form – whether these are abstract, like symmetry and solid geometry, or logical, like the spatial requirements for particular uses, or cultural, like style. It is as if all the discussion of functionality and stylistic consequences given rise to by the concept of irregularity has been incorporated and dissolved within the original picturesque idea of architectural form that gives way to the pure form of phenomenal experience.

As well as being picturesque, we can also understand the promenade as being cinematographic – the two concepts are not unrelated. In retrospect, we can see the eighteenth-century picturesque as pictoriality with movement added. The problem of how the temporal form of film and the composition of its shots are related has strong parallels with the description of the promenade I have made. The film has sequence and duration as a given and needs to give this a kind of spatial form. This is the axiom of 'road movies': space is traversed as the time of the film elapses. Conversely, architecture has space and position as givens, and in the strong cases of the picturesque garden or Le Corbusier's architectural promenade, tries to give space sequence, direction and even narrative. Beatriz Colomina has shown how implicit photography and film were in the presentation and dissemination of Le Corbusier's architecture. She suggests that we should fold photographic and cinematographic techniques back into readings of how the buildings were designed and experienced, and she writes of Villa Savoye: 'the house is no more than a series of views choreographed by the visitor, the way a filmmaker effects the montage of a film'.[160]

The premise of Colomina's argument lies in Walter Benjamin's work on the distinct mode of modern cultural experience. Benjamin admired the work of Le Corbusier and other modern architects, who, he writes, express the 'poverty of experience' – a necessary condition of modern times and modern art.[161] Experience was impoverished, according to Benjamin, by urbanization, capitalism and the appropriation of high culture by conservative forces. By his ambivalent praise for 'poor experience', Benjamin means that modern architects (and filmmakers) deal with experience as it happens, rather than with the accumulation of experience as collective wisdom. In German, Benjamin has the advantage of distinguishing experience-as-it-happens, *Erlebnis*, from accumulated experience, *Erfahrung*. This distinction is much the same as the two ways that 'experience' is used in English. (My 'experience' of being nearly knocked down while crossing the road is different to that of the driver, who has enough 'experience' of such situations to be able to avoid me.) This distinction allows us to further specify the experience of the promenade. It is 'poor' in what we have been calling form: in a collective and accumulated culture of architecture that we already know and to which we can add our experience of Le Corbusier's buildings. Le Corbusier describes the promenade at the Villa Savoye as even rendering the concept of 'house' irrelevant:

> The visitors, till now, turn round and round inside, asking themselves what is happening, understanding with difficulty the reasons for what they see and feel: they don't find anything of what is called a 'house.' They feel themselves within something entirely new. And . . . they are not bored, I believe![162]

For Benjamin this inability to make buildings connected to an ongoing culture of great architecture is a tragedy but an historical fact. Not to recognize it would be to ramify the problem, and thus moderns must focus on what is particular to their situation. As pre-existing templates of experience are not usable, one is thrown back onto concrete matters of unmediated perception. The temporality of experience is reduced to just that of perception. The time of my experience can no longer be registered against the time of culture.

Benjamin thought that the mode of viewing cinema is, at a certain level, tactile. He meant that the cinema audience sees the film in the same unmediated way they see objects to hand. In the cinema, the popular audience Benjamin admired does not distinguish culture from entertainment, or cinema from other aspects of social life in the city. Most importantly, the audience is not self-conscious of the way that cinema represents them by exhibiting newsreels and dramas of everyday life, and by making the preferences of the masses apparent in their cinema-going choices. All this is in stark contrast to the sacralized experience of high culture, surrounded by an aura of its own history and the institutions of cultural value that require great paintings or plays to be regarded across a distance. Auratic artworks test the quality of our immediate experience against the *Erfahrung* that they embody. At this point, Benjamin gives architecture an historically crucial role. Traditionally, we think of buildings the way Benjamin would have us think of all art. Contemplative looking across a distance at building is the look of the tourist – a less valued mode of perception than the look of the native, who is familiar and close to the building. One must know the building in use; it must be rubbed up against in a semi-conscious way, incidentally and over time, before one can 'look' at it and also at one's relation to it. For Benjamin, architecture provides the model for an unmediated tactile vision, free from the weight of tradition, and at the same time critical. This is one explanation for the historical condition of perceptual immediacy that Le Corbusier seeks in the promenade.

There are obvious risks of anachronism in understanding the architectural promenade as picturesque. It is useful to consider both as cultural strategies that valorize visual empiricism. However, there is no simple way of defining a visual empiricism that is constant under changing cultural circumstances. Ideas about perception are themselves historical, varying with the broad social construction of the perceiving subject and their training in particular visual acuities. What Price and others grasped was that if connoisseurship of pictures is a particular kind of visual training, then gentlemen could apply this training elsewhere. In his picturesque strolls, Price not only saw cottages in their roughness and variegated tints, he saw the system of genres and the 'keeping' of depths, which are the medium of painting. Who Price and his readers become, through this exercise, is also clear: they are judges, displaying to one another their judgements of what would or would not make a good picture. By contrast, the architectural promenade is 'shot' through an eye trained in photographic images, and by persons self-conscious of how modern visual experience has been changed by cinema. If the picturesque aesthete undertakes these reflections in a moment of judgement, Benjamin suggests that the modern vision makes us all critics; not judges of merit of artworks but critics of the means of their production and historical necessity. When we are in a critical position, Benjamin says, we 'wake-up' from the dream of thinking that the present was inevitable and foretold in the past. Having outlined these significant differences in the meaning of the picturesque, we can nevertheless speak of a modern picturesque delimited to issues of apperception. It is the techniques for producing self-conscious of the act of perceiving which do develop across the modern period, and which also maintain the memory of and exemplary status of the original picturesque.

Richard Etlin argues for a history of the picturesque in which Le Corbusier is the apogee.[163] The more broadly accepted argument about Le Corbusier's patrilineage, however, is led by Colin Rowe, Alan Colquhoun and others, who see his planning as a creative variation on techniques implicit in nineteenth-century Beaux Arts architecture. If the latter were shown to be correct, Le Corbusier would have reached a 'picturesque-like' position in a reaction to classicism, just as the eighteenth-century picturesque did, but there would be no important historical relation between them. I think that both accounts are viable without much contradiction. Putting them together, in fact, sharpens my argument. Etlin follows the history of irregularity and freedom in planning as it became increasingly concerned with visual experience. Those who find Le Corbusier's sources in the Beaux Arts are concerned with the way that figurative planning opens a space of technique. We have only to recover the fact that the historical picturesque was about the plan and not against the plan, to show how these two histories articulate.

Etlin shows that Le Corbusier's knowledge of the picturesque came from two sources: Auguste Choisy and Camillo Sitte. Choisy, in his *Histoire De L'architecture* of 1899, made several astute observations about the 'irregularity' of classical Greek architecture. Le Corbusier (then Charles Edouard Jeanneret) knew this book. When he visited the Athenian Acropolis, he saw the place through picturesque eyes. He later included illustrations from Choisy in his treatise *Towards a New Architecture.* Choisy was summarizing and organizing a theory of the Greek picturesque that goes back to the eighteenth century. The fact that Greek temples, while largely uniform in themselves, were arranged in a contingent manner on their sites, had been remarked upon by Le Roy and Stuart, but became a matter of great interest to the architects of the early nineteenth century, who had incorporated the picturesque. I mentioned the pattern-book architects Papworth and Thomson earlier. Another connection was John Pennethorne, who was apprenticed to Nash with his elder brother James (who probably had a large hand in the design of the Park Villages). In 1844, John Pennethorne published his argument that the Greeks had made optical adjustments to their regularly conceived forms, curving plinths and columns so that they would appear straight.[164] He also believed that the temples were meant to be seen from particular viewpoints.[165] Etlin shows how this idea of a Greek picturesque, along with numerous archaeological studies that it inspired, were widely propagated through the canonical histories of James Fergusson in Britain and Emmanuel Violet-le-Duc in France.[166] Choisy's *Histoire* is the culmination of this line of thought, and is greatly persuasive of picturesque principles, because of his analytic drawings that show perspectives and accompanying plans with the viewpoints marked. Choisy argued that the apparently negligent placing of the acropolis structures was, in fact, the purposeful design of a processional route. As evidence for this, he shows how the views of buildings along this route were themselves composed. For instance, seen from a particular angle, the Caryatid porch of the Erechtheion is as visually prominent as the large porch on the other side, making an apparent symmetry in the view of an irregular building. This phenomenon of parallax is not treated so specifically in British picturesque theory, although it is implied in Price and other interest in real and apparent recession. In any case, it is clear that Choisy's analysis of the Athenian Acropolis provides a model of sequential spatial experience for Le Corbusier, that is given form not by volumes but by visual composition.

Evidence for Le Corbusier's second source on the picturesque is less circumstantial. When still named Jeanneret, and living in Germany in 1910 and 1911, Le Corbusier worked on a manuscript titled 'La construction des villes'. This text, which has never been fully published, was greatly inspired by extensive readings in German theory of aesthetic urbanism, or *Stadtbaukunst*, including the work of Sitte.[167] The *Stadtbaukunst* literature is deeply imbued with values of *Malerisch* or 'painterliness' – the usual German translation of picturesqueness. The picturesque was brought to Germany by tourists through the importation of texts such as that of Price, and was then greatly popularized by Karl Friedrich Schinkel.

By the turn of the century, it was transformed by the new aesthetics of empathy theory, and in the texts of Heinrich Wölfflin, the picturesque became a major tool of formal description, a subject to which we will return in Chapter 6. Sitte's work parallels Choisy's use of the picturesque. He aimed to show that the apparently haphazard form of medieval towns had an order in visual experience. Sitte opposed the manner of treating ancient buildings by disencumbering them of subsequent additions and neighbours, restoring a lost order to their form. He showed how the complex order of form, additions and the irregular squares that framed ancient cathedrals were more picturesque as an ensemble than the building restored to a particular period of its life with space all around it. Christoph Schnoor has shown that to a substantial extent, Le Corbusier takes his readings of *Stadtbaukunst* into his published book, *Urbanisme*, of 1925; albeit, he reverses his values and is a proponent for rationalism over picturesqueness in city planning.[168] Etlin's view is that, after he renounced them as urban principles, Le Corbusier's early interest in picturesque form and route finding were incorporated into his building planning.

The purpose of this description of Le Corbusier's picturesque sources is intended to bolster the formal parallels that I made earlier. This understanding of a broadly diffused interest in the relation of visual experience to architecture and other arts is also consistent with the idea that Le Corbusier's architecture is cinematographic. There is, however, a differing account of Le Corbusier's relation to the history of architecture that complicates this picture. In 1947, Rowe published an argument that Le Corbusier's planning, however much it valued functionality and spatial expression, was based on inversions of classical architectural principles.[169] There are many things at stake in Rowe's article, but for our purposes the point is that if this were the case, the picturesqueness of the architectural promenade would be neither an aim nor a concept of architectural space or affect; it would be the result of technical procedure. Rowe argued that Le Corbusier's free plan was an implicit inversion of the 'free-façade' of classical buildings. Colquhoun and Michael Dennis show more explicitly how Le Corbusier inverted neo-classical planning principles.[170] Classical planning shaped rooms and put service spaces out of sight in the *poche* or leftover space, whereas Le Corbusier tended to shape the smaller, less significant spaces, leaving the main spaces as an extensive, lightly formed field. Dennis writes:

> The traditional plan articulates the difference between spaces, while the free plan articulates the difference between objects. The consequential emphasis on spatial continuity and the unity of the whole is bound to be at the expense of the identity of the part.[171]

Antony Moulis applies the same logic to the promenade, seeing it as an explicit alternative to the Beaux-Arts principle of the *marche*, or walk.[172] In the Beaux-Arts practice, which Le Corbusier explicitly rejected, the *marche* is, at once, an axial line drawn in the process of designing and building, and an imagined affect of a visitor who would walk this axis with spaces unfolding in a pleasing and intelligible manner. While both the *marche* and the promenade are concepts of visual experience, the *marche* strongly prescribes experience as an access to the realm of architectural forms, and the promenade offers an affected freedom to wander in the absence of forms. Moulis goes on to show that, however much this freedom is felt, Le Corbusier produced the promenade from a vocabulary of spiral and meander forms that preoccupied him his entire career. Just as in the practice of the *marche*, Le Corbusier drew human movement patterns around which the architectural plan and the scenography of the promenade grew. This is, to an extent, obvious in Le Corbusier's later projects, when the ramps utilized in the villas of the 1920s became monumental objects to be regarded from a distance – as in the Carpenter Centre (Harvard, 1962). Moulis shows how this figural quality is imminent in Le Corbusier's techniques of drawing and diagramming experience from early in his career.

Moulis strengthens this argument for a figural understanding of plan experience by analysing a series of largely unbuilt projects for buildings with spiral plans. In the design drawings and over-drawings of movement paths, they begin with the same planning technique as the promenade but exaggerate and formalize this. In its most extreme versions – the Mundanium (1928–9) and Museum of Unlimited Expansion (1939) – the visitor is intended to feel as if they are wandering in a free plan when in fact their experience is thoroughly determined by a square spiral. In the promenade, the feelings of freedom to wander and spatial unfolding are, of course, carefully planned, and the logic of that planning is concealed to foreground visual experience. Ordinary mundane aspects of 'house' are the main determinates of the Villa Savoye, and yet Le Corbusier is able to master these to such an extent that they are occluded, leaving the observer without the rationalization of picturesque form that Loudon favoured. All the same, these determinates are material, practical matters like room uses, structure and servicing, and they are manifold. In the spiral projects, by contrast, the spatial determinate that has been elided is a single device – formal, abstract and without purpose, which is only appreciable in viewing the plan.

We can conclude this section by making a parallel between the spiral museum projects of Le Corbusier and Malton's triangular museum that I analysed earlier. In a drawing remarkably like Malton's in its intent, Le Corbusier shows a disoriented wanderer in the labyrinth and a plan of the building (Figure 4.28). It is unclear if the plan is a vignette within the frame of the view or a representation of a plan hung on the wall of the museum. Is the man consulting a plan of the museum that makes up the informational deficit in his experience? Or is Le Corbusier notating the first drawing with another, to explain that although the man is apparently lost in attention to the museum's artefacts, in fact, his experience is planned, formed and cued? Le Corbusier's spiral museums critique the necessity of converging the plan and the form of the experience of the building, but this is conducted through a regularization of the plan as a figure.

Picturesque minimalism?

In part this chapter has been arranged so as to also offer a critique and supplementation of one of the most insightful modern essays on the picturesque, Yve-Alain Bois' 'A Picturesque Stroll around Clara-Clara'. Bois makes a strong case for the relevance of the picturesque in contemporary art, especially in that strand called minimalism or post-minimalism. He connects Le Corbusier's architecture to the picturesque in a way that is less historically informed than Etlin, but much more explicit about the formal, perceptual and aesthetic description of the picturesque. Unfortunately, Bois caricatures the architectural plan as something opposed to the picturesque. This is, at least, unsubtle, as the body of this chapter has shown. In this last section, I want to go past correcting the details of architectural history in Bois' argument, and to conclude my chapter as he does his article but considering the relation of the picturesque to the perceptualist strategies of Minimalist art. Bois' article is a catalogue essay for an exhibition by the sculptor, Richard Serra, at the Centre du Pompidou in 1980. In the essay, Bois is concerned with what Serra's art reveals about the previous decades, and particularly, the resources that Serra and the picturesque might offer to argue against Michael Fried's dismissive critique of the Minimalist artists of the 1960s.[173] Since the 1990s there has emerged a new style or mode in architecture, also called minimalism. Some of the proponents of architectural minimalism explain it in relation to Minimalism in the visual arts, and in the experiential terms that Bois and Rosalind Krauss developed since the 1970s. Other accounts of architectural minimalism relate it to the lineage of classical formalism. My point is that these apparently competing explanatory frameworks are not inconsistent; that one can have an experiential formalism, as I argued about the triangular picturesque. This not so unusual argument is, however, underlaid with some large premises about the nature of interdisciplinarity in the arts, and the history of the interaction of visual arts and architecture since the picturesque.

Bois describes the mode of Serra's sculptures (Figures 4.29 and 4.30) as picturesque. He defines this picturesqueness as a practice in which a Gestalt reading of the form is disabled to foreground the phenomenal experience of the work. The German word *Gestalt* means shape, but in English, it is generally reserved for strong figurative form 'incapable of expression simply in terms of its parts', and thus it requires to be understood as a whole.[174] Serra describes the point of avoiding a Gestalt reading of his *Rotary Arc* when he says that a viewer cannot 'ascribe the multiplicity of views to a Gestalt reading of the Arc. Its form remains ambiguous, indeterminable, unknowable as an entity'.[175] I could have used 'Gestalt' earlier when I wrote of the figurative aspects of classical planning. A Gestalt is exactly what irregularity is intended to avoid and could be taken as the opposite principle to Price's 'variety'. However, the Gestalt psychology that interested perceptual psychologists and art theorists at the beginning of the twentieth century has a more particular meaning. Gestalt psychology supposes that we first recognize a form as a whole in its limits and distinction against a ground; that the task of perceiving has to be preceded by recognition of the thing to be perceived. Then, as we examine the object, we place the perceptual data gained within an already existing totalized form. If this were the case, cognition, or rather re-cognition, would always precede perception, which would be a kind of colouring-in, and, arguably, a less than replete experience of perception. Bois assumes that any plan figure will necessarily be experienced as a Gestalt, and indeed, that the concept of the architectural plan is a concept of Gestalt. Serra says, and Bois agrees, that architects can never be site-specific enough.

> Architects suffer from the same studio syndrome. They work out of their offices, terrace the landscape and place their building into the carved-out site. As a result the studio-designed then site adjusted buildings look like blown-up cardboard models.[176]

Bois recommends that architects move from an *a priori* designing in plan to designing in elevation, which would require them to attend to the situation in which they build. Bois lays out a history of the picturesque that moves from eighteenth-century garden theorists, through Piranesi and Choisy to Eisenstein, arriving at Le Corbusier and his promenade. Bois then argues that the un-totalized viewing of Serra's sculptures is the *Erlebnis* or experience-in-the-now described by Benjamin, which we earlier identified with Le Corbusier.[177] For Bois, Le Corbusier is the only modern architect able to draw on this repressed picturesque history, to understand its role in modern visuality. 'For just as Le Corbusier's kinetic intelligence was exceptional, so the understanding of that intelligence among architects today remains the thing least shared in the world'.[178]

It is worth insisting that irregular planning for sequential spatial experience was the major invention of architectural culture as a whole over this period. If we took Bois' definition of picturesqueness in unfolding sequenced experience, unclosed by figure, then his heroes ought be Richard Norman Shaw, Victor Horta, H. H. Richardson, Edwin Lutyens, all of whom produced more elaborate and nuanced planning for visual experience than Le Corbusier. Bois' passing over of the whole of the nineteenth century might be explained by ignorance of these buildings, or by a degree of hyperbole in his enthusiasm for Le Corbusier, but it is also a particular view of modernity that takes the presence or absence of the category of style as a watershed. What denies Art Nouveau or historicist architecture its 'kinetic intelligence', presumably, is that it was polluted with issues of the form of the architectural object, issues that Bois does not see in Le Corbusier. To make the difference that Bois must make between Le Corbusier's Maison la Roche and, for instance, Hector Guimard's 1909 house not so far away on Avenue Mozart, means placing a great deal more importance on what links the visual forms of architecture and cinema in some general modern 'visuality', than on techniques of contriving visual forms within architecture.

Bois is also wrong to think that the lessons of Le Corbusier are not heard. Apart from Le Corbusier's own books, most scholars have recommended a study of his experientialist point-of-view planning since Sigfried Giedion's *Building in France* of 1928. Poor architects and bad cities are problems caused by the same rarity of talent and prevalence of cliché afflicting all art disciplines. Arguably the architectural promenade and aformal experientialism have become clichés in modern architecture: planning for point of view collapsed into creating affects in a subject, which then transmute from an empirical account of visual experience into a supposition of archetypal human responses to space.[179] While I am not suggesting that Bois' ideas of the picturesque open onto this kind of romantic humanism, he does not seem to understand that the most dangerous essentialism for modern architecture lies not with ideal object forms but with suppositions about the subject. Simplistic phenomenology evokes Le Corbusier's name only because of a failure to recognize the figural form in his planning, or because this is mistaken for idealism. What separates Le Corbusier from Guimard in a history of picturesque planning is not the quality or mode of visual experience created. It is that in Le Corbusier the experience is registered against a figure that does not prescribe it; and also gives out onto a particular kind of objecthood of the architectural work. For instance, Bois writes of the ramp that cuts through the centre of the Villa Savoye as a cost that Le Corbusier is prepared to pay – a degree of awkwardness in planning to produce the promenade.

> a simple staircase [. . .] would have posed fewer problems. Now the very subject of the Villa Savoye is the penetration of a vertical section into a horizontal grid [. . .] It is this vertical penetration by the passageway into the arrangement of the plan, this disturbance of the plan by the elevation and by the movement of the stroller, that creates the richness and intricacy of the Villa Savoye (and in a certain way one could say that the aim of the free plan corresponds in Le Corbusier, despite what he says about it, to a wish to free his architecture from the generating tyranny of the plan).[180]

What is the thing disturbed? Bois writes as if it is planning as a concept or facility, not a particular plan figure. The planning of rooms and spaces in the Villa is, indeed, loose; they are more strongly related through visual experience than they are through spatial definition. Bois, however, has neglected the fact that the Villa's plan perimeter is, notionally, *square.* The plan is a square grid of columns (with some displaced column positions for pragmatic reasons) but the floor plate has small cantilevers that take it slightly out of square in one axis. The generic-ness of the plan figure of the Villa is important – it signals that this is not a unique work of art, but an instance of a series; as Le Corbusier puts it in one of his more constructivist moments, the house is 'a machine for living'. It is this reproducibility that separates them from Guimard – or, an even closer example – the arty modernism of Robert

Figure 4.28 Le Corbusier, sketch of interior of the Museum of Unlimited Expansion, 1937.

Figure 4.29 Richard Serra, *Intersection*, Kunstmuseum, Basel, 1992. An example of Serra's geometrically derived forms in the series of torqued ellipses. © Richard Serra. Licensed by VISCOPY, Australia, 2007.

Figure 4.30 Richard Serra, *The Gate in the Gorge*, 1986, Louisiana Museum, Humlebaek, Denmark. An example of Serra's site-specific works. © Richard Serra. Licensed by VISCOPY, Australia, 2007.

Mallet-Stevens. According to Rowe's analysis of the Villa's planning geometry, the cantilevers, apart from demonstrating the construction of the free, columnless, elevation, serve to de-emphasise the centredness and thus, classical formality, of the plan figure.[181] The squareness, or near squareness of the plan is thus not a geometrical ideal, but the kind of normalization of shape that results from mass production. The significance of these inferences is clear if we think on the fact that planning the house would have been considerably less awkward if Le Corbusier had not been constrained by the square figure; if he had added another bay or increased the reach of the cantilevers. As it is, the ramp really does 'pinch': each landing pushes hard at the spaces, particularly in the arrival onto the main level, and also in the bite that the ramp takes out of the main bedroom. The ramp runs in the same axis as the cantilevers, so we could, in one light, see these as ameliorations of the clash of the ramp with the *a priori* figure of the square plan. Here, the figure's 'squareness' is not the master term; it is not the concept into which one's percepts are loaded. This is not the Beaux-Arts, where the *marche* delivers one's experience to the building's axial ideals. Bois, and most architects, think of the Villa Savoye as the epitome of route-based, point-of-view planning. Contrary to this I am suggesting that its merit over, say, the earlier Maison la Roche, lies in the combination of the promenade with the plan's figure. Le Corbusier shows that the architecture of experience does not lie in an ever more precise choreography, but in increasing the tension between perception and cognition. At the Villa Savoye, we experience, in the poor sense, the building's abstract concept at the same time and at the same level that we become self-conscious of, and conceptualize, our experience as the promenade – as picturesque.

What is slightly strange about Bois' article is that this possibility of unideal figurality is also at stake in Serra's sculpture. Bois writes as if Serra could teach architects about subject position, vision and movement, about which they possibly know too much. What, in fact, Serra could teach architects is that planning for experiential affects need not exclude figural form. Serra's sculptures tend to fall into two groups: those that are entirely site-specific (see Figure 4.30), and those that are based on geometric forms such as *Intersection* (see Figure 4.29). Bois makes the unlikely claim that the geometries of the latter are not apparent:

> *Sight Point*: even though this sculpture is constructed on a series of similar elements, nothing acts to forewarn the observer that it is, in Serra's words, 'a truncated pyramid' delineating an equilateral triangle at its top. Or again, when Serra, with some reluctance, describes the placing of the three slabs of *Spin Out* in geometric terms, he says nothing about what the spectator's experience will be: he pretends to give the key to that experience, and this key is not the right one: 'The plates were laid out at twelve, four and eight o'clock in an elliptical valley, and the space between them forms an isosceles triangle'. I have spent some time surveying Spin Out, trying in particular to determine whether some sort of geometry was at work there, and never was I able to come to that conclusion (on the contrary, it seemed to me that any a priori geometry was absent and that the work, like *Shift*, was a function of the topography).[182]

Bois' overly simplistic opposition between ideation and experience causes him to deny a geometry that is self-evident in photo documentation of the work and which is confirmed by the artist's description. I agree that Serra is concerned with heightened but de-sacralized experience, however, Bois has not attended to the possibility implicit in his own experience: that is, the experience of the uselessness of forms – a tactic by the artist to foreground experiential aspects of the work. Bois says of Serra's use of geometry: 'he pretends to give the key to that experience, and this key is not the right one'.[183] Serra does not pretend to give the key, he does give the key – it just does not unlock some plenitude of experience. One is left to construct that for oneself in parallel with the artist's geometric construction of the art object. At the end of the article, Bois recalls the experience of *Spin Out* slightly differently, saying: 'The pleasure I felt in walking in *Spin Out* did not occur in spite of my inability to grasp its geometrical form but because of that inability'.[184] Precisely so: the geometry did exist, Bois deduced this from his experience – but he could not experience it. This divergence of Bois' experience from the formal concept of the work structures his experience of the work.

Clara Clara, the main topic of the article, is one of the *Tilted Arc* family, which are segments of cones. When Bois describes it, he writes approvingly of the affects it produces in an observer: the 'strange impression [which an observer has] that one wall goes faster than the other, that the left and right sides of his body are not coordinated'.[185] In this description, we imagine the sculpture as a device acting directly on the human body's spatiality: the body's uprightness, its frontal dorsal directionality, its lateral symmetry, its experience of gravity, and the relative horizontality of the visual field. Bois explains, for the reader, how the sculpture creates these affects: the kissing arcs of steel form an 'X' in plan and are segments of cones, arranged so that one is inverted with regard to the other. Bois writes as if it is very difficult to deduce this geometry from visual experience, but I do not find it so. Rather, if one thinks, as Bois does, that Serra's art touches a spatiality that belongs *only* to the body, then deducing its geometric forms is no more relevant than estimating the weight of its steel. Bois insists that Gestalt form is the cause of architecture's failings, and that it is Gestalt form that Serra's sculptures rigorously eschew. A better explanation of the role of Villa Savoye's squareness and *Clara Clara's* cone-ness is found in a dictum of minimalist Robert Morris. Morris states the reason for his simple Platonic solids:

> the characteristic of a gestalt is that once it is established, all the information about it, qua gestalt, is exhausted. (One does not for example seek the gestalt of a gestalt.) [. . .] One is then both free of the shape and bound to it.[186]

This discussion of form and formed experience in Serra and Le Corbusier has helped to sharpen some of my earlier descriptions of the interest in geometric planning that paralleled the invention of irregularity. In the first place, this is an issue of technique driving changes in concept. Having 'seen' the irregular as a plan and hence as a figure, uniform closed figures changed, subsuming their concept to the new paradigm of visual empiricism. The picturesque is not aformal; it is a concept of the aesthetic utility of weakness in form, whether shapeless unclosed forms or strong forms acting weakly – underdetermined and unideal. This is barely a concept; it cannot be understood outside techniques like 'irregularity', which can, in turn, only be understood in their disciplinary and historical context.

Today, the architecture of Le Corbusier, Alvar Aalto and others, to whom the term picturesque might be applied, is somewhat out of fashion – a degree of formalism in the old sense of object form marks the most progressive practices. There is a degree of frisson over buildings such as Herzog and de Meuron's triangular Barcelona Forum. This is because of its resiling of the kind of spatial choreography that is identified with good planning. But the position that Herzog and de Meuron have reached was already implicit in picturesque planning from its first emergence; as we saw with the short career of a less talented architect, James Malton and his triangular museum. This cultural shift in architecture is partly trival, a reaction against the over-familiarity with point-of-view planning and the kind of sickly humanism with which it has been falsely advertised. On the other hand, this could be the point at which picturesque *regularity*, nascent in the pattern books and Le Corbusier's spiral projects, emerges as a mature means of making architecture. I am not suggesting that we should extend the word picturesque so as to apply it to the Barcelona Forum, but rather the opposite: arcane concepts of form from the beginning of picturesque architecture might help explain the current formalism outside the too easy oppositions of form and experience.

Some of the difficulty in making an empirical account of the perception of geometric forms comes with the term minimalism, which emerged around 1990 to describe a new reductive tendency in architecture. There are two common descriptions of minimalism against which I want to pitch my picturesque regularity. The first, and most common, is minimalism as an elegant abstraction to the essentials of space and material. This is a position with little to stop it collapsing into idealism and results in ahistorical claims such that anything simple – a Cistercian Abbey, for instance – is 'minimalist'. Against this undoubtedly naïve view is usually counter-posed a more sophisticated account, drawing on Minimalism in art and the writings of Bois and Krauss.[187] It begins by explaining that Minimalist art, for example that of Donald Judd or Sol le Witt, which looks like minimalist architecture, is resolutely anti-idealist, being concerned with phenomenal experience and the category of art. A right description of minimalist architecture, then, is a matter of felt-experience and disavowal of the object. As, however, these are the same terms with which Bois lionizes Le Corbusier in the picturesque essay, where does the specificity of minimalist architecture lie? The best contemporary architecture provides an experience of forms shorn of idealism and concepts; this is what distinguishes it from the simple choreography of subject position. This is also what distinguishes it from the visual arts, and why Bois' account will not work. This last point is more complex; it has to do with the objecthood of architecture, and opens another aspect of Bois' essay.

Bois's underlying argument in the picturesque essay is with Michael Fried's idea of the historical role of art disciplines. Fried is a conventionalist who thinks that each art proceeds through an internal problematic; that to a large extent, the viewers of paintings and architecture are different, even if empirically they can appreciate both paintings and architecture, and call them both 'arts' for convenience. Bois is responding to Fried's famous 1967 article, 'Art and Objecthood', where Fried claims that art requiring the durational experience of an observer becomes merely 'theatre', destroying both the difference between art objects and quotidian objects, and the difference between art forms. Bois' recuperation of the picturesque and architecture as an historical and disciplinary context to Serra's sculpture is, thus, opposed to Fried: it shows that visuality in duration is a proper concern across all arts and through their history; visuality in duration rides across the materiality of the work and the material history of the art discipline in which it was created. Bois accepts Fried's description of the mechanism of objecthood, but does not think it is a problem. Indeed, most contemporary artists and critics would side with Bois on this. Bois does not, however, consider that 'objecthood' might be different in architecture. Whether rightly (Bois) or wrongly (Fried), large parts of twentieth-century visual art put into crisis the assumed differences between artworks and quotidian objects. But this is what architecture has been doing since the eighteenth century, in fact, since the discovery of vernacular 'architecture' by the picturesque. By the late nineteenth century, architecture's profile as an art discipline lay in its claim of applicability to the whole built environment. Architecture was an art the products of which were not artworks, but everyday objects. The difference between building and architecture did not lie in the material differences between everyday buildings and architectural works but, rather, in process and knowledge. In 1903, Hermann Muthesius proposed to change the name of the profession to *baukunst* or building art, to make this relation clear.[188] In modernist architecture, buildings were serial objects: instances of an architectural capacity in terms of production volumes and social effects, as in any object form. The reductive formalist architecture of today, while equally opposed to idealized form as the generic forms of Judd or Morris, cannot play on experience in the same way. This is for historical reasons. There is no jolt, no space, no paradox, no theatre in saying 'this work of architecture is an object among other objects, look to your sensorium if you want architecture'. In architecture, this refusal of the specific architectural object was institutionalized in modernism, and stretches back to the orginal picturesque discovery that calling ordinary buildings architecture has a certain aesthetic force. When architects today present indubitably architectural objects, this is the same risky nominalism that Carl Andre played at in calling rows of bricks 'art'. The claim that a building is categorically, rather than necessarily, architecture seems just as unlikely. The game with categories may be, as with minimalist art, a provocation to experience the work, but that provocation works by reversing poles of the art object and the quotidian object.

This is the most 'architectural' of this book's chapters, and a part of its point has been to insist that picturesque visual experience is not some general mode. The picturesque idea lends itself to generalization, appropriation and defusion, but matters of architecture (and landscape architecture) are irreducibly a part of it; are necessary for understanding the picturesque. It is not possible to use the picturesque as a concept without supposing a visual experience based on the experience of buildings and gardens. Like Bois, I think that the picturesque works through knowing and foregrounding aspects of visual experience, such as subject position and field of view, that are natural or at least able to be described separately to their contrivance by architects, sculptors or gardeners. It does not necessarily follow that such experiences are a class that can be set against ideation. I have shown that the palpability of experience is shot through with the question of the palpability of forms that have no basis in natural experience. The picturesque is interdisciplinary, as the other chapters of this book show. This interdisciplinarity, however, is a history of exchanges between disciplines, not some ground of visual experience underlying architecture and the visual arts. The picturesque did begin in the eighteenth century with sketching, connoisseurship, and gardening, and subsequently worked its way into modern architecture. This does not mean that it is some meta-art of experience, which has had a long life because it deals in a particularly direct way with visual experience. It has had this long life because of its uptake in a discipline with an historical trajectory of its own. In the late eighteenth century 'irregularity' bundled together in an unlikely way the possibility of an art of experience with concepts of style and techniques of social discipline. Irregularity is, thus, incoherent as a concept; we need to understand it as a technique within a discipline. While we can understand 'the' picturesque, said with the definite article, as space of articulation between art disciplines and historical moments, this does not mean constructing it as a self-consisting concept or body of practices. There can be no picturesque visuality without remembering its architectural irregularities.

5
Appropriation

A degree of ownership is irreducible in the picturesque. Looking involves searching for information, finding our way, attending to the actions of another, but to look at something as if it were a picture is also to imagine it as a product of viewing; a thing to be had. The momentary flattening of space in the picturesque is not simply an occasion for a person of taste to demonstrate visual propensities and skills; nor is it only an affect for architects and gardeners to arouse. In the eighteenth century a picture was a particular kind of image. Unlike a mural, a picture was cut from its context by a frame and made on a transportable surface. We now use 'picture' quite generally for many kinds of images, but something of the sense of picture as moveable property has remained in the picturesque. The landscape gardener Humphry Repton used the term 'appropriation' to describe this aspect of the picturesque.

Historically, appropriation is one of the most important concepts and techniques that the picturesque offers modern culture. Eighteenth-century aesthetes and gardeners made this concept when they decided that what was outside of the park could be made to seem a part of the park. Aesthetic unities could be a different size and shape to the property on which they were created. In Repton's theory a small appropriation of real property, sufficient to control and compose a foreground, could enable a greater, if more ephemeral, property in the whole of one's view. From these techniques of appropriation arises the modern concept of context. Henceforth, buildings and gardens are rarely seen outside their relations with the landscapes and cities in which they are sited. Eighteenth-century theorists were largely concerned with how consulting the context could improve garden or building design. In the theory of urban design as it developed through the nineteenth century, the emphasis gradually shifted from how a building could make use of the greater site beyond the property boundaries to how a building could change and inflect the whole 'Townscape'. In some ways, this was a simple application of the landscape principle. The role that ornamental buildings had in landscape parks, in providing goals, making sequences, marking out thresholds of territories, was transferred to the city as a whole. If the city was a 'built environment' – buildings and roads determined almost naturally by need and land value – then the architectural building made visible the city's structure; celebrated its strengths, improved them, and delivered it as an aesthetic experience. Since the picturesque, the question put to every building is how much does it act beyond its site? Visually, narratively and conceptually, how much of the landscape or city can be had from this place?

In this chapter, I explain Repton's theory in terms that assist us to understand more of the history of the picturesque, but also to understand what has happened since. The chapter, then, focuses on the Townscape movement from the 1940s to the 1970s and its aftermath. Townscape was the vehicle with which Sir Nikolaus Pevsner and others reintroduced the picturesque to England as a source of modern architecture and urban design. It is also the case that Townscape's appropriation of the picturesque is a substantial development of the concept. Townscape, like the picturesque, has been unfashionable at least partly because of its unseemly interest in appearance. By contrast, the movement that followed – 'contextualism' – focused on the plan and seemed to place building type and urban structure above the trivialities of the picturesque. But as I established in the last chapter, the picturesque is this oscillation of plan and view. Repton and Price's distinction of landscape from prospect adds to my description of the picturesque as a rotation of the viewpoint downward toward the horizontal plane of the earth.

It is now common to think that the whimsical decorousness of the picturesque acts strongly to naturalize land ownership, acquistion and colonialism. In my view, there is no overarching ideology of the picturesque, only the uses to which it has been put in building planning, the politics of taste and aesthetic interest, and in landscape design and urban planning. However, it is easy to see why some might think of a coherent 'politics of the picturesque'. Picturesque discourse is shot through with political metaphors, and I will show how the gap between real and visual property regularly opens into a dizzying abyss of simplistic political theory. There is a case for reversing the usual arguments and seeing the 'politics of the picturesque' as an issue of the aesthetic appropriation of schemas of politics. In Chapter 2, I explained how the possession of taste was thought of as analogous to political franchise. Here we broaden that picture by considering how viewpoint was held to be an issue of sovereignty, and how these grand analogies to governance served the picturesque's own imperialism in urban planning.

Repton's theory of appropriation

I have already discussed, in passing, two aspects of Repton's 'appropriation'. In Chapter 2 we saw that Repton's picturesque involved editing out of the scene inappropriate objects so that the view conformed to genre. For example, Repton excluded the butcher's shop in the view from his own living room. In Chapter 3, I discussed how this was also a reproach to Price's more piquant taste. Here, I will place these ideas of visual editing within a broader account of Repton's theory of landscape design. My main point follows the previous chapter's argument on the plan: as with building, landscape architecture that creates views does so through the plan; and Repton's technique of visually acquiring the property of others began with a concern about the boundary and extent of landscape. Repton thought that the main difference between his ideas of landscape and the picturesque as defined by Sir Uvedale Price and Richard Payne Knight was 'appropriation'. Repton claims to have coined the term as it applied to landscape, its usual meaning being 'the making of a thing private property, whether another's or (as now commonly) one's own; taking as one's own or to one's own use'.[1] For Repton, the picturesque, and any other kind of visual practice, was based on a natural propensity to enjoy looking at what one owns, and imagining ownership of what one looks at. For Price and Knight, the visual acuity learned through painting was a way of making what was already theirs seem more so. Conversely, when Repton advised clients on the creation of landscape parks and gardens, picturesque appropriation could not be separated from the real appropriation of property that the design required.

> Appropriation. A word ridiculed by Mr Price as lately coined by me, to describe extent of property; yet the appearance and display of such extent is a source of pleasure not to be disregarded; since every individual who possesses anything, whether it be mental

> endowments, or power, or property, obtains respect in proportion as his possessions are known, provided he does not too vainly boast of them; and it is the sordid miser only who enjoys for himself alone, wishing the world to be ignorant of his wealth. The pleasure of appropriation is gratified in viewing a landscape which cannot be injured by the malice or bad taste of a neighbouring intruder: thus an ugly barn, a ploughed field, or any obtrusive object which disgraces the scenery of a park, looks as if it belonged to another, and therefore robs the mind of the pleasure derived from appropriation, or the unity and continuity of unmixed property.
>
> A view into a square, or into [city] parks may be cheerful and beautiful, but it wants appropriation; it wants that charm which only belongs to ownership, the exclusive right of enjoyment, with the power of refusing others should share our pleasure: and however painful the reflection, this propensity is part of human nature.[2]

Repton's idea is so familiar, that we need to remember that, while some aspects of the idea are a 'part of human nature', others are particular to the enclosure of parks within great estates, and to the history of landscape gardening.

That vision is a kind of possession is an ancient idea. Sir Henry Wotton, in the first English treatise on architecture, expresses well the possibility of exercising this acquisitiveness in design:

> A well chosen Prospect: which I will call the Royalties of Sight. . . . There is Lordship likewise of the Eye (as of the feet) which being a raunging and Imperious, and (I might say) an usurping Sense; can indure no narrow circumscription; but must be fedde, both with extent and varieties.[3]

Wotton makes clear that the pleasure of viewing implies the possibility of moving into the scene, and that such a pleasure can be spoiled by a refusal of access, visual or pedestrian. Wotton's sight from a prospect point does not invite actual movement. The garden or countryside is traversed by an eye offended by concavities and walls that halt its imagined peregrinations. The revolution of the English garden, begun by Charles Bridgeman and William Kent, was to put a certain interval into this imperious sight; to articulate sight with motion.[4] One of the most significant aspects of the paintings called landscapes, when taken as models for gardens, is their low horizon. The royalty of sight is frustrated by the occlusions of a foreground, but then rewarded when one walks into the scene and finds status confirmed by a further scene to appropriate. Hence, the recipe for any garden without a ritual itinerary is that famously put by William Shenstone: 'The foot should never travel to [the object] by the same path which the eye has travelled over before. Lose the object, and draw nigh obliquely.'[5]

This technique of exchanging vision and destination, sight and movement, was developed in gardens and 'pleasure grounds' of the early to mid-eighteenth century. They differ from the later picturesque landscapes in two ways. First, they are emblematic in structure. Like the pictorial emblems common to Baroque culture, they suppose an exchange between word and image (or vision). Second, the poetic garden is a 'garden', while what Lancelot Brown and Repton later in the century work on are 'parks'; that is grazing land. Whately put it thus, in 1770: gardening has been 'lately brought to perfection' in England and is 'no longer confined to the spots from which it borrows its name, but regulates also the disposition and embellishments of a park, a farm or a riding'.[6] Together, these two aspects of the emblematic garden meant that there was not, early in the century, the principal issue that engaged Repton: the extent of the landscape as cadastre and viewing field.

The garden at Rousham in Oxfordshire is a useful example of an earlier gardening style that used some of the techniques of picturesque visuality but was both smaller than the majority of Repton's designs and lacked a way for its use of the land to be understood within the design. Rousham, designed by Kent and constructed in the late 1730s and the 1740s, relied on a verbalized reading because of its metrical sequence and the necessity to interpret emblems.[7] The garden was designed to have its parts interrogated to produce verbal constructs. While admitting Rousham's great charm, some of this results from its strangeness. Looked at with modern visual values, the garden appears crowded with structures, making it fall too easily into object and setting. Compared to the sense one has of the emblematic garden as *topoi*, the spatial disposition seems weak. Other emblematic gardens such as Stowe or Stourhead are very much larger than Rousham and this allowed more figures, larger elements, more elaborate sequences, but the land consumed was not of primary significance.

Brown's innovation in landscape design was to empty out the allegorical structure of earlier gardens, so that the experience was purely that of sight and destination, and then to apply principles of gardening to the larger areas called 'parks'. A park is pasture for the keeping of deer, the hunting of which was an aspect of the hospitality of a great house. In pre-modern times, owners could not forbid access to their land except where it had been 'emparked', which meant fenced and patrolled for the protection of the game over which the owner did have exclusive property. The original purpose of the acts of enclosure was to create parkland; we could say the logic of emparkment precedes the agricultural significance of enclosure discussed in the previous chapter. By 1800, deer hunting had become less fashionable than fox hunting, which occurred in the agricultural countryside rather than in parks, and made better exposition of horsemanship. From this time, parks were as likely to be grazed by cattle or sheep as deer, but the analogy of the preservation of game and of the chase remained important. What one 'took' in the picturesque park was scenery. Similarly, the contract of hospitality and the display of wealth involved in a park continued. A park is that part of a landholding not let to tenants nor farmed by the proprietor but left outside the calculations of profit for the enjoyment of guests. Thus the size of a park is indicative of the size of the whole estate and the wealth of its owner. As Repton puts it, the park's 'actual dimensions should bear some proportion to the command of property by which the mansion is supported'.[8] When Wotton says that the eye refuses 'narrow circumscription', he is referring to the nature of visual attention, and in so far as this concerns design, the number of things to attend to.[9] But by Repton's time, this eye had become cadastral: not so much roaming freely as calculating the area of its dominion; offended not by the concavities of a valley but rather by those fences and walls that marked the limit of real property. The propensity to understand the park by area is what Repton battled against, and, at this basic level of view orientation, the elevational view of landscape is opposed to the cadastral view of plan area.

> So natural is the partiality for extent or greatness of dimension, that I have constantly been asked, How large is a park? How many miles is it round? And since I visited Woburn, everybody talks to me concerning the length of the park wall. I can only answer, that I do not estimate places by measurement; and that I never go round the extremity of a place to form an idea of its beauty. With respect to the boundary, whether it be a wall or a pale, my business is to hide it not to lead a drive so near as to display it.[10]

At the same time that Repton decried the simplicity of understanding landscape by area, he assumed this was an irreducible structure of visual desire to be played and deceived. Landscape, with its way of valuing what is occluded, could play a trick on area:

> By LANDSCAPE, I mean a view capable of being represented in painting. It consists of two, three, or more well marked distances, each separated from the other by an unseen space, which the imagination delights to fill up with fancied beauties; that may not perhaps exist in reality.[11]

Landscape still served a sovereign eye, but Repton saw the challenge as one of exclusivity rather than quantity:

> the situation of a house in the country is more or less defective, in proportion as it is more or less bounded or incommoded by alien property. Thus a high road, a ploughed field, a barn, or a cottage adjoining a large house, has a tendency to lessen its importance.[12]

'Extent' had a part of its logic in pushing away the neighbouring productive farm. The practice of Brown had been to plant the boundary of the park with a belt of trees so that one could not see the park and farm contrasted. Repton comments:

> One of the great errors of Mr Brown's followers, has been the unnecessary extent of parks. It is my opinion that, provided the boundary can be properly disguised, the largest park need not exceed two to three hundred acres, else they become farms with in a pale, or they are forests rather than parks.[13]

> When by this false taste for extent, parks had become so enlarged beyond all reasonable bounds of prudence and economy in the operation, it became advisable to allot large portions of land for the purposes of agriculture, within the belt or outline of this useless and extravagant enclosure; and thus the interior of a park is become an arable farm.[14]

There are two problems implied in Repton's examples: the embarrassed owner forced to resort to farming inside the park because his eyes were larger than his pocket book; and the boundary belt which reveals what it is in any case – a sign of the limit of property. As Repton understands it, 'one of the fundamental principles of landscape gardening is to disguise the real boundary'.[15] A park should 'give the appearance of extent and freedom by carefully disguising or hiding the real boundary'.[16]

The difference between Brown's and Repton's landscape styles is quickly grasped through an analysis in John Claudius Loudon's *Treatise on . . . Country Residences*. Loudon shows four plates that constitute a graphical history of landscape design in Britain. The first is an area of farmland with small fields, a brook and scattered farm houses and cottages representing a countryside that might be emparked. The second shows the gardening style of a 'century ago', in the Anglo-Dutch semi-formal style, with avenues leading to a central house, reflecting pools, parterres, and an irregular 'wilderness' in one corner. The third plate (Figure 5.1) is of a Brown-style design, showing his characteristic style applied to the same area of land (in fact a Brownian park would likely be larger than earlier ones). The house is placed centrally with its services, stables and kitchen garden hidden in a wood. The brook running in front of the house is fattened by a weir into the appearance of a river, and the entry drive crosses this mighty stream as it makes a serpentine journey towards the house. The park is uniform smooth pasture spotted with Brown's famous 'clumps' of trees. There is a densely planted belt with a carriage drive that at various points opens inward to view the house across the park. The belt screens out the view of the arable farms that support this display, and the workers are gathered together and rehoused in a prim Georgian row.

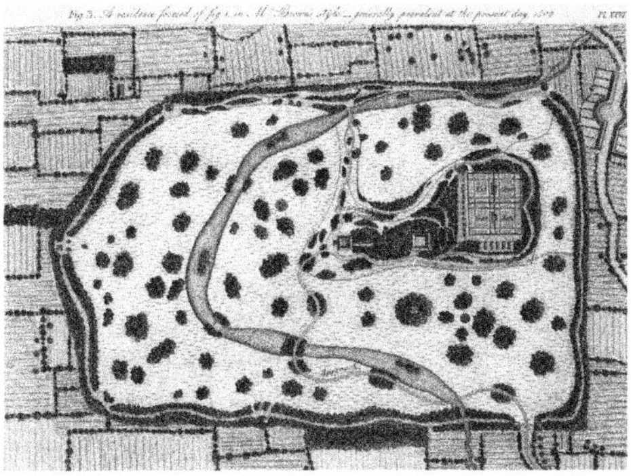

Figure 5.1 J. C. Loudon's diagram of Lancelot Brown's landscape style, 1806. By permission of La Trobe Rare Books Collection, State Library of Victoria.

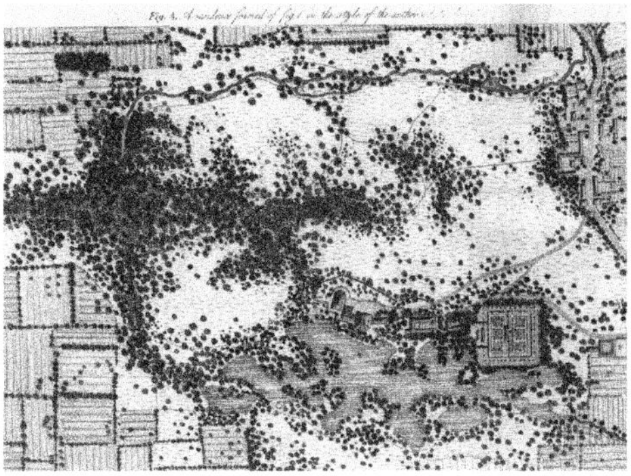

Figure 5.2 J. C. Loudon's preferred landscape style, 1806. By permission of La Trobe Rare Books Collection, State Library of Victoria.

The final plate is a modern scheme of Loudon's devising (Figure 5.2). As he was only 23 in 1806, most of his original work lay ahead of him, and this scheme was greatly indebted to Repton. Therefore the plate serves equally well to illustrate the latter's ideas, which Loudon later did much to propagate with his cheap and definitive edition of Repton's texts of 1840. The Repton/Loudon scheme has an irregular mansion placed off-centre in the park and opening onto a terrace garden overlooking a lake. The entry is through gates that stand at the edge of a picturesque village and the drive passes subsidiary buildings and service areas before arriving at the house. Repton wrote of such arrangements:

> In ancient Gothic structures, where lofty walls and various courts intervened between the palace and the neighbouring village, there was sufficient *dignity* or seclusion, without that apparent extent of domain which a modern mansion requires.[17]

Rather than clumps, the plantation is one large wood with fingers that softly divide the grounds into areas with scattered single trees and small groups, consistent with shade trees in pasture. The park is arranged so that from the house one cannot see out to the fields, but there is no belt, and while the boundary is planted in some points, at others the boundary fence is visible. The figure of the boundary is further obscured by Loudon's having some pasture beyond the boundary and the odd tree remaining in the ploughed fields. At the top of the image we see a typical device of Repton: the brook has been redirected parallel to the boundary and thus seems like a natural division of the land, pre-existing property boundaries. But the park continues on the far bank for a little way, and thus one boundary, a faux natural one, is overcome to please the eye's appetite for extent. To stop the property boundary becoming a major feature of the park, Repton reduces the contrast between park and agricultural countryside, and then, in the last instance, allows the boundary to be permeable to view and movement.

To an extent (which I will qualify a few pages hence), Repton should be understood as having developed a theoretical possibility outlined in William Gilpin's account of Stowe of 1745. The pamphlet is an adroit exposition of the uses of a landscape park given in the form of a dialogue, where Gilpin has one of the *Dialogue*'s characters notice and prefer the woods beyond the park.

> Callophilus. . . . We have a good View into the Country from hence. Those Woods are extremely elegant in their kind; we must certainly contrive to take a Ride thither some Evening. They are laid out in a very fine Manner, and cut into very beautiful Ridings
>
> Polypthon. Ay, that is the kind of Improvement that takes most with me [. . .] I am altogether of the Poet's Opinion, that
>
> Tis Use alone that sanctifies Expense.
>
> Were I a Nobleman, I should endeavour to turn my Estate into a Garden, and make my Tenants my Gardiners: Instead of useless Temples, I would build Farm-houses; and instead of cutting out unmeaning Vistas, I would beautify and mend Highways: The Country should smile on my Labours, and the Public should partake in my Pleasures. What signifies all this ostentatious work? Is any Man the better for it? Is it not Money most vilely squandered away?[18]

The complainant, Polypthon, has returned from 'the Northern Circuit' and compares Stowe with the wilderness of northern England, and Stowe's artificial waters with the River Stirling.[19] Yet Stowe did not suffer under this distant comparison as it did from the immediate contrast quoted above. The question of the North is a comparison of equally weighted concepts – Art and Nature. The quoted passage, on the other hand, questions the very idea of a landscape park as an object closed and distinct from the countryside. Polypthon's sight of the wood includes a knowledge that it is beyond the park, that he and Callophilus must go there another time. The problem is not that they might enjoy both the park and the country, but rather that the park itself should suggest that they exchange their conversation on antique art for horses; that the park is suddenly reduced to a representation.

Repton's attitude to appropriation changed through his life. While in his first publications he courted the landholder with claims to enrich a sense of possession, after much experience he became jaundiced with the cupidity of the rich and with what this was doing to the greater landscape of England.

> I have too frequently witnessed a greater satisfaction in turning a public road, in stopping a foot-path, or in hiding a view by a pale and a screen, than in the most beautiful improvements to the scenery; and sometimes have contended in vain against the firs and poplars, which, on the verge of a forest, presented more agreeable objects to the proprietor than the scenery of the forest itself; one acknowledged that he would rather look at a young sapling of his own, than the most venerable oaks belonging to the Crown.[20]

But underlying his changed attitude to real property, Repton's position about visual property and its limits remained constant.

In his design for Brandsbury published in *Sketches and Hints* of 1795, Repton made a humorous critique of the Brownian boundary (Figures 5.3 and 5.4). A polite party in the park come up against the boundary pale, an arbitrary limit that property put on their stroll. Their natural curiosity is frustrated and the gentleman levers himself up to look over the fence while the ladies squint between the pales.[21] Repton's solution is to open the park to the agricultural countryside beyond it, in this case, park-like land with grazing cattle. One presumes that now the party need not go there; they can look across the sunken fence and their eyes will extend where the park does not. Twenty-one years later in *Fragments*,

Figure 5.3 Humphry Repton's critique of the boundary, 1795 (state 1). By permission of State Library of New South Wales.

Figure 5.4 Humphry Repton's critique of the boundary, 1795 (state 2). By permission of State Library of New South Wales.

Repton made a different critique from a point of view outside the boundary, ironically titled 'Improvements' (Figure 5.5). Repton tells a fable about returning to visit a place he had admired years previously. There he met an old labourer who was forced by a newly enclosed park to 'walk a mile further round, every night after a hard day's work'.[22] The park had not been extended, but the new owner had planted up its boundary with the Scotch firs Repton thought so alien to England, and policed the boundary with a 'lofty close paling' and 'cautions against man-traps and spring-guns'.[23] The illustrations show that beyond the park is the source of the proprietor's wealth: a scene of endless wheat fields with harsh striated furrows. Repton recalls in a further image what the park had been like before it was 'improved'. The ancient park had no closed fence on the boundary, but an open one with a stile to assist in crossing it. The countryside beyond the park was not intensively farmed by big plough teams, but used lightly, perhaps for common grazing. Thus, the insult of the fence of the 'improved' landscape and the excessive sentiment of appropriation harmed three kinds of person: the labourers whose former patrons held them in antagonism and fear; the owners with their taste distorted from being pressed against the limit of their property; and Repton who we see in the image of the ancient park, sitting on a bench talking to the old cottager and looking into the park.

Figure 5.5 Humphry Repton, 'Improvements', 1816. By permission of Rare Books and Special Collections, State Library of New South Wales.

In these examples, so far apart in his career and attitudes to his profession, Repton's problem stayed the same at a formal level: the figure of the boundary made the division of property a constraint on the eye. It was not Repton's intention that, in the circumstances described, the labourer should be able to get into the park, or the gentry should be granted their wish to leave it. It was only Repton, the professor of landscape, and his readers, who actually had occasion to both aestheticize the countryside and visit the parks and homes of the aristocracy. Thus, Repton's regret at the old labourer's increased journey needs to be qualified. Repton did not design parks with free access for field labourers. He regretted that the park was made myopic through constraint by the property boundaries; it was not fitting into the tissue of the countryside, maintaining its flows, understanding its functions and economies. In Repton's landscape conceptions, the old labourer need not curse the enclosing landlord because he need never cross the boundary. The walk along the boundary would be the natural and obvious path to his work. Just as Repton did not allow for labourers to cross the boundary of the park, nor was there any special provision for the gentry to do so. Repton would have the spaces of park and country seem contiguous when in fact they were different types of space with different ways of opening and closing for different subjects. The problem of the park as property was that it loads boundaries with this impossible difference. A gentleman of taste needed to end his walk at the park boundary. To cross it meant exchanging Virgil for accounts of rent and crop yields, sketch-books for guns, the ideational games of status for the sheer coercive power of class difference. Repton's theory supposed that the park constructed a subjectivity that seemed to go beyond it. Thus taste was the natural consort to power; in no one moment could it have been seen that taste and ownership appropriated objects differently.

Repton's theories were based on the grand country houses and extensive parks that had been the paradigm of the landscapes of Kent and Brown, and on which he hoped to be commissioned. As his career progressed so too did the suburban villas and gardens that I discussed in the previous chapter. Repton's great influence on the history of landscape is at least partly because he was able to adapt his ideas to smaller projects. The gardens and terraces that he (like Price) recommended for great houses gave him control of the foreground from where he could also control the distant views. But this same technique was applicable without an extensive park. In these smaller commissions, the meaning of appropriation changed from describing the 'natural propensity' to look at what one owns, to a landscape technique where Repton supplied the boundless appetite of vision while using the property of others.

A good example of the technique of appropriation is a villa in the North of England (Figures 5.6 and 5.7) on which Repton reports.[24] There was the problem of extent, as the

Figure 5.6 Humphry Repton, 'A Common Improved in Yorkshire', 1816 (state 1). By permission of Rare Books and Special Collections, State Library of New South Wales.

Figure 5.7 Humphry Repton, 'A Common Improved in Yorkshire', 1816 (state 2). By permission of Rare Books and Special Collections, State Library of New South Wales.

view from the villa was of common land not owned by Repton's client. There was also a problem of character in 'a row of mean tenements [and] some of those places of worship too apt to disfigure the neighbourhood of all great manufacturing districts'.[25] The tenements and the non-conformist chapel not only shared the common with the villa, but were unsuitable ornaments to the landscape. These buildings were doubly 'unsightly': they should neither be looked at, nor should they share in the view. What was more, the villagers' use of the common, which in the illustration appears to be coursing with their dogs, brought them close enough to view into the garden of the villa. The solution advised by Repton is an act of enclosure that allowed the villa to have legal possession of the common, to drain it and plant it as a park forming the middle ground of the view from the villa. Then, by hiding the village with planting, the owners of the villa possessed the full scene as a landscape picture. In this case, the common had to be enclosed because the plantation hiding the houses could not have been made in the foreground – the problematic dwellings and chapel were directly opposite the house. However, simply planting the boundary to hide them could have had the effect of drawing attention to the limit of the landscape. It was thus essential that the real property boundary appear to be a natural feature of the topography rather than a limit to the purchasing power of the proprietor. Repton's boundary of trees was naturalized by appearing to line the bank of a river, which, in fact, was formed while draining the common. On the far bank of this 'river' stands an ornamental temple that must have been hard on the edge of the property, but because it was on the other side of the faux-river, the temple suggested a continuation of the property out of sight. Visible in the wood above are grand 'gentlemen's seats', socially and topographically superior to the villa, but after Repton's work they appeared to be neighbours with a common boundary. The 'appropriation' at the northern villa was this double 'taking' of real property and visual form, the latter enabled by the former.

Appropriation worked on four levels of referent. The first was the natural propensity of the client to love of possession. The second was the conventional signification of this as kind, quantity and proportion of property. Repton matched this social display to the actualities of the topography and the pocket book, but this work of matching – the sleights of hand about the actual extent of property and the antiquity of the landholding – are supposed to have disappeared in the finished design. Yet, Repton's publications explained the tricks. Thus, at the third level of remove, appropriation became visible again as a technique to be admired. In individual cases, we might imagine that proprietors would also have wanted to display their hiring of Repton through their possession of one of his famous Red Books, which showed how cleverly the landscape was done. Those who commissioned Repton, or those connoisseurs in reduced circumstance who knew his work only in publication, would have appreciated the art of the landscape appropriation because it demonstrated a kind of economy between art and the world. To understand landscape gardening as an art implied knowledge of principle and a consequent facility for the command of material in a kind of equation with the proprietor's mastery of resource. The final, fourth level of appropriation is again a kind of propensity, familiar to the modern world through the picturesque. We can all, by looking at the structure of the landscape, know how topography, ownership and investment in building constrain it. In this apprehension of structure, we have a kind of ownership.

Repton's final account of appropriation is in the final 'fragment' of *Fragments of the Theory and Practise of Landscape Gardening*, which is titled 'Hare Street: of quantity and Appropriation'[26] (see Figures 3.4 and 3.5). Hare Street is the name of the village in Essex where Repton lived in a cottage that he bought in 1786 and where he died in 1818, two years after the publication of the *Fragments*. The topic is announced as 'the little consequence of quantity or value' but it soon becomes clear that this is a vehicle for moral and autobiographical remarks. He intimates that he has accepted his approaching death; he draws for readers the lesson that the beauty of gardens is inalienable pleasure; and he concludes with an assessment of his character by an 'able statesman' – a somewhat early obituary. He then describes how appropriation made him a home with very little quantity of property.

> I obtained leave to remove the paling twenty yards further from the windows; and by this appropriation of twenty-five yards of garden, I have obtained a frame to my landscape; the frame is composed of flowering shrubs and evergreens; beyond which are seen, the cheerful village, the high road, and that constantly moving scene, which I would not exchange for all the lonely parks that I have improved for others.[27] [. . .] in improving places for others, I must consult their inclinations; at Hare Street, I follow my own. Others prefer still-life – I delight in movement; they prefer lawns fed by their own cattle – I love to see mankind; they derive pleasure from seeing the sheep and oxen fatten, and calculate on the produce of their beef and mutton: perhaps they might not object to the butcher's shop, which I have taken some trouble to hide, giving preference to a basket of roses. This specimen may serve to shew how much may be effected by the foreground; how a very small object, aptly placed near the eye, may hide an offensive object ten times as large [. . .] Such is the lesson of quantity and appropriation.[28]

Through the resource of a frame, Repton turned the village into a landscape as we see by comparing the views. The frame introduces a new balance to the pictorial composition. The existing framing trees are strengthened by some low shrubs to the right, the foreground now flows out as a lawn to the mid-ground and the mid-ground becomes a mixture of Repton's property and the houses of others. However, the frame also hides those objects that were inappropriate because they are disgusting, like the crippled beggar and the butcher's shop with its legs of mutton hanging over the dusty road. In the first picture, every person, including the passing outside passengers on the coach, can see onto Repton's porch; they are within a few steps of joining the beggar. The improvement removes everyone to a distance where no eye contact is possible. The powerful foreground frame of the two trees in the unimproved scene is, in the improved scene, relieved of its coercive fence, and is now hidden in the mid-ground shrubbery. The other village houses, which previously opened onto a space that faced the Repton cottage, now look into his garden across a boundary hedge, but the place for looking at the cottage has been removed.

In the earlier chapter on disgust I argued that there is a sub-text to Repton's remarks: his differences with Price, and particularly, with Price's explanation of his ideas about disgust which use the example of a butcher's shop. Price thought that all sensations including negative ones could be exercised in the improvement of taste. Repton did not. But on the larger issues of the picturesque they agreed. Price's interest in disgust was merely an extreme form of his argument that one could have a taste for the ordinary and everyday, even the agricultural countryside. He proposed that rather than pull down villages and replace them with high-genre ornamental buildings, landholders could accept the village as an object of taste rather than of economic necessity, and tactically improve it.

> Should he, however, choose to preserve the look of a farm or hamlet [. . .] any building of good form, rising higher than the rest amidst them, would probably answer to that purpose, and serve at once to vary and unite the whole group [. . .] There may be cases

> also where an improver, with great property all round, may have only a small piece of ground in such a hamlet, and be unable to purchase any more: a building of the character I mentioned, might do all that a lover of painting wish for, and give him a sort of property in the whole; and I know that manner of appropriating objects to be the source of much pleasure.[29]

Repton followed Price in these ideas, and Blaise Castle Hamlet was a clear case where the client, Harford, did not own the village, but gave himself the feeling of ownership. He overcame the closure of his park pale by building the ornamental cottages at the edge the neighbouring village. As we saw in Loudon's cartoon and Repton's remarks, a hierarchy of building was a way of telling (or making up) the character of a great house. Repton's remarks about his cottage at Hare Street put this idea through a further turn, because Repton appropriated the village from a position within, not outside of it. When Repton looked onto 'the cheerful village, the high road, and that constantly moving scene' what he saw was what was significant in the situation of his cottage: it was off the highway; it viewed the other houses and the inn; and it had a garden that maintained the privacy of the house while offering amenity to his neighbours.[30] The things that the appropriation edited out of view – the butcher's shop, the coach passengers and the beggar – were all things that Repton did not want 'to call his own'.

> And, after all, the most romantic spot, the most picturesque situations, and the most delightful assemblage of nature's choicest materials, will not long engage our interest, without some appropriation; something we can call our own; and if not our own property, at least, it may be endeared to us by calling it our own home.[31]

The Oxford English Dictionary's definition of appropriation makes a subtle distinction: 'the making of a thing private property, whether another's or (as now commonly) one's own; taking as one's own or to one's own use'.[32] At Hare Street, Repton used the more common modern significance, that is, he took what was already his own with a greater 'endearment'. What was already his own was not real property, but the situation of his property in relation to that of his neighbours and the social world that made. Repton was writing about what would become the concept of urban context. Price's idea for tactical intervention in existing towns was put into practice by John Nash in Regent Street in the 1810s. Price's passing remark and Nash's concrete practice are revolutionary; they no longer supposed that architecture acted on buildings and towns or cities with equal criteria and strength. Nash showed that relatively few buildings, acting in concert, could have the effect – weak although nevertheless sufficient – of 'unit[ing] the whole group' and appropriating a whole area of London to a design idea. Nash was designing a street and park, Price was imagining the appropriation of a hamlet; both are units larger than a single building site. Repton's proposal was even more radical in its modesty: even a single site could provide opportunities for the designer to reorder and revalue its relations with its surroundings; every site, every building, is a picture of its context.

From landscape and prospect to landscape and power

In Chapter 2, I outlined a disagreement between Repton and Price about the use of pictorial concepts in gardening. Repton attempted to refute Price's 'picture-gardening', stating that the gardener's art must include the making of prospects, or views from high places, which

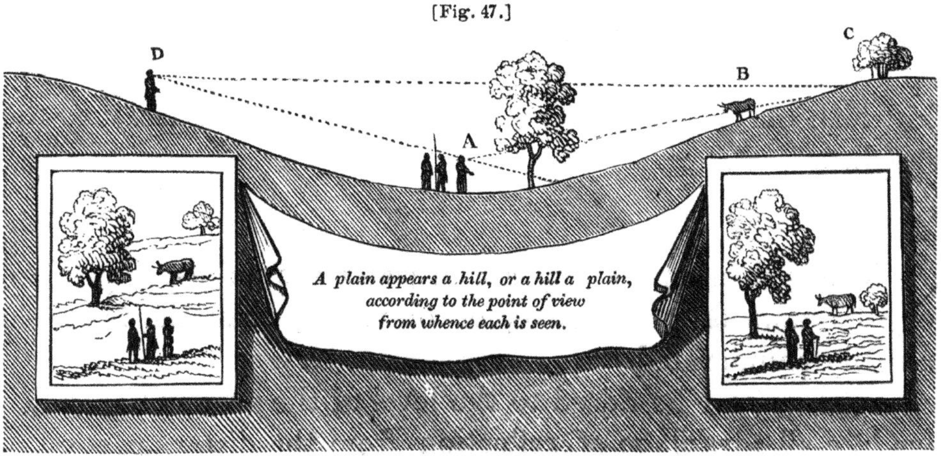

Figure 5.8 Humphry Repton, 'A Plain appears a hill . . .', 1803 (1840).

Figure 5.9 Humphry Repton, 'General View of Longleat from the Prospect Hill', 1816. By permission of Rare Books and Special Collections, State Library of New South Wales.

could not make successful pictures. This is somewhat obtuse of Repton, as he invented the term 'landscape gardening' for his practice, and he has a role for 'prospects'. His diagram, 'A plain appears a hill, or a hill a plain, according to the point of view from whence each is seen'[33] (Figure 5.8), explains this articulation well. Repton even went some way to showing that a prospect might be painted in the charming picture of a 'Picnic at the Prospect Point above Longleat', except that, as a picture, it relies on the foreground made by the prospect-takers (Figure 5.9). The debate between the two theorists about viewpoint, painting and gardening was also likely to have been something of a staged bout as it was an echo of Whately who decades earlier wrote:

> Painting, with all its powers, is still more unequal to some subjects, and can give only a faint, if any, representation of them; but a gardiner is not therefore to reject them; he is not debarred from a view down the sides of a hill, or a prospect where the horizon is lower than the station, because he never saw them in a picture.[34]

I will show how Repton used prospects before I return to Price's reply. Their discussion of viewpoint and horizon can be used to open broader issues of the politics of the picturesque, and the mechanism by which landscape concepts become one of the bases of urban design.

Prospect bears directly on the extent of the landscape and the problematic of proprietorship that I have been describing. John Barrell has shown that in the early eighteenth century, prospect and landscape were opposed as kinds of views on the model of the general and particular.[35] Landscape as a genre of painting but also view, was concerned with the detail and hence the incidental and accidental aspects of nature and the particularity of life as it was lived by necessity. Prospect, by contrast, partook of a noble generality: an aptitude for oversight, analysis and higher understanding that assumed freedom from necessity. As Barrell shows, this understanding of prospect is based on an ideology in which land was understood as a secure form of property that guaranteed objectivity in judgement and suitability to govern (as I discussed in Chapter 3). Eventually pictures of landscape came to have, by virtue of their frame and their being property, an element of what real views of the particularity of the world lacked: a way of being outside and above – a way of being a prospect. By the end of the century, Barrell suggests, new understandings of credit meant land lost some of its symbolic power and had become less a franchise in the civic realm and more a simple possession that would make it vanity to display publicly. The simple contrast of the display of extent in Brown and Repton, which I discussed earlier, was an issue of social change as much as the internal development of a formal problem. The extent of Brown's parks had a meaning anterior to wealth, but this was greatly weakened by Repton's time. In some ways, this fading of the discourse of civic humanism is merely historical context to the issues of design and visual form; but significations of property and responsibility continue in the way that we use the term 'landscape'. As it became generalized from a genre of painting to its current use, 'landscape' swallowed something of the meaning of prospect. The social and political significances of landscape and prospect are important in the later history of a politics of landscape, but so too is contrast of viewpoints which is the basis of the political identification – the fact that, as Whately put it, a prospect could not be a picture. There is another historical aspect of the contrast of landscape and prospect at which this discussion must begin, and it is a point that Barrell does not open: landscape and prospect were not simply different kinds of views that required different kinds of representation; for the picturesque theorists, a prospect was a kind of view that could not be a picture.

Repton makes the distinction when describing two views at Heathfield Park, the first being a landscape:

> numerous objects so wonderfully combined in this extensive view; the house, the church, the lawns, the woods, the bold promontory of Beachy Head, and the distant plains bounded by the sea, are all collected in one splendid picture, without being crowded into confusion.
>
> This view is a perfect *landscape*, while that from the tower is rather a *prospect*; it is of such a nature as not to be well represented by painting: because its excellence depends upon the state of the atmosphere which is very hostile to the painter's art. An extensive prospect is most admired when the distant objects are most clear and distinct; but the painter can represent his distances only by a certain haziness and indistinctness, which is termed aerial perspective.[36]

For Repton, a landscape can be extensive and suggestive of those connections between its elements that invite higher thought, but it is nevertheless distinguishable from the prospect.

The first reason that prospects could not make good pictures was that their viewpoints were too high and therefore as pictures, their horizons would be too high or too low. From a prospect point one looks out or down, but not 'into'. Painted prospect pictures were produced at the time and are now often called 'topographical landscapes'. In terms of traditional expectations of landscape, they look unsatisfyingly flat because looking down from a high place gives too much plan information and lacks the articulation of successive depths, which achieves the spatial illusion of looking into a picture. Without foregrounds, their surface distributions look very similar to one another. The differences between them are geographical rather than pictorial: all are governed by the line of the horizon splitting sky from earth. In fact, the flatness of topographical 'landscape' painting has much in common with twentieth-century painting, a point to which we will return. On the problematic of extent and appropriation that we have been following in Repton's work: the distinction between landscape and prospect is important because extent was a matter of view in landscape and cadastre in prospect.

In the *Red Book* for Tendring, there is a rare statement on the double problem of the view to and from a house that, according to Repton, was sited too high.[37] In remarks titled 'Character', Repton informed Sir William Rowley that the new house designed by John Soane was completely inadequate.[38] Repton accused Soane of not understanding the role of buildings in the country. The architect sited the house prominently on a hill, and compressed it into a small volume on three levels. The result was too small for the visual field in which it was subject: 'the house is not apparently of sufficient importance for the park, I should rather look forward to a period when [by the addition of attached wings] the mansion may be made to correspond with the grounds'.[39] This is another instance of an argument about character and extent of property that runs through all of Repton's works. What is of particular interest in the *Tendring Red Book* is that Repton goes on to describe the problems of the disunity of character in the view from the house. This section is headed 'Situation'.

> the difference betwixt a prospect and a landscape, I shall [attempt to show] with views from the Saloon, presently . . . the point of view is so high compared with the horizon, that it is impossible to hope for any foreground of trees to raise above it, the ground under the eye is spread out as in a map, and all inequalities of surface are lost by looking over them, consequently the view must be considered as a prospect; [this must] lead the eye to distant cornfields which should not form the principle object of a view from the house. To remedy this, I propose the removal of many trees yet by the help of others in the more distant avenue, and a plantation near the lodges, we shall preserve a kind of rich park foreground to appropriate and enrich the prospect.
>
> [The effect of this is shown with the removal of the slide. Repton then shows a third view, without a slide, taken from a lower angle.]
>
> The foregoing sketch presents nearly the same objects as those seen from the house, but being viewed from a different level to what I considered before as a prospect, then becomes a Landscape. The opposite hill is indeed lower. The Town of Nayland, the Lodges and distant objects are more compressed, but the shapes of the ground are more conspicuous and the trees in the second distance rise above the horizon.[40]

Soane's compact three-storey house looked small compared to the extensive park, but this problem was the more confounding because from inside the house the park looked inadequate.

The prospect accidentally created from the drawing room included property outside the proprietor's control, i.e. 'to cornfields which should not form the principle object of a view',[41] and this gave Repton a second reason to propose lowering it. If that had been undertaken (sensibly it was not), then the 'inequalities of ground' would have given Repton a way of using earthworks and planting to control the foreground, break the horizon and reconcile real property and property in view. The tricks of appropriation are revealed in the prospect, but if the place was well designed, these tricks are irrelevant. Some of these issues could be made clearer in an analysis of one of Repton's designs: Blaise Castle Estate near Bristol.

At Blaise, Repton reworked an existing park that contained a prospect tower as at Heathfield. At Blaise, this triangular mock Gothic shell on top of the hill was the basis for calling the place 'castle', despite the prim Georgian house below it that Repton disliked. Repton's design involved changing the approach to the house so that instead of coming into its carriage court directly from the village of Henbury and off the road from Bristol, one entered from the further London road, through an irregular crenellated gate house and a long drive. The drive passes through a forest, and the house is first seen across the roof of a woodsman's hut, which makes a pleasing and contrasting foreground. Very soon after this point, a steep gorge is revealed and one's expectation of a smooth and rapid arrival at the house is exchanged for a much longer precipitous descent through hanging woods and past a ruined mill, before the drive climbs back into the sunlight, and the cheerful hospitality of the house. The house's court opens directly onto the village of Henbury, in an image of the building hierarchy of former feudal times that Repton recommended. In fact, Harford, the owner, was a Bristol merchant whose family's money came from the slave trade, and not from ancient estates. The philanthropic hamlet, which Nash and George Stanley Repton built at the edge the village, assuaged some of Harford's guilt about the origins of his wealth and also further supported the image of his paternal possession of the village.[42]

In the *Red Book* for Blaise, Repton gave a clear demonstration of his use of pictorial composition, that is consistent with his remarks at Attingham where he contrasted the proportions of pictures with the wider viewing field of human vision and the landscaper's art. In a watercolour, Repton shows the view from the house in a wide format. On one side, we glimpse the prospect tower on the ridge, but, even with its strong depths, there is insufficient focus to make a view. When one lifts Repton's famous 'slides' to see the painting of the improved view, the woodsman's hut appears. The two buildings, then, provide the objects of two 'pictures', one indicating a prospect and the other a landscape. At Attingham, he had quipped that 'picture gardening' would be like so many paintings by Claude, fixed together end to end, but Repton's qualification of 'picture gardening' was quite simple and minor. Human vision being what it is, the gardener cannot make pictures, but he can supply the depths, to which a coincidental foreground, or object in the background, could be sought by the viewer to complete the picture. If, at Blaise, one is enticed to walk from the house to revisit the woodsman's hut, one moves closer into the 'landscape' of strong foregrounds and high horizons of the gorge. But if one chooses the castle as a destination, a different experience opens. With a bird's-eye view from the prospect tower, one can see the relative proximity of elements of the landscape and the park wall. The relatively small size of this suburban estate can be compared to the greater extent of the landscape experience that Repton had contrived. One also sees beyond the property: the village of Henbury beyond the hamlet; the neighbouring farms; and the gentlemen's seats. But these do not impinge on the prospect as they would on a landscape because the view is dominated by the sky, the estuary of the Avon and the Bristol Channel – which is to say – transcendent territories beyond possession.

When Repton attacked Price's picturesque as 'picture-gardening', his argument followed this line: the gardener is obliged to include prospects because of an innate propensity to wish to see from the highest point.

> In the valley a thousand delightful subjects present themselves to the painter, yet the visitors to this place [Matlock Bath] are seldom satisfied till they have climbed the neighbouring hills, to take a bird's eye view of the whole spot, which no painting can represent.[43]

As I have shown with the example of Blaise Castle, Repton used prospect points as the culmination of the sequence of the design. Cadastral information was withheld within the 'landscape', so that the extent and the adjacencies of passages of the design were not apparent until the final prospect: a plan-like view. Repton's description also supposes an anthropological basis for the formalization of view types. The park visitors had an inchoate desire for the high point and the most extensive view. Repton's task was to delay them – have them dally in the culture of landscape to civilize their sensibilities.

In reply to Repton, Price professed that he too loved a prospect, having several at his estate, Foxley, to which he took guests.[44] Like Repton, he wrote of prospects as necessary accompaniments to landscape; he decried the false taste that apparently led some of his contemporaries to affect a disdain of prospects to better show their understanding of landscape. Price agreed with Repton that a prospect could not be painted, but expressed bemusement at why this would lead his interlocutor to think that prospects could not be included in a picturesque design. Price then makes a quite sophisticated argument, showing that viewpoint, the angle of vision and foreground were at stake in the prospect landscape distinction. 'With regard to prospects, they are for the most part taken from the highest and openest part of a hill, where there is the least obstruction, and consequently where there is seldom either foreground or second distance.'[45] Price proposes a mental experiment where one takes the foreground from a master's painting and applies it to a 'mere prospect'. A beautiful landscape will result, he claims. Price proposes that:

> With respect to the point of sight being taken high, *that* has frequently a very grand effect; and that Titian thought so, [. . .] may be proved by the height of the horizon line, he has supposed himself on a considerable eminence. Where beauty is the painter's object (as was the case with Claude) it is certainly more judicious to place the horizon line lower, which he accordingly does.[46]

Price thought the high horizon line in Titian's landscapes showed that his paintings strove for grandeur. By taking a high viewpoint, looking slightly downwards rather than out, and by introducing foreground, Titian employed a touch of sublimity in a landscape. The lower horizons of Claude's paintings assumed a lower viewpoint and an aesthetic value in beauty. Although he was not explicit on this point, we can take it as implied that for Price, the picturesque was an horizon lower still, like the paintings he admired of Salomon van Ruysdael or Meindert Hobbema in which a great expanse of sky is divided and arranged by an incidental foreground of twisted trees, cottages and boats. We could extrapolate a broader theory from Price's remarks: that the angle of vision and the extent of vision had a certain reciprocity. Some landscape artists that Price admired – Salvator Rosa, some Ruysdaels, Gainsborough – drew the foreground even closer so that the horizon was high in the picture plan but the extent of view was reduced. Implicit in Price's remarks was the idea that the extent of view and height of viewpoint interact. A picturesque landscape could have a low horizon and thus represent the distance, if much of this was obscured by the foreground. The picturesque could have a high horizon, if the viewpoint was low and the objects all close at hand. The paintings of Titian and Claude, despite a degree of picturesqueness in their foreground, were grand and beautiful because they represented not only the distance but the recession by which our eye traces a path from the foreground into the mid- and backgrounds, and thus matched an understanding of topographic structure to the pictorial structure.

One way to understand this issue of viewpoint is as a rotation of the viewpoint that was implicit in earlier geometrical gardens. Allan Weiss has done much to overcome the clichés of simplicity and over-determination of the French garden inherited from English commentators such as George Mason.[47] André Le Nôtre's gardens at Vaux-le-Vicomte and Versailles do not subjugate lived experience to abstract pattern as has so often been suggested, rather their experience is of surprises and allegories that Le Nôtre contrived through optical theory. The flatness of the garden means that relatively small changes in level have dramatic effects in the field of view. There is a prospect that we can deduce from the plan of the garden, but the point at which it would be visible would not be on a hill but almost vertically above looking down, which is to say, from an inhuman position. Versailles is an exercise in sheer power, through extent and expense, but the optical aspect of this power is not a crushing of human experience *per se*, it is rather an emblem of the encompassing power of the King. One is not subjugated by geometry or figure; the figure that one could not see except anamorphically is the cipher of Monsieur. For Repton, the usual picturesque condition of visuality was to be within the landscape, and when he offered access to a prospect that saw outside this, it was not a requirement of having been in the landscape; it was an addendum. The prospect was a reflection on a normative landscape experience. By contrast, Le Nôtre's gardens supposed not a norm but an epitome of seeing: the super-prospect of the King's aerial view.[48] In relation to this, scratching around on the surface among the parterres is incidental. The inference that the King is outside the garden looking down onto it is not only due to our anamorphic view of the figures, but also to the overall impression that the garden is a flat tray of space, bounded by a low horizon and under the larger space of the sky.

The picturesque, with its celebration of contingency, cannot be assimilated to this master allegory of Kingship, and the prospects that Repton and Price wrote of were not suppositions of oversight but real hills and real views. The naturalism of the picturesque meant that topography was not flattened to make the garden. To an extent, any view into rising ground was a landscape, any view down a hill could be a prospect. As well as foreground, it is this active topography and the variable position of the horizon that contrasts so sharply with the geometric garden, and allows us to think beyond the opposition of landscape and prospect to see them as degrees of elevation and inclination of view.

In different ways, both Price and Repton stretched the usage of the word 'landscape' and developed the remit of the pictorial as it describes actual views. When Repton and Price included the making of prospects in 'landscape' gardening, they were contributing to the radical generalization of the word as we now use it. If today deserts, rainforests and glaciers; parterre or water gardens; farmland and freeways; can be called landscapes, it is not so much because of an analogy with the subjects of painters as the idea that each 'landscape' brings into relation the extent of the view with its contingencies or foreground. This significance for landscape begins in the later eighteenth century as the social and political significance of prospect weakened, and it became possible to think of landscape, a new kind of liberality not based on a property franchise, but on the autonomy learned in judging pictures.

Repton's concept of appropriation can also be understood in the light of this folding of prospect into landscape. His idea of using the view of areas beyond the park in his designs had famous precedents. William Kent was the first to leap the fence, as Horace Walpole puts it, to see landscape as a relation of garden, park and countryside.[49] Gilpin seemed to announce something of the idea of appropriation in his *Dialogue upon Stowe*, where the characters looked out of the park. However, the owner of Stowe, Viscount Lord Cobham, had, by his nature and office, an extensive view; when he looked beyond the park he saw England at a high level of generality. By contrast, appropriation is a prospect that only appears by virtue of a qualification, a foreground that allows the eye to command the distance, but at the cost of remaining particular. Appropriation is not that majesty of sight that belongs to and betokens exceptional individuals suited to government; it is a decentred prospect contingent on position, not person. To call a place a landscape still implies a kind of property, a claim to being outside of a situation and to be able to perceive its connections in a way that those that are within it cannot. Landscape is an aesthetic of ownership in the sense that to see in this way encourages us to mentally command and to reorder what we see, to place the hill and the bay on the parallel thirds, to leave the fishing boats and sink the jet skis. But at another level, this landscape still contains something of the civics of prospect, if an eccentric one. To see landscape is to see structure and connection; even if this is pictorial, it is not completely disconnected from a responsibility to govern what one sees.

I am going to explore this issue of appropriation, with its strange mix of aesthetics and government, by looking next at the revival of the picturesque in British town planning and architecture from the 1940s to the 1960s. This is an obvious enough route to take because the post-war revival of the picturesque as a guide to design practice is the main way in which Repton's and Price's ideas survived and were developed. However, this is not the usual way in which visual proprietorship is discussed in the literature. In the studies of cultural history, the picturesque is generally held to have had actual power in the subjection of people and places.

Stephen Copley and Peter Garside introduce a very useful and varied volume of essays titled *The Politics of the Picturesque*, with this clear summary:

> The picturesque translates the political and the social into the decorative, and so, as the route to the naturalisation of the picturesque image. The clearest instance of this translation is the picturesque deployment of motifs for aesthetic effect which in other circumstances are the indicators of poverty or social deprivation [. . .] recent criticism has also questioned the extent to which the picturesque initially and specifically a domestic landscape aesthetic – can be seen to shape British (or wider European) accounts of colonial landscapes and cultures.[50]

W. J. T. Mitchell takes an even stronger line, arguing that the study of landscape is a matter of 'a historical, political, and (yes) aesthetic alertness to the violence and evil written on the land, projected there by the gazing eye. [. . .] What we know now is that landscape itself is the medium by which this evil is veiled and naturalized'.[51] Mitchell is critical of most revisionist accounts because, in his mind, they fail to sufficiently distinguish viewing landscape from representing it, leaving open a false supposition that the European nexus of painting and land is the origin and model for other cultures and circumstances. Mitchell argues that we need to posit 'landscape' as a cultural artefact based on viewing, and anterior to the kinds of picturing practice representing 'landscapes'.

I think that ideas of a powerful and oppressive picturesque are exaggerated, because of the landscape prospect distinction that I have been examining and because of loose uses of the concept of ideology. Much of Repton's and Price's writing is clearly ideological in the sense that it bolstered existing beliefs, giving a logic and apparent inevitability to the tastes of landholders. The picturesque, thus, naturalized the hegemony of the landholders or colonists as Mitchell, and Copley and Garside, and many others write. In this and the previous chapters, I have built on this understanding of the politics of the picturesque. But I have also tried to show how attenuated this politics is, how class relations are an occasion for ideational games such as the aesthetics of disgust and the hierarchy of genre in painting. The thrust of my Chapter 2 shows that poverty and social deprivation are not transmuted into the decorative in the picturesque but maintained in the mechanism by which disgust gives a profile to aesthetical feeling. In the same way, appropriation, the fact and feeling of acquisition, clearly has a reference in the actual appropriations of the enclosure of common lands in England. The landscape design and the role that it has in feelings of appropriation must have contributed a common cultural base to those engaged in the clearances of the Scottish Highlands and the Black Line in Tasmania. But how the cultural self-consistency of imperialists is actually served in these very different circumstances is a moot point.

The English landscape painter John Glover, who emigrated to Tasmania in the early nineteenth century, included Aborigines in his paintings in a manner similar to the figures in his earlier English landscapes.[52] Glover was taught by John 'Warwick' Smith, who accompanied William Gilpin on his Tours and provided some of his illustrations.[53] What are we to make of this common template of pastoral arcadia, when the actual mechanism of the genocide against the Tasmanians was so different to the enclosure of commons in England? Of course, Glover's paintings cannot be extricated from the land tenure, agriculture, surveys, fences, roads, militia and landscape gardening that made parts of Australia look like parts of Britain in the nineteenth century. If there are aesthetics of sight operative in fences and surveys, it is not landscape but prospect – those affects of possessing not organized by culture but anterior to it. Much of the discussion of visual objectification and imaginary possession that heads full of the picturesque were supposed to have taken to subdue the wilds of New Zealand or Canada, in fact, speaks of this older idea of prospect. The sovereignty claimed by sight was the external referent point of landscape, which was not landscape. It is simpler and closer to modern usage to call both parts of this relation 'landscape'; but beyond historical accuracy there are issues in the distinction that continue to concern us today. Mitchell argues against the British authors that we ought not conflate the picturesque landscape of late eighteenth-century Britain with landscape *per se*, or with the landscape of other imperialists such as the ancient Romans, or the Chinese. But his point here is not inconsistent with that the picturesque theorists make themselves in distinguishing the new sense of landscape that they were developing from prospect. In prospect, the viewer was implied to be a sovereign of what was seen. In landscape, the viewer stood to one side; sovereignty was vicarious and fleeting. Landscape plays at power and possession, always contingent to the prospect point, but flitting past it. It seems to me that what was significant in the politics of the picturesque at this more general level was the illusory aspects of Repton's appropriation. Landscape appropriation was thus the name for what had failed to be appropriated in fact. Repton bought twenty-five yards of road verge and the illusion of owning, or at least being at home, in his village. The elegiac picturesqueness of Glover's paintings lay in the fact that they named for him a Tasmania that he did not own, where he imagined himself the benevolent governor of a landscape park peopled by Aborigines. In each of these circumstances, 'landscape' holds the imprint of power relations, and it does so with a degree of nuance that allows us to see a critical potential in the paintings and design. But the picturesqueness of these scenes is a relation within culture, not an instrument of domination.

Although the prospect–landscape distinction seems arcane today with the vast extension of the latter term, it does show how the power to dispose territory comes to be incorporated in picturesque culture of the time. Then and now, claims of the power of landscape to enable conquest and to reorder the world run in the face of the most obvious facts about the sumptuary role of art in all societies. Landscape, like painting, architecture, music and dress, is in the first place an economy of the display of wealth; the critical or ideological potential that its practitioners might seek in it are at a second order, and in the first place marginal. The problem of landscape and architecture is that they are almost tautological as arts, being made out of what they are displaying: land and building that are already thoroughly determined. In the end, claims that complex concepts of viewing land like picturesqueness functioned in colonialism, display an anxiety about the triviality of landscape. Landscape risks the kind of satiation-induced disgust that was discussed in Chapter 2, if its only role is to insist that one should be affected by one's possessions.

In my view, there is another reason, outside the discussion thus far, for why landscape is thought to be so strong in appropriating otherness to familiar forms: it obscures the more significant project of applying landscape ideas at the centre of Western culture – in the design of cities. This, too, is a project in which the effects of landscape are much weaker than the claims made for it, but where that weakness has something to tell us – landscape is as much about the theory of governance as the actual exercise of power.

Ivor de Wolfe's picturesque, or, who and what was Townscape?[54]

One of the main reasons that the picturesque has resisted being subsumed into broader and arguably more sophisticated ideas about spatio-visual experience is that it was explicitly revived as a touch-stone of national culture in post-war England. The agency for this lay largely with a professional architecture journal, the *Architectural Review* (*AR*), its owner Hubert de Cronin Hastings, and its editorial team, including the émigré art historian Nikolaus (later Sir Nikolaus) Pevsner. Price would have thoroughly approved of the purpose of this revival: to create a new sensibility of 'Townscape' that could carry picturesque ideas and techniques into the problem of rebuilding and expanding post-war British cities. Although the scholarly activity that supported the polemic of the *AR* constitutes a good part of the literature on the picturesque, few today realize how close Townscape and the picturesque are as concepts. Nor is it apparent to most how much our present ideas of the picturesque were shaped by its development in Townscape, and the later critique of Townscape. Further entangling the picturesque's reception and development was the nationalistic bent of the *AR*'s enterprise (which began just before World War II) and a chauvinistic modernism that caused the more obvious developments of the picturesque in the nineteenth century to be disregarded. Appropriation of the picturesque is one of the issues in Townscape but the larger theme of appropriation in Repton's sense of the relation of real and visual property remains the main theme of this chapter.

The idea of the picturesque as a potentially productive mismatch between actual and imaginary control of territory continues in the twentieth century, and so too does a discussion of the sovereignty of sight. While I have argued that it is close to tautology to say that landscape has had political effects, there is no doubt that the picturesque was conceived as if it did have particular powers of possession. These were not the real politics of arrogation of land, nor an ideology required to justify this. It was not so much an aestheticization of politics as of political theory. The rational and the empirical in architecture planning and landscape can be thought to confront one another, as do the French and English systems of state and law.

Modern theories of the state evolved at roughly the same time as landscape architecture and the contrast of the geometric French garden from the irregular naturalism of the English was celebrated from the eighteenth century onward as an analogy of national characters and differing concepts of government. Townscape's theory of city planning based on opportunity and contingency was contrasted with planning based on system; in the same pattern of binary opposition in which codified law was opposed to case-based law, and the republican sovereignty of the people was compared to the vicarious sovereignty of constitutional monarchy.

It is worth insisting at the outset what a very strange relation of art and politics this was. The control of territory is one of the basic tasks of government and is innately political as is obvious in the many occasions where governments change rights of development and land tenure systems, or provide more or less infrastructure and thus change the value of land. Architecture, which is premised on a right to develop property, exists within a more general governance of land supply and value, the limits on uses of buildings, on their size, demography, transport infrastructure and so on. One would expect a political relation between architecture, planning, the capacity to govern these matters, and the actions of governments that wield these powers. However, Townscape proposed that what architecture and planning required to intersect productively was a visual analysis and order, found in picturesque theory and its supposed foundation in liberalism. Townscape, then, was not so much politics by other means as it was an illustration – a picture – of a liberal political comportment that might also be the comportment of the architect or artist. Thus, the first and central point to note about Townscape was the absence of actual problems, technologies and politics of land and planning. Before land economy and transport engineering, Townscape proposed that the primary 'political' problem to address was the ability to picture urban life.

In 1949, the *AR* announced a programme for the renewal of architecture and town planning under the title 'Townscape: A Plea for an English Visual Philosophy founded on the true rock of Sir Uvedale Price'. The author was Ivor de Wolfe – a pseudonym of the owner-editor Hubert de Cronin Hastings who was greatly influenced by Christopher Hussey's *The Picturesque* of 1927. Hastings recruited Pevsner to the editorial team in 1942 and the historian later recalled that about that time Hastings remarked to him that there was much in common between the picturesque and the work of the journal in modern architecture and urbanism.[55] The 1947 article was accompanied by a 'Townscape Casebook', which is an essay in photographs, and diagrams by the magazine's art director, Gordon Cullen (Figure 5.10). Cullen's graphic interpretation and his later book *Townscape* had the largest influence on Townscape's reception, which still has adherents today. However, Cullen's work was something of a simplification of the idea, and his success has obscured something of the orginal aims of 'Ivor de Wolfe', as have the scale and variety of Townscape as a publishing phenomenon. Mathew Aitchison has identified over 200 articles in the *AR* that argue the Townscape case, from the 1930s through to the 1960s and 1970s, when the idea was reprised in numerous special editions such as, 'The Functional Tradition', 'Outrage', 'Counter-Attack', 'The Italian Townscape', 'Civilia' and lastly, the fabulous 'SLOAP' (an acronym for 'space left over after planning'). While Pevsner and Hastings' work lies at the core of the Townscape idea, not only Cullen but also Ian Nairn and Kenneth Browne were key figures in developing the idea; and Aitchison has identified over 20 other contributors.

The 1949 'Townscape' article was something of a post-rationalization of a tendency emerging in the journal before the war. In 1944, 'the Editor' published the core of the argument later called Townscape, under the title 'Exterior Furnishing or Sharawaggi: The Art of Making Urban Landscape'. Pevsner laid out the main historical and scholarly arguments for

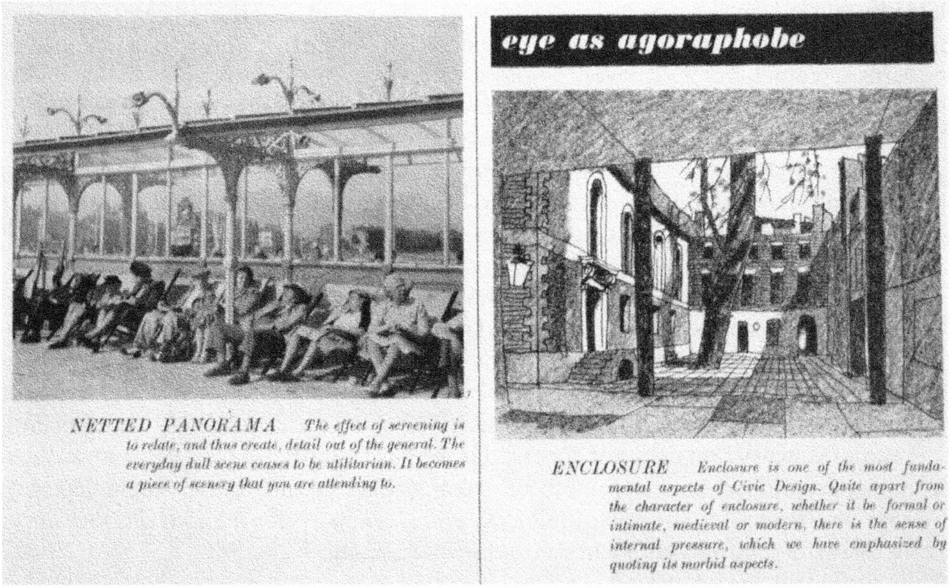

Figure 5.10 Gordon Cullen, 'Netted Panorama' and 'Enclosure', from 'Townscape Casebook', 1949.

Townscape in his paper 'The Picturesque in Architecture', read to the RIBA in 1947. The origins of the project were probably in a commission that Hastings gave to Pevsner sometime early in the 1940s, to produce a book tentatively entitled *Visual Planning*.[56] The book was never completed but drafts contain the notes that Pevsner used in a number of historical and exegetical essays on Sir Joshua Reynolds, Price, Knight, Repton and on the 'genesis' of the picturesque, which began to appear during the war.[57] Pevsner also made analyses of Oxford, Cambridge and Bath as urban structures: 'sequences of buildings – interior and exterior spaces which can reveal their aesthetic qualities only to the roving eye. The immoveable eye of the camera cannot catch them'.[58] These analyses were to be illustrated by sequential photographic views keyed to plans, a technique that Cullen later made famous.

While 'Ivor de Wolfe' was Hastings' pseudonym and it is most likely that he put the words on the page, there are several reasons for hearing both men's voices in 'de Wolfe'. The manuscript, *Visual Planning*, seems to have been one of de Wolfe's major sources. De Wolfe's voice was also the next incarnation of 'the Editor', who was the author of 'Exterior Furnishing', the first full articulation of the 'Townscape' argument in 1944. Pevsner was the editor at the time along with Hastings and J. M. Richards, who was absent serving the Ministry of Information during the war. Pevsner used other pseudonyms, and wrote regularly as 'Peter F. R. Donner', perhaps to give the appearance of a greater depth of contributors than the *AR* could actually muster during the war. Not only ideas but actual phrases from de Wolfe's articles later appeared in *The Englishness of English Art*, where Pevsner is given as sole author.[59] When Basil Taylor attacked the picturesque revival and the *AR*'s promotion of it on the BBC in 1954, it was Pevsner, not de Wolfe, who replied.[60] When Peter Reyner Banham, another enemy of the picturesque revival, recounted the period, it was Pevsner, his former PhD supervisor, who was the main player.[61] De Wolfe's texts were most likely composed by Hastings, and with a degree of polemic and irascibility uncharacteristic of Pevsner. But behind this lay Pevsner's research, his notes, and his historiographic suppositions of *kunstgeographie*, along with an Hegelian idea of artistic progress and the historical inevitability of modernism. Pevsner's histories were intended to be partisan promotions of the revealed historical destiny of modernism, as David Watkin has shown at length.[62] Whether Pevsner, de Cronin Hastings, or a combination of the two, 'de Wolfe' was the moment about which Pevsner's history became operative.

'Exterior Furnishing or Sharawaggi: The Art of Making Urban Landscape' (Figure 5.11) by the Editor, is retrospectively considered to be de Wolfe's first outing. The author distinguishes his ideas about what we would now call urbanism from those of his contemporaries.

> Planning theory at the moment might be described as a fight between three groups: the garden city people, the Bauhausians, and the County Councils. The garden city people . . . have on their side a keen sense of the cosy life, but they have little understanding of the metropolitan scene or of the intricacy of social contacts or even of the variety of human tastes and types. The Bauhausians have boldness and architectural imagination. But their new world does not appear to incorporate any of the old ones, and to many quiet people it seems that, like other revolutionaries, they may destroy more than they can possibly create. They have no tolerance of accident. As for the councils, they are as a rule all out for Bankers' Georgian and road-widening.[63]

De Wolfe wanted a *civitas* unavailable in the Garden City, and unlike the Bauhausians, he favoured the maintenance of historic structures. The word 'Sharawaggi' in the title is a clue to the major argument of the essay. This imagined Chinese word was used by Sir William Temple to describe the Chinese taste for irregular landscape in his *Gardens of Epicurus* of 1685 and the word became synonymous with the early picturesque and an irregular form

Figure 5.11 Illustration for 'Exterior Furnishing or Sharawaggi: The Art of Making Urban Landscape', 1944.

of landscape. In the *AR* 'sharawaggi' became a shibboleth for those who thought picturesque theory could be the means of making operative a modernism reconciled with tradition. By 'picturesque' de Wolfe means the power of pictorial composition to unify disparate elements: 'to *reconcile visually* in the mind's eye what would appear to be irreconcilable elements in any town plan: quaint bits, new bits, monuments, traffic, tall buildings, short buildings, flat blocks, individual cottages, etc., etc.'[64]

At the level of technique, all Townscape theory prescribed was the design of urban architecture with reference to actual views and sequences of views, rather than to only functional organization and constructional logic. Townscape was an attempt at a pragmatic aesthetic encompassing both modern and historical architecture. Townscape's view of urban history was coloured by 'anti-scrape' views of architectural conservation and was quite unsentimental and unjudgemental about the past. It proposed to include both buildings with architectural merit and those without that are none the less valuable through necessity, sentiment, or simply as instances of the different tastes of the past. This empirical approach to architectural value is partly explained by the circumstances of the war and its damage to British cities. One of the important immediate precursors to Townscape was the *AR*'s special issue on rebuilding the St Paul's Cathedral precinct, which had been largely flattened.[65] As opposed to a doctrinaire modernism based on the logic of building type and construction, the *AR*'s team gave an example of modernist architecture that was somewhat syncopated: determined in part by *genius loci* and tested against actual viewpoints. The illustrations were by Hugh Casson and have something of the gaiety of his Festival of Britain designs. Equally important were the problems of reforming mass housing and building new towns, and Fredrick Gibberd's design for Harlow was a principal example of this.

Townscape attempted to address what the *AR* saw as major problem of modernism in rebuilding and in new building – its unpopularity and a divergence of taste between the public and the profession. In 'Exterior Furnishing', de Wolfe imagined an everyman 'Bill Brown' who is asked to choose between a Garden City, which de Wolfe and his readers assumed to be socially and technically out of date, and the modern 'machine to live in', which de Wolfe identified with the modernist group MARS (Modern Architecture Research). Brown chooses the Garden City:

> And so Bill Brown goes for the ideal he knows, because what he wants is a picture that makes sense to him. It isn't that he is a fool; he is quite capable of imagining the complications inherent in planning, even of making sacrifices for the greater good of the greater number, but he cannot, he feels, be expected to do his part without being given an idea, a pretty clear idea, of what it is all leading up to. He wants a picture of the kind of world the physical planner will make, and up to date he has been given nothing between Port Sunlight and MARS. Roses round the Door is a picture which contrives to summon a range of far cosier associations.[66]

Thus, according to de Wolfe, the popular choice of familiar building forms was not only based on uncritical sentimentality but also on the failure of doctrinaire modernists like the MARS group to provide a 'picture'. The reason for this failure was familiarly picturesque: de Wolfe held that the modernists were idealists and their ideal could not be constructed whole, and to the extent that it might have, it stood in stark contrast to the actual conditions of cities. De Wolfe reminded the reader of the great English tradition of the picturesque, and then explicitly repeated its formula. Architects and planners, de Wolfe writes, need to learn from painters, in this case from contemporary British painters: John Piper, Paul Nash and others, who show that 'a music-hall or a Victorian pub or a pylon, or a wild Gothic four-cornered lamp-post are what correspond in our urban scenery to the grotto, the umbrello, the tumble-down cottage and the sunk lane . . .'.[67] The painters knew that the picture could give unity to disparate objects, even those that in a different view would be considered repulsive. In a near perfect iteration of the issues of my chapter 'Disgust', de Wolfe alluded to Price's argument made with Rembrandt's painting, *Carcase of an Ox*. (Unfortunately de Wolfe made an error and misattributed the idea to Richard Payne Knight.) This extreme example sets de Wolfe's 'critical' picturesque apart from the naïve sentimentality of 'Bill Brown', and at the same time, it is an attack on the idealism of the modernists. He anticipates a charge that the picturesque revival was historicism, writing:

> Amongst architects unfortunately even the most eager and progressive believe that the defence (for instance) of Victorian fantasy is reactionary, and stigmatize such goings-on as flippant. They have forgotten – or never discovered – their Uvedale Price, perhaps the first man in history to reveal that an object may be 'ugly' in itself and yet in a suitable context have aesthetic possibilities. Payne Knight, it will be remembered, brought up the carcass of an ox as an instance of a revolting object which could evoke painterly delight – could produce, that is to say, a picturesque effect . . . In their development of a visual aesthetic capable of including the awful and the odd (Sublime and picturesque) the eighteenth century intelligentsia cut right across the centuries linking Salvator Rosa with Salvador Dali.[68]

In retrospect, Townscape is considered one of the cracks in the dam of high modernism and it has been frequently misunderstood as proposing historicist architectural forms. This is close to true of one tendency in the journal marked out by John Betjeman's arch and titillated appropriations of popular taste,[69] and later J. M. Richard's celebration of suburbia in his *Castles on the Ground*, and Cullen's *The Concise Townscape*. Indeed, the doyen of post-modernism, Robert Venturi, had his first publication in the *AR* as a Townscape study of the Campodogolio, and both *Complexity and Contradiction* and *Learning from Las Vegas* have considerable debts to Townscape.[70] However, Hastings, Pevsner and de Wolfe were completely committed to modernism in architecture, and in the first place, Townscape was an attempt at persuading architects to take a more empirical view of the actual context in which modern architecture was seen. The case studies emphasized the variety of elements combined; apart from people and vehicles they tended to include historic building, modern building and signage flags or ephemera. In part, as with the Festival of Britain, this involved an attempt to make modernism more popular by making it less austere. But as much, it assumed that modernism was historically destined to be popular, and would be sooner, if modernists had sympathy with, rather than antagonism to, the obsolete world.

In the article 'The Second Half Century' of 1947, the editors of the *AR* announced a campaign of 'visual re-education' that was to become Townscape, and followed this with a retrospective, 'The First Half Century', which attempted to encapsulate the editorial direction since 1897. Here, as in the later 'Townscape Casebook' (Figure 5.10) it is clear that the *AR* was attempting to provoke by including Victoriana and popular culture and especially when something in ghastly taste could be shown to demonstrate an admirable spatial or visual arrangement.[71] This was consistent with Townscape's liberalism in urban planning: while pluralism would never be accepted in modern architecture it might be in Townscape which did not require the demolishing of historic buildings, leading, rather, to strong visual contrasts. But in Townscape, the historic fabric rarely includes buildings of value as architecture – not Pugin, nor Cockerell, but lumpish churches of indeterminate age with eroded details and chintz Victoriana. In principle, Townscape accepted historic buildings for their historical, rather than their architectural, value, and aimed to show that modern architecture could cleverly accommodate old buildings that had been maintained for their associations or curiosity even if completely devoid of architectural merit.[72] But in practice, it was the clash of the past and present building stock that gave Townscape its particular visual style. As de Wolfe puts it in a rather racy phrase: Townscape is a place where 'the Victorian dolls-house must be politely encouraged to lie down with Mr Fredrick Gibberd's flats'.[73] In a kind of spoof of stream of consciousness writing he raps: 'one bus stop, two public lavatories, one Underground entrance, one manhole cover . . . six plane trees . . . and a hundred and fifty horizontal windows . . . From such assortments the radical planner has to produce his practical surrealist picture'.[74]

Today Townscape is best known not through de Wolfe and Pevsner's articles but the later books by Cullen, who was the *AR*'s art director and who 'realized' several of their polemical proposals such as 'Westminster Regained', of 1947.[75] Cullen used high viewpoint perspectives and plans annotated to successive views in what can be seen as the full realization of the picturesque techniques of Repton. From 1949 and the eponymous article, *AR* carried regular Townscape features by about twenty contributors, the most prolific of whom were Cullen, Ian Nairn and Kenneth Browne. In the mature version, such as 'The Midlands Experiment' of 1954, the *AR* made a persuasive case for what is now called contextualist urbanism.[76] While the new buildings proposed were not historicist in their appearance, in their placement on their sites and their scenographic consideration of the sequence of visual experience they formed a spatial whole with the pre-existing fabric. In retrospect, it is necessary to point out that this too was a kind of historicism – what would become the 'typological' historicism of the architectural urbanism of the 1970s – because the buildings' plans were constrained by pre-existing size and organization of the lot structure of the town. Nevertheless, in their time, the intent was more like that of Price or Repton. When Price wrote of the scenic potential of villages neighbouring landscape parks, his idea was radical because a village was considered ugly and not able to be assumed into the classical ideals of the Claudian landscape. The *AR* is not only Pricean in its technique of minor interventions based on extensive analysis, it is similar in its intent: modern buildings frame the urban events with which we have become overly familiar. The idiosyncrasies of past buildings are made visible by modernism and this allows them to be appropriated to the modern.

The picturesque sensibility was, by the twentieth century, endemic in British culture and its artistic possibilities well demonstrated in most of the architecture, landscape and much of the city planning of the nineteenth century. However, the *AR*'s explicit revival of the sensibility as definite concepts and techniques, and the representation of this in pictures and diagrams, made the picturesque visible in a way unseen since the heyday of the picturesque controversy in 1795. The language of Townscape, both textual and visual, was at once the fulfilment of the picturesque idea and a substantial development of it. Price's books were unillustrated and his descriptions quite conversational, not affecting in the manner of the 'word paintings' of nineteenth-century stylists such as Sir Walter Scott or John Ruskin. Repton's 'Red Books' had a very high quotient of images and plans closely keyed to the text, but these were manuscripts in private hands. The printed works in public circulation are beautifully illustrated with hand-coloured engravings that also reproduce Repton's before and after 'slide' technique. However, these books were extremely rare and expensive and his work was generally known through Loudon's crudely illustrated editions of his *Works*.[77] By contrast, the *AR* had a very wide distribution and almost immediate impact, and Cullen's inventive and expressive graphic layouts had a higher proportion of images of a greater variety: photographs and orthography as well as views; and a mixture of full colour and two and three colour printing on large format. In their structure of analysis and proposition, and their combination of pictures and spatial description through views and orthography, the *AR*'s Townscape segments are the apogee of the picturesque idea.

The graphics also rely on Cullen's superb drawing skills, which use the rhetoric of 'sketching' in a way not uncommon in twentieth-century art but with its origins in Gilpin and his contemporaries. As I showed in Chapter 2, Gilpin proposed that one should sketch in order to form one's own sensibilities and powers of observation. One might later display cleaned up versions to one's friends, but this should be done modestly, without suggesting that art was the principal objective. Cullen's drawings have an apparent negligence about them, as if speed of execution and making the point to the reader were more important than final form. We see this in the use of collage and the resulting unevenness of representational verisimilitude. It is also noticeable in hand lettering and the use of a typewriter for captions, as well as the general lack of a sense of the page as frame. These graphic techniques imply a comportment of the designer as observer and collator of found materials, who values these over composition. This is a kind of painterliness, where indefinite outlines and a sense of movement or succession imitate visual attention directly rather than finished representation of the thing seen. De Wolfe's text and Cullen's paper architecture suppose a visual order to pictures understandable independently of content. They think that we can extend this learned idea of pictorial composition to phenomenal visual experience. Through the *AR*'s visual re-education we can learn to momentarily forget the abstract or insensible aspects of urbanism, such as land-use, transport and cultural symbols, so that we can reduce urbanism to the purely visual. Then, we can understand potential connections before returning with new vigour and insight to the fuller conditions of actual city design, or so it is claimed.

Part of the problem in understanding the reception of Townscape is understanding the difference between Cullen's two books of that title, which include materials developed for the *AR* and later. The 1961 *Townscape* is very handsome, with some three-colour printing and gloss stock, and a section containing Cullen's proposals for the *AR* that show modern buildings and urban 'fabric' in the manner I have described (Figure 5.12). Although there was no subsequent edition of this book, in 1971 there appeared *The Concise Townscape*, consisting entirely of scenographic and spatio-visual analyses of traditional urban forms; the 'proposals' had been dropped (Figure 5.13). It is this volume that has been massively reprinted. Whether this editorial decision was based on production exigencies alone, or a change of heart, *The Concise Townscape* left the concept unable to be differentiated from later admonishments of modernism in the name of traditional urban structure. A further issue is less important historically but closer to our theme. Among those aware of the differences with the *AR*, it is usual to say that Cullen emptied the theory out of Townscape, allowing it to become a facile technique in the hands of others. This was not quite the case. Cullen's book is hardly intellectual; it does not mention the picturesque nor the political philosophy and national character issues that drove de Wolfe's introduction of the term. However, this intellectual context has its own problems and instabilities. The greater difference with the *AR* is that Cullen's avoidance of picturesque terminology makes clear how much the whole Townscape project relies on later pychologized concepts of vision. A quotation from Cullen's text accompanying a 'serial vision' analysis of Ludlow is an example:

> And, as if echoing or continuing the space enclosed by the portico, the narrow alley disappears to its own mysterious destination. Branching right, however [. . .] the scene

Figure 5.12 Gordon Cullen, 'Bankside Regained', 1961.

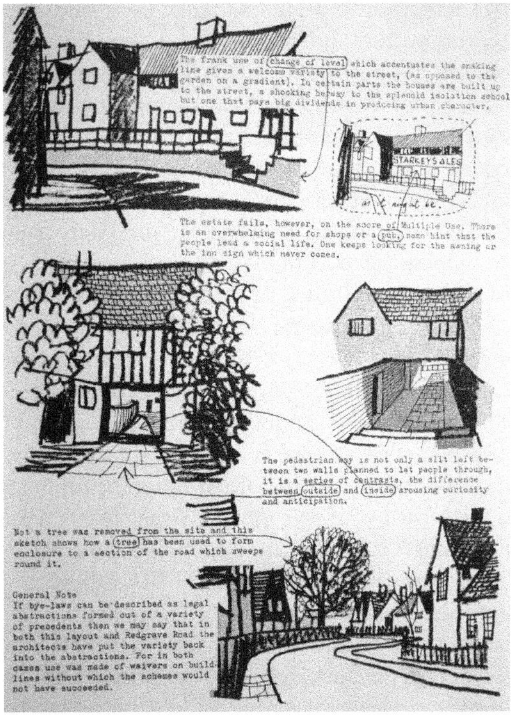

Figure 5.13 Gordon Cullen, '1915 Well Hall Estate, Eltham', 1961.

> is quite different; dark and intimate, with a pub on the right, the path passes through an archway, to a sunny distance. It is hard to realize that the two streets are but 30 ft. apart, and it is partly this variety of character in so small an area which enhances the delightful air of intrigue.[78]

The language here is deeply marked by the idea that visual perception is empathetic. That Cullen could write that the alley is possessed of 'its own mysterious destination' is not picturesque, or at least, not in the first order. This use of poetic metaphor in description is what Ruskin decried as 'the pathetic fallacy', that is the moment when description fails the object and turns to the subject's feelings instead.[79] But when Cullen was writing British architects might well have thought this a strength, as 'subject-objectification' was one of the modes of recently translated works of European art history such as Wilhelm Worringer's *Form in Gothic*, and Heinrich Wölfflin's *Principles of Art History* or *Classic Art*.[80] In Wölfflin, buildings are described as almost animate – an imaginary projection of the subject's sequential inspection onto the object. These ideas originated in the German empathy theory of the late nineteenth century and were introduced to Britain as a new art history and relation of art to everyday life by major figures of English modernism, including Herbert Read, who wrote introductions to translations of Worringer and Wölfflin. In architecture schools in the twentieth century, various psychological accounts of form perception have displaced aesthetics based on the concepts of form internal to the disciplines. Figures such as Rudolf Arnheim and Christian Norberg-Schulz, in different ways, merged psychological and phenomenological theories of sense perception into a programmatic experientialism where, as Mark Jarzombek puts it, '"reading the object" becomes an exercise in self-referentiality'.[81]

There are two points to make here, and the first is a differentiation. The eighteenth-century picturesque was objective aesthetics: it was concerned with the actual qualities of objects and how they provoked or constrained pictures made of them. Eighteenth-century landscape gardeners made and conceptualized an art of programmed visual experience in duration. But this is not exactly the same as the aestheticization of one's own experience typical of the 'aesthetic experientialism' of the twentieth century. In the latter, the subject is one of affects and aesthetic experience based on immediacy of feeling. In Price's description of the village in the 'Dialogue on the Picturesque' (which is perhaps the original, primitive and unillustrated form of Cullen's 'serial vision'), there was no role for the metaphorical life of buildings and lanes, or for the gap between the subject's bodily and visual apprehensions of space.[82] The category of feeling in the eighteenth century is simple: it is visual pleasure located in the eye and visual nerves. Price's analysis was a formal description and nomenclature for the different causes of this one feeling. His example was meant to show that with a humble village, one might achieve the same comportment – that of the judge of one's own pleasure – that one might achieve with a painting by Claude. We can see this difference from modern attitudes in the organization of Knight's *Principles of Taste*, the last third of which is concerned with why most feelings are not aesthetic, but associative: 'The passions . . . do not come within the scope of my present inquiry; it being only by sympathy, that they are connected with subjects of taste.'[83] In Cullen's more psychological account – marked at least at the level of the text by the concept of empathy – the relation of visual and spatial awareness led to a variety of feelings in which the whole body is at stake. By the mid-twentieth century, a variety of psychological accounts of aesthetics became known through emotive descriptions of the experience of art and architecture, both by art historians and popular educators. The phenomenological idea of perception as an act proceeding outward from a lived body is the best way to conceptualize what Cullen was doing. However, this was often conflated with Freud-esque ideas of vision and images being driven by desires of which we are unconscious; and empathy theory, in which the aesthetic experience of sensations received gets transferred onto other senses or the body's motor capacity in kinesthesis and synaesthesia. There is no reason to think that Cullen's ideas were driven by these concepts. It is more likely that he simply grafted a popular understanding of the modern aesthetic self onto eighteenth-century visual empiricism. The second point to make begins with the fact that someone else did know all this theory and must have realized what modifications were being made to the picturesque, but chose not to make this apparent.

Pevsner lectured on English art and culture while a young academic in Göttingen in the late 1920s.[84] He studied under Wilhelm Pinder, a former student of August Schmarsow, one of the generation of German aestheticians and scholars, including Wölfflin and Alois Riegl, who (pretty much) invented modern art history. Some of the key debates at the turn of the century in Germany were concerned with how perceptual categories related to the history of art. Schmarsow held (against Wölfflin) that space was an object of sense and the basis for comparing all architectural achievement. There can be no doubt that Pevsner had a sophisticated understanding of the issues surrounding visual perception and art history through German empathy theory before he thought on the picturesque. Forced from his academic post by the Nazis in 1933, Pevsner moved to Britain and made English architecture and culture his principal concern. He was deeply impressed by Herbert Read's *Art and Industry*, which must have seemed to him as the Bauhaus returning to reform its Arts and Crafts origin, and he began a life-time's work attempting to further reconcile Britain to modernism. In 1936, he published *Pioneers of the Modern Movement: From William Morris to Walter Gropius*, which argued that England was the source of the latest European ideas. But even this enthusiasm for his new homeland was insufficient to save him from being briefly interned as an enemy alien in 1940. Thus, Pevsner's involvement in the origins of Townscape during the war added a particular poignancy to the nationalism with which it was presented. The situation was not as simple as de Wolfe's jingoism being a compensation for Pevsner's German background. As Brian Harrison puts it: 'Pevsner was exploiting the refugee's prize asset: alertness to cultural contrast. He was familiarizing Britain with art-historical ideas already widely accepted in Germany'.[85] And we might add – appropriating England and the picturesque as examples of German art history concepts.

In 1946, Pevsner wrote a text entitled *Visual Pleasures from Everyday Things* that was addressed to teachers of art and product design. In this it is implicit that skills and sensibilities of design can be understood and developed in themselves as well as in their interaction with social and technological circumstances. Design was not only a symptom of historical forces; it could be a social act. This was a very English idea, going back to A. W. N. Pugin, Thomas Cole, Ruskin and William Morris, as Pevsner states in *Pioneers* and also in *An Enquiry into the Industrial Art of England*. *Visual Pleasures* was introduced by Read and published by the Council for Visual Education. It was the 'visual re-education' that became the catch-cry of *AR*'s special retrospective, 'The First Half Century', in 1947; it was through visual re-education that Pevsner was able to graft a German art historical concept of style to the relatively simple visual empiricism of the picturesque. Pevsner was not prone to discussions of methodology, but in 1949, in a review of Sigfried Giedion's *Space, Time and Architecture* and *Mechanization Takes Command*, he discussed Giedion's teacher Wölfflin, and the latter's purely visual accounts of style. Pevsner then remarked on the lack of this in Giedion's more determinist social and technological histories. The implication is that while Giedion had turned more towards a social basis for explaining art history (one that Pevsner identified with his own teacher Pinder), he had put aside too readily the idea of style or aesthetic sense as an historical agent. It can be no coincidence that this review was in the same volume of *AR* that concluded with the announcement of Townscape.

Put most strongly by Wölfflin, an historical account of style supposed that the life world of old art remained present in the work, crystallized in its forms and in the way that those forms continued to order the perception of later observers. Thus, the eighteenth-century picturesque could be shorn of its social meaning in an agrarian class society and still be put to work by Pevsner and de Wolfe in an egalitarian, industrial, modern Britain. Price's interest in the mundane as a limit case of judgement became consumed into the possibility that mass production offered (and which the Bauhaus advertised) the total design of material life. And perhaps most significantly, Pevsner, like his teacher Pinder (and to a degree Wölfflin), was an Hegelian: he assumed that art proceeded dialectically, each age expressing its identity and in doing so leaving problems that delimited the possibilities of the succeeding age. Hegelianism licensed Pevsner to use historical research in the partisan manner of de Wolfe, and justified Townscape's reaching back to the eighteenth century in its reaction to the nineteenth century.

That England was more than a field of exemplification for Pevsner is clear from the start of his career and in the *Buildings of England* guidebooks that came to occupy much of it (and which have been renamed *The Pevsner Architectural Guides* in his honour). His affection or obsession is especially marked in the iteration of his title for his Reith Lectures on BBC radio in 1955 and subsequent book *The Englishness of English Art*, which itself quotes the title of an article of 1934, 'Das Englische in Der Englischen Kunst'. That there was more than art history going on here is evident in the book when Pevsner has to confront contradictions of *kunstgeographie* in the time frame he uses, which is longer than the existence of England as a nation, and in which the creation of Britain is a late event with which he has difficulty. (In one tortured section, he raises but fails to resolve the problem that one of the great architects of England, Robert Adam, happened to be Scottish.)

This historiographical superstructure and Pevsner's status as an enemy alien led to two important elisions in Townscape's historical imagination: the importance of German aesthetic urbanism and the nineteenth century. The issue here was not anachronism *per se*, as the *AR* was not inconsistent in its claim to be able to raid the whole of architectural culture for its purposes. A little scepticism about the historical claims helps bring into profile a more important aspect: in claiming progenitors writing on landscape design around 1800, de Wolfe was apparently disowning some closer relatives. There was a double elision of a German and a British intellectual context. Camilo Sitte's *Der Städtebau nach seinen Künstlerischen Grundsätzen* of 1889 stood at the head of the movement of *Stadtbaukunst*, which emphasized the visual aspects of town planning. Arguably, Sitte's ideas were developments on earlier British city aesthetics and movements to preserve historic city centres.

The picturesque was popular in Germany in the eighteenth century, where it was received as an English invention, with numerous parks laid out on 'English' principles. Perhaps more importantly, the picturesque was also received as an aesthetical account of form making by Friedrich Gilly.[86] Gilly's teacher Friedrich Wilhelm Freiherr von Erdmannsdorf was an aristocratic amateur who had visited England and Rome and established neo-classical building and English landscape at once in Germany with his palace and park for Prince Leopold Friedrich Franz von Anhalt-Dessau at Wörlitz Park from 1764. Christian Hirschfeld's *Theorie der Gartenkunst* (1779–85) explained the current fashions and helped turn Germany from the Baroque.[87] Gilly himself read widely in the new landscape aesthetics, and visited English-style parks in France and wrote a commentry on Bagatelle, designed by the Scottish gardener Thomas Blaikie, but substantially redesigned by François Joseph Bélanger who had worked at Bowood. In this Gilly expresses dissatisfaction with the English formula, and he references his opinion to that of Price whose book he owned in an early and unattributed translation.[88] Gilly's student, Karl Friedrich Schinkel, developed the irregular planning techniques of British architects like Nash after his visit to Britian. By the early nineteenth century the picturesque was widely known to a lay public through Prince Hermann von Pückler-Muskau's publication of his *Tours*, and the Prince also commissioned Humphry and John Repton.[89]

Sitte's work was punctuated by the word *malerish*, literally meaning painterly, but which is typically used to translate picturesque. This was also the case with Wölfflin, who used 'picturesque' in a highly nuanced way to describe some of the problems of form, as we will see in the next chapter. Sitte was very well known in Britain through Raymond Unwin's extensive references and reproductions of Sitte's diagrams in his *Townplanning in Practice* of 1909, and both Pevsner and Rudolf Wittkower reviewed Charles T. Stewart's translation of *Der Städtebau* in 1946.[90] The scholars were highly critical of the faults in translation, but Pevnser writes: 'Sitte teaches something that still needs as much emphasis today as it did in the last century. He teaches visual planning as opposed to drawing-board planning, and the informal as opposed to uniformity . . .'.[91] Given the history of exchanges between Britain and Germany on 'visual planning' and Pevsner's knowledge of this, it is remarkable how little Sitte appeared in the Townscape articles. It is almost as if this more complex history was suppressed to serve the 'Englishness' argument. For instance, in *The Englishness of English Art*, Pevsner gave Frederick Gibberd's design of Harlow New Town as an example of a modern picturesque.[92] But Gibberd's book *Town Design* of the same year (1955), which has a photo narrative technique like that of the *AR*, claimed Sitte as his precedent.[93] De Wolfe (who was pure Hastings by this time), finally gave Sitte his due in the article and later book *Italian Townscape* and Pevsner finally put Sitte in the context of Townscape in 1967.[94]

From reading the 'Visual Planning' manuscript across Pevsner's work for the *AR*, Aitchison has argued that Pevsner's main concern was to show the contribution of English picturesque planning to Western culture.[95] Pevsner thought England had been consistently ignored in urban planning histories such as Pierre Laveden's *Histoire de l'urbanisme*. Thus espousing the theory of the picturesque is important in showing that the English predilection for the informal was underwritten by a principle comparable to the Grand Manner and Baroque planning in France. It is possible that in looking for the 'theory' of the urbanisms of Bath or Oxford, Pevsner was simply avoiding the confusion that might be caused by working from later more apposite theories in German. But whatever his motivations, it is clear that Pevsner did not discover the picturesque in the manner of an ethnographer – describing it as an outsider. His ability to abstract the picturesque into aesthetic and art historical principles was a result of his already knowing it at one remove – in German.

The second elision of 'English' urban practice is, perhaps, best understood as an elision of the nineteenth century. The problem for de Wolfe was that the actual development of landscape into Townscape had been conducted in the discourse of historicist styles, and in particular, the Gothic Revival. Pevsner can, in academic discourse, mention G. G. Scott, the Edinburgh New Towns, and the picturesque in Ruskin; de Wolfe, in the pages of a professional journal, cannot, for fear of being misunderstood as betraying the modernist refusal of history. The nuances here are fine, as the *AR* was proposing the use of history, but a history of what we would now call 'visualities' rather than form, style and ornament. At the same time, there was a revival of interest in classicism through the research of Wittkower and the polemic of Colin Rowe, that proposed that there were syntactical issues of form common to classicism and modernism underlying their different lexicons. Both non-revivals preferred the eighteenth century to the nineteenth century, because the former was more abstract. In the eighteenth century, the classical 'language' of architecture was simply assumed, and when in the second half of the century the first revivals of medieval and vernacular buildings occurred these were not exactly exercises in style. They combined technical issues such as the possibilities of asymmetrical planning with an interest in the theatrical affects of associations with a barbarous past. Finding origins in the eighteenth century and in the analogous discipline of landscape was, thus, not a surprising gambit; it avoided the anathema of nineteenth-century style in its full-blown form. As the Editor puts it in 'Exterior Furnishing': 'Anytime he so desires the modern town-planner is free to pick up picturesque theory at the point before its corruption by the Gothic Revival; pick up the theory, rediscover the prophets, and apply the principles'.[96] Later, de Wolfe put this same argument in more clearly dialectical terms:

> According to the present thesis the full implications of the modern movement with all its baffling ambiguities can only be brought out by reference to the eighteenth century, in which, and not the nineteenth, were set up those basic contradictions which were to form the stuff of the modern dilemma.[97]

Pevsner's own work on the picturesque was not inconsiderable, however its greater significance lay in making the original ideas available in the new context of Townscape. Hussey, in his *The Picturesque* of 1927, had already made a brilliant synopsis of the picturesque as an aesthetic theory and cultural practice, in terms quite subsumable to today's ideas of an historical understanding of the visualities of past cultures. However, Hussey was a cultural conservative committed to the continuity of tradition; most of his considerable scholarly work was conducted in a mode of connoisseurship in the journal *Country Life*. Hussey was an admirer of Sir Edwin Lutyens who had been a talented architect in the later picturesque, Art and Crafts manner. But Lutyens, about the same time that Gropius turned to modernism, joined and led the revival of the classical and Baroque as the style of the British establishment and its empire. Pevsner's contribution was the generalization, through formal and historiographic concepts, of the picturesque to make it available to the readers of the *AR* as well as *Country Life*. Clearly, he saw his role as popularizing the picturesque and making it operative. In the pages of the *AR*, under his own name, he published excerpts and assessments of the major eighteenth-century figures in the same kind of page layout as other articles on the patrimony of English culture. These same notes, passed over Hasting's desk, transmuted into de Wolfe's polemical 'visual re-education'. In 1947, two years before the Townscape article appeared, Pevsner addressed the Royal Institute of British Architects on 'The Picturesque in Architecture'.[98] Chaired by John Summerson and with a response by Hussey, Pevsner argued cogently for what the *AR* was doing by showing that the picturesque foretells the inevitable rise of modernism and its destiny. These arguments were taken up again in 1954 in an article 'C20 Picturesque', which answered Basil Taylor's criticism of the *AR*'s picturesque revival;[99] and they had their fullest form in 'Picturesque England', one of the Reith Lectures on BBC radio in 1955, which was published in *The Englishness of English Art* in the following year, and dedicated to 'H de C', as Hastings was familiarly called. The overriding themes in these works are that the picturesque is English, modern and practical. The most important of these is modernity.

Pevsner argues that picturesque irregularity is required by functionalism, and hence by modernity itself. If we look past the cubic forms and large openings of the work of modernist masters such as Gropius and Le Corbusier to their other aesthetic qualities, we see something quite picturesque, according to Pevsner:

> the free grouping of the individual building, a mixture of materials, synthetic and natural, rough and smooth, and, beyond that, the free planning of a whole quarter, [. . .] with interaction between landscape and building and between buildings of different shapes and heights. Do not these qualities define the difference between the free exercise of the imagination, stimulated by the disciplines of function and technique [. . .] and academic rule of thumb, within whose strait-jacket architecture was confined before the modern movement set it free? And do they not show that, albeit unconsciously, the modern revolution of the early twentieth century and the picturesque revolution of a hundred years before had all their fundamentals in common? The qualities of the modern movement were not developed to please the eye, but because without them no workable, no functioning, no functional architecture is possible in our age. Impose symmetry, impose axiality and grids, impose rules even where the artist is feeling his way, and you reduce usefulness. [. . .] no other existing aesthetic theory fits the demands of modern architecture and planning so well as that of Price and Knight.[100]

Pevsner's argument is quite subtle; he does not suggest that the irregularity of Price was based on or even cognizant of function in the modern sense. In fact, as I discussed in the previous chapter, there is quite a lot of evidence for a nuanced concept of planning in relation to use that developed in the historical picturesque. But Pevsner, if he knew this material, was not so interested in it. For instance, his 1944 commentary on excerpts from Price did not include the passages I quoted earlier on the tactical improvement of villages, nor the description of the Parsonage house made irregular through additions, which would have strongly supported his argument.[101] Instead, Pevsner prefers the less prescriptive passages from Price because they accord with his idea that the picturesque is empirical and even experimental, and independent of its eighteenth-century rusticity. It was in Pevsner's hands as much as anyone's that the picturesque became the felt absence of *a priori* spatial concepts. His claim is that the picturesque provides concepts that are relatively indifferent to the art and taste of their time – the picturesque was in fact a preparation for later generations who would appropriate functional forms to aesthetic interests. The converse of this way of thinking is the implicit claim that functionalism was lacking a means to achieve an aesthetical becoming. While functional rationalism was the true self-identity of the modern, once that identity had been made, it was opened to history, and the picturesque could be shown to be immanent in it; a resource waiting to fulfil modernism and make it popular.

In the earlier address to the RIBA, Pevsner is much more circumspect, regularly prefacing his remarks by acknowledging the audience's greater experience with the exigencies of planning, buildings and cities.[102] What is interesting here is how much he emphasizes the conservation of historic buildings, pointing out that modern schemes for the rebuilding of Whitehall, like earlier classical schemes for London, would have involved the loss of buildings of merit or of historical value, because unlike the picturesque, the modernist planner had no place for contingency. Therefore, the Townscape strategies based on compromise and impurity had the flexibility to be robust in the face of difficult land acquisitions. Pevsner speaks of this as a matter of practicality. However, Townscape also answered the need for a cultural consensus among architects and with the community. Hussey rose to thank Dr Pevsner at the end of his address and took the opportunity to demand that modern city planning not destroy England's patrimony. Thus, the sense of nationalism in the picturesque as a native aesthetic theory doubled itself in the resources it offered for a kind of cultural continuity.

It would be possible to over emphasize this historical conservation aspect of Townscape. Traditionalism is, perhaps, the most remembered aspect of it, as I remarked earlier when discussing Cullen's *Concise Townscape*. But in fact, in the documents of the 1940s and 1950s, Townscape was resolutely modernist. For instance, Pevsner's examples of the new picturesque in *The Englishness of English Art* include Roehampton housing estate and an early scheme for the Barbican housing and arts centre. Only a decade or so later, these would be considered prime examples of modernist megalomania completely at odds with traditional urban form. There is a case, however, for understanding the picturesque as a visual aesthetic arising in a dialogue with the historical sensibility of building conservation. In 1787, James Wyatt 'restored' Salisbury Cathedral by removing almost all of the structures that had accreted to it, including the bell tower, to better show what he considered to be the architectural merit of the thirteenth-century building. In response, Richard Gough made some of the first arguments that restoration ought to respect the historical complexity of the building's life. He later resigned from the Society of Antiquaries in protest to Wyatt's election in 1797. The arguments of Gough and other antiquaries around the aesthetic value of mutability in building might well have been a source for Price's thinking on the complexity and variety of building form. This was the beginning of a debate that continued through the nineteenth century about whether it was conscionable to 'scrape' buildings back to a conjectured original state. Salisbury continued to be at the centre of this debate in England, as G. G. Scott's restorations of it from 1863 were the object of an articulate critique by J. J. Stevenson, and then by William Morris and Philip Webb, who set up the Society for the Protection of Ancient Buildings around 'anti-scrape' principles in 1877.[103] There were similar reactions to Eugene Violet-le-Duc's 'restorations' that removed most of the subsidiary buildings of Nôtre Dame de Paris. Brian Ladd has argued that Sitte should be understood in part as being in opposition to the disencumbering or *Freilegung* of churches. Sitte says of disencumbering: 'it really is a foolish fad, this craze for isolating buildings'; and, 'Such an exposed building will always appear like a cake on a serving platter'.[104] He goes on to count 255 churches in Rome of which only six were freestanding. The much-reproduced diagrams of monumental and accretionary buildings are evidence for this view as much as they are the descriptions of contingent public spaces.

That 'anti-scrape' was not merely a matter of preserving historical evidence was put strongly in the *AR* in 1947, in a long article and photo essay by the painter John Piper entitled 'Pleasing Decay'. Piper introduces the reader to some of the history of 'anti-scrape', identifying it with Ruskin's definition of the picturesque as parasitical sublimity, and quoting John Thomas Smith. Piper uses one of Smith's drawings of decrepit cottages and the same passage about the pictorial quality of decay that I quoted in the previous chapter. More to my present point, Piper adds:

> Architects and townplanners have another task to add to their present ones: to re-educate themselves visually, taking note of these characteristics. But just as we have learned [. . .] to appreciate Utrillo as well as Cotman, there are other characteristics that can, and must be added to Ruskin's elements of 'picturesqueness' to-day; and if he himself had lived to-day he would certainly have added them. The incorporation of Picasso and Matisse, Ernst and Miró into our visual philosophy may mean an uncomfortable stretching of the word 'picturesque' to embrace our beliefs; but it is certain that if the lessons of these painters are properly learned 'pleasing decay' will be found to have a very large place in our present-day visual consciousness. [. . . For] the visually re-educated planner, it will not merely be a question of retaining and incorporating the *best* existing buildings [. . .] but a question of using existing buildings [. . .] that will be an enrichment, or allow an area of rest, or even note of agitation, in a new planning and building scheme.[105]

While on one side, the picturesque-ness of townscape was advertised as a compromise of modernism with tradition, for Piper, the picturesque is assimilable to modern art, collage and the as-found. Piper lists buildings of significance to architects, those with 'circular white and blue plaques on their façades' and implies that these are not as interesting as old buildings available to architects in the same way as Picasso used pieces of old rattan, or Ernst cut up mail-order catalogues.[106]

Townscape was not so much a way of planning but a sensibility based on the historical complexity of cities that, if respected, always put them beyond planning and introduced an externality proper to architectural design. Historic buildings were valued not for their history but for a value they obtained when the specific history they embodied was obscured by their becoming 'historical', and thus a useful constraint in form making. We can make this point clear by contrasting Townscape with what immediately followed it, the so-called 'contextualist' urbanism of Rowe, Aldo Rossi, Rob and Leon Krier. This later development in the 1960s and 1970s is truer to Sitte, by proposing to constrain modern building by the lot, and street patterns of traditional urban structure and building form by historically constituted typologies. I have more to say on the relation of Townscape and urbanism a few pages hence, but here the point is that Townscape proposed modern building and historic building would occur within modern planning. Undoubtedly, this was because modern planning was seen as essential to modern urban infrastructure, as indeed it is, but the position that this put old buildings in also rewarded a certain sensibility of obsolete things that I remarked on earlier in relation to de Wolfe's evocation of the 'surrealism' of Townscape.

Much of these aesthetic and historical issues are obvious in the first article that announced the picturesque revival, the curiously named 'Exterior Furnishing or Sharawaggi'. The article runs two arguments for a new picturesque. The first is its Englishness, here represented by the whimsical usage 'sharawaggi' for picturesqueness. The second is a semi-anthropological argument about taste and furnishing that brings us back to surrealism and collage. This second idea has a strong parallel with a passage in Sitte, and it is possible that entitling an essay largely concerned with the picturesque 'Exterior Furnishing' was a nod to those who knew Sitte's opinion that: 'It is precisely the external use of interior architectural elements (staircases, galleries, etc.) that is an essential ingredient in the charm of ancient and medieval designs'.[107]

Transposing an historical argument onto an anthropology, the Editor argues that the mixed aesthetic with which unpretentious people furnish their homes, is a model for urban design. In the home, each item is valued for itself whether that value is in design quality, functionality, or sentimental associations.

> The fear of one's modern cupboard clashing with the Victorian atmosphere of a room, or one's Victorian chandelier looking out of place in an Aalto environment is wholly unjustified. Even more undesirable is the fear that any object, in itself not up to a discriminating contemporary aesthetic standard, would be a blot on a whole interior. The aesthetic qualities of the individual items are quite irrelevant. Let them be ugly, let them be incongruous. What matters alone is the unity and congruity of the pattern. A frankly vulgar little bronze poodle on an Italian marble pedestal might even hold a place of honour on the mantle shelf, either because of its value as an accent in a picturesque whole, or – and here is a new argument – because of some equally legitimate sentimental value.[108]

Sitte's argument is for tolerating the oddities of old buildings with external stairs and open loggia and his examples are of buildings with great status and artistic merit, such as the town hall at Brussels. De Wolfe's 'vulgar little bronze poodle' is a different intersection of associative and aesthetic values. At the level of form, Townscape's use of historic fabric is like the collages of Kurt Schwitters or Max Ernst, or the contemporary paintings of Roland Penrose. Here, fragments are dissociated from their original role and reassembled so that visual unity is always made unstable by the possibility of deciphering the original meaning of the pieces. There is a further level for the role of art and architecture in these surrealist allusions. The painter Paul Nash, who was involved in British surrealist movements, wrote an essay for the *AR* in 1936 titled 'Swanage, or Seaside Surrealism', and this, along with Nash's photograph of a monumental concrete swan in a provincial town, became something of an emblem in the journal's own mythology. The swan appears in 'The First Half Century' along with (among other images): a formalist photograph by Moholy-Nagy; aerial photographs of 'the pattern made by bulldozers putting a landing ground out of use in the desert' (it is tempting to speculate that this might have been contributed by Richards who was in Cairo in 1942); and an ugly villa by the picturesque architect Peter Frederick Robinson, whose butcher's shop I discussed in Chapter 3. Under the heading 'Architectural Review employs shock tactics to stimulate visual awareness' (Figure 5.14), the Editor writes:

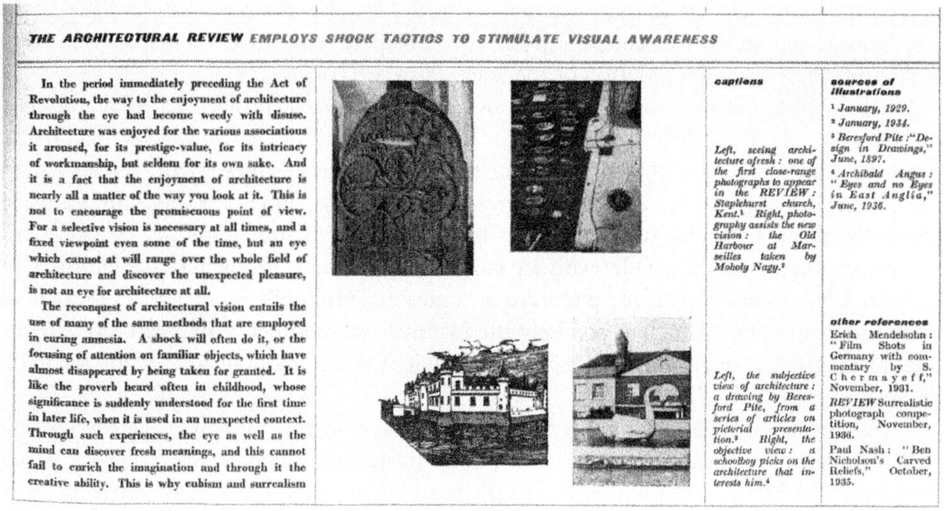

THE ARCHITECTURAL REVIEW EMPLOYS SHOCK TACTICS TO STIMULATE VISUAL AWARENESS

In the period immediately preceding the Act of Revolution, the way to the enjoyment of architecture through the eye had become weedy with disuse. Architecture was enjoyed for the various associations it aroused, for its prestige-value, for its intricacy of workmanship, but seldom for its own sake. And it is a fact that the enjoyment of architecture is nearly all a matter of the way you look at it. This is not to encourage the promiscuous point of view. For a selective vision is necessary at all times, and a fixed viewpoint even some of the time, but an eye which cannot at will range over the whole field of architecture and discover the unexpected pleasure, is not an eye for architecture at all.

The reconquest of architectural vision entails the use of many of the same methods that are employed in curing amnesia. A shock will often do it, or the focusing of attention on familiar objects, which have almost disappeared by being taken for granted. It is like the proverb heard often in childhood, whose significance is suddenly understood for the first time in later life, when it is used in an unexpected context. Through such experiences, the eye as well as the mind can discover fresh meanings, and this cannot fail to enrich the imagination and through it the creative ability. This is why cubism and surrealism

captions

Left, seeing architecture afresh: one of the first close-range photographs to appear in the REVIEW: Staplehurst church, Kent.[1] *Right, photography assists the new vision: the Old Harbour at Marseilles taken by Moholy Nagy.*[2]

Left, the subjective view of architecture: a drawing by Beresford Pite, from a series of articles on pictorial presentation.[3] *Right, the objective view: a schoolboy picks on the architecture that interests him.*[4]

sources of illustrations

[1] *January, 1929.*

[2] *January, 1934.*

[3] *Beresford Pite: "Design in Drawings," June, 1897.*

[4] *Archibald Angus: "Eyes and no Eyes in East Anglia," June, 1936.*

other references

Erich Mendelsohn: "Film Shots in Germany with commentary by S. Chermayeff," November, 1931.

REVIEW Surrealistic photograph competition, November, 1936.

Paul Nash: "Ben Nicholson's Carved Reliefs," October, 1935.

Figure 5.14 'The Architectural Review employs shock tactics to stimulate visual awareness', from 'The First Half Century', 1947.

> The reconquest of architectural vision entails the use of many of the same methods that are employed in curing amnesia. A shock will often do it, or the focusing of attention on familiar objects, which have almost disappeared by being taken for granted. It is like the proverb often heard in childhood, whose significance is suddenly understood for the first time in later life, when it is used in an unfamiliar context. Through such experiences, the eye as well as the mind can discover fresh meanings, and through it the creative ability. This is why cubism and surrealism were such important movements to architects . . .[109]

At one level, the Editor is saying that the pre-modern is a kind of cultural childhood that remains in memory. But we could also think that here, Townscape comes close to Walter Benjamin's concept of the dialectical image. In the eighteenth-century picturesque, the value of ugliness and deformity was not in its affect but in its avoidance. Not being disgusted evinced a level of disinterestedness that suited one to government. The ugliness of Townscape was instead a kind of historical awareness that arose through a critical understanding of the affects of nostalgia and the violence that it does to the past. Having 'the Victorian dolls-house lie down with Gibberd's flats' was, like surrealist collage, one way to realize that the people of the past dreamed the present, but not the one that has occurred.[110] The persistence of buildings after their functional and social obsolescence was one way to experience these past dreams, and this put a shock into the self-evidence of the present. This interest in surrealism was much more likely to have been Hastings', Nash's and Piper's, than Pevsner's, but the idea that the English were in some way particularly tolerant of, and interested in, incongruity joins them.

In this section introducing Townscape, I have tended to analogize 'appropriation', making a theme of the kind of taking that saw Pevsner make England his, and that enabled him to return *Stadtbaukunst* to its origins. The themes of nation and national culture might thus seem simple, useful generalizations of the actual facts of the life of the picturesque idea and Pevsner. But there is a further aspect that thus far I have downplayed: the political ideology with which Townscape was introduced and in which Englishness is also at stake. This aspect of Townscape was almost certainly Hastings, and at one level, it was simple nationalism best ignored. However, understood in reverse – not as national character with aesthetic consequences, but as an analogy between political theories of sovereignty and the powers and limits of art – it links our earlier discussion of Repton's appropriation with the disenfranchisement from urban form that designers feel today.

The politics of viewpoint from *Civilia* to *Collage City*

There was a degree of jingoism in the Englishness arguments of 'Exterior Furnishing' and 'Townscape' which is largely explained by wartime patriotism and the rhetoric by which the nativeness of the picturesque was expected to make modernism popular, once it had been explained that they were the same in principle. But at the same time that de Wolfe exhibited some boisterous chauvinism, writing of 'those who have the misfortune not to be English – Scots, Germans, Americans', he also states that ' – national flags are wagged here merely for brevity's sake'.[111] What the names of nations and peoples are, in brief, for, according to de Wolfe, are different kinds of liberal political philosophies with different kinds of architectural corollaries. De Wolfe's starting point is Mason's idea in his *Essay on Design in Gardening* of 1768: that the irregularity of the English garden is the consequence of a native English passion for independency standing in contrast to the tyranny accepted by the French and demonstrated by the forms of their geometrical, rule-governed gardens. De Wolfe admits that Mason's argument is simplistic, given that the French became violently democratic shortly afterwards, but he does not disavow it. Instead, in a discourse on the history of political theory that is remarkable for its length in an illustrated professional architecture journal, de Wolfe starts with the Greeks, and then spends time with Machiavelli, Hobbes, Shaftesbury and Humboldt, to demonstrate that English liberty and French tyranny continued as a dialectic between the liberal democratic positions of Rousseau and Voltaire (the former being English for the purpose of the argument). He calls these Radical and Rational Liberalism:

> we now have the rational canon of French democracy defined as the assumption that liberty by making the individual free to get at the truth, which is *one*, will end by establishing universal conformity; and on the other hand what for want of a better word what I have called the radical canon, of English democracy, based on the belief in individualism *per se*; as a departure from conformity, as a means of differentiation in the biological sense – of achieving, that is, an increase in complexity, or organization, equivalent to that which occurs when differentiation takes place in the embryo and the organs appear.[112]

'Differentiation' in the biological and political sense de Wolfe gives it here, is used to develop Price's aesthetics:

> English artists, . . . have shown an inclination throughout the styles and the centuries to treat life objectively and empirically and in the eighteenth century under the war-cry irregular (meaning 'let's have more character,' i.e., significant differentiation) this urge was brought into consciousness.[113]

Price's terminological project, differentiating the causes of visual pleasure as beauty or picturesqueness, is ultimately an attack on beauty. Price denies this vehemently throughout his text, but de Wolfe is correct to insist that ideality is irreducible in beauty, and that the picturesque doctrine of irregularity must ultimately be antithetical to it. Price insists that, empirically, we experience beauty and picturesqueness as mixed. In his rhetoric, this has the role of ameliorating the more challenging aspects of picturesqueness to maintain it within the 'republic of taste'. But the converse is also true: if empirically, beauty is always mixed with picturesqueness, it can never be ideal. I earlier quoted de Wolfe's word-painting of the 'practical surrealist picture' that the planner must make from the collage materials of the city, and this passage is also framed in political terms.

> From such assortments the radical planner has to produce his practical surrealist picture. If it is good it will have what the good interior scene has, an overall character – conformity even – yet founded, not as with rational Liberal theory on the effort to achieve congruity through harmony but on the effort to achieve a new kind of organization through the cultivation of significant differences. Not any old differences. The significant ones. By concentration on the urge of the parts to be themselves to make a new kind of whole.[114]

De Wolfe's presentation begins with political theory, moves through picturesque theory, and then makes the arguments for Townscape that I have already discussed at length. At the hinge point he writes:

> Everything so far has really been introductory; but now the great, the crucial question has to be posed. It is this. Supposing it to be agreed that these are some of the forces which dictate the pattern of politics, can they be distinguished in action out there on the surface of the land?[115]

This grand deduction is, however, hedged with cautions and much smaller claims, and is presented with confusing irony. The essay finishes as if its only purpose is to introduce Cullen's pictorial 'Casebook' following it. In contrast to the extensive scope of the essay, the argument seems quite minor; just as the legal codes of Napoleonic Europe can be contrasted with English case-based law, so urban design should proceed by precedents rather than principles.[116] De Wolfe actually begins the article with a very strange aside on the provisional nature of his argument. He cites Charles Baudelaire citing E. T. A. Hoffmann's experience of synesthesia: 'when he "breathed the odour of red, or brown nasturtiums" he seemed to "hear far off, the grave deep note of an oboe".'[117] The inference seems to be that the discussion of political theory and architecture is synesthetic. If we sweep away all of the contingent reasons that England is in the discussion, we might well agree that the connection is no more likely than the idea that we smell political theory and hear architecture.

However, two more serious points remain. In the first we should understand the matter the other way around. Here politics provides some concepts that assist the development of the picturesque as an aesthetic and a way of making art. De Wolfe's political dichotomy made clear the incompatibility of beauty and the picturesque as concepts. His idea of significant differentiation as the model of organic social development and urban development was not exactly original, but linking it to Price's ideas of haphazard buildings did help to make the picturesque more available to a modern audience. In this light, political theory was no more apposite than simple English nationalism. Like the appropriation of linguistic theory in the following decades, or the new biology today, political theory was simply consumed by architects into new differentiations and articulations within a familiar concept of form. The second reason to forgive Townscape's hyperbole would be to say that de Wolfe marked out a kind of necessity: that the socio-political would always be the horizon of architectural discourse – its limit. At a certain level, this is a banal thing to state because, compared to arts that merely cost money and reproduce prestige, the use of territory in city planning and architecture will always have more self-evident relations with government and the limits of its capacity. It is this immanence of issues in the governance of space that makes architecture, landscape architecture and urban design quite different to the other arts. Ballet and painting are political in the sense that, from the suburban school hall to the great state companies and collections, they affirm social structures and reproduce prestige with more or less spectacular costs. But the material from which dance or paintings are made is not immediately social and politicized in the way that land is. In an analogy I am going to develop through the remainder of this chapter, I will suggest that the issue of the politics of the picturesque collapses onto and rises again from the same question that confronted Repton. Appropriation is a way to interpolate from the partial possession that we have of the world to a totalized view that we can call 'our own'. How best, then, to appropriate the socio-political, in prospect or in landscape? The manner of viewing territory, ideally, contingently, from within, from above, is not a simple allegory of politics; it is a single comportment towards land and government. What is irritatingly capricious in the Townscape essay is that, to continue my analogy, the height of the horizon goes up and down a lot. As I have argued in this and the previous chapter, it is actually thoroughly in the spirit of picturesque practice to locate 'the embodied, the differentiated, the phenomenal'[118] in the imagination and rejection of a concrete experience of an ideal.

In the remainder of the chapter, I will substantiate my observation by showing a certain compulsion to aestheticize the political in the work of Colin Rowe, whose 'Collage City' of 1975 has generally been understood as critiquing and surplanting Townscape. Many of the differences between de Wolfe and Rowe will be shown to be less significant than a very simple point. Rowe's great innovation over de Wolfe is his visual understanding of the city by looking down from a great height, using aerial photography. To stress the closeness of the overlap, I will analyse de Wolfe's last iteration of Townscape in a largely forgotten book that appeared only four years before 'Collage City'.

In 1971, Hastings' Architectural Press published a volume entitled *Civilia: The End of Sub Urban Man: a Challenge to Semidetsia*. The editor, who also contributed the majority of the text, was Ivor de *Wofle*. In the intervening twenty-seven years since its first pronouncement, Townscape became a regular feature in the *AR* and developed under other campaigning titles such as 'Outrage', 'Counter-Attack', 'Manplan' and 'SLOAP' (Space Leftover After Planning). Ian Nairn and Kenneth Browne were responsible for many of these features. *Civilia* was published in the same year as Cullen's *The Concise Townscape*, which, as I mentioned earlier, was very successful on account of Cullen's dropping the modernist aspects and making Townscape into a kind of nostalgia for traditional communal forms. If the consolations of tradition gave Townscape its edge, and became its historical destiny, *Civilia* shows that this is certainly not what de Wolfe intended. I think that we should understand the ultimate development of the concepts of Townscape to lie in *Civilia* because of its patrimony in The Architectural Press, and because it is conceptually consistent with the idea, back to 'Exterior Furnishing'.

Civilia (Figures 5.15 and 5.16) was 'realized' by Browne with the assistance of Priscilla Baschieri-Salvadori, is introduced by Nairn, and has a long essay and commentary on the design by 'de *Wofle*'. (Apparently, this typo amused the contributors so much that they made it consistent throughout the volume. However, to simplify things I will stick to the original

Figure 5.15 Kenneth Browne (with Priscilla Baschieri-Salvadori), 'Swan Wharf, Civilia', 1971.

Figure 5.16 Kenneth Browne (with Priscilla Baschieri-Salvadori), 'The Quay and University, Civilia', 1971.

pseudonym.) De Wolfe's line on architecture and planning had not changed since 'Exterior Furnishing', and although neither the picturesque nor Townscape are mentioned, the mixture of political theory and pictures is very similar. *Civilia* supposes that urban architecture and planning do not so much arise out of solutions to problems, but rather from a picture of a life to be led and a grand explanation of the benefits of that life. De Wolfe begins, again, with the story of Hoffmann's synesthesia and Baudelaire's idea that genius can be defined as the ability to create a new commonplace. If liberalism had the smell that provoked Townscape, *Civilia* begins by citing Adam Smith's *The Wealth of Nations* and goes on to state:

> In the absence of a cliché peculiar to planning, and the genius who could run one up, I propose to move in on the phrase that has worked so well for economics in order to grab it for the environment. If supply and demand does something to the economists why shouldn't it answer the needs of planners?[119]

In *Civilia*, de Wolfe's ideas about planning *per se* are framed within the rise of environmental issues, particularly pollution and over-population. The city of Civilia is described in the present tense as being 'located in the heart of the Midlands at the centre of the nation's communication system' on the site of a disused quarry. The scenario of the book is a documentation of the design and building of Stage 1 Civilia, which is expanding to become a new high-density city. At a regional level, the *Civilia* 'Planner's Report' argues for high-density new cities 'which take the adverse pressure off the existing centres, allowing their identity to remain' and which also save the countryside from de Wolfe's real nemesis: the suburbia spreading out across England like 'the sprawl of the mining camp'.[120] De Wolfe claims that the fault of suburbia – its destruction of the countryside without creation of urbanity – is the result of a false merging of 'two antipodal impulses in Man':

> Society, like a man, is in tension between two contradictory claims, the herd instinct and the demands of the individual – the need to identify with one's kind and the impulse to differentiate from it. On the face of the land these contradictory urges materialise as town and country.[121]

The residents of super-dense Civilia look out across beautiful rural England to which they have an equality of access. De Wolfe explains the relation as that of a beehive to its territory:

> Opposition of 'town' and 'country' perpetuates one of those false antitheses that obscure the real issue, better illustrated, in the beehive and its territory where the emptiness of the territory and the congestion of the hive have significance insofar and only insofar as they illuminate the bee polity, the bee way of life.[122]

Civilia's argument is, thus, a quite familiar one in which higher density building and living reduce land use and transport costs and foster social interaction. What is unusual is the mode of presenting this argument, which is entirely pictorial. The designers present no plan of Civilia, only an isometric view of an area of land, which looks like discarded chewing-gum. Neither are there plans of buildings or types of buildings, nor figures for population density or floor areas to be achieved. There is no diagram of a system of transport, water supply or sewage disposal, and no discussion of the ownership of land and buildings, their procurement, or the government of the city and its building programme. *Civilia* is the extreme development of de Wolfe's idea, three decades earlier, that 'Bill Brown', in order to become urbane, needs a picture to aspire to.

Given the complete lack of planimetric and quantitative information, Browne's designs are remarkably well-developed images of the public places of Civilia. The images are grouped in chapters describing the life and urban character of different precincts of the city. Reading de Wolfe's commentary with Browne's designs, we can picture how high-density living, shared outdoor space and grade-separated public transport systems would feel, even if we know nothing about what makes them possible or viable. Browne's images are, thus, further demonstrations of the one real power that de Wolfe had previously claimed for the picturesque: 'to *reconcile visually* in the mind's eye what would appear to be irreconcilable elements in any town plan: quaint bits, new bits, monuments, traffic, tall buildings, short buildings, flat blocks, individual cottages, etc., etc.'.[123] The problem of Townscape had been that these elements did have actual relations and causes, but that these were insensible matters of history, economics and the taste of past generations. Picturesque techniques allowed the historical city to be appropriated into new unities of visual experience and modernity. Civilia is all new and modern and we are to suppose that 'supply and demand' and 'planning' produced a city that was already reconciled. But, following the spirit of the picturesque, the experience of Civilia is imagined entirely in its own terms, split from cognition of the rational planning imperatives that brought it into existence.

Browne's means of producing images of this utopia, constructed *ex novo* and yet picturesque, is a brilliant conceit. It seems he swept the floor of the Architectural Press and collaged together photographs of the best buildings of recent decades with images from de Wolfe's *Italian Townscape* of 1963 (on which Browne had also worked). Favourites that appear in several of the realizations are Churchill College Cambridge (Sheppard Robinson and Partners), Moshe Safdie's Habitat at Montreal, the student housing at Durham University by Dick Raines of the Architects Co-partnership, Queen Elizabeth Hall, the Hayward Gallery, Harry Seidler's Killara house, and in an echo of de Wolfe's political allegory, Basil Spence's 'Beehive' extension to the New Zealand Parliament. There is only one old building in Civilia, a sixteenth-century farmhouse, which de Wolfe, in the fictional mode of historian of Civilia's construction, describes as a token victory for conservationists:

> The passionate determination to save Grange Farm, [. . .] genuine 16th century black-and-white, had awkward consequences for practically everybody in the vicinity – the Provost, the University, the halls of residence, the town wall, the galleria, the street pattern and of course Grange Farm. It can be seen now nestling in an elbow of the town wall, 92, with, left, the Habitat-style halls of residence . . .[124]

This last remnant of the problematic of Townscape in the megastructural picturesque of Civilia serves to insist, yet again, how the problems of buildings of historical value and traditional urban forms were the pretexts of Townscape, not its aim.

Townscape supposed that we could develop a visual acuity that would allow us to see the clash of the modern and the obsolete as surrealism. In Civilia, the process is inverted: dozens of uniformly excellent buildings, largely constructed in the heavy off-form concrete of late Brutalism and thus equally historically advanced, are jumbled together into something that alludes to both the megastructures popular at the time and the picturesque irregularity of historically developed cities. It is the process of collage that generates the irregularity. Each element of Browne's pictures already has within it a viewpoint and a viewing distance of the original photograph, and thus the slight shifts of the perspective mean each image maintains an instability where it comes together as a picture at the same time as one senses the individual elements into which the picture might dissolve.

Civilia is a largely forgotten book because of its own faults, but more so because of the conceptual revolution of 'contextualism', the apogee of which was the publication in book form of Rowe and Fred Koetter's *Collage City* in 1978. *Collage City* was a watershed in architectural thinking about cities, and about modernism. It contains a strongly worded critique of Townscape and is generally thought to have supplanted it. However, the differences between *Collage City* and Townscape are much less than are usually thought, at least if we understand Townscape's ultimate form to be *Civilia* rather than Cullen's populist *The Concise Townscape*. In a letter to the Editor of the *AR* in 1975, Peter Reyner Banham quipped that the true author of *Collage City* was Ivor de Wolfe.[125] Banham was attacking the cultural conservatism that they had in common, but, as well as this, many of the apparent differences between the books can be resolved by the similarities in their political rhetoric and by the concept and technique of collage. These similarities are all the stronger if we understand a simple formal difference: Townscape was conducted in imagined landscape views from terrestrial viewpoints while *Collage City* rotated the axis of view to look down on the plan from above.

Rowe's early essay, 'The Mathematics of the Ideal Villa', was published in the *AR* in 1947 and its mix of history and design theory made him an influential teacher and began his dedication to putting the embodied knowledge of architectural history in the hands of modern designers. This attempt at a conceptual reconciliation of modernity and tradition, and the consequent debunking of the millennialist tendency in modernism, is quite at odds with Townscape. It meant that Rowe was a major figure in what was to become post-modernism. Rowe's ideas and taste are perhaps best exemplified in the work of his friend and former pupil James Stirling. Rowe had been taught at the Warburg Institute in London by Wittkower, whose book, *Architectural Principles in the Age of Humanism*, provided much of the conceptual base for 'The Mathematics of the Ideal Villa'. A small amount of the opposition of Rowe to Townscape must have gone back to the rivalry between the differing re-appropriations of the Classical and the Romantic/Gothic/picturesque that were themselves connected with Wittkower and Pevsner. Mark Linder has argued that, as much as architectural history, Rowe was influenced by American art theory and in particular Alfred Barr's account of the role of collage in modernism.[126] Rowe was British but taught longest in the United States, while his urban ideas mostly grew out of his regular residence in Italy. From the early 1960s, when he began teaching at Cornell University, Rowe and his students were developing the conceptual base of *Collage City* in design studios. Thus, there was considerable historical overlap with the later manifestations of Townscape. In 1975, the *AR* gave over a whole issue to Rowe for a long essay titled 'Collage City', which made the argument that was greatly extended in the book three years later. In the article, Rowe makes a negative assessment of Townscape that is quite circumspect compared to the scorn of the later book, *Collage City*, although the argument is basically the same. Rowe contrasts an image of Archigram's Plug-in City with Frederick Gibberd's Harlow New Town Square:

> As an exhibition of townscape, the Harlow town square involves a conscious attempt to placate and console. The first image [Archigram] is ostensibly forward looking, the second deliberately nostalgic; and, if both are highly random, the randomness of the one is intended to imply all the vitality of an un-prejudiced imaginary future, while the random-ness of the other is intended to suggest all the casual differentiations which might have been brought about by the accidents of time. The implication of the second image is of an English market place [. . .] which, though it is absolutely of the moment (the moment being 1950) is also a product of all the accumulations and vicissitudes and of history.[127]

This reasonable summary of the aims of Townscape is then quickly and unfairly interpolated into a further opposition between Superstudio's complete transcendence of building, and Disneyland's 'Main Street'. In the book, Rowe extends this discussion and claims that the situation of architecture and urban life has been reduced to a non-choice between modernist technological millennialism and the administered popularity of Townscape. These are: 'two alternative prisons for the human spirit . . . one of them is a fortress with electronic controls while the other is an open gaol conducted on compassionate principles'.[128] *Collage City* appears to be much more sophisticated than the works of de Wolfe. Rowe has none of the patronizing bonhomie and ironic argot of de Wolfe, and instead expresses the intellectual and culturalist aspirations of the architects of his time. Whereas de Wolfe offers to simplify philosophy and history for a reader who is a commonsense architect keen to put ideas into practice, Rowe's fireworks of references assume a reader who is, or aspires to be, very widely read in the history of architecture and philosophy. Nevertheless at a certain level, the template is the same. Like de Wolfe, Rowe sets up a dichotomy, winds it up to a point of crisis, and then demands the good sense of compromise, and he does this in a space where architecture and political theory become almost interchangeable.

Rowe's dichotomy is that of the closed and the open, by which he means both concepts of form and political systems. The closed form is the ideal that de Wolfe identified as totalitarian. Just as de Wolfe appropriated Rousseau, Voltaire and Smith to explain different aspects of architectural form, Rowe introduces Karl Popper:

> The *philosophe engagé*, dedicated via experience to attack upon all doctrines of historical determinism and all assumptions of the closed society: it is in terms of this background that Popper, the apostle of scientific rigour, further presents himself as the critic of Utopia and the exponent of tradition's usefulness; and it is in these identical terms that he may also be seen to emerge as, by implication, the greatest of critics of modern architecture and urbanism.[129]

Popper's idea that scientific advances come not through pure rationality but through the critique or falsification of existing knowledge, is used by Rowe to argue for an architecture that looks backward in a lively and critical relation to tradition. Rowe deploys Popper's critique of Hegelian historical determinism in *Open Society and its Enemies*, to argue against architecture as an instrument of socialist government. If this looks like Townscape's liberalism, it is. But Rowe raises another problem with 'openness': the dictatorship of the majority into which democracy might fall, if it has no ideal.

> The architectural proponents of populism are all for democracy and all for freedom; but they are characteristically unwilling to speculate as to the necessary conflicts of democracy with law, of the necessary collisions of freedom with justice. They address themselves to what they believe to be (and to a large extent are) concrete evils – economic evils, stylistic evils, cultural and ethnic abuse; but they are so much (and so properly) concerned with specifics as to be typically unable to place libertarian detail in what, for the want of a better world, must be complementary context of legal and legalistic abstraction. In other words, the populists (like some of the devotees of townscape) are apt to vitiate an entirely plausible argument by their unwillingness to consider the matter of ideal reference . . .[130]

> in practice, townscape seems to have lacked any ideal referent for the always engaging 'accidents' which it so promotes; and, as a result, its tendency has been to provide sensation without plan, to appeal to the eye and not to the mind and, while usefully sponsoring a perceptual world, to devalue a world of concepts. It may be argued that these limitations are not intrinsic to the approach, that townscape can be detached from what too early became an undue preoccupation with beer and yachting . . .[131]

Rowe misunderstands, or misstates, the centrality of modern art to Townscape, by writing that, for a time in the 1930s, 'the possibility was open of seeing the townscape idea as affiliated to Cubist and post-Cubist tradition'.[132] This possibility was lost, according to Rowe, because of the war and nationalism, but his remarks also suggest that it is this latency that *Collage City* fulfils.

Rowe argues that modern urban planning supposes that buildings will be arrayed simply in grids in an open field, so that, while some (good) modern buildings have complex and nuanced forms, urban planning tends to encourage isolated buildings, where form is found in the object rather than the space. In a famous observation, Rowe shows that the court of the Uffizzi could be imaged as the spatial inverse of Le Corbusier's Unite d'Habitation. Rowe develops a neat and powerful schema to explain this contrast. The modern city has two formal conditions: building and isomorphic spatial field. The traditional city has two kinds of building: monumental (read architecture) and ordinary building. In the traditional city, external spaces are closed because of high density, and they fall into two types: the figural spaces, squares and the like; and the purely contingent 'Townscape' arising out of the interplay of buildings. The quality of 'collage' that Rowe identifies lies in the pieces of ideal building and idealized open spaces that always have their spatial qualities rivalled by the incidental and unforseen. To show this, *Collage City* is greatly dependent on figure-ground drawing techniques and aerial photography. Rowe's alternative to Versailles is not the English Garden, but something that inspired Richard Payne Knight's ideas of a picturesque architecture – in many ways the cipher of the Collage City idea: Hadrian's Villa at Tivoli, which he presents through a high viewpoint photograph of a model:

> There is unambiguous, unabashed Versailles. The moral is declared to the world and the advertisement, like so many things French, can scarcely be refused. This is total control and the glaring illumination of it. It is the triumph of generality, the prevalence of the overwhelming idea and the refusal of the exception. And then, compared with this single-minded performance of Louis XIV, we have the curiosity of Hadrian who is, apparently, so disorganized and casual, who proposes the reverse of any 'totality', who seems to need only an accumulation of disparate ideal fragments . . .[133]

According to Rowe, it is the interplay of the four kinds of form, rather than 'picturesqueness', that explains the experiential richness of the traditional city. In fact, there is little about cities in this account that was not already in Sitte (to whom Rowe gives no more credit than does de Wolfe). But Rowe does schematize Sitte-esque values at a higher order, giving a much greater flavour of theory than the empiricism that Townscape valued in the picturesque. Most of Rowe's concepts come from modern art, as I will show, but *Collage City* is also marked by the rise of architectural semiotics, which Françoise Choay and Diana Agrest were encouraging about this time. Rowe writes that the double condition of architecture and building is like literary language and everyday speech, and while he does not acknowledge it, this is surely a version of Roman Jakobson's 'poetic function of language', just as the two-by-two factor analysis of urban form resembles Algirdas Greimas' 'semiotic square'.[134]

The implications for design are simpler than Rowe's argument might suggest, but they do mark a real turning point in architectural history. This is not because there are any fresh design techniques or concepts. *Collage City*, like townscape and Sitte, concerns a visual judgement of form in which cities are material in the sense of an artist's material, and the book is relatively indifferent to the social and technical aspects of urban design. Like Sitte, but unlike Townscape, *Collage City* finds a model in the bounded figural urban spaces typical of medieval and pre-industrial Europe. What made *Collage City* so important in the 1970s was the context in which these ideas were presented and taken to be an explicit critique of modernism: first, not all building could or should aspire to be architecture; and, second, there is a mode of historicism open to architecture but other to appearance, an historicism of the plan rather than the elevation. Urbanism became the opening out of the closed system of modernism, making it possible to keep faith with one's times – with technology and appearance of buildings – while maintaining continuity with the past by acceding to the same plan constraints of traditional buildings.

Much of my summary of Rowe's position is hard to evidence in his extravagantly argumentative and digressive book, and very much clearer in an exegesis by one of Rowe's students and collaborators, William Ellis. It is something of a cliché to say that '*Collage City* equals Sitte plus modern art' but, among other clarifications, Ellis shows how this is not a trivial point. I earlier quoted Rowe on the possibilities of modern art combined with Townscape. Ellis describes one of the Cornell studio's schemes: 'the Buffalo project takes the Baroque idea of a system of connected nodes and places it under the compositional auspices that typified Suprematist and Elementarist painting. It is the Quirinale complex executed by Malevich, Philadelphia by Van Doesburg . . .'.[135] He goes on:

> The traditional city is more interesting as a pattern of buildings and spaces, and with its uniform roof heights, more susceptible to two-dimensional representation. Although figure-ground is a pictorial device involved with *Gestalt* assumptions and the procedures, it is not picturesque in the scenographic sense. It suggests the abstract painter rather than the painter of scenes, relationships rather than objects, pattern rather than picture. It betrays Rowe's inclination toward the totally activated field of much modernist painting. Thus it unites two of his great enthusiasms: traditional urban space and certain aspects of modernist art. It also allows him to work with pattern structures at a scale as grand as Le Corbusier's. These patterns are abstract – and anti-picturesque – in a further way: their huge size enables them to be imagined from the plan, but prevents them being seen as pictures in front of the eye.[136]

The whole thrust of this book has been to show that what Ellis (and Rowe) thought was anti-picturesque is, in fact, picturesque. There is more than a thread tieing Rowe's interest in the visual form of the plan to picturesque architecture of the early nineteenth century. As I showed in the previous chapter, the architectural speculations on picturesque irregularity had already discovered the possibility of an empirical unidealized experience of pure form and the broken and collided forms of what will later be called collage. But before reintroducing some of my former arguments to show that Rowe is more, not less, picturesque than de Wolfe, there is a more obvious point to be found in Ellis' exegesis. How do we see these pictorial but anti-picturesque patterns? Alongside orthographic plans of cities, *Collage City* is packed with aerial photographs and bird's-eye views, that is to say, with experiential views of these abstract matters. For Rowe to illustrate the spatial qualities of the closed defined spaces of traditional cities, his principle device is not a photograph or drawing taken from a place that anyone could occupy. If he had done this, *Collage City* would have appeared either like *Civilia* or *The Concise Townscape*. The modernity of *Collage City*, its viewpoint outside of, and onto tradition, is at about a thousand metres from a high incident angle, where what we see is a shallow tray of space laid horizontally.

Horizontality and modern art

In opposing abstract art and the picturesque so simply Ellis overlooks the possibility that the difference might not lie in representation so much as the orientation of the canvas and viewer. Ellis mentions the model of visuality found in modern painting throughout the text, but its importance can be grasped at a more fundamental level in the numerous figure-ground drawings and aerial photographs in *Collage City*. These look like the 'field painting' manner of late modernist painting, characterized by flatness, pattern and an 'all-over-ness', that imply the painting is not a composition of elements, but a single indivisible expanse. The particular marks and the sense of space or event in such a painting are, then, instances of this 'field' condition. These concepts are the basis for the more successful design explorations in *Collage City*, such as Graham Shane's 'field analysis of central London'.[137] What Rowe asks us to admire in an 'aerial' photograph of a conjectured reconstruction of Hadrian's Villa is not the particular arrangement of the buildings and courts; it is rather the sense with which, and the differing degrees to which, the elements conflict or co-exist with one another, or attend, or not, to the topography. The varied and contingent causes of the Villa have, in fact, formed a general condition that can continue to unfold across a field. This idea is not only an idea in painting. Field studies dominated the large-scale architecture of the post-war period, and Rowe illustrates many of these. In opposition to the mega-structure idea of deep hierarchies and coordination, Alison and Peter Smithson, Cedric Price, Josic Candillas and Woods, and many others, experimented with semi-organic grammars of site organization based on sociological data or organization theory. In these experiments space requirements, enclosure systems and servicing technology interact and give rise to autochthonous spatial organization. There were doubtless many and complex ways in which the formal logic of painting, possible formal architectural languages, and sociological and organization theory interacted in this period; but one of these was primary and simple: the argument that *Collage City* presents to the reader depends, as did post-war painting, on a rotation of the viewpoint.

When Jackson Pollock painted on the floor and then hung the canvas on the wall, a certain horizontalness remained in the geometry of the paint dribbles, as well as in the coins, cigarette butts and detritus that were doubly indexical of the horizontal and the floor. The viewing conditions of such a painting are like those of any picture, except that canvas is no longer *facing* the viewer. Unlike the upright posture of the viewer, the position of the canvas can only be understood as a convention of the gallery space, not of painting. Pollock's innovation was the largest shift in the spatiality of the painting surface since portable pictures overtook mural painting, and it also bears more generally on the spatiality of painting. Formalist proponents of abstraction, particularly Clement Greenberg, celebrate the non-representational aspect of abstract painting as a movement towards purity; as painting addressing matters of its own condition, colour, shape and the flatness of its surface.[138] In challenging this formalist account, Rosalind E. Krauss developed a different narrative for modern art, one that places greater historical emphasis on surrealism and greater interpretive attention to the phenomenological and pyschoanalytic aspects of art. For Krauss, the problematic of surface is an aspect of its horizontality, and it is not a movement towards purity, but an attack on the Gestalt concept of form as native to human perception.

> The power of Pollock's mark as index meant that it continued to bear witness to the horizontal's resistance to the vertical and that it was the material condition of this testimony – the oily, scabby, shiny, ropey qualities of the self-evidently horizontal mark – that would pit itself against the visual formation of the Gestalt, thus securing the condition of the work as formless.[139]

This quote is taken from Krauss' essay 'Horizontality' in which she goes on to describe works by Andy Warhol including the *Oxidation Painting* that Warhol produced by having friends urinate onto a canvas prepared with metallic paint and placed on the floor. The essay is a chapter of a book, *Formless*, written with Yve-Alain Bois about the explanatory power of Georges Bataille's concept of *informe*, or formlessness. *Informe* they state to be an inverse of form, a bad form that opposes and undoes the 'good form' of Gestalt, which is why Warhol's piss paintings, with their transgressive relation to sexuality and to the institutions of art, suit their argument well.[140] Their argument reaches into psychoanalysis, mentioning Jacques Lacan's relating the phallus to the Gestalt. It also reaches outward to an anthropological dimension, fundamental to Bataille and Freud: the bifurcation of vision

> into two distinct functions: with the vision of animals focused on the horizontal ground on which they and their prey both travel. A vision that is therefore, in certain ways, merely an extension of the sense of touch; but with the sightedness of mankind recharacterized as 'beholding.' Qualified by its acknowledgment of the distance that separates the 'beholder' from his object, the gap built into the human perceptual relation is what provides a space for all those varieties of vision which separate man from animals: contemplation, wonder, scientific inquiry, disinterestedness, aesthetic pleasure.[141]

Krauss' and Bois' (and Bataille's) position is rather strange, as they do not think that *informe* disproves the existence of Gestalt form, or that 'horizontality' has any power to demystify the vertical. They simply praise the transgressive term and thus risk a kind of Gnosticism. In my view, their argument would be more viable if it was limited to art history and Gestalt was understood without a psychological dimension, as simply figural form. The rotation of the viewpoint that they take to be so significant could then be given a greater historical context. In a much earlier essay by Bois, it is the picturesque that opposes the Gestalt.[142] My discussion here takes up from my argument with Bois in Chapter 4, where I criticize his assumption that architectural plans are irreducibly Gestalts and that the picturesque concerns only elevations or the 'vertical' (in the terms of the present discussion). Similarly, in my chapter 'Disgust', I explain Price's theory of the relation of the liminally formed and the disgusting (which relies to a small extent on Virgil's use of the Latin word *informe*). Pointing out that the picturesque is concerned with *informe* and what Bataille calls base materialism; and that viewpoint rotation is also at stake in Price and Repton's debates and in the contemporary architectural developments of planning; we are close to supplying a broader historical context to Bois' and Krauss' book. More to the present point, with a couple more steps in the argument, I can show that what makes the visual language of modern painting apposite to the view of cities from above is the picturesque.

Krauss' argument about the significance of the horizontal in art history derives in part from a 1972 paper by Leo Steinberg, whose formulation is slightly different, as is the valency he gives to the idea. Steinberg's ideas arise from his contemplation of the works of Robert Rauschenberg, which he describes as having a 'flatbed picture plane'.[143] Steinberg chose the term from printing – the horizontal tray in which the type is held – and this has several felicities. It helps him contrast the indifference to orientation in our treatment of printed text compared to painting. The analogy to a shallow tray is also a good description of Rauschenberg's work. Rauschenberg placed found objects, such as a clock or a ladder along with newsprint and photographs, amongst the paint, making both the paint and the painting object-like. As Steinberg puts it: 'The picture's "flatness" is to be no more of a problem than the flatness of a disordered desk or an unswept floor.'[144] Horizontality is not, in the first place, a relation of the viewer to the work, but of the work to the objects within it, which are laid down – a horizontality made apparent through gravity and before any opposition to an upright viewer. This is a mundane flatness of floors and desks, anterior to the specialized flatness of the painting support. The appliqué of the objects is not a transgression of some pure flatness, but the relief any ordinary surface has by being used as such. Why Steinberg thought this significant is quite different to Krauss. Rather than presenting some kind of challenge to form, or the phallus, or the affirmative role of art in which such a myth of the upright exists, Steinberg thinks that what Rauschenberg invented is:

> a pictorial surface that let the world in again. [. . .] The picture conceived as the image of an image. It's a conception which guarantees that the presentation will not be directly that of a worldspace, and that it will nevertheless admit any experience as the matter of representation. And it readmits the artist in the fullness of his human interests, as well as the artist-technician.[145]

Rauschenberg thus affirms a millennial role for art by finding a place for content within a visual language that developed by abstracting itself from representation. The problematic of painting is not my topic, but the spatiality of the picture is, and this detour through Krauss' and Steinberg's ideas of horizontality gives me some terms to return to urbanism: the 'flatbed' of space and the idea of 'letting the world back in'. The view from which we look across a space that is so extensive that its elevational and pictorial character is lessened, so that it appears flat and below us, is a prospect. For most of the past, prospects have connoted power – the royalty of sight. What would it be to 'let the world' into a prospect? For it to become liberal and modern?

Aerial photography has played a significant role in modern art and urbanism. From an aeroplane, the world does indeed look like a shallow tray of space, and photographs from the air have a particular kind of flatness that has made them models for painters. But most significantly, flight and photography make a double index of modernity. Matisse urged his students to fly, saying that the aerial view 'gave the optical key the world'.[146] Kazimir Malevich's paintings, which Rowe mentions and illustrates, are based not only on the new spatial concepts of the Cubists but on aerial photographs of cities and his experience of flight. According to Richard Wohl, some of his works, usually understood as abstract compositions, are actually designs for airports.[147] Early modernists thought that aerial photography gave a proof from nature of the new pictorial problematic. The lack of fore- or mid-ground in an aerial photograph seems to produce the transposition of depths into surfaces of modern painting. An increase in altitude looks like a process of pictorial abstraction.[148]

The use that Rowe makes of aerial photography – to explain urban principles – has precedents in the early twentieth century. In 1919, Captain Gordon H. G. Holt, RAF pilot and photographer, wrote in the *Architecture Review*, explaining that the techniques of aerial photography, developed during the war for mapping battlefields, would become an important tool in the architectural understanding of cities.[149] Holt uses his photographs of well-known urban set pieces to demonstrate that – as well as being dimensioned surveys – aerial photography provides 'complementary data' for the planning of towns and for the study of existing cities. He describes photographing Trafalgar Square – first in ortho-corrected plan and then obliquely

> showing the ordnance of the square or the "volume" of the fabric in three dimensions and in relation to features nearby. Characteristic details, anomalous or unusual effects, which with the spectator on the ground would perforce escape attention, reveal themselves instantly.[150]

Holt's sense of figure-ground pattern shows that his sensibilities were trained in Sitte or Unwin, but his use of the bi-plane already solves, at a rhetorical level, the problem of de

Wolfe and Rowe. A discourse on the city, based on historical examples, faces the paradox of tradition. How can one use the past without either traducing it, or blinding oneself to history? Holt can fly into the past. At one level, the aeroplane, special lenses and fast exposing film merely mark out a temporal position: the agency by which urban traditions might be wrenched from history to make fundamental statements on the timeless principles of city design.

The franchise of architecture, or looking down with the picturesque

There is a rhetoric of civics and political theory that dominates architectural understandings of cities where we might expect to see discussions of the actual politics of land value, the delivery of services and the citizen's role in the government of space. The political talk of Rowe and de Wolfe does not so much exclude this real politics of cities as disguise the scandalous disarticulation of architecture from town planning and from the actual government of space. Even then, the political theory of Townscape and its successors, despite its unanchoredness, is not entirely spurious. In the last instance, in the formal issues of the angle of vision and the position of the viewer and the scene, there is an issue of political imagination, of belonging and taking, of having with and without exclusivity, of actual and visual appropriation.

In the earlier sections of this chapter, I showed that in the eighteenth century the distinction of landscape and prospect alluded to different kinds of ownership and responsibility for the scene viewed. Prospect connoted the elevation of the viewpoint and was a kind of kingship where the power to see analogized the power to dispose. Landscape relied on contingency: the viewpoint had no significance in itself but allowed a surreptitious appropriation, a proprietorship, that relied on opportunity rather than rights, and a power that did not exist in exclusivity of possession so much as in position. Aerial photography is, then, a peculiarly modern viewpoint, not only because of the technology involved, or the issues of urban form discussed above, but because aerial photography makes a landscape from a prospect. Here, I return to the earlier argument about view orientation. I have described the spatiality of Le Nôtre's gardens as shallow trays of space to suggest what they might have in common with late modern painting and Steinberg's description of the 'flatbed' picture plane. Now I want to return briefly to the *ancien régime* and to do so through Louis Marin's analysis of royal maps.[151] Marin's careful analysis of the enunciative structure of such maps as allegories of sovereignty adds to my description of the modernity of the aerial photograph. It is a commonplace notion that the form of politics in the modern world is governed by the end of the divine rights of Kings to the dispersal of sovereignty in various forms of political franchise. The ongoing question of the abstraction or corporeality of the sovereign means that aerial photographs and maps cannot but be allegories of the forms that political franchise takes.

The practical significance of prospects becomes quite complex at a semiotic level. Militarily, the high ground is significant for the scope of information and the space for strategic manoeuvre that it allows, and it had an obvious connection to the power of captains and Kings who held the high ground. But the even higher viewpoints of city plans and maps were significant because they could not be occupied, thus connoting a superhuman abstraction of information and power. As Marin has shown, such views were an imagined experience of the abstract by an extra-human figure, the King, who commissioned maps and who constituted the single point at which such a mass of data could be significant. The high-viewpoint maps that combine plans with axonometric-like views of buildings and places survived long after the difference of plan and view was conceptualized. For Marin, this is evidence that city plans and maps had always described the viewer as much as the view. Aerial photographs are, thus, not merely a new means to see the city; they are the first palpable view of what had been an abstraction only seen by Kings: human society.

In 1858, as part of a project to develop aerial map-making as a surveying tool, Nadar took the first aerial photograph from a balloon over Paris.[152] Balloons first had military uses in the American Civil War and by the end of World War I, the military value of aerial views and aircraft was clear. By then, aerial photographers such as Holt (and Colonel Edward Steichen, the art photographer who commanded the US aerial survey)[153] were able to produce, for their colleagues in the artillery, orthographically corrected and dimensioned photographs of the kind that Nadar proposed. However, Nadar's first aerial image does not look directly down, but out across Paris, and clearly the power and interest of the image then and since are in the occupation of a viewpoint which was once absolute and unreal, but which has become actual. We should also see Nadar's photograph as concordant with the problematic relation of democracy and authority that shook the European nations and cities over the previous decade. In France in 1848, after the violent failure of a radically democratic republic, Louis-Napoleon Bonaparte, largely on the basis of his family name, was popularly elected to an effective dictatorship. In 1852, the government had become the Second Empire that declared him Napoleon III and sovereign in his own right. Nadar's photograph might stand for the problem of democracy, for how it can avoid collapsing into tyranny if power is no longer sacred. The photograph is very much like the aerial viewpoint plans of the *ancien régime*, except that the viewpoint is actual. If the viewpoint of the King's map is in reality impossible (there is no position in space where one can see that view), it is true of the power to which the view is directed (in Marin's terms, it is utopic). By contrast, Nadar's position is concrete, indisputable, but still unknowable. With a helicopter, we could probably find the position of Nadar's balloon by trial and error and use the aircraft's instruments to measure height and inclination; but there is insufficient information to do this with the photograph alone. Just as in the maps of the *ancien régime*, the instrumentality that lay in information about the dimensions and concrete position of buildings is given up for a narrative; but a narrative of contingency rather than divine right.

Collage City proposes a critique of both popularism and science; of democracy without aim (Townscape) and of ideals realized at the cost of lived life (socialism/modernism). In terms of political theory, this is a problem of sovereignty: in the name of who or what does government occur? *Collage City* is something like the theory of constitutional monarchy. Rowe writes: 'Collage . . . seems to be a technique for using things and simultaneously disbelieving in them, it is also a strategy which can allow Utopia to be dealt with as image, to be dealt with in fragments without our having to accept it *in toto*'.[154] Ideas of the practical compromise of the English Garden are often seen (including by Pevsner) as an analogue of the 'Glorious' Revolution. In 1688 the English Parliament threw out the Catholic King James II, and rather than rule directly as Parliament had done during the radical protestantism of the Commonwealth, invited the protestant William of Orange and Mary Stuart into a limited monarchy where Parliament held executive power. Price uses this analogy to sovereignty when he argues for the partial reintroduction of formal gardens and terraces within the picturesque:

> I shall probably be accused by Mr Brown's admirers, of endeavouring to bring about a counter-revolution, and to restore the *ancien régime*, with all its despotism of strait lines and perpetual symmetry. It is true that I have some attachment to the old monarchy,

> though I should not like to have it restored without strict limitations: but my wish in this instance is to combat the despotism of modern improvers, as resembling in a great degree that of religious intolerance; for they allow no salvation out of their own pale.[155]

The idea of a constitutional monarchy is that effective removal of kingship requires the King to be maintained.[156] For the people to exercise power over themselves, sovereignty without power must exist in the place of power, to stop it up, vouchsafing it against expropriation by demagogues and tyrants. Power can belong to the people only because sovereignty is still vested in a single unique body, a body which is constrained never to act for itself but that sees all in the name of all. The aerial photograph represents the city as it once was: whole in relation to a position outside of itself, but no longer owned in that view. Modernity might be understood as a certain democracy of viewpoint, or at least, the end of the absolute privilege of view. In aerial photographs we can each know the incidental, organic, everyday life of cities in which we live and we can experience the excitement of possessing them as total image. The aerial photograph is a vicarious sovereignty of the city. Like constitutional monarchy, it proposes that the most effective removal of kingship requires the King to be maintained. When *Collage City* shows us both dimensioned figure-ground plans and oblique aerial photographs, the role of the photograph is not to add further information about the roofs of buildings, it is to express the actuality of our franchise: that the only King and the only utopia is the sum of our individual experiences.

Popular books of aerial photography are worthy inheritors of the picturesque idea, and they reward the same sensibility towards which *Collage City* is directed. As I write, Yann Arthus-Bertrand's folio *Earth From The Air* is immensely popular in several editions of differing size, as a touring exhibition, website, calendars and diaries. There are a legion of such lavishly printed books continuing the publication of picturesque travel accounts going back to the eighteenth century. Just as in the past when travel was expensive and adventurous and the publishing of images by etching, lithography or photo-engraving was technologically advanced and expensive, so too, the luscious modern four-colour printing and the use of an aerial viewpoint connotes expense, technical prowess, and a certain amount of daring-do in achieving the image. More to my point here, Arthus-Bertrand's project is to make the whole of the globe visible, but only visible. His readers are perhaps like de Wolfe's 'Bill Brown': they require a convincing picture and then everything else will follow. The photographs do not tell us more about the world's ecologies and human action on them, they let us appropriate what we already know within a model of visual experience that comes from modern art. Arthus-Bertrand shows us that the slums of Nairobi look like analytic cubism. The gap between what we know or imagine of how such a city came to be, and the visual acuity under which we appropriate it, is at once trivial and affecting. It is picturesque.

Postscript: sharawaggi now

The current discourse on architectural urbanism is dominated by the ideas of Rem Koolhaas, a fierce critic of the contextualism of the later twentieth century. Koolhaas mounts two critiques of contextualism that attempt to show its irrelevance, but that, again, explode upwards into the heady world of political theory. In 'Bigness', Koolhaas makes an argument against context in its own terms of visual empiricism, and it is radically simple.[157] He points out that many buildings being commissioned today are simply so large that they fill the visual field, and no context is visible. The experience of the city is not of a collage of buildings varying in age or in instrumental or ideal qualities, but simply of one building and then another. Similarly, in 'Generic City', Koolhaas shows how the conservation of 'urban character', in the context of the vast acceleration in urbanization, means that 'the past will at some point become too "small" to be inhabited and shared by those alive'.[158] The problems of a heritage of urbanity exist only in a small part of a small number of cities, mostly in Europe. Not only is it an abrogation of responsibility for architects not to understand the booming cities of Asia, South America and Africa, it makes the idea of 'identity' more of a prison (for reasons similar to Rowe's critique of Townscape). Instead, Koolhaas praises the freedom from cultural determination of the Generic City.

> The Generic City is what is left after large sections of urban life crossed over to cyberspace. It is a place of weak and distended sensations, few and far between emotions, discreet and mysterious like a large space lit by a bed lamp. [. . .] Instead of concentration – simultaneous presence – in the Generic City individual 'moments' are spaced far apart to create a trance of almost unnoticeable aesthetic experiences: the color variations in the fluorescent lighting of an office building just before sunset, the subtleties of the slightly different whites of an illuminated sign at night.[159]

While not stated, it is fairly clear that the Generic City is modelled on Singapore, and the essay is preceded by a photo essay of blurry images taken through a car window of a high-rise city in a monsoonal downpour. Koolhaas' rhetoric against contextualism is in the space of geo-politics: the globalization of the economy, communication and architecture; the speed of urbanization; the demography of markets breaking down the control of governments over territory; and the rise of a modernity that is not Western. These are all serious matters, but whether to act on them or know more of them through architecture is a moot point. What interests me is how much the style of Koolhaas' essays is like that of de Wolfe's, with his blasts of pop political theory in some kind of crazy equation with a highly individuated visual empiricism. Despite its size and genericness, one can see Singapore from the air, but Koolhaas chooses not to and instead intersects a world of statistics and graphs with his view from a cab window, in a 'practical surrealistic picture'. More recently, Koolhaas directed a studio on contemporary Chinese urbanism in the publication of which his student Kate Orff quotes Price and feigns to own copyright of the word PICTURESQUE©.

> PICTURESQUE© revenge of the anti-idealist. A mode of making and perceiving space, invented by Chinese gardeners in the sixteenth century, which insists on the juxtapositions and relationships of between objects rather than their singular presence.
>
> an aesthetic based on harmonizing disparate elements, the PICTURESQUE© facilitates the overall development of southern China by visually preparing the viewer to receive any and all chaotic fragments of construction by integrating them into a pleasing inhabitable vision.[160]

In the footnotes, Orff goes on to compare the rebellion of the eighteenth-century English against French geometric ideals and totalitarianism with the growth of economic and political liberalism in China.[161] This is, perhaps, a greater irony than was intended. I presume that the picturesque here is just the vehicle for the larger amusement of framing, within this older story of cultural exchange, the impetus that China's present urban explosion might offer to Western architects. But this does not quite do justice to the picturesque, that may or may not have its origins in China, but which does not stop with Price. If Koolhaas and the Harvard students know of *sharawaggi*, Sir William Temple and the theory of the origin of picturesque in China, this is because these old ideas have a modern history in that other spoiled un-utopic modernism: Townscape. To forget the modernity of the picturesque elides the new perfect rotation of phenomenal view into plan view and back in de Wolfe's, Rowe's and Koolhaas' alternating views on modern urbanism, and what the history of architecture has to do with it. Through this succession of ideas the question of whose picture this is, and whose the picturesque is, continues to open out questions of viewpoint onto questions of politics – albeit at the trivial level of visual appropriation.

6
Movement

What makes the picturesque something other than the pictures to which it alludes, is movement. Pictures represent spaces in which one can imagine moving. They also have their own position as objects hung on the wall and are related spatially to a mobile observer. However, since the dominance of framed easel pictures, this viewing position has been a disembodied gaze. The critique of the picture in later twentieth-century painting brings back the body in only the most abstract sense. By contrast, our visual experience of gardens, buildings and cities is as embodied subjects: we are not merely changing position but are walking, driving, passing by, arriving, entering, staring, glancing . . . These eye and body movements are varyingly complex sets of gestures and locomotion, forming whole 'movements' that can be identified and named. It seems obvious that planning for such movements is the business of architecture, urbanism and landscape architecture: to move the viewer, to make 'movements' that are as identifiable as everyday activities such as walking to the shop, but to construe these movements as art. Hence the common and not inconsiderable charge against the picturesque in architecture, gardening and urbanism that it stills the viewer, removes the particularity of viewing in motion and duration, and flattens space.

Michel Conan, having remarked on the scarcity of discussion of movement in gardens, organized a symposium at Dumbarton Oaks in 2003 to redress the situation. In his Introduction to the subsequent book, Conan writes: 'The first part of this volume, "Beyond the picturesque" [. . .] demonstrates vividly how much attention to the experience of motion rules out the still-dominant picturesque aesthetic in landscape design.'[1] Now, it is hardly the case that practices of picturesque gardening were 'against movement'; they aimed to break the pattern of successive topoi that characterized earlier allegorical gardens. One contributor to the Dumbarton Oaks symposium, John Dixon Hunt, discusses this open form of movement as a 'ramble'.[2] I showed in an earlier chapter that irregularity in building assumes a peripatetic apprehension of form thought to be picturesque. I also showed how the concept of pictorial composition arrived relatively late, and weakly, and can hardly act strongly to fix the subject through views. And yet, at the level of concepts, Conan is correct. There is remarkably little discussion in the theory of the picturesque as to how pictures were to guide the design of sequential or continuous spatial experience. The putative opposition of the picturesque to movement was already present in Humphry Repton's charge that Sir Uvedale Price promoted 'picture gardening'. Price insisted that the picturesque lay in the visual acuity gained from the study of painting, rather than the garden being like a painted landscape. But in Price's generation and since, it is usual to see this as too fine a distinction; that a certain stillness is irreducible from the picturesque. How is it, then, that the earliest attempt at an art of visual experience in duration grows out of a concept of stillness? In fact, there is a marginal discussion of movement in the literature of the picturesque but it does not concern the motion of people through the landscape. Rather, it proposes that under picturesque conditions, buildings appear to possess movement. This whimsical idea arises out of a concept central to Western culture – the theory of mimesis, or the idea that an innate human propensity to imitate is the basis of all artifice and the means to differentiate the arts by type and nobility. Thus, to propose that buildings can have movement is to assert that architecture (and gardening) are imitative arts that mimic our movement.

Despite movement being crucial to the bundle of concepts that make up the picturesque, there is less written about it, and its historical status is most ambivalent. The very few mentions of movement in the eighteenth century texts are nevertheless of great importance. Sir Joshua Reynolds and Robert and James Adam used movement to characterize the kind of art that architecture is, and in an apparent digression about the picturesque of bridges, Price made an early and remarkably modern description of the movement of visual attention and the apprehension of space. The concept of movement that architects have today comes largely from the extensive German literature on art history, aesthetics and psychology at the end of the nineteenth century. Heinrich Wölfflin developed contemporary ideas of movement and the perception of form into an influential description of Baroque architecture, and subsequently a general description for all arts in all periods. Wölfflin's student Sigfried Giedion made movement fundamental in his argument that modern architecture was a necessary historical development, making space the proper medium of architecture and allowing us to experience it empathetically through movement. What links this major body of thought with the earlier scattered remarks of picturesque theorists are some historical details, which open larger conceptual issues. When the Adam brothers, Reynolds and Price describe picturesque architecture (of the grander kind) and its basis in movement, they refer to the work of Sir John Vanbrugh, the English Baroque architect. This puts the phenomenon that interested Wölfflin at the origin of picturesque theory. Wölfflin uses the German word for picturesque, *malerish*, to describe both an unreflective picturesque sensibility and his own superior concept, which is usually translated as 'painterly'. I mentioned this in Chapter 2 where I showed how disgust at the picturesque as an aesthetic category is the mechanism by which it has propagated historically. The role that Wölfflin gives to what he calls 'the picturesque movement-effect' can be used in the reversed direction to help us understand why the picturesque of buildings lies in the idea of these most static and fixed artworks moving. For Wölfflin, movement in architecture is a matter of empathic relations with the building, which are not to do with the body's capacity for spatial extension and locomotion so much as matters of posture, pose and gesture. While the major importance of this account is that it uses empathy theory to reorient and reinvigorate a millennial tradition of anthropomorphism in architecture, for us it is interesting because it returns movement to an issue of imitation. Architecture imitates us in our capacity for movement, but not our actual passage through space, rather, the gestures through which we give movement a communicative and affective form.

Picturesque and Baroque

In 1773, in the first volume of *The Works in Architecture of Robert and James Adam*, the authors write of their admiration for the Baroque architecture of Sir John Vanbrugh. This was:

> of the first class in point of movement, novelty and genius . . . *Movement* is meant to express, the rise and fall, the advance and recess, with other diversity of form, in the different parts of a building, so as to add greatly to the picturesque of the composition.[3]

The Adams' sense of the picturesque had been formed in the library of their architect father William and by the brothers Paul and Thomas Sandby, with whom they had drawn the old castles and new forts of Scotland.[4] The Adam brothers were expressing newly fashionable ideas that the role of architecture was to raise feelings and excite the imagination. Key members of the Scottish Enlightenment such as Adam Smith, Lord Kames and David Hume were known to the family, but Robert and James were more artistically than intellectually talented and it is as likely that they knew ideas of aesthetics through Thomas Sandby and through their time in the circle of the French Academy in Rome during their 'Grand Tours' (1755–7 and 1760–3 respectively). The brothers were taught drawing by Charles-Louis Clérisseau, and Robert was greatly influenced by Giovanni Battista Piranesi. Thomas Sandby became the first Professor of Architecture at the Royal Academy and in his lectures also praised Vanbrugh, stating, in 1771, in the language of the Burkean sublime, that: 'the prodigious dimensions, large divisions and succession of various forms at Blenheim in Oxfordshire [Figure 6.1], when seen at a proper distance, never fail to excite the strongest ideas of grandeur and magnificence'.[5] At one level we might think Sandby's a clearer account; 'movement' being forms seen in succession. However, the Adams' expansive statement includes the more ambiguous matters of the picturesque, the relationship of architecture to painting and of movement in painting, which, in any plain sense, is just as motionless as architecture. Movement and the picturesque are bound together by the theory of mimesis, as we see in the much richer account of Reynolds. Caroline van Eck has argued that Reynolds' and the Adams' ideas of movement bear comparison with passages in Quintilian where movement was a rhetorical category that linked the formal qualities of artworks and affects.[6] While the picturesque movement is a matter of empirical perception, van Eck is not incorrect. For Reynolds it was one way after the victory of aesthetics over rhetorical concepts of the visual arts to reconnect the ancient problem of mimesis to the emotions.

Reynolds praises Vanbrugh in his XIIIth Discourse to the Royal Academy in 1786 and in terms similar to Sandby and the Adams:

Figure 6.1 John Vanbrugh, Blenheim Palace, Oxfordshire, design c. 1705.

> he had originality of invention, he understood light and shadow, and had great skill in composition. To support his principal object, he produced his second and third groups or masses; he perfectly understood in *his* Art what is the most difficult in ours; the conduct of the Back-ground, by which the design and invention is set off to greatest advantage. What the back-ground is, in Painting, in Architecture is the real ground on which the building is erected; and no Architect took greater care, that his work should not appear crude and hard. That is, it did not abruptly start out of the ground with-out expectation or preparation.[7]

The topic of Reynolds' Discourse is a comparison of the arts, and his argument is that such a comparison reveals that there is a general concept of art beyond the particularities of painting, drama, landscape and architecture. This is 'to supply the natural imperfection of things, and to often gratify the mind by realising and embodying, what never existed but in the imagination'.[8] Reynolds' cautious introduction of romantic concepts of imagination is intended to relativize imitation and to show that it serves a greater task in which art can 'make an impression on the imagination and feeling'.[9] The status of imitation in the other arts will show, Reynolds thinks, the fallacy of understanding painting as the servile imitation of appearances. The XIIIth Discourse is of fundamental importance to the picturesque as Reynolds' statements and his authority gave the impetus and much of the agenda to Price's theories. It is also a very subtle and complex essay because, although Reynolds says that architecture is not an imitative art, his argument implies otherwise. He suggests that, as an art, architecture has an inverse condition to that of drama in which the actor begins with imitation and must break from it. I will return to these matters later in this chapter; my point here is a simpler one – the high architecture that seemed picturesque to the theorists of the late eighteenth century was Baroque.

In 'Essay on Picturesque Architecture and Building,' Price supposes two classes: 'those splendid artifices which may be called the picturesque of regular and entire architecture, in contradistinction to that of irregular buildings and ruins'.[10] Price's ideas about the irregular category are the more interesting and historically important, particularly as the addition of the adjective 'picturesque' allows Price to consider vernacular buildings as a kind of architecture. But it is significant to the present argument that the examples of the splendid regular picturesque were the buildings of Vanbrugh and the Italian Baroque. Taking his agenda from Reynolds here as elsewhere, Price spends some thirty pages rambling around Reynolds' remarks. His observations about Vanbrugh are, however, quite astute and elaborate Reynolds' view of the architect's painterliness.

> [Vanbrugh's] first point seems to have been massiveness, as the foundation of grandeur. Then, to prevent that mass from being a lump, he has made various bold projections of various heights, which from different points serve as foregrounds to the main building. And, lastly, having probably been struck with the variety of outline against the sky in many Gothic and other ancient buildings, he has raised on the top of that part, where the slanting roof begins in many houses of the Italian style, a number of decorations of various characters. These, if not new in themselves, have at least been applied and combined by him in a new and peculiar manner; and the union of them gives a surprising splendour and magnificence, as well as variety, to the summit of that princely edifice.[11]

Price describes the appearance of Blenheim from various viewpoints and distances, and in conjunction with the passage above, we get a sense of what the 'movement' of Robert and

James Adam might have meant. For a modern reader trained in these matters, it is difficult to grasp the extent to which a concrete description of human locomotion and its effects on vision are absent from Price's text. One might think that Price's topic of landscape design would leave him free from discussing the orders and canons that make architectural descriptions of the period so abstract, and would allow him to develop the observations of the Adams and Reynolds. But he does not. Despite the abundant exemplifications and quite concrete descriptions of successive viewpoints throughout the three volumes of *Essays*, there is only one point where Price says what human movement has to do with the picturesque. This passage is at once startlingly modern and laconic, positioned as it is in a section about bridges. Nevertheless, what Price describes about the sequential visual inspection of bridges must apply to all that he has to say.

> Whatever gives the idea of easy and rapid motion, gives in the same proportion that of lightness: and, on the other hand, whatever impresses the idea of resistance to motion, in the same proposition also impress that of massiveness. It is true that all solid buildings, though not equally immoveable, are in themselves motionless; but where the surface is even, the eye glides easily along it, and that ideal motion of the sight, is in some degree transferred to the object itself: all easy transitions, therefore, from one object, or from one part of an object to another, which constitute so principal a cause of beauty, are equally a cause of lightness; and it may be observed, that many of the such occasions, are borrowed from those of motion.[12]

Price is saying that perception includes the bodily aspects of eye movement. To Edmund Burke's neurological thesis (that sharp and rounded objects excite the nerves of vision differently) Price is adding an aspect of the ancient doctrine of mimesis. The movement of the eyes is a kind of imitation of the form of the object, moving across it to follow its form. It is in this imitation of the inanimate object, which happens in time and in the never-still human body, that the sense of movement arises. In imagination we then transfer this movement to the object that we are imitating. The most remarkable aspect of this passage is how close it is to late nineteenth-century German empathy theory, and I will return to this matter, and the meaning of the rarity of discussion of movement shortly. For the moment, my point is to show how imbricated the picturesque is with the terms we use to describe the Baroque, and with Baroque architecture itself.

Price travelled to Italy in 1767–8, but when describing the appearance of buildings three decades later, he usually does so through examples in paintings (Veronese, Titian, Raphael, Michelangelo), which he could have examined in prints while writing. He rarely mentions particular buildings, but notes of Pietro da Cortona: 'some churches in Rome built after his designs, are highly esteemed.'[13] He does recall that he disliked the curvelinear façades of high Baroque, writing:

> At one period, the architects throughout Europe, were extremely fond of waving lines. I recollect many public edifices in Rome and at Naples in that style, the false taste of which struck me at the time; of it is obvious that the first principle in all architecture, whatever its style, must be the appearance, as well as the reality of firmness and stability.[14]

Amongst his rather tedious list of paintings with interesting buildings in them, there are a couple of points at which Price comes close to explaining how a regular and splendid architecture could be picturesque. Picturesqueness can be caused by the 'abruptness of ornament'.[15] By this it is possible that Price means the contrast of a plain massive wall surface with extravagant ornament that later commentators point out in the Baroque. Second, and more significantly, picturesqueness in regular buildings results from seeing them on incidental angles, and a refusal of frontality, or at least of the primacy of frontality. Since Wölfflin, it has been common to argue that this planning for oblique and concrete viewpoints is a major motif in Baroque architecture. Paolo Portoghesi's book *Roma Barocca*, makes this point in the rhetoric of its photographs, and is heavily illustrated with neck-craning views up and across the face of buildings, while almost entirely avoiding frontal elevations. Price explains, by reference to a Titian painting, the *Madonna di Ca' Pesaro* (see Figure 2.2).

> The Roman school may sometimes condescend to take lessons from the Venetian, though in general so much superior to it in dignity. I have in my mind a composition of Titian, respecting the Virgin and child placed on an altar in a sort of portico, with other figures on the steps of the altar: only two columns are seen, the tops of which are supposed to be out of the picture. The manner in which this architecture is introduced, produces a very grand, and at the same time a very picturesque effect; these columns, from being brought near the eye, and in their full proportion, present an imposing mass; and as their bases are placed on different levels, their symmetry, though not doubtful, is not obvious: sufficient to impress the idea of magnificent architecture.[16]

This paragraph is important in a number of ways. First, a footnote reveals that Price is referring to a passage in Reynolds' *Journey to Flanders and Holland*, and although Price neglects to mention this, he is in disagreement with it. Reynolds is comparing Rubens and Titian and gives proof of the latter's superiority by recalling the *Madonna di Ca' Pesaro*, of which he writes: 'Rubens' manner is often too artificial and picturesque for the GRAND STYLE. Titian knew very well that so much formality or regularity, as to give the appearance of being above all the tricks of art, which we call picturesque, is of itself grandeur'.[17] Price, without wishing to be read as correcting Reynolds is nevertheless claiming that the picturesque and the grand can be combined, that Titian has grand subjects in a grand building but also a picturesque viewpoint full of movement. In Chapter 2 I discussed Thomas Puttfarken's claim that the *Madonna di Ca' Pesaro* itself marks an epoch in the development of the concept of the picture. Titian uses perspective to represent the space within the painting, unlike earlier paintings, Raphael's *School of Athens* for example, where perspective had the task of uniting the represented space with that of the observer. The independence and indifference of the painting's spatiality to an observer makes viewing it all the more affecting. Nevertheless, it seems likely that Titian also planned for this oblique viewpoint, which apparently fortuitously individuates the observer, making viewing the painting concrete rather than abstract. It is exactly this play between phenomenal experience and ideation that Price and Reynolds are noticing with their different prejudices. Second, Price's description of this picturesque but grand character brings it very close to what modern commentators say about the contrast of the Baroque with the logical presentation of geometric forms in the Renaissance. Borromini constructed the plan of S. Carlo alle Quatro Fontane on the figure of Vesica Pisces, but the pure figures of the circles and triangles are not perceptible, subsumed into the interceding impure oval. Price's description, that the symmetry, 'while not doubtful, is not obvious', is a phrasing true to Baroque architects' attitudes to geometry in general.[18] The last point is that, most likely, Price has a source for these ideas in William Hogarth's *Analysis of Beauty*, where the painter writes:

> It is a constant rule in composition in painting to avoid regularity. When we view a building, or any other object in life, we have it in our power, by shifting the ground, to take that view of it which pleases us best; and in consequence of this, the painter if he is left to his choice, takes it on the angle rather than in front, as most agreeable to the eye; because the regularity of the lines is taken away by their running into perspective, without losing the idea of fitness . . .[19]

Ronald Paulson, in his introduction to the *Analysis of Beauty*, argues that the picturesque is a development of the ideas of Hogarth: 'Gilpin's picturesque is essentially a retitling of Hogarth's Beautiful/Novel . . . what came to be known as the picturesque in many ways carries on the Novel, especially Hogarth's version of it . . .'.[20] Paulson argues for too complete an identification here. In Chapter 2, I showed how Gilpin's ideas grow from his reading of Roger de Piles. I would also distinguish Hogarth's humour and satire from the aestheticization of disgust in the later picturesque of Price and Knight. Nevertheless, it is Hogarth who gives a model of the mixture of aesthetic theory, criticism and advice on art-making that characterizes William Gilpin and Price. What is more, 'intricacy' and 'variety' were both Hogarth's terms before Price's, and the passages compared above suggest a close reading of Hogarth by Price. Price's debts to Hogarth are obscured, because, while Burke, one of Price's main sources, praises Hogarth and endorses his theory of the curving line of beauty, Price's greater admiration is for Reynolds, who places Hogarth with the lowness of the Dutch love of verisimilitude.[21] The passage I quoted above, condemning the wavy façades of Italian Baroque buildings, is introduced with a remark about the 'line of beauty' 'so ingeniously set forth by Hogarth; and since more fully considered by Mr Burke'.[22] Price then makes a footnote where he tells an anecdote of his father, who knew Hogarth, sarcastically contrasting the painter's person and posture with the serpentine line of beauty. Price's opposition to Hogarth was, thus, a complicated one. Price and his father loved and collected 'Dutch' art but Price wished to place this within the hierarchy of genre that Reynolds laid out, not to celebrate the comedic history painting of Hogarth. Price does locate a real conflict in Hogarth's thought between his empirical methods of observation and the ideality of the line of beauty which the painter discovered everywhere. But Price cannot afford to correct and refine Hogarth's argument because he is committed to the critique of the Rococo. This meant hunting out the pretence of naturalism in Lancelot Brown's artificial waters with their serpentine forms, and Hogarth fell under this same prejudice. Nevertheless, Paulson is right to draw our attention to the commonalities in aspects of the aesthetic theory. This does not merely serve to add a further detail to the consideration of the origins of the picturesque. Hogarth's theories of mimesis and the depiction of action in painting are interesting in themselves for our topic, and we will return to them shortly.

Many of the ideas of the picturesque theorists can be understood in terms of the later pictorial formalism of Wölfflin. Particularly, Knight's idea of picturesqueness as the suppression of linearity and the accurate depiction of things in favour of atmospheric breadth, seems to anticipate Wölfflin's contrast of the linear and the painterly.[23] Price's remarks about architecture and the role of 'massiness' and movement in its picturesque qualities are also remarkably similar to the much fuller and more sophisticated account of Baroque architecture developed by Wölfflin. In *Renaissance and Baroque* of 1886, Wölfflin's aim is to distinguish the two periods on the basis of style. This distinction is one that would have appeared artificial to Price or Reynolds and is confusing today because Wölfflin's examples are what are now typically called Mannerist. However, the terms of his description are very similar to Price's ideas of the beautiful and picturesque in architecture; of how Blenheim, while splendid and regular in plan, might also be picturesque. For Wölfflin, 'Renaissance art is the art of calm and beauty' while the Baroque is a 'painterly' style:[24]

> What does 'painterly' mean? It would be simple enough to say that painterly is that which lends itself to being painted, that which without addition would serve as a motif for the painter. A strictly classical temple, if it is not in ruins, is not a picturesque object. However impressive it may be as a piece of architecture, it would look monotonous in a picture. An artist painting it on a canvas today would have great difficulty in making it look interesting; in fact he could only succeed with the aid of light and atmospheric effects and a landscape setting, and in the process the architectural element would retreat completely into the background. But a rich baroque building is more animated, and would therefore be an easier subject for a painterly effect. The freedom of line and the interplay of light and shade are satisfying to the painterly taste in direct proportion to the degree to which they transgress the rules of architecture. If the beauty of a building is judged by the enticing effects of moving masses, the restless, jumping forms or violently swaying ones which seem constantly on the point of change, and not by balance and solidity of structure, then the strictly architectonic conception of architecture is depreciated. In short, the severe style of architecture makes its effect by what it is, that is, by its corporeal substance, while painterly architecture acts through what it appears to be, that is, an illusion of movement.[25]

This definition of the painterly qualities of a temple in ruin is remarkably like Price's first definition of the picturesque as a ruined temple,[26] which I discussed in Chapter 4. In the following section, I will consider at length the extent to which we should identify the painterly with the picturesque as concepts, but for the moment, let me continue to lay out the strong parallels and connections of the picturesque and Baroque. Like Hogarth and Price, Wölfflin thinks that painterly qualities can be observed not only in ruins but in incidental views of whole buildings. As he writes: 'to gain an even greater sense of movement, all or most of the composition is placed obliquely to the beholder'.[27] Wölfflin goes on to define Baroque architecture in the two moments of massiveness and movement.

> The baroque required broad, heavy, massive forms. Elegant proportions disappeared and buildings tended to become weightier until sometimes the forms were almost crushed by the pressure. The grace and lightness of the Renaissance were gone; all forms became broader and heavier.[28]

Price continually stresses the 'massiness' of Blenheim, its lack of grace, which, at the same time, constitutes its power to affect the viewer. He writes:

> no mansion of regular, finished, ornamental architecture that I have yet seen, has [. . .], so grand an appearance as Blenheim; and never was the reproach of heaviness so unceasingly applied to any building. How far the heaviness of the ancient temples or of the modern palace might be diminished, without diminution of their grandeur, may be a question; but I – believe it is very clear, that after a certain point, as in lightness, they would become less majestic, and, beyond that again, less beautiful.[29]

Price goes on to a parallel in painting: 'the Caracci [use] a peculiar word (sagoma) to express that fullness and massiveness of form, as opposed to the meagreness of Mantegna, Pietro Perugino, and almost all the earlier painters'.[30] This parallels Wölfflin writing:

> Annibale Carracci finds a late figure by Raphael 'as hard and as sharp as a piece of wood' [. . .] As early as Vasari the dryness of Bramante's early Roman style of the Cancelleria is criticised; 'secchezza' was something hated by the baroque.[31]

Movement, for Wölfflin, is the principle opposing massiveness. He writes:

> In contrast to Renaissance art, which sought permanence and repose in everything, the baroque had from the first a definite sense of direction. It expressed an urge for upward movement, and so the vertical force was opposed to the broad massiveness that we have already described . . .[32]

Wölfflin goes on to make a rich and complex description of movement in architectural form emphasizing upward orientation; rhythmic rather than equally spaced sequences of elements; the 'unfilled' sense of the column immured in the wall which seems to want to burst forth; and the overlapping and partial concealment of one element by another (Figure 6.2). All this is compatible with the earlier British writers.

Figure 6.2 Immured columns in the façade of S. Susanna, Rome. Carlo Maderno, 1597–1603.

It is possible that Wölfflin drew on Price directly, but there are only textural parallels to suggest this. The scholars treating Wölfflin's intellectual biography make clear that his orientation to Italian art comes out of the work of Jakob Burckhardt, his predecessor in the Chair of Art History at Basel, and that he understood his own project by comparison with contemporaries such as Alois Riegl, August Schmarsow and Adolf Hildebrand.[33] However, it is of interest to realize that the English texts were well known in Germany, including a 1798 translation of Price, as I have had cause to describe in Chapter 5.[34] British aesthetics was greatly developed in Germany, both in philosophical aesthetics as with Immanuel Kant's reading of Burke, and in cultural criticism. Gotthold Ephraim Lessing was greatly impressed by Hogarth: he paid for the printing of the translation of the *Analysis of Beauty*,[35] with his own introduction and arguably, his *Laocoön* develops Hogarth's theory of pose and posture. If Wölfflin ever thought of the picturesque as an explicit, and English, theory he might well have done so through John Ruskin as he is known to have read *The Stones of Venice* and *The Two Paths* with admiration.[36] The catalogue of the University of Basel library shows holdings, from the period of Wölfflin's tenure, of most of the significant British writers. These connections and the textual parallels are not sufficient to argue that Wölfflin's theories grew out of a consideration of picturesque theory. A more likely explanation of the commonalities is the sources that both Wölfflin and the English writers had in the battle between the *Poussinistes* and the *Rubénistes*, that is, between the values of line and colour in the French Academy of the seventeenth century. However, when Wölfflin uses the German *malerisch* – the usual translation of picturesque – to describe Baroque architecture, this cannot be understood as entirely distinct from the ideas of Reynolds and Price.

Wölfflin, *malerisch* and the picturesque movement-effect

My claim is that we can understand Wölfflin as giving the concept of the picturesque a new valency in the early twentieth century and at the origins of modernism. This would be more apparent to English readers if it were not for an issue of translation. In Kathrin Simon's translation of *Renaissance and Baroque*, Wölfflin writes of 'picturesqueness' and 'painterliness' fairly interchangeably, but in the later books – *Classic Art*, and more so, *Principles of Art History* – Wölfflin systematizes a distinction that is translated as between picturesqueness and painterliness. Wölfflin (in translation by M. D. Hottinger) writes: 'The really interesting question now is this – what is the relation between the painterly style of treatment and the picturesque quality of the theme?'[37] This is indeed a fundamental question for the picturesque and for the argument of this chapter, and it relies on the opposition within Wölfflin's sentence. Yet in the German this is a difference of tone; orginally Wölfflin wrote: 'Die eigentliche interessante Frage ist nun diese: Wie verhält sich geschichtlich der malerische Darstellungsstil zu diesem Malerischen des Motivs?'[38] Wölfflin's text and the German language in general, do not make a lexical distinction between picturesque and painterly, and nor for that matter, 'pictorial'. In German, all are derived from the word *maler* or painter. Although German has the naturalized word *das Pittorescke*, the regular translation of 'the picturesque' is *das Malerische* or *die malerische Schönheit*.[39]

Herbert Read, in his introduction to the 1952 translation of Wölfflin's *Classic Art*, writes as if 'painterly' was a neologism, entirely omitting the common meaning of *malerisch*:

> One word, however, calls for comment – the word 'painterly', which has been invented to convey the meaning of the German word *malerisch*. It is a word absolutely essential to the discussion of stylistic problems in art, and purists must admit it into our language,

> for no other word is exact enough. It stands for that depreciation and gradual obliteration of line (outline and tangible surface) and for the merging of these into a 'shifting semblance of things' – it is an attempt to represent the vague and impalpable essence of things. English readers who are familiar with the distinction which Blake makes between 'the hard and wiry line of rectitude' and the 'broken lines, broken masses, and broken colours which he denounced as 'bungling' will have already seized the full meaning of the word.[40]

Perhaps connecting the familiar 'picturesque' with the difficult 'painterly' appeared to Read as a threat to the progressive potential of Wölfflin's books for modern art; for it would be equally possible to connect everything Wölfflin says about the painterly to Ruskin and to Price and Knight. In arguing for the specificities of the translation (by Peter and Linda Murray) Read is trying to avoid the imputation that the newly rigorous art history, with its laws of development, has anything to do with a naïve taste for charming views of the poor. The translation issue can be confirmed in its reciprocation. The *Oxford English Dictionary*'s entry for 'painterly' says: 'Like, or pertaining to, a painter; characteristic of a painter, artistic; spec. of a style of painting, characterized by qualities of colour, stroke, and texture rather than of contour or line.' The second clause is pure Wölfflin, as is clear from the Dictionary's usage citations. There is one sixteenth-century and one nineteenth-century example, and then fourteen from 1978 back to 1932, the year of publication of the translation the *Principles of Art History*, when the *Times Literary Supplement* writes, '"painterly" (a translation of the German word *malerisch*, which can also mean picturesque)'.[41]

Joan Hart has traced Wölfflin's usage of *malerisch*, claiming that his usage in Renaissance and Baroque is a significant addition to the significations of the word.[42] She cites Grimm's *Deutsches Wörterbuch* of 1885, defining *malerisch* as: '1) anything connected with the painter's profession (in both a narrow and broad sense) and 2) things which, by their manner and organization, provided a good subject for a painter'.[43] Authors such as Schiller and Goethe regularly use *malerisch* in relation to landscape. Wölfflin's main source and inspiration for his work on Baroque architecture was Burckhardt's *Der Cicerone*, and Burckhardt uses *malerisch* frequently in describing architecture. Burckhardt developed an opposition of *malerische* to *plastische*, or sculptural, that became the basis for his stylistic distinction of the painterly Baroque from the solidity of earlier Renaissance forms. Hart claims that this project of formal description of styles that Burckhardt began and Wölfflin took up is the point at which *malerisch* parts company with its everyday meaning as picturesque. However, I maintain that the reference against the everyday lower picturesque is fundamental to Wölfflin, as it is in English.

Wölfflin inflects *das Malerische* so that it is used positively or pejoratively, in exactly the same way that 'picturesque' can have, or not, the pejorative meaning of simplistic or sentimental taste in English, and for exactly the same reason that Ruskin resorts to the adjectives 'lower' and 'noble' to condition his use of the word 'picturesque'. The translators' use of painterly is not incorrect; it is Wölfflin's point to specify a concept that is more definite and more broadly applicable than 'picturesque'. The point is rather that through translation, English has come to have a difference in kind between painterly and picturesque that is merely a matter of degree in German. Wölfflin's denigration of the picturesque is, thus, rather less nuanced in English than he intended. When combined with the influence of his ideas and his language in the rise of modernist formalism, this has coloured the twentieth-century reception of the picturesque even more than Ruskin's hysteria about its moral ambivalence.

In *Principles*, Wölfflin's contrast between 'linear' Renaissance architecture and the illusory painterly qualities of Baroque buildings becomes a master dialectic that includes plane and recession; closed and open forms; multiplicity and unity; clarity and unclearness; and is applicable to architecture, painting and sculpture across the Renaissance to modernism. For Wölfflin, the history of art is the unfolding of this dialectic – the painterly excesses of Baroque architecture already have within them the corrective linear strictures of neo-classicism, just as Impressionist painting demands the return of planes and lines in Cezanne and Mattise. Wölfflin's art history, with its formal description of movements and tendencies and its determined ignorance of iconology, artist careers and social conditions, has been enormously influential. This is because his formal descriptors provide a kind of matrix in which historical art and architecture and new developments can be placed together, as we see with 'movement', which Wölfflin's pupil Giedion took to be the origin and telos of modern architecture. The present point, however, is a simple one: the painterly is the picturesque, or rather, the picturesque cleaned of baseness. It is also important, methodologically, to Wölfflin: for the painterly to become an abstract transhistorical category rather than something located in the Baroque, it needed an empirical moment. The rise from sensibility to true artistic discernment in an individual mirrors and explains the progress of art at a phylogenetic level. My claim, then, is that we should understand Wölfflin's use of the picturesque in the same way that I earlier described Ruskin's disgust at the picturesque: as a kind of pre-text for theory.

Wölfflin distinguishes the picturesque from the painterly in terms which would be familiar to readers of Ruskin, and which fold back to eighteenth-century debates about the role of low subjects and disgust in art. When Wölfflin says, the 'picturesque theme is more or less only a preliminary stage to the higher forms of the painterly taste', he goes on to evidence this in the career of Rembrandt, who earlier preferred 'the ragged beggar' and 'the rugged faces of old men', but 'later the "picturesque" vanishes and in the same ratio the real painterly content increases'.[44] Just as with Ruskin, picturesqueness is a naïve and unwitting enslavement to sensory pleasure in degradation, which Wölfflin can help us overcome.

> We call the ragged beggar, with his weather-beaten hat and gaping shoes, a picturesque figure, while the boots and hats which have just come out of the shop are regarded as unpicturesque. They lack the rich rustling life of form which we might compare to the ripple of the waves when a breeze ruffles the surface of the water. And if this illustration does not suit the beggar's rags very well, we have but to think of more costly costumes, where, with the same effect, the surfaces are broken up by slashes or brought into movement by the mere cast of the folds.[45]

The discomforting person of the beggar is underlined in the passage by comparison with the boots and hats coming out of the shop, which are strangely empty, or are perhaps those of the polite reader. We have already met this beggar in Price, Repton and Ruskin. Wölfflin follows the same path as Price, who in the 'Dialogue on the Picturesque', after one of his more challenging descriptions of a filthy gypsy hovel, relieves the reader with the statement: 'handsome well-dressed men and women, and handsome horses with gay caparisons, [. . .] admit of effects of light and shadow, and harmonious colouring, as well as Gypsies, asses and panniers'.[46] We can imagine the beggar, desperate and lice ridden, catching at our sleeve and insisting on sympathy and charity: he is an object of phobic disgust. Someone insensible of visual qualities would be disgusted at this specimen of humanity become pathological; but a person of sensibility would be able to separate the empirical facts and possible trajectories of the beggar from his appearance with its 'rich rustling life of form'.[47] However, this adept of picturesqueness is weak; remaining bewitched by the distancing that aesthetic appropriation makes. Such a person is affected by not only visual qualities but also by the magic of their production from dirty materials. Rembrandt and Wölfflin, having been at that point themselves, are able to transcend the picturesque to a further state, the painterly, where visual qualities belong to their pleasure and the history of painting, and they are indifferent as to whether the subject is rotting rags or costly fabrics.

Movement has a role in this distinction between grades of picturesqueness, and Wöfflin describes this in a section which in the English edition bears the title 'The Picturesque and its Opposite', as a translation of '*Das Objektiv-Malerische und sein Gegensatz*', literally, 'the objective picturesque and its contrast'.[48] For Wölfflin, the fault of the low picturesque is its objectivity, not in the sense of unbiased opinion, but in finding aesthetic qualities in the physical existence of the object. His explanation is obscure:

> the 'painterly' is treated essentially as a matter of perception in the sense that it does not matter about the object, but that the eye [. . .] can perceive everything in one way or the other, painterly or not painterly. But it cannot be denied that there are in nature certain things and situations which we denote as 'picturesque'. The character of the picturesque seems to be inherent in them apart from perception by a painterly eye. Naturally there is no absolute 'picturesque' [. . .] but for all that we can still isolate as something special those themes whose picturesque character consists in actual conditions which can be demonstrated. These are themes in which the single form is so entwined in a great context that an impression of all-pervading movement arises. If real movement[49] is present, so much the better, but [. . .] there will always play the stimulus of a movement which does not reside in the object, and that also means that the whole only exists as a *picture* [*Bild*] for the eye, and that it can never, even in the imaginary sense, be grasped with the hands.[50]

The sense of this difficult passage can be reduced to the following propositions. The picturesque is the empirical existence of the painterly. This is not in itself a fault. Its inferiority lies in the confusion it allows between aesthetic interest and an interest in the actual existence of the object. It might seem that here, Wölfflin is simply following Kant who thinks that we refer our sensual experience to the imagination, to determine whether or not it pleases us, and therefore it is a faulty aesthetics to compare our sensory experience to the object.[51] However, in Wölfflin's account, we still need the object and we do indeed compare it to the representation that our senses make of this, but the point of this is not to make a judgement, rather it is to experience an aesthetic affect that is the movement between the two, the visual form lifting off and separating from the object form. Wölfflin does not think that this movement is caused by the object; it is rather an innate mental power and a fundament of perception – but there are some empirical circumstances that are more susceptible to this aesthetic power than others, and he calls these the 'objective' picturesque. Although a practised aesthete can experience the painterly in any percept, weaker minds might only find it in beggars, cottages and old boots, and mistakenly think that the painterly, the true picturesque, has an objective cause. The picturesque can be a good thing if these easy examples in which painterliness seems inherent can lead on to a more developed aesthetic sense and a realization of the subjective nature of aesthetic experience.

Wölfflin gives this movement a name, 'the picturesque movement-effect,' and explains it with an architectural example, one already familiar to us from Hogarth and Price, of the view of a building on an incidental angle.

> Everyone knows that, of the possible aspects of a building, the front view is the least picturesque: here the thing and its appearance fully coincide. But as soon as foreshortening comes in, the appearance separates from the thing, the picture-form [*Bild-form*] becomes different to the object-form, and we speak of a picturesque movement-effect. Certainly, in such a picturesque movement-effect, recession plays an essential part in the impression – the building moves away from us. The visual fact, however, is that in this case objective distinctness retreats behind an appearance in which outline and surfaces have separated from the pure form of the thing.[52]

This example makes the picturesque movement-effect deceptively simple if we do not focus on the radical reduction of what movement refers to; it is totally confined to the relation of perception and imagination, the non-objective painterly, and does not include the embodied acts of perceiving that we might expect. Price, as early as 1810, thought that there was such a relation that the 'motion of the sight, is in some degree transferred to the object itself'.[53] This idea of an imaginary projection of the actual motion of the body and organs of perception onto the building is assumed in Wölfflin's earlier ideas of the painterly/picturesque in *Renaissance and Baroque*. The distinction of picturesqueness from the painterly seems to have led Wölfflin to a point where movement is an image, apparently unrelated to perceptual acts or the position of the body in space. I can put the strangeness of this more bluntly by pointing out that nowhere in his books does Wölfflin consider where one looks at buildings from, or the procession of the body through space, matters which are fundamental to the concept of movement in modern architecture.

Movement, space and modernity

Recovering the picturesqueness of Wölfflin's ideas is, in part, an argument for the significance of the picturesque in the formation of the concepts of modern art and architecture with which Wölfflin is identified. At the same time, however, it shows the idiosyncrasies of Wölfflin's thought, and some instabilities in modernism. In particular, those who read Wölfflin and his contemporaries and took the idea of movement into architecture overrode Wölfflin's reluctance to connect movement with locomotion in space.

It is generally accepted that a strong concept of space as a felt quality of architecture emerged out of the analysis of Baroque architecture and subsequently became fundamental to modern architecture, allowing it to break the deadlock of stylistic formalism. Geoffrey Scott's influential book, *The Architecture of Humanism* of 1914, combines English inclinations towards an empirical understanding of classical order with concepts of German art history. He argues that picturesqueness and the Baroque are related understandings of movement, which reveal the essence of spatial understanding.[54] Scott learnt German language art history in the circle of Bernard and Mary Berenson at I Tatti in Florence. In the 'Preface', Scott acknowledges his debt to Wölfflin's *Renaissance und Barock*, but according to Richard M. Dunn, he drew on a variety of modern theories of spatial perception: Theodore Lipps, Adolf Hildebrand and the English empathy theorist Vernon Lee.[55] In fact, Scott's relation of space and movement is closest to that of Wölfflin's rival, August Schmarsow. Scott writes:

> Aesthetically space is [. . .] supreme. The architect models in space as a sculptor in clay. He designs his space as a work of art; that is, he attempts through its means to excite a certain mood in those who enter it. What is his method? Once again his appeal is to

> Movement. Space, in fact, is liberty of movement. That is its value to us, and as such it enters our physical consciousness. We adapt ourselves instinctively to the spaces in which we stand, project ourselves into them, fill them ideally with our movements.[56]

This concept of space as the felt or imagined extension of the body is fundamentally modern, but unlike Wölfflin. Nevertheless, Scott follows Wölffin's idea of the historical succession of Renaissance and Baroque and he gives picturesqueness a new role there. Scott generally uses 'picturesque' ahistorically, as a neutral description of a relation that closely follows Wölfflin's *malerisch*. But he also thinks that the picturesque has an historical origin in Italian Renaissance painting, with its inclusion of mundane objects and scenes in the backgrounds.[57] These assumptions lie behind the apparent anachronism of his claim that the Baroque intellectualized the picturesque.

> It was not only in painting that the picturesque could be favourably included; it was not only in its farms and hill-town buildings, pictorial as their beauty is. The Renaissance ended by reconciling the picturesque with classic architecture itself. The two were blended in the Baroque. It is not the least among the paradoxes of that profoundly great style that it possesses, in complete accord, these contrary elements. To give the picturesque its grandest scope, and yet to subdue it to architectural law – this was the baroque experiment and it is achieved. [. . .] It enlarged the classic formula by developing within it the principle of movement. But the movement is logical. For baroque architecture is always logical: it is logical as an aesthetic construction, even where it most neglects the logic of material construction. It insisted on coherent purpose, and its greatest extravagances of design were neither unconsidered nor inconsistent. It intellectualized the picturesque.[58]

In Wölfflin's version of historical development, the Baroque added movement to the Renaissance, which then made it 'painterly'. Scott thinks of the picturesque as a pre-existing and almost innate interest in the aesthetic effects of 'movement' – 'unexpected, wild, fantastic, accidental', which were excluded in the effort to produce the order of Renaissance architecture, but were readmitted in the Baroque to complete the edifice of a humanist (by which he means humane) architecture.[59]

Harry Mallgrave and Eleftherios Ikonomou's introduction to the German aesthetics of the late nineteenth century, shows that similar concepts of space emerged in the work of many individuals. Schmarsow made the clearest argument that spatial perception was the basis of art writing:

> The less we are willing to behave like exclusively visual beings and be satisfied with only one viewpoint, the more freely will we make use of the change of position in order to grasp the material individuality of the object from as many sides as possible.[60]
>
> The linguistic terms that we use for space, such as 'extension,' 'expanse,' and 'direction,' suggest continuous activity on our part as we transfer our own feeling of movement directly to the static spatial form. We cannot express its relation to ourselves in any way other than by imagining that we are in motion, measuring the length, width, and depth, or by attributing to the static lines, surfaces, and volumes the movement that our eyes and our kinesthetic sensations suggest to us, even though we survey the dimensions while standing still. The spatial construct is a human creation and cannot confront the creative or appreciative subject as if it were a cold, crystallized form.[61]

These ideas of movement as the experience of spatial unfolding became fundamental in modern architecture, not so much through Scott, who continued to be read as a proponent of classicism, but through Wölfflin's student Sigfried Giedion. Giedion used the analytic concepts of art history in a polemical promotion of modernism and its historical necessity, connecting Baroque movement to Le Corbusier's architectural promenade in his seminal *Space, Time and Architecture* of 1941, and to mechanized culture in general, in *Mechanization Takes Command* of 1948. Giedion introduces his approach by saying that he tries to follow Wölfflin's method, by which he means, largely, contrasting styles and the 'life of a period'; but he also emphasizes the Baroque and its qualities of movement as being prescient of modernism. For instance – an illustration of the spiral lantern of Borromini's S. Ivo della Sapienza is captioned: 'culminating point for the movement that penetrates the whole design' and is accompanied by a drawing of Vladimir Tatlin's spiral Monument to the Third International.[62] The 'Space–Time' concept of Giedion's title is, he says, a development from the spatial analysis of Cubism, the movement analysis of Futurism, and a rather confusing allusion to Einstein's physics; but in one of his principal examples – Le Corbusier's Villa Savoye, with its famous architectural promenade – he returns to the Baroque:

> It is impossible to comprehend the Savoie house by a view from a single point; quite literally, it is a construction in space-time. The body of the house has been hollowed out in every direction: from above and below, within and without. A cross section at any point shows inner and outer space penetrating each other inextricably. Borromini had been on the verge of achieving the interpenetration of inner and outer space in some of his late baroque churches.[63]

To a significant extent, Giedion's citation of his teacher is honorific; his ideas of space registered in locomotive movement are much closer to Schmarsow's. At the turn of the century, Wölfflin was in competition with Schmarsow over the principal terms of Art History – the former championing issues of form over those of space. Wölfflin's limitation of 'movement' to an issue of affective relation with the form of the art object – to the 'picturesque movement effect' – must be understood as a refusal of the idea of space founded on the potential of bodily extension. By the time Giedion wrote, the issue had been resolved. Mallgrave and Ikonomou claim Paul Frankl showed that form and space could be complementary concepts, in 1914,[64] but we could say that this resolution is also clear in Scott's book of the same year.[65]

If the picturesque were what it is commonly said to be then, Scott's book would be a good place to end this consideration of movement. The eighteenth-century picturesque ideas of specificity of viewpoint, with their tentative perceptual psychology, would have been fulfilled and rationalized by Scott, who used aspects of German aesthetics to forge an elegant and simple resolution of the picturesque sensibility with the formal tradition of anthropomorphism. The picturesque would have discovered movement in pictures, and then movement would have led to the discovery of space. Why, then, have I spent so much time with Wölfflin, with his arcane idea of the picturesque and with his highly abstract concept of movement? This is because there remains a question about 'movement' in the texts of Price and Reynolds, and Wölfflin. How could these thinkers, a century and a culture apart, have such similar insistence on a pictorial concept of movement and such little interest in connecting this with actual motion? The answer lies in a distinction between motion and movement at the heart of the picturesque. Motion and the potential for the extension of the body is an all-pervasive condition of existence, indiscernible except when it is formed into those wholes that we call movements. This forming is a kind of stilling.

To an extent, the prestige that movement has had in architecture should be understood in relation to cinema. The distinction between the fact of motion, say trees swaying in the wind, and purposive movements, such as swinging a golf club or flying to America, is not hard to grasp. But the history of image technologies makes motion and movement seem integral. It is the motion of an image that is required for images to take on the narrative form of cinema. Giedion's *Mechanization Takes Command* gives a key role to Eadweard Muybridge's serial photography for this reason. Walter Benjamin's claim that cinema and architecture are parallel modern arts of experience is a sophisticated version of the widespread belief in the technological determination of cultural forms.[66] The cinematic image, which is also a highly spatialized image, seems to combine the distinct culture of twentieth-century modernism with a clear technological watershed. Part of the attraction of the picturesque as a moment in European cultural history is understanding it as having been fulfilled in the technology and art of cinema, or rather in this and what a cinematic understanding of the image does in architecture. It is not irrelevant to our inquiry that Wölfflin's ideas of perception and art were formed before the invention of the moving image, and that his later more formalist book, *Principles*, was written at the time of the emergence of cinema as an art. (D. W. Griffith's *Birth of a Nation*, one of the first comprehensive uses of camera movements and editing to tell a story, was also produced in 1915.) To the landscape panel paintings that fascinated Price, it might seem that the history of visual technology has added, first, the indexicality and verisimilitude of photography, and then the motion, duration and spatialized point-of-view of cinema. Should, then, we understand the connection of the picturesque and movement, from the brothers Adam to Wölfflin, as being an attempt to describe the experience of a cultural form that they could only imagine but which has since arrived?

It has been reasonable to understand the movement aspect of the picturesque as cinemagraphic for most of the twentieth century. Arguably the situation has now changed as the moving image undergoes technological and cultural change. Special effects-based 'blockbuster' movies have much in common with the pre-narrative cinema of spectacle, as Tom Gunning and others have shown.[67] Streaming video on the internet has attributes of both still and moving images, and the so-called Virtual Reality image has even more so. Video installation art has developed a whole new genre. Artists including Thomas Struth and Bill Viola have produced images that are still, in the sense that the people in them do not move, but nevertheless are filmed in duration. This idea goes back to Andy Warhol's long duration films of the 1960s, but video and flat screen displays have allowed this idea to develop outside of the cinematic apparatus of the darkened box and screen, and to be much more pictorial. Thus, while the history of the picturesque in modernity might well be understood in terms of cinema, it is tempting to now re-read the 'picture' in the picturesque in the terms of Viola's video tableaux.[68] Such a project must wait for another occasion, but this present context gives us further reason to examine Wölfflin's apparently motionless movement. In his time, Giedion was correct to cut through the empathy theory of his teacher and tie the movement of the Baroque to movement through space and a cinematic concept of the image. Much of the great architecture of modernism resulted from thinking such as this. However, for us, after cinema as it were, there is some utility in returning to the point immediately before the moving image was a given. Wölfflin has more to tell us about picturesque movement, which is not (or at least not in the first place) to do with space and the human ability to traverse it, but with gesture and pose, or the *form* of movement. To explore this proposition, we need to return to the empathy theory underlying *Renaissance and Baroque* and Wölfflin's earlier doctoral thesis.

Imitating movement

Wölfflin's ideas on movement begin in his doctoral thesis of 1886, which is largely incorporated into *Renaissance and Baroque* of 1888. The book's description of the form of Baroque buildings is the outcome of the psychological analysis of style formulated in the dissertation, which was titled 'Prolegomena to a Psychology of Architecture'. The psychology referred to is the theory of *Einfühlung* or empathy, which dominated German aesthetics in the late nineteenth century.[69] Wölfflin's problem is how art could be both a period style and then appreciable to later generations. He did not believe that the unity of art historical periods could be understood by their context in social form or the development of the sciences, which would mean we would have to be historically situated to appreciate them. Nor did he believe that art could express ideas, and while ideas about art could be communicated across history, such ideas are not themselves open to artist apprehension. Artworks, and the unity that art possessed in a period like the Baroque, could only be understood as the expression of feelings. Wölfflin supposed that there was an affective relation between artworks, the persons who perceived them, and art as a whole in a period. Styles and their formal aspects, such as movement, had, Wölfflin thought, a double root: first, in the expression of the native demeanour of a people and an age; and then in fundamental psychological processes of perception. The movement of Baroque architecture is, then, both inherent in the spirit and the whole cultural orientation of the artists and people of seventeenth-century Rome. Movement also speaks to psychological mechanisms in all people at all times, which allows us today to perceive and participate in this style. What is common between people of different times is their bodily-ness, but this is also the point of empathetic relation between people and art objects. This is why Wölfflin thought that the fundament of art was the object character of artworks rather than their spatial form; that the basis of artistic feeling is an objecthood shared between the human body and the art object. Such assumptions underlie the Baroque principles of massiveness and movement, but are given slightly different terms in the earlier dissertation:

> Matter is heavy; it presses down and wants to spread out formlessly on the ground. We know the force of gravity from our own body. What holds us upright and prevents a formless collapse? It is the opposing force that we call will, life, or whatever. I call it force of form [*Formkraft*]. *The opposition between matter and force of form*, which sets the entire organic world in motion, is the principal theme of architecture. Aesthetic perception even transposes that most intimate experience of our own body onto inanimate nature. We assume that in everything there is a will that struggles to become form and has to overcome the resistance of a formless matter.[70]

Mallgrave and Ikonomou explain that Wölfflin drew on Fredrich von Hausegger's theory of the emotions, which in turn drew on Charles Darwin's *The Expresssion of the Emotions in Man and other Animals*.[71] In such a theory, emotion is never entirely mental and inseparable from its expression in the face and the posture of the body, and one can arouse emotions in one's self by imitating these known expressions. Mallgrave and Ikonomou continue:

> Wölfflin describes his anthropopathic theory in the following way: (1) Every emotion has an expression, the physical manifestation of the mental act; (2) when we imitate the

> expression of the emotion, we also experience this emotion; (3) we then unconsciously transfer our emotional response to the person or object.[72]

Wölfflin is extending the anthropomorphic tradition in architecture into psychology and physiology of perception. When architects design buildings, they do not merely imitate the static proportions of the human body but also the mechanics of posture by which we hold ourselves erect under the force of gravity. The human body expresses movement even when motionless because that very lack of motion is achieved through the same interplay of skeleton and musculature that makes motion and extension into space possible. The converse of this idea is stranger, but cuts to the heart of our discussion: the feelings of movement that we might experience in buildings are, then, a result of us imitating the expression of movement in the building. The armature of perception – the eyes, head and body – move literally, in a visual inspection that is given its agenda by building. These pyscho-motor events affect the emotions directly. We are excited because our eyes move quickly, we are impressed by tall spaces because as we look up our chest movements are constrained:

> Of great interest is the relation of the proportions to the rate of breathing. It cannot be doubted that very narrow proportions produce the impression of an almost breathless and hurried upward striving. Naturally we immediately associate them with the idea of tightness, which makes it impossible to continue to breathe deeply with the necessary lateral expansion. Thus Gothic proportions are oppressive . . .[73]

As Wölfflin developed his position, there was less and less role for psychology, and by the publication of *Principles of Art History* in 1915, the master dialectic of linear and painterly, with its other avatars, had become largely a way of formally identifying historical periods and contrasting them. What remains, the question of how we perceive art and whether affect is a matter of perception as well as of the art object, is confined to the discussion of the picturesque movement-effect. It is as if all the earlier discussion of embodied states of perception had collapsed into the picturesque and the act of transcending it. While the eighteenth-century English theorists were not concerned with expression, which had yet to arrive as a concept in art, there is a point at which these theories overlap. This is in the concept of mimesis. Price's one perceptualist description of movement, where the 'motion of the sight, is in some degree transferred to the object', is quite ocular, more like Riegl than Wölfflin, in that the eye alone imitates the object. But Reynolds' remarks are more complex, and support, for different reasons, Wölfflin's contention that movement in architecture is a mimetic relation, and one linked to the body.

The descriptive note (there are no titles) to Reynolds' XIIIth Discourse says: 'Art not merely imitation. In what manner Poetry, Painting, Acting, Gardening, and Architecture, depart from Nature.'[74] The Discourse is part of a continued defence against the idea that painting is founded in appearances and thus limited in its claims to be a liberal art. Reynolds is largely a conventionalist about art disciplines and much of the Discourse is an argument that painting has its own internal and coherent account of imitation, which need not answer to a general concept of mimesis. Reynolds introduces architecture, gardening and also drama, in order to show that each art strikes its own relation to appearance and ideality. Architecture is good for Reynolds' argument because, while generally considered below painting in the hierarchy of the arts, its relation to utility, he points out, means that 'Architecture [. . .] does not come under the denomination of an imitative art. It applies itself like Musick (and I believe we may add Poetry) directly to the imagination without the intervention of any kind of imitation.'[75] On the other side of the question of mimesis lies 'The Theatre, which is said to *hold the mirror up to nature*'.[76] But Reynolds points out that the problem of theatre and acting is that their illusion could collapse if too complete; if one did not understand that Reynolds' friend, David Garrick, was playing Hamlet, was not the Dane in reality. Reynolds argues that the very aim of illusion in theatre requires deviations from nature.

> Hence the deliberate and stately step, the studied grace of action which seems to enlarge the dimensions of the Actor, alone fill the stage. All this unnaturalness, ridiculous and affected as it would appear in a private room, is right and proper in its place.[77]

Reynolds is using imitation in a complex and ambiguous way because in each of the arts, he supposes a bad mechanical imitation of appearances and a higher imitation, one that begins in appearance but ends in the imagination and higher ideals. His argument is more consistent if we understand him to mean that architecture lacks this first lower imitation. Reynolds places painting between the two other arts, each understood as a particular state of the mimetic contract. The actor is totally given over to the imitation of the role and yet must make a gap or interruption of person and gait, which introduces a self-evident conventionality to the performance. Architecture cannot appear to be anything other than building, but to be art, to be more than building, it must speak to the innate human capacity for imitation on which the idea of art is founded. What Reynolds and Wölffin are assuming for different reasons in their different projects, is that architecture is a form of resemblance which cannot be sensed directly. To understand this, we need to turn to Walter Benjamin.

Benjamin and the non-sensuous imitation of movement

In 1915, Wölfflin lectured from the final form of the text of *Principles*, which was then in press; one of those listening was Benjamin, then aged 23.[78] While empathy theory and his early postural account of it are no longer apparent in *Principles*, throughout the text, Wölfflin still assumes that artworks are expressive of emotions and create feelings in us. Wölfflin himself is said to have been a spellbinding speaker who had the ability to evoke in the audience the feelings that they would have had if the artworks described were present to them. Benjamin knew Wölfflin's earlier works, certainly *Classic Art*, which he praised in a letter to Herbert Belmore in 1912 writing: 'Wölfflin's book is one of the most useful I have ever read about concrete art.'[79] It is likely that Benjamin hoped to find a teacher in Wölfflin as this was the time that he was beginning his study of Baroque culture and the first essays that would become *The Origin of German Tragic Drama* were written some time shortly after 1915.[80] However, on hearing Wölfflin, Benjamin was bitterly disappointed,

> I did not realise right away what Wölfflin was up to. Now it is clear to me that what we have here is the most disastrous activity I have ever encountered in a German university. A by no means overwhelmingly gifted man, who by nature has no more of a feel for art than anyone else, but attempts to get around this by using all the energy and resources of his personality.[81]

What offended Benjamin in Wölfflin's performance was a stultifying mixture of connoisseurship and instructed feeling, an impression that has struck many readers of *Principles* since. For Benjamin, the demand that one be affected halted any self-knowledge that might be gained in visual inquiry. 'He [Wölfflin] does not see the artwork, he feels obliged to see it, demands that one see it, considers his theory a moral act; he becomes pedantic [. . .] and thereby destroys any natural talents his audience might have.'[82]

Benjamin's opinion is perhaps typical of the reaction to the doctrine of artistic expression that would become one of the main fault lines through modernism. Benjamin's most constructivist essay, 'The Work of Art in the Age of its Mechanical Reproducibility', while sharing aspects of Wölfflin's historicism, is a completely inverted model of artistic reception. Benjamin contrasts a modern artistic reception that is immediate and socially progressive with a cult of art, where works are not understood only for themselves but in the context of a ritual role. Wölfflin would be the priest of such a cult of art history. The idea that the artwork acts to affect me accords the artwork a kind of mystical power and introduces a fundamental unapproachablity. The discipline Wölfflin worked to establish, explains to those affected the historical forces by which art possesses this power. Benjamin says that this cultic power functions through aura, which is one of his most difficult concepts. At one level, it means that we perceive art not as it is but as the immanent weight of tradition; in the 'Work of Art' essay, it means that we falsely worship the glow around art rather than the work itself. But Benjamin also has a non-pejorative use of aura, and writes that the experience of aura in art is modelled on the aura of natural appearances. In this he is quite close to Wölfflin's picturesque movement-effect.

Benjamin describes aura thus:

> the unique phenomena of a distance, however close it may be. If, while resting on a summer afternoon, you follow with your eyes a mountain range on the horizon or a branch which casts its shadow over you, you experience the aura of those mountains, of that branch.[83]

Benjamin goes on to claim that such experience of aura can no longer be a model for art because of:

> the desire of contemporary masses to bring things 'closer' spatially and humanly, which is just as ardent as their bent toward overcoming the uniqueness of every reality by accepting its reproduction. Every day the urge grows stronger to get hold of an object at very close range by way of its likeness, its reproduction.[84]

This is the thesis of the essay: that reproduction technology destroys uniqueness but with that distance and inaccessibility. It will allow modern people to 'pry the object from its shell'.[85] Benjamin's historical analysis of the situation of art and his prognosis for its future, is, thus, very different from Wölfflin's. However, if we attend to the basis of aura in perception, Benjamin's definition is not so different from Wölfflin's, or, for that matter, Price's. Both Price and Wölfflin thought that the movement of the eyes, when scanning the visual field, was a kind of fundamental imitation of visual appearances that also relates to touch. In *Principles*, Wölfflin precedes the discussion of the picturesque movement-effect by writing:

> The tracing out of a figure with an evenly clear line has still an element of physical grasping. The operation which the eye performs resembles the operation of the hand which feels along the body . . . just as the child ceases to take hold of things in order to 'grasp' them, so mankind has ceased to test the picture for its tactile values. A more developed art has learned to surrender itself to mere appearance.[86]

Again, we can find this idea anticipated in Price, who claims that touch is yet another way in which picturesqueness can be distinguished from beauty, picturesqueness being a visual quality that does not lead us to desire touch.

> As the eye borrows many of its sensations from the touch, so that again seems to borrow others from the sight. Soft, fresh, and beautiful colours, though not sensible to feeling as to sight, give us an inclination to try their effect on the touch; whereas, if the colour be not beautiful, that inclination, I believe, is always diminished; and, in objects merely picturesque, and void of all beauty, is rarely excited.[87]

Benjamin and Wölfflin have different values and teleologies arranged around the same basic distinction between a purely visual seeing (for Wölfflin, one based in the experience of pictures), and a mode of seeing articulated with touching, as is the case in embodied perception, where both touch and sight partner one another in the perception of objects close at hand. This distinction of optic and haptic visuality is usually attributed to Alois Riegl, who developed this contrast in *Late Roman Art Industry* of 1901. In turn, Riegl was drawing on the kinesthetic aspects of *einfühlung* or empathy theory of the preceding decades, which Wölfflin also knew. Riegl's terminology appears in Benjamin's first essays of the *trauerspiel* project in 1916 and in his curriculum vitae of 1928 he states Riegl as an important source for his method.[88] However, it is likely that he first heard of the contrast through Wölfflin in 1915, in terms that he found unpalatable which led him to Riegl and to his own account.[89] Riegl was concerned to show that the concept of space was constitutive of architecture, but he believed that it was a relatively recent invention of culture rather than a fundament of perception. Riegl argued that it is only in late Roman art of the second and third centuries that we find art with an aim other than presenting objects as material entities. In the 'Work of Art' essay, Benjamin explains how cinema could be non-auratic and 'tactile' yet still recognizably art. He also uses the example of architecture. Architecture, says Benjamin, has always been accepted as high art and has always been understood through tactile perception. He instances this superiority in the common prejudice that a tourist's rapt contemplation of a famous building is a lesser thing than its apprehension by a local person whose visual perception is founded on a day-to-day habitual or tactile experience of the building in its context. Benjamin is drawing different conclusions than Riegl, while adopting his terms.

> Tactile appropriation is accomplished not so much by attention as by habit. As regards architecture, habit determines to a large extent even optical reception. The latter, too, occurs much less through rapt attention than by noticing the object in incidental fashion.[90]

For Riegl, the telos of architecture is an optical sense of space based on a consciousness of subjectivity. By contrast, Benjamin is celebrating the distracted semi-consciousness of architecture that remains palpable and at hand. For Wölfflin, we can separate the painterly from painting as such because we can experience a building visually, and separate this from our use of it, and even from its material existence. But notice Benjamin's description of the incidental nature of architectural perception. It is the partial occlusion of symmetry in incidental viewpoints that is the basis of the picturesque, according to Price and Wölfflin. But for Benjamin, this incidentality is not purely a matter of viewpoint; it is a relation to lived life. In a review essay of 1932 'The Rigorous Study of Art History', Benjamin explains the merits of the Vienna school art historians over Wölfflin.[91] He praises an article by Carl Linfert about architectural drawing which 'does not take the pictorial detour'. This sheds another light on the tactile apperception of the later 'Work of Art' essay, because in 1932 this is clearly a reversal of the values of Wölfflin's picturesque movement-effect. According to Benjamin the imaginary world of architecture differs from that of painting because:

> architecture is not primarily 'seen,' but rather is imagined as an objective entity [*Bestand*] and is sensed by those who approach or even enter it as a surrounding space [*Umraum*] *sui generis* – that is, without the distancing effect of the edge of the image space [*Bildraum*]. Thus, what is crucial in the consideration of architecture is not seeing but the apprehension [*durchspüren*] of structures.[92]

In proffering Linfert as a correction of Wölfflin's painterly architeture, Benjamin's argument strongly parallels that of Reynolds and Price over the interplay of architectural and pictorial form.[93] In the *Madonna di Ca' Pesaro* Titian made use of an incidental perspective in the architectural setting of the Virgin. Price thought that because there was insufficient detail to gauge the metrics of the structure that the painting gave a model as to how architecture could move into the realm of pure painterly appearance. Reynolds on the other hand, like Benjamin, thought that the tangibility of architecture, its 'imagination as an objective entity' is what saved the painting from being merely a picturesque play of sensations.

Both Wölfflin and Benjamin use phylogenetic arguments to support their historiography. Wölfflin opposes the tactile to visual perception to explain the historical and conceptual succession of the painterly over the linear, of Titian over Botticelli, of Michelangelo over Bramante. He writes 'just as the child ceases to take hold of things in order to "grasp" them, so mankind has ceased to test the picture for its tactile values'.[94] The linear is not wrong, nor is earlier art to be less valued; indeed, the power of the dialectic relation of the linear with the painterly is the periodic return of the less sophisticated and more direct approach. For Benjamin, the childhood of art is in the cultic aspects of aura, the belief that the artwork has an autonomous life and is inapproachable. Where Wölfflin sees the history of visuality as a movement from the tactile to the conceptual, Benjamin sees a gradual liberation from magic and religion, until art can parallel life and be touched. Despite different values and prognoses for the art of their times, Benjamin and Wölfflin share the supposition of an underlying history of perception and a common interest in how aspects of that past persist in modernity.

Similarly, Benjamin is fascinated by aura because for him, it is part of an unresolved problem in the concept of art. This is the idea of non-sensuous resemblance of which movement in architecture is an example, as would be the description of visual experience in poetry. In each case, it is not possible for the artwork to present itself to the same part of the sensorium as the object. Buildings cannot move, a poem is made of sounds and not sights. There is a tradition of making this structural impossibility constitutive of a kind of art; *ekphrasis*, the genre of poetry in which works of art are represented is an example. This might mislead us to think of movement in architecture as the designation of an externality, a limit that constitutes the discipline. However, Benjamin's meaning is stronger than this; it is to do with the concept of mimesis itself before the question of its application. Again, the childhood of art is instructive; Benjamin reminds us that: 'The child plays at being not only a shopkeeper or a teacher but also a windmill and a train'.[95] There is a difference in degree between the adequacy of the representation that a child might make of an adult person and a machine or building, but as acts of imitation, they are equivalent. In Benjamin's interest in non-sensuous resemblance, he attempts to understand an archaic aspect of mimesis, other to representation. The goal of this imitation is not to re-present the visual form of the object, but to approach the object. When the child takes a pose in imitation of a windmill, all the meaning is in the appearance that the child makes, but none of it in the adequacy of the image to the thing. Semblance is a movement towards the object, or of the object onto the subject, not the deceit by which the appearance might be taken for the thing.

Benjamin's interest in non-sensuous mimesis arose in relation to his thoughts on language. He thought that underneath the use of language as a conventional representation of the world there remained an ancient concept of correspondence. This is not the onomatopoeia of 'tick-tock' and the like where language imitates sounds, but rather a non-sensuous resemblance, the idea that words have a secret similarity with a thing that they name and that language as such is an imitation of the world. This is one of the aspects of Benjamin's work that most intrigued Theodor Adorno, who folded it into his theory of aesthetics as a dialectic between mimesis and rationality, at the basis of the concept of art.[96] We know what an art work is because of its internal logic, its pattern or construction, its sense of being whole or divided, but we also need to know that it is art and what art is, and we can know this because of a fundamental mimetic orientation in humans. Adorno thinks that, like a musician playing a score or a person sub-vocalizing while reading a poem or the eye ranging over a building, every artwork requires us to copy and repeat it at a semi-sensuous level that engages our mimetic faculty. Nevertheless, art remains enigmatic because what we are assimilating ourselves to in such imitations is a non-conceptual, non-discursive language; the language of things. Rationality gives us the distance to know that art is enigmatic and that we do not understand it. However, this dialectic is not one of experience and critical reflection on experience; it is not a version of the *homo duplex* of mind and body. Reason does not undo art's enigmatic quality and reveal conceptual knowledge. The non-conceptual logic that we can appreciate in artworks is inseparable from mimesis; it tells us that what we are imitating, or feeling, *has been made*.

We might speculate that Benjamin read some of this problematic of mimesis in *Renaissance and Baroque*, and that it was the lack of this that troubled him in *Principles* as much as his distaste for Wölfflin's rhetoric, with its demands of complicity. Wölfflin's theory of empathy, when it was still psychological in *Renaissance and Baroque*, was in equal part imitative: the body takes a posture from the building. Whereas in *Principles*, what remains of empathy theory is a mere subject–objectification: the object is a site for projecting and recognizing ourselves. This is why Wölfflin's equivocation on the 'natural' occurrence of the painterly as the picturesque movement-effect is so interesting: it is a remainder of the earlier argument based on mimesis. Rather than movement being with the painterly in the reveries of the cultured subject, the picturesque movement-effect puts movement back into the object and the perception of *it*. Having made these connections, we could then elaborate Benjamin's 'tactile' appropriation of architecture to include those eye-movements and raised breathing, that arrest of the attention, which Wölfflin describes as architectural movement. This would not be a projection of ourselves onto the building in a simple anthropomorphism; it would be a kind of mimesis. Our responses to a building that limits and governs our motion and field of view are a kind of imitation of it, an objectification of our body as affected by architecture.

Benjamin's ideas of affect draw on Henri Bergson's *Matter and Memory*, and Bergson's theory of the bodily-ness of emotions has commonalities with some of Wölfflin's sources for his postural account of movement as an affect in the Baroque. Bergson defines affect as 'a motor tendency in a sensory nerve'.[97] By this he means that the sensation of being affected occurs when one moves, outwardly as it were, the parts of the body which are normally experienced as a perceptive surface, a surface which receives the world and takes it into the body. Action and extension are somehow lost to the limbs, the body is motionless and instead, perception and sensibility are felt to move out from the body. The tears and erratic breathing of the person who grieves are actions which show the futility of actions, because the locomotive body is still or at least directionless, while the body of sensations enters a self-affecting process where, instead of perceiving, it extends outward tears, cries and hot breath.

Gilles Deleuze in his Bergsonian account of the cinema analyses the close-up, which functions in cinema by facial expression, being a kind of imitation of an action that the character sees but which we do not. Deleuze calls this the 'affection-image'; it has the properties of being at once still – in the sense that the face is a singular stable organization – but also animated by the micro movements of the facial expression that reflects the action happening out of shot.[98] Deleuze, who used Wölfflin extensively in *The Fold* to describe the characteristics of Baroque space, also cites his dialectic of linear and painterly to explain the formal qualities of the 'close-up' in cinema. Deleuze writes that an apprehension of the linear outline of the face and its features constitutes a minimum of facial movement and the expression of admiration, while the sense of the face as overlapping planes and 'brilliance of the look that rebels against outline' is painterly. The 'affection-image' has more to tell us of movement in architecture than Deleuze's concept of the 'movement-image'. The movement-image is inseparable from the fact of the motion of the cinematic image while movement that is at stake in architecture and its perception is an affect. To return Deleuze's terms to their origin, we could say that the Renaissance buildings have about them a linear 'faceification' – the stillness of them facing us – while in the Baroque, a painterly 'faceicity' (Deleuze's *visagéité*) gives a sense that the building watches and yearns for the movements we make in relation to it. Wölfflin's movement, if it were a theory of affect, would follow this logic: movement is some whole of which we have an image and which is directed to the image of our body. The motion or motionlessness of the subject in the experience of architecture has nothing (necessarily) to do with movement. Movement is when the building becomes present to a body that has an image of itself as affectable, causing in the body a kind of movement between sensation and action.

Bergson, and following him Deleuze, distinguish movement from the space covered in the action of moving. This is to say that movement is in the present and it is whole and indivisible, while the space one has traversed is in the past and it is a section or sections of homogenous space. Bergson shows that sections of space and a temporal structure of succession is merely a relation of positions; it cannot constitute movement. In our present inquiry, this means that the experience of moving through 'this room' followed by 'that room' and so on, is not movement, no matter what relation between the spatial qualities of the rooms. Movement requires that the rooms are not merely a set but a whole, present at each moment of the movement. Bergson argues that in our immediate perception of things moving, say a leaping cat, there is no *a priori* division of the movement observed into a body that moves and a change in position which it makes. Neither is there a scientific reason to do so. He writes:

> A moving continuity is given to us, in which everything changes and yet remains: why then do we dissociate the two terms, permanence and change, and then represent permanence by bodies and change by homogeneous movements in space? This is no teaching of immediate intuition; but neither is it a demand of science . . .
>
> [he claims that such a division makes sense in geometry but not in physics.]

> Besides consciousness and science, there is life. Beneath the principles of speculation, so carefully analyzed by philosophers, there are tendencies of which the study has been neglected, and which are to be explained simply by the necessity of living, that is, of acting. Already the power conferred on the individual consciousness of manifesting itself in acts requires the formation of distinct material zones, which correspond respectively to living bodies: in this sense, my own body and, by analogy with it, all other living bodies are those which I have the most right to distinguish in the continuity of the universe. But this body itself, as soon as it is constituted and distinguished, is led by its various needs to distinguish and constitute other bodies. [. . .] Whatever the nature of matter, it may be said that life will at once establish in it a primary discontinuity . . .[99]

We could take Bergson to support the idea that movement in architecture is imitative. There is no distinction between the movement of my self, my eye and objects in the world, and hence no distinction between real and imagined movement, except by virtue of the fundamental perception of having a body, and then introducing that distinction into the world. To say that a building possesses movement connotes that something in it makes an articulation like that between the permanence of the organization of my body and my capacity for movement or change. However, this analogy is not a simple anthropomorphism, because, according to Bergson, perception is not something that proceeds from us, it only seems to do so because of memory.

> Our perception [. . .] is originally in things rather than in the mind, without us rather than within. The several kinds of perception correspond to so many directions actually marked out in reality. But, we added, this perception, which coincides with its object, exists rather in theory than in fact: it could only happen if we were shut up within the present moment. In concrete perception, memory intervenes, and the subjectivity of sensible qualities is due precisely to the fact that our consciousness, which begins by being only memory, prolongs a plurality of moments into each other, contracting them into a single intuition.[100]

It is this idea of an involuntary memory and the unconsciously habitual nature of perception that interested Marcel Proust and Benjamin; and it brings us to my final point. The imitations that we make of buildings, that produce them as bodies and hence capable of movement like our own, are habitual, gestic. Imitation is not blind to itself. It is acting.

Interruption

I argued above that in the XIIIth Discourse, Reynolds places architecture on one side of painting and acting on the other. While he writes that acting is all imitation and architecture all imagination, each participate in both, and we could put Adorno's concept of non-conceptual logic in the place of Reynolds' imagination. While architecture is in a simple sense incapable of mimesis, Reynolds suggests that by sheer imagination, it can imitate the movement of animate life. What, then, of acting? Reynolds says that theatre is not simple imitation because what pleases in the 'studied grace of action' is unnatural and would appear ridiculous in ordinary social life. Hogarth has a much fuller account of the same issue, but broadened to comportment in general. It may be that Reynolds has this in mind and his insistence on the different grades of theatric art is a rebuke to Hogarth, whose Plate II of the *Analysis of Beauty* has a wonderful scene of a country dance, the comedy of which is exactly what

Reynolds complains of in both theatre and painting. However, Reynolds is in substantial agreement with Hogarth's text, in which the latter argues that comportment and gesture are cultural artefacts that can be misconstrued in an inappropriate context.

> For altho' the muscles of the body may attain a pliancy by these exercises, and the limbs, by the elegant movement in dancing, acquire a facility in moving gracefully, yet for want of knowing the meaning of every grace, and whereon it depends, affectations and misapplications often follow. Action is a sort of language which perhaps one time or other, may be come to be taught by a kind of grammar-rules; but, at present, is only got by rote and imitation . . .[101]

Because the history painting of their time supposed that a narrative sequence could be represented on canvas in a *coup d'œil*, it suits Reynolds and Hogarth to think that gesture is not so much a part of a bodily movement as an image of that movement, one that is already self-conscious so that we can recognize it in a picture and imitate it in our actions. But Hogarth goes further than Reynolds by suggesting that to approach true gracefulness, we must know that there is no natural grace, only those conventions that we imitate gracefully. Hogarth writes:

> What can be more conducive to that freedom and necessary courage which make acquired grace seem easy and natural, than the being able to demonstrate *when* we are actually just and proper in the least movement we perform; whereas, for want of such certainty in the mind, if one of the most finish'd gentlemen at court was to appear as an actor on the public stage, he would find himself at a loss how to move properly, and be stiff, narrow, and aukward in representing even his own character . . .[102]

Walter Benjamin takes this traditional problematic of the actor through a further turn in his essays on Brecht's theatre, and recently Samuel Weber has made a study of theatre as a medium that draws in part on Benjamin's idea that interruption is the basis of the gesture as a theatrical medium.[103] Brecht's theatre rejects empathy with the characters and the Aristotlean principle of unity of action, and it does this, according to Benjamin, through gesture understood not as communication but as an interruption of action. Here the 'aukwardness' that Hogarth's gentleman might feel on stage, the impossibility of mimesis, is the resource that Brecht uses to move theatre from drama to a modern epic.

> the epic theatre, being based on interruption is, in a specific sense, a quotable one. [. . .] 'Making gestures quotable' is one of the substantial achievements of the epic theatre. An actor must be able to space his gestures the way a typesetter produces spaced type. This effect may be achieved, for instance, by an actor's quoting his own gesture on the stage. [. . .] Epic theatre is by definition a gestic theatre. For the more frequently we interrupt someone in the act of acting, the more gestures result.[104]

In his reading of this passage, Weber disagrees with 'quotable' as the translation for *zitieren*, which is etymologically closer to the English verb to 'cite'. 'Citable' gestures are closer to the problematic of mimesis that we have been following. The quotation is 'direct speech', where we take the actor to be gesturing, whereas what interests Benjamin is that the audience has a sense that an action, or acting is happening; that the actor is mimicking a gesture made elsewhere. To cite is to refer and as Weber shows, this is a matter of movement.

> Epic theater is not just gestural; it is citational. It renders gestures *citable*. This is not quite the same as 'quotable', which is how it has been rendered in English. This is all the more true in German, where even today the verb *zitieren* still carries with it etymological resonances from its Latin root, *citare*, to set in movement. In English, this resonance is buried in verbs such as 'incite' and 'excite.' And yet setting-into-movement is only half the story here. In both German and English 'to cite' has another meaning that is decisive for Benjamin. To cite means not simply to set something in movement, but also – as American drivers know only too well – to arrest movement by diverting it, as in the sense, of course, of receiving a traffic citation, a summons to appear before a tribunal in order to account for an excess of speed.[105]

The political potential of Brecht's gestic theatre is this kind of pause or diversion; as Weber puts it: 'citability means recalling the past as the possibility of a future that would be different from the present'.[106] Gesture in Brecht is not expressive of character; it is mimetic in Aristotle's sense of learning through repetition, and it becomes a kind of form.

> Unlike human actions and undertakings, [gestures have] a definable beginning and a definable end. This strict, framelike enclosing of every element in a posture [*Haltung*] that as a whole is caught up in a living flux is one of the basic dialectical phenomena of gesture. From this an important conclusion can be drawn: gestures are obtained all the more someone engaged in an action [*eines Handelnden*] is interrupted.[107]

In one way, Brecht was simply exaggerating the necessary unnaturalness of theatrical representation that Reynolds and Hogarth observe. But Brecht did so to the point of destroying any illusion or image that places the audience; they are in the same place as the actors, not outside of it. Benjamin's point is that this occurs neither through heightened realism nor a heightened conventionality. There is no grammar or lexicon of gesture. It is the direct uncommunicative language of mimesis, the basis of meaning, which itself means nothing. While gesture might interrupt the action and reveal the constructed nature of plot, gesture itself is constructed, 'citable', and at a double level shows the ties of mimesis and rationality in theatric art. To continue extrapolating Reynolds' parallel, we could say that what Brecht did to theatre was to make it architectural.

Buildings are still and no one sees them move. What we might see is a stillness like the human body in gesture. Gesture is an interruption of the continuity of the body's motion; small movements of the muscles of the face and hand are not acts of extension or of passage. Certain facial expressions and postures might token an imminent embrace or attack, but they are not integral with such actions, distinguished from them in their aim in affecting a viewer, and in their learned conventionality. The sense that a gesture is an interruption means that it always puts the action-movement under question. Gesture refers to the movement that has ceased, and to a resumption of movement, but not necessarily the same one. But what are the consequences of understanding movement in architecture as matters of gesture rather than locomotion? It is to reverse the usual argument and to say that the human capacity for movement relates to building at a primary level in the object character of the body and its capacity for motion, for the gestures of the body to signify movement, a state before any particular movement that a 'you' or an 'I' might make. The movement of architecture is not something that we take from ourselves and project on the building by a feat of the imagination; it is something the building does to us, stilling us, returning to us something anterior to subjectivity. By interrupting the 'moving continuity' of which Bergson writes, the stillness of architecture shows what is given to us.

Architecture and the picturesque

That architecture implies some sense or illusion of the movement of building has always been one of the more curious ways in which the picturesque is instanced. If pictures and visual experience are to be contrasted, one of the principal axes must be the stillness and fixedness of the picture when compared to durational experience. The historical importance of the picturesque is often said to lie in the discovery of visual forms in space and duration, and in this, pictures perhaps function as a simple contrast, as everything the picturesque is not. From early in the twentieth century, in the works of Scott, Giedion, Christopher Hussey, later Nikolaus Pevsner, and recently Yve-Alain Bois, we see the picturesque as a humble beginning of the idea that durational spatio-visual experience is a kind of material that can be formed in architecture, landscape and urban design. In this story, the picture analogy of the picturesque is a cranky origin that can be honoured but left behind in the development of what would be more logically called 'cinema-esque'. I agree with the importance of these matters, and much of Chapter 4 is devoted to concepts of space and passage through it, developed from the pictures. But as I argued there, these are architectural ideas implicit in the concept of the building plan as much as they are a consideration of the perception of space and movement. An attentive reading of the eighteenth-century British sources with Wölfflin and his 'picturesque movement-effect' has shown their references to architectural 'movement' are not some simple or general allusion to what would become a more substantive account of progress through space. The arcane aspects of empathy theory and Giedion's championing of 'space-time' in the name of Wölfflin's method have obscured the fact that Wölfflin's concept of architectural movement does not refer to the motion of the human subject. At the same time, the overly axiomatic translation of *malerisch* has left readers of Wölfflin in English without a realization that it is the picturesque that is at stake in this motionless movement. For much of the last century, we have thought of buildings, cities and gardens as things that move us; devices to construct certain kinds of visual and spatial experience, to construe the visitor as the subject of spatial sequence in a similar way as cinema. But currently, the mood in architecture is returning from space to form, from a kind of cultural augmentation of the subject, to a more traditional subject–object relation. If the architectural object is to make a perhaps unlikely escape from becoming a simple consumer product, then issues such as those of non-sensual mimetic relations with the human form may provide some resources for architects.

For a couple of centuries, spatialized and flattened visual experience have tumbled over one another, and it is hard to predict whether new image cultures will extend or dissipate this productive exchange. But the questions raised by the spatiality of images, the superiority of disgust over beauty in representation, the perception of the architectural plan, the analogies of possession and politics that seem irreducible in any viewpoint, and the self-imitating aspects of the body are all there in the picturesque to be recovered and refreshed.

Notes

1 Introduction

1 The Editor, 'Exterior Furnishing or Sharawaggi: The Art of Making Urban Landscape', *The Architectural Review* 95, 565 (1944), fn p.6.
2 Thomas Puttfarken, *The Discovery of Pictorial Composition: Theories of Visual Order in Painting 1400–1800* (New Haven, Connecticut and London: Yale University Press, 2000); Geoffrey Scott, *The Architecture of Humanism: A Study in the History of Taste*, 2nd edn (London: Constable, 1924).
3 Sir William Temple, *Gardens of Epicurus* (1685).
4 R. L. (Marquis d'Ermonville) de Girardin, *An Essay on Landscape*, trans. Daniel Mathus (New York and London: Garland, 1783).
5 Dora Wiebenson, *The Picturesque Garden in France* (Princeton, New Jersey: Princeton University Press, 1978).
6 Leon Battista Alberti, *On the Art of Building*, trans. J. Rykwert, N. Leach and R. Travernor (Cambridge and London: MIT Press, 1988).
7 Jerome Stolnitz, 'On the Significance of Lord Shaftesbury in Modern Aesthetic Theory', *Philosophical Quarterly* 11, no. 43 (1961).
8 Quote from 'Gardens of Epicurus' in Nikolaus Pevsner, 'The Genesis of the Picturesque', *The Architectural Review* 96 (1944): 140.
9 Joseph Addison, *The Spectator*, 25th June 1712, quoted in ibid.: 141.
10 Horatio Walpole, 'On Modern Gardening', in *Anecdotes of Painting* (London: 1762–4).
11 John Barrell, *English Literature in History 1730–1780: An Equal, Wide Survey* (London: Hutchinson, 1983); John Barrell, *The Idea of Landscape and the Sense of Place 1730–1840: An Approach to the Poetry of John Clare* (London: Cambridge University Press, 1972).
12 Murray Krieger, *Ekphrasis: The Illusion of the Natural Sign* (Baltimore and London: Johns Hopkins University Press, 1992); Rensselaer W. Lee, *Ut Pictura Poesis; the Humanist Theory of Painting* (New York: W. W. Norton, 1967).
13 Charles Alphonse du Fresnoy, *De Arte Graphica. The Art of Painting, . . . With Remarks [by Roger De Piles]*, trans. John Dryden (London: 1668); Charles Alphonse du Fresnoy, *The Art of Painting of Charles Alphonse Du Fresnoy Translated into English Verse |by William Mason, M.A. With Annotations by Sir Joshua Reynolds, Knt President of the Royal Academy* (York: 1783).
14 William Mason, *The English Garden*, 3 vols (1772–82).
15 Andrew Charlesworth, *An Atlas of Rural Protest in Britain 1548–1900* (London and Canberra: Croom Helm, 1983).
16 E. P. Thomson, *The Making of the English Working Class* (New York: Vintage Books, 1963).
17 The literature on enclosure is extensive. A good summation is J. M. Neeson, *Commoners: Common Right, Enclosure and Social Change in England, 1700–1820* (Cambridge: Cambridge University Press, 1993).
18 Stephen Daniels and Charles Watkins, *The Picturesque Landscape: Visions of Georgian Herefordshire* (Nottingham: Department of Geography, University of Nottingham, 1994).
19 John Berger, *Ways of Seeing* (Harmondsworth: Penguin, 1972); Ann Bermingham, *Landscape and Ideology: The English Rustic Tradition 1740–1860* (Berkeley: UC Press, 1986); Simon Pugh, *Reading Landscape: Country–City–Capital* (Manchester: Manchester University Press, 1990).
20 Humphry Repton, *The Landscape Gardening and Landscape Architecture of the Late Humphry Repton Esq.*, ed. John Claudius Loudon (London: 1840), 104–9.
21 Walter John Hipple, *The Beautiful, the Sublime and the Picturesque in Eighteenth-Century British Aesthetic Theory* (Carbondale: Southern Illinois University Press, 1957).
22 Andrew Ballantyne, *Architecture, Landscape, and Liberty: Richard Payne Knight and the Picturesque* (Cambridge and New York: Cambridge University Press, 1997). See also Michael Clarke and Nicholas Penny, *The Arrogant Connoisseur; Richard Payne Knight 1751–1824* (Manchester: Manchester University Press, 1982); S. Lang, 'Richard Payne Knight and the Idea of Modernity', in *Concerning Architecture: Essays on Architectural Writers and*

Writing Presented to Nikolas Pevsner, ed. John Summerson (London: Allen Lane, The Penguin Press, 1968).

23 Stephen Daniels, *Humphry Repton: Landscape Gardening and the Geography of Georgian England* (New Haven: Yale University Press, 1999); Daniels and Watkins, *The Picturesque Landscape*.

24 Richard Payne Knight, *An Account of the Remains of the Worship of Priapus* (London: 1786).

25 Richard Payne Knight, *An Analytical Inquiry into the Principles of Taste*, 4th edn (London: T. Payne and J. White, 1808). Although his ideas are probably the best known today because of Sir Nikolaus Pevsner's précis and popularization of them in the mid-twentieth century.

26 Hipple, *Beautiful, Sublime, Picturesque*, 224.

27 'The Poetry of Architecture' was published as the work of 'Kata Phusin'. John Ruskin, *The Library Edition: The Works of John Ruskin*, ed. E. T. Cook and Alexander Wedderburn (London: George Allen, 1903–12), I, 1–188.

28 *Modern Painters* in John Ruskin, *The Library Edition*, VI, 9–26.

29 John Ruskin, *The Library Edition*, XXII, 493–507.

30 John Ruskin, *The Library Edition*, IX.

31 See Stanford Anderson's Introduction in Hermann Muthesius and Stanford Anderson, *Style-Architecture and Building-Art: Transformations of Architecture in the Nineteenth Century and Its Present Condition* (Santa Monica, California: Getty Center for the History of Art and the Humanities; Distributed by the University of Chicago Press, 1994).

32 Heinrich Wölfflin, *Renaissance and Baroque*, trans. Kathrin Simon (Ithaca, New York: Cornell University Press, 1966).

33 Heinrich Wölfflin, *Principles of Art History: The Problem of the Development of Style in Later Art*, trans. M. D. Hottinger (New York: Dover, 1950).

34 Harry Francis Mallgrave and Eleftherios Ikonomou, *Empathy, Form and Space: Problems in German Aesthetics 1873–1893* (Santa Monica: Getty Center for the Arts and Humanities, 1994).

35 Sigfried Giedion, *Space, Time and Architecture: The Growth of a New Tradition* (Cambridge, Massachusetts: Harvard University Press, 1967).

36 David Watkin, *Morality and Architecture* (Oxford: Clarendon, 1977).

37 John Barrell, *English Literature in History*; John Barrell, *The Dark Side of the Landscape: The Rural Poor in English Painting, 1730–1840* (Cambridge: Cambridge University Press, 1980); John Barrell, *The Idea of Landscape and the Sense of Place*; John Barrell, *The Political Theory of Painting from Reynolds to Hazlit: The Body of the Public* (New Haven and London: Yale University Press, 1986); John Barrell, 'The Public Prospect and the Private View: The Politics of Taste in Eighteenth Century Britain', in *Projecting the Landscape*, ed. J. C. Eade (Canberra: Humanties Research Centre, Australian National University, 1987). Raymond Williams, *The Country and the City* (London: Chatto and Windus, 1973). John Berger, *Ways of Seeing*, based on the BBC television series with John Berger (Harmondsworth: Penguin Books, 1972).

38 This work has since been developed by others. See Malcolm Andrews, *The Search for the Picturesque: Landscape Aesthetics and Tourism in Britain 1760–1800* (Stanford: Stanford University Press 1989); Ann Birmingham, *Landscape and Ideology: The English Rustic Tradition 1740–1860* (Berkeley: University of California Press, 1986); Denis Cosgrove and Stephen Daniels, eds, *The Iconography of the Landscape: Essays on the Symbolic Representation, Design and Use of Past Environments*, Cambridge Studies in Historical Geography 9 (1988); Simon Pugh, *Garden – Nature – Language* (Manchester: Manchester University Press, 1988); Simon Pugh, *Reading Landscape: Country – City – Capital* (Manchester and New York: Manchester University Press, 1990).

39 Jean-François Courtine et al, ed., *Of the Sublime: Presence in Question* (Albany: State University of New York, 1993); Jean-François Lyotard, *Lessons on the Analytic of the Sublime: Kant's Critique of Judgment, [Sections] 23–29* (Stanford, California: Stanford University Press, 1994); Jean-François Lyotard, *The Inhuman: Reflections on Time* (Cambridge: Polity Press, 1991).

40 Iñaki Ábálos, *Atlas Pintoresco – Vol. 1, El Observatoria* (Barcelona: Editorial Gustavo Gill, 2005, 2006); Iñaki Ábálos, 'Le Corbusier Pintoresco: El Pintoresquismo En La Modernidad', *Massilia* 3, no. 2 (2004); Ákos Moravánszky, 'Forced Spontaneities. Sitte and the Problem of the Pittoresque. Erzwungene Ungezwungenheiten. Sitte Und Das Paradox Des Malerischen', Paper presented at the Symposium Camillo Sitte, TU Wien – Prechtlsaal. 2003; Phillipe Nys, 'Le Pittoresque Généralise Ou De L'unité Critique De La Fabrique Du Monde Contemporain', *L'Architecture d'Aujourd'hui* no. 363 (2006): 48–55; anon. 'Sul Pittoresco,' *Parametro: rivista internazionale di architettura e urbanistica*, no. 264–265 (2006).

2 Pictures

1 Clement Greenberg and John O'Brian, *Clement Greenberg: The Collected Essays and Criticism* (Chicago and London: University of Chicago Press, 1986).

2 Thomas Puttfarken, *Roger De Piles' Theory of Art* (New Haven: Yale University Press, 1985); Thomas Puttfarken, *The Discovery of Pictorial Composition: Theories of Visual Order in Painting 1400–1800* (New Haven, Connecticut and London: Yale University Press, 2000).

3 Michael Baxandall, *Giotto and the Orators: Humanist Observers of Painting in Italy and*

the Discovery of Pictorial Composition (Oxford: Clarendon Press, 1971); Michael Baxandall, *Painting and Experience in Fifteenth Century Florence* (Oxford: Clarendon Press, 1972); E. H. Gombrich, *Means and Ends: Reflections on the History of Fresco Painting*, Walter Neurath Memorial Lectures (London: Thames and Hudson, 1976); E. H. Gombrich, *Norm and Form* (London: Phaidon, 1966).

4 Caroline van Eck, *Organicism in Nineteenth Century Architecture: An Enquiry into Its Theoretical and Philosophical Background* (Amsterdam: Architectura & Natura, 1994).

5 Robin Middleton, 'Introduction', in *The Genius of Architecure; or, the Analogy of That Art with Our Sensations*, ed. Nicholas Le Camus de Mézières (Santa Monica: The Getty Center, 1992), 31.

6 Michael Clark. 'Poussinisme', in *Oxford Reference Online: The Concise Oxford Dictionary of Art Terms*, Oxford University Press, http://www.oxfordreference.com/views/ENTRY.html?subview=Main&entry=t4.e1365 (accessed 2 June 2005).

7 Middleton, 'Introduction', 28–31.

8 Roger de Piles, *Cours De Peinture Par Principes* (Paris: 1708); Roger de Piles, *The Art of Painting, and the Lives of the Painters: Containing, a Compleat Treatise of Painting, Designing, and the Use of Prints: . . . Done from the French of Monsieur De Piles. To Which Is Added, an Essay Towards an English-School, . . .* (London: J. Nutt, 1706). Roger de Piles, *The Principles of Painting, . . . In Which Is Contained an Account of the Athenian, Roman, Venetian and Flemish Schools. To Which Is Added, the Balance of Painters. Being the Names of the Most Noted Painters, and Their Degrees of Perfection . . . Written Originally in French by Mons. Du Piles [under the Title Of 'Cours De Peinture Par Principes' And Now First Translated into English by a Painter.]* (London: Osborn, 1743).

9 De Piles, *Principles of Painting*, 5.

10 Ibid., 59.

11 Ibid., 64–5.

12 Ibid., 76.

13 Puttfarken, *Discovery of Pictorial Composition*, 272–3.

14 De Piles, *Principles of Painting*, 8–10.

15 Meyer Schapiro, 'On Some Problems in the Semiotics of Visual Art: Field and Vehicle in Image-Signs', *Semiotica* 1, no. 3 (1969).

16 Gombrich, *Means and Ends.*

17 Ibid., 39.

18 Maurice Henri Leonard Pirenne, *Optics, Painting and Photography* (London: Cambridge University Press, 1970).

19 Baxandall, *Giotto and the Orators.*

20 David Rosand, 'Titian in the Frari', *The Art Bulletin* 53, no. 2 (1971), 196–213.

21 Puttfarken, *Discovery of Pictorial Composition*, 144.

22 Deborah Howard, 'Titian's Painted Architecture', in *The Cambridge Companion to Titian*, ed. Patricia Meilman (Cambridge: Cambridge University Press, 2004), 146–62.

23 Joshua Reynolds and Harry Mount, *A Journey to Flanders and Holland (Art, Patrons, and Public)*. (Cambridge and New York: Cambridge University Press, 1996), 60.

24 Uvedale Price, *Essays on the Picturesque: As Compared with the Sublime and the Beautiful and, on the Use of Studying Pictures for the Purpose of Improving Real Landscape*, 3 vols (London: J. Mawman, 1810), II, 298.

25 Anthony Ashley Cooper Shaftesbury, Gerd Hemmerich and Wolfram Benda, *Standard Edition: Complete Works, Selected Letters and Posthumous Writings (Standard Edition: Samtliche Werke, Ausgewahlte Briefe Und Nachgelassene Schriften)*, vol. 15 (Stuttgart: Frommann-Holzboog, 1981).

26 Shaftesbury, Hemmerich and Benda, *Standard Edition*, I, 5:74.

27 Monika Schmitter, 'Falling through the Cracks: The Fate of Painted Palace Façades in Sixteenth-Century Italy', in *The Built Surface: Architecture and the Pictorial Arts from Antiquity to the Enlightenment, Architecture and the Pictorial Arts from Romanticism to the Twenty-First Century*, ed. Christy Anderson and Karen Koehler (Aldershot, Hants and Burlington, Vermont: Ashgate, 2001).

28 Sebastiano Serlio quoted in ibid., 130.

29 Joseph Rykwert, 'Leon Battista Alberti: AD Profiles 21', *Architectural Design* 49, nos 5–6 (1979).

30 Michel Foucault, *The Order of Things: An Archaeology of the Human Sciences* (London: Tavistock Publications, 1970).

31 Pirenne, *Optics, Painting and Photography*, 84.

32 Karsten Harries, *The Bavarian Rococo Church: Between Faith and Aestheticism* (New Haven, Connecticut: Yale University Press, 1983), 53.

33 Ibid., 139.

34 Ibid., 60.

35 Ibid., 256.

36 Ibid., 10.

37 Ibid., 236.

38 Ibid., 250–5.

39 Hl. Kreuz church in Etwashausen 1741–5. Ibid., 244.

40 Friedrich Melichoir Grimm in the Correspondance littéraire for 15th December 1756 cited in Michael Fried, *Absorption and Theatricality: Painting and Beholder in the Age of Diderot* (Chicago, Illinois: University of Chicago Press, 1988), 89.

41 William Gilpin, *An Essay Upon Prints: Containing Remarks Upon the Principles of Picturesque Beauty; the Different Kinds of Prints; and the Character of the Most Noted Masters: Illustrated by Criticisms Upon Particular Pieces to Which Are Added Some Cautions That May Be Useful in Collecting Prints*, 2nd edn (London: J. Robson, 1768).

42 De Piles, *The Art of Painting*, 66, 54–68 passim.

43 Charles Alphonse du Fresnoy, *The Art of Painting of Charles Alphonse Du Fresnoy Translated into English Verse by William Mason, M.A. With Annotations by Sir Joshua Reynolds, Knt President of the Royal Academy* (York: 1783); William Mason, *The English Garden: A Poem*, 4 vols (York: 1781).
44 Gilpin, *Essay Upon Prints*, 1.
45 Ibid., 1–3.
46 Ibid., 3.
47 Ibid., 8–10.
48 Ibid., 1.
49 Ibid., 3.
50 Carl Paul Barbier, *William Gilpin: His Drawings, Teaching, and Theory of the Picturesque* (Oxford: Clarendon Press, 1963), 36–40.
51 Cf. ibid., chs V and VI.
52 William Gilpin, *Observations Relative Chiefly to Picturesque Beauty Made in the Year 1772, on Several Parts of England; Particularly the Mountains and Lakes of Cumberland and Westmoreland*, 2 vols (London: The Richmond Publishing Company, 1786), II, 91.
53 It maybe that we should also understand Gilpin in the context of Horace Walpole's *Ancedotes of Painting* of 1762. Walpole's compendium of remarks about artists concludes with his influential essay 'On Modern Gardening', a semi-historical, connoisseur's account of English gardening practice. Gilpin dedicated the *Essay upon Prints* to Walpole, and what is innovative in Gilpin's tours could be understood as fulfilling the synthesis that Walpole had implied by publishing his considerations of the skills of painters and improvers in one binding.
54 Gilpin, *Observations on Mountains and Lakes*, 119.
55 William Gilpin, *Observations on the River Wye, and Several Parts of South Wales, &C. Relative Chiefly to Picturesque Beauty: Made in the Summer of the Year 1770*... (London: 1789), 2.
56 Barbier, *William Gilpin*, 101.
57 William Gilpin, *Three Essays: On Picturesque Beauty: On Picturesque Travel: And on Sketching Landscape: To Which Is Added a Poem on Landscape Painting* (London: R. Blamire, 1792), 34–6.
58 Price, *Essays on the Picturesque*. The first essay was published in 1794.
59 Gilpin, *Three Essays*.
60 Gilpin, *Essay Upon Prints*, 1.
61 The sublime stretches these cords beyond their normal range. Gilpin, *Three Essays*, 131–2 and Part 4 passim. See also the discussion in Walter John Hipple, *The Beautiful, the Sublime and the Picturesque in Eighteenth-Century British Aesthetic Theory* (Carbondale: Southern Illinois University Press, 1957), 91–2.
62 Gilpin, *Three Essays*, 5.
63 Ibid., 4.
64 Ibid., 6.
65 Gilpin, *Essay Upon Prints*, 3.
66 Gilpin, *Three Essays*, 8.
67 Ibid., 7.
68 Ibid., 16.
69 Ibid., 17.
70 Ibid.
71 Ibid., 16.
72 Ibid., 19.
73 Gilpin, *Essay Upon Prints*, 17.
74 Cited in Barbier, *William Gilpin*, 26.
75 Gilpin, *Three Essays*, 69.
76 The idea of grading works of art and literature by kind is ancient. The modern system of a hierarchy of genres of painting was introduced by André Félibien in the 1660s. Genre hierarchy is the foundation of Reynolds' *Discourses*. Some modern inquiries include: Mieke Bal and Norman Bryson, 'Semiotics and Art History', *Art Bulletin* 73, no. 2 (1991); Alastair Fowler, *Kinds of Literature: An Introduction to the Theory of Genres and Modes* (Oxford: Clarendon, 1982); Anne Freadman and Amanda Macdonald, *Four Essays in the Semiotics of Genre* (Mount Nebo, Queensland: Boombana Publications, 1992).
77 Reynolds 'Letter' in Gilpin, *Three Essays*, 35–6.
78 André Félibien, *Conférences De L'académie Royale De Peinture Et De Sculpture* (Paris: 1669); André Félibien, *Sieur Des Avaux Et De Javercy Seven Conferences Held in the King of France's Cabinet of Paintings between Mr Le Brun, Mr Bourden, Mr De Champagne, Mr Perrault & C* (London: 1740).
79 Sir Joshua Reynolds, *Discourses on Art*, ed. Robert R. Wark (New Haven and London: Published for the Paul Mellon Centre for Studies in British Art (London) Limited by Yale University Press, 1975), 63.
80 For instance Reynolds places Hogarth's comic observations of 'low and vulgar characters' above the 'cold painter of portraits'. By this he means portraits the values of which lie in verisimilitude alone, rather than (I assume) his own thematicized portraits which are semi-Grand. Ibid., 51–52.
81 Reynolds, *Discourses on Art*, Discourse IX, 171.
82 Charles Crammer shows how this reductive empiricism underlies Gilpin's and Cozens' work. Charles A. Crammer, 'Alexander Cozens's New Method: The Blot and General Nature', *The Art Bulletin* 79, no. 1 (1997).
83 Reynolds, *Discourses on Art*, Discourse IX, 171.
84 Reynolds had, much earlier, offered comments on the manuscript of the 'Essay on picturesque Beauty', which he read in 1776. But these comments are rather confusing. Reynolds there told Gilpin 'everything in nature that is beautiful I hold to be picturesque. But beauty in art ought not be so called; for it is not to art, but to nature which the painter applies, as his object of imitation. Whatever works of art are introduced in a picture, they are there to assist or explain: they make not the bulk or principal of his composition: if they do the work must class among the lowest in art'. It

seems that Reynolds understood the picturesque to involve the copying of landscape pictures. From a modern perspective this seems unfair to Gilpin, but for Reynolds there appears to have been little significant difference between generalizing the techniques of landscape painting as an object of imitation, and simply copying pictures. Reynolds, July 1776, cited in Barbier, *William Gilpin*, 101.

85 Uvedale Price, *Essay on the Picturesque*, 1st edn (Hereford: 1794), passim, 142.
86 Ibid., 39.
87 For a discussion of this problematic in twentieth-century art see Thierry de Duve, *Kant after Duchamp* (Cambridge, Massachusetts: MIT Press, 1996).
88 Stephen Daniels and Charles Watkins, 'A Well-Connected Landscape: Uvedale Price at Foxley', in *The Picturesque Landscape: Visions of Georgian Herefordshire*, ed. Stephen Daniels and Charles Watkins (Nottingham: Department of Geography, University of Nottingham, 1994); Beryl Hartley, 'Naturalism and Sketching, Robert Price at Foxley and on Tour', in *The Picturesque Landscape: Visions of Georgian Herefordshire*, ed. Stephen Daniels and Charles Watkins (Nottingham: Department of Geography, University of Nottingham, 1994).
89 Reynolds, *Discourses on Art*, Discourse XI, 197.
90 Price, *Essays on the Picturesque*, I, 113–46. The discussion of pictures with reference to Reynolds starts on page 127.
91 Ibid., 145.
92 In a later text ('A Dialogue on the Distinct Characters of the picturesque and the Beautiful') Price does show an understanding of Burke's sublime, which he thinks 'more generally admitted than those of the beautiful . . . we have been used to consider the terrible as a principal source of the sublime in poetry'. Price, *Essays on the Picturesque*, III, 188.
93 Price, *Essays on the Picturesque*, I, 140–41.
94 'Again, by its variety, its intricacy, its partial concealments, it excites that active curiosity which gives play to the mind, loosening those iron bonds with which astonishment chains up its faculties.' And footnoted to this the remark 'This seems to be perfectly applicable to tragi-comedy, and is at once its apology and condemnation. Whatever relieves the mind from a strong impression, of course weakens that impression.' Ibid., 89. Shakespeare and Fielding are mentioned early (I, 6) not particularly because of their use of comedy, but their observation of character. It is interesting that he chooses them rather than Pope or Milton.
95 Ibid., 140–41.
96 Crammer, 'Alexander Cozens's New Method.'
97 Price, *Essays on the Picturesque*, I, 157. Price makes this point again comparing butcher's shops, by Rembrandt and Teniers. Price, *Essays on the Picturesque*, II, 335.
98 Price, *Essays on the Picturesque*, II, 171–369.
99 Ibid., 342–43.
100 Ibid., 325–27.
101 Ibid., 328–29.
102 Martin Price, *To the Palace of Wisdom: Studies in Order and Energy from Dryden to Blake* (Carbondale: Southern Illinois University Press, 1970), 381–2.
103 Ovid, *The Metamorphoses of Ovid: A New Verse Translation by Allen Mandelbaum* (New York, San Diego and London: Harcourt Brace & Company, 1993), Book VII, 272–7.
104 Price, *Essays on the Picturesque*, I, 147–55.
105 Ibid., 153.
106 De Piles, *The Art of Painting*, 296.
107 Richard Payne Knight, *An Analytical Inquiry into the Principles of Taste*, 4th edn (London: T. Payne and J. White, 1808), 150.
108 Hipple, *Beautiful, Sublime, Picturesque*, 261.
109 Knight, *Principles of Taste*, 155–6.
110 Nigel Everett, *The Tory View of Landscape* (New Haven, Connecticut: published for the Paul Mellon Centre for Studies in British Art by Yale University Press, 1994), 103–15.
111 Humphry Repton, *The Landscape Gardening and Landscape Architecture of the Late Humphry Repton Esq.*, ed. John Claudius Loudon (London: 1840), 104–9. Also cited in full in Price, *Essays on the Picturesque*, III, 3–21.
112 The *Red Book* for Attingham has been published as a facsimile. Repton, *Landscape Gardening*, 224–30; Humphry Repton, *The Red Books of Humphry Repton* (London: Basilisk Press, 1976).
113 Repton, *Landscape Gardening*, 227.
114 Ibid.
115 This is not, in fact, a position Repton holds strongly. His Whigish-ness in the Attingham *Red Book* is in contrast to later opinions where he often recommends hierarchies of building as an expression of social cohesion between classes, see especially the *Red Book* on Sherringham also reproduced in Repton, *The Red Books.*
116 Attingham *Red Book* plate N: II.
117 Repton, *Landscape Gardening*, 227–8.
118 Richard A. Etlin, *Frank Lloyd Wright and Le Corbusier: The Romantic Legacy* (Manchester: Manchester University Press, 1994). Yve-Alain Bois, 'A Picturesque Stroll around Clara-Clara', in *October: The First Decade*, ed. A. Michelson et al. (MIT Press, 1987).
119 I simplify a complex dispute that also concerned lighting and how the putative succession of Purism over Cubism was to be expressed. Nevertheless, according to Tim Benton, the significant aspect of the dispute is the density of the hanging as it affects the visibility of the architecture. The dispute is documented in letters between Le Corbusier, La Roche and Ozenfant. See Tim Benton, Charlotte Benton and Dennis Sharpe, *The Villas of Le Corbusier: 1920–1930* (New Haven and London: Yale University Press, 1987), 65–70.

120 Le Corbusier, letter to Ozenfant 16th April 1925, Dossier La Roche, Doc.506, quoted in ibid., 67.
121 La Roche, letter to Le Corbusier, 24th May 1926, Dossier La Roche, Doc.506, quoted in ibid.
122 Rosalind Krauss, 'Leger, Le Corbusier, and Purism', *Artforum* 10, no. 8 (1972), 52.
123 J. L. Sert, F. Léger and S. Giedion, 'Nine Points on Monumentality', in *Architecture Culture, 1943–1968 : A Documentary Anthology*, ed. Joan Ockman and Edward Eigen, Columbia Books of Architecture (New York: Columbia University Graduate School of Architecture, Planning Rizzoli, 1993), 29–30.
124 Gerhard Mack and Valeria Liebermann, *Eberswalde Library: Herzog & De Meuron*, vol. 3, Architecture Landscape Urbanism (London: Architectural Association, 2000).

3 Disgust

1 Mark Cousins, 'The Ugly (Part 1)', AA Files, no. 28 (1994); Mark Cousins, 'The Ugly (Part 2)', *AA Files*, no. 29 (1995); Mark Cousins, 'The Ugly (Part 3)', *AA Files*, no. 30 (1995); Paul Rozin, Johnathan Haidt and Clark R. McCauley, 'Disgust', in *Handbook of Emotions*, ed. Michael Lewis and Jeannette M. Haviland (New York and London: The Guilford Press, 1993).
2 Charles Darwin, Paul Ekman and Phillip Prodger, *The Expression of the Emotions in Man and Animals*, 3rd edn (Oxford: Oxford University Press, 1998 [1872]), 250–77.
3 Rozin, Haidt and McCauley, 'Disgust', 591.
4 Cousins, 'The Ugly (Part 3)', 68.
5 William Ian Miller, *The Anatomy of Disgust* (Cambridge, Massachusetts: Harvard University Press, 1997), 8.
6 Ibid., 7.
7 Winfried Menninghaus, *Disgust: Theory and History of a Strong Sensation*, trans. Howard Eiland and Joel Golb (Albany: State University of New York Press, 2003); Miller, *Anatomy of Disgust*.
8 Miller, *Anatomy of Disgust*, 11.
9 Darwin, Ekman and Prodger, *Expression of Emotions*, 257.
10 Gilles Deleuze, following Henri Bergson has a useful way of schematicizing affect as: 'a motor tendency on a sensible nerve'. Gilles Deleuze, *Cinema I: The Movement Image*, trans. H. Tomlinson and B. Habberjam (London: Athlone Press, 1986), 66. By this Bergson/Deleuze mean that we experience affect as an action that has no effect as it is taken by an organ of sense. This is the case with crying, in which in grief or laughter, the eyes, which we understand as a place that visual impressions enter, attempt to act, like a limb or some other part of the body of actions, but cannot, except to exude and project tears.
11 Rozin, Haidt and McCauley, 'Disgust', 584.
12 Ibid., 583.
13 Roland Barthes claims that Charles Fourier's utopian system of pleasures is better understood as an attempt to stop one's disinclinations from transferring to the persons whose pleasures we do not share. Barthes describes a situation where his 'core' disgust at eating couscous prepared with rancid butter, if exhibited, would have risked insulting his hosts. Roland Barthes, *Sade, Fourier, Loyola* (London: Jonathon Cape, 1976), 78.
14 Miller, *Anatomy of Disgust*, 206–34.
15 Cousins, 'The Ugly (Part 1)', 63.
16 Miller, *Anatomy of Disgust*, 20, Ch. 6, 109–42.
17 Menninghaus, *Disgust*, 18.
18 Miller, *Anatomy of Disgust*, 20.
19 Kolnai cited in Menninghaus, *Disgust*, 18.
20 Ibid., 19.
21 Ibid.
22 Ibid., 84 and 84–91 passim.
23 Cousins, 'The Ugly (Part 2)', 5.
24 Julia Kristeva, *Powers of Horror: An Essay on Abjection* (New York: Columbia University Press, 1982).
25 Pliny et al, *Natural History*, Loeb Classical Library (London: Heinemann, 1940), Book XXXV.
26 *OED* 'A painter of mean or sordid subjects.' [f. late L. *rhyparographos*, = Gr., f. filthy: see -GRAPHER. Cf. F. *riparographe* (Cotgr.).]
27 Gotthold Ephraim Lessing, *Laocoön: An Essay on the Limits of Painting and Poetry*, trans. Edward Allen McCormick (Baltimore and London: Johns Hopkins University Press, 1984), 13.
28 Aristotle, *Aristotle Poetics* (Ann Arbor, University of Michigan Press, 1970), 48b12–19, p. 20.
29 Norman Bryson, *Looking at the Overlooked: Four Essays on Still Life* (Cambridge, Massachusetts: MIT Press, 1990).
30 Ibid., 60.
31 Miller, *Anatomy of Disgust*, Icelandic 144–9, Catherine 58–63.
32 François Rabelais, Thomas Urquhart and Peter Anthony Motteux, *Gargantua and Pantagruel*, Newly annotated edn (London: Oxford University Press, 1934). Author's Prologue to the Fifth Book.
33 Edmund Burke, *A Philosophical Enquiry into the Origins of Our Ideas of the Sublime and the Beautiful* (London: Routledge and Kegan Paul, 1958), Section XVI, 45.
34 Knight, 'Note annexed to The Landscape' cited in Uvedale Price, *Essay on the Picturesque*, III, 256–7.
35 1642, Oil on oak, 39.8 × 53.8 cm, Museum of Fine Arts, Budapest, or *Peasants outside a farmhouse, butchering pork*, 1641.
36 Arthur Schopenhauer, *The World as Will and Representation* (New York: Dover Publications, 1969), 207–8. He has the same objection to nude figures.
37 Richard Payne Knight, *An Analytical Inquiry into*

the Principles of Taste, 4th edn (London: T. Payne and J. White, 1808), 75.

38 Richard Payne Knight, 'Note Annexed to the Second Edition of the Landscape', in *Essays on the Picturesque, as Compared with the Beautiful and the Sublime; and, on the Use of Studying Pictures, for the Purpose of Improving Real Landscape*, ed. Uvedale Price (London: J. Mawman, 1810), 255–6.

39 Knight, *Principles of Taste*, 83.

40 Ibid., 87–8.

41 Knight, 'Note Annexed to The Landscape', 252.

42 Knight, *Principles of Taste*, 72.

43 Menninghaus, *Disgust*, 38–45

44 Lessing, *Laocoön*, 17.

45 Uvedale Price, *Essays on the Picturesque: As Compared with the Sublime and the Beautiful and, on the Use of Studying Pictures for the Purpose of Improving Real Landscape*, 3 vols (London: J. Mawman, 1810), II, xiv.

46 John Ruskin, *The Library Edition: The Works of John Ruskin*, ed. E. T. Cook and Alexander Wedderburn (London: George Allen, 1903–12), VII, 363.

47 Immanuel Kant, *The Critique of Judgement*, trans. James Creed Meredith (Oxford: Clarendon Press, 1952), 42–3.

48 Menninghaus, *Disgust*, 7.

49 Kant, *Critique of Judgement*, §48, 174.

50 Georg Wilhelm Friedrich Hegel, *Introductory Lectures on Aesthetics*, trans. B. Bosanquet (London: Penguin, 1993).

51 Jacques Derrida, 'Economimesis', *Diacritics*, June (1981): 9.

52 Ibid., 13.

53 Ibid., 21.

54 Ibid., 25.

55 Ibid., 22.

56 Immanuel Kant, 'Inquiry Concerning the Distinctness of the Principles of Natural Theology and Morals', in *Theoretical Philosophy, 1755–1770*, ed. David Walford and Ralf Meerbote (Cambridge, New York: Cambridge University Press, 1992), 252. Menninghaus, *Disgust*, Ch. 3, passim.

57 Menninghaus, *Disgust*, 29.

58 Ibid., 116.

59 Kant, 'Principles of Natural Theology and Morals', 252. Cited in Menninghaus, *Disgust*, 116. In fact there is a lot of interpretation required to take us from Kant's text to Menninghaus' summation. Kant's passage concerns the difference between philosophy and mathematics, and especially the large number of philosophical concepts which cannot be assayed or demonstrated. Disgust is an example: 'Other concepts can only be partially analysed, for example, the concepts of space, time and the many different feelings of the human soul, such as the feeling of the sublime, the beautiful, the disgusting, and so forth.'

60 Menninghaus, *Disgust*, 117.

61 Jacques Derrida, 'From Restricted to General Economy: An Hegelianism without Reserve', in *Writing and Difference: Essays 1950–69* (Chicago: University of Chicago Press, 1978).

62 Menninghaus, *Disgust*, 15.

63 What is more, that it is made on the floor but presented upright on the wall intimately connects its abasement with the role of the horizontal picture plane in late modern art (an issue to which I will return in Chapter 5).

64 Menninghaus, *Disgust*, 125–7.

65 Pierre Bourdieu, *Distinction: A Social Critique of the Judgement of Taste* (Cambridge: Harvard University Press, 1984), 491.

66 J. G. A. Pocock, *The Machiavellian Moment: Florentine Political Thought and the Atlantic Republican Tradition* (Princeton, New Jersey: Princeton University Press, 1975); J. G. A. Pocock, *Virtue, Commerce, and History: Essays on Political Thought and History, Chiefly in the Eighteenth Century*, Ideas in Context (Cambridge, New York and Melbourne: Cambridge University Press, 1985).

67 John Barrell, *English Literature in History 1730–1780: An Equal, Wide Survey* (London: Hutchinson, 1983).

68 John Barrell, *The Political Theory of Painting from Reynolds to Hazlitt: The Body of the Public* (New Haven and London: Yale University Press, 1986), 63.

69 Jerome Stolnitz, 'On the Origins Of "Aesthetic Disinterestedness"', *Journal of Aesthetics and Art Criticism* 20 (1961), 132–3.

70 Jerome Stolnitz, 'On the Significance of Lord Shaftesbury in Modern Aesthetic Theory', *Philosophical Quarterly* 11, no. 43 (1961).

71 Stephen Daniels and Charles Watkins, *The Picturesque Landscape: Visions of Georgian Herefordshire* (Nottingham: Department of Geography, University of Nottingham, 1994).

72 William Marshall, *A Review of the Landscape, a Didactic Poem: Also of an Essay on the Picturesque: Together with Practical Remarks on Rural Ornament* (London: 1795); William Marshall, *On the Landed Property of England, an Elementary and Practical Treatise; Containing the Purchase, the Improvement and the Management of Landed Estates* (1804).

73 Sherringham in Norfolk in Humphry Repton, *The Landscape Gardening and Landscape Architecture of the Late Humphry Repton Esq.*, ed. John Claudius Loudon (London: 1840), 575.

74 When Thomas Coke, Earl of Norfolk, one of the fathers of the Agrarian Revolution took to stocking the park of Holkham with his improved breeds of sheep, he was careful to advertise this as science.

75 Repton, *Landscape Gardening*, 575.

76 See also: Peter Frederick Robinson, *Designs for Farm Buildings* (London: 1830); Peter Frederick Robinson, *Designs for Ornamental Villas*

(London: 1827); Peter Frederick Robinson, *Rural Architecture, or a Series of Designs for Ornamental Cottages* (London: 1823).

77 Peter Frederick Robinson, *Village Architecture, or a Series of Designs [. . .] Illustrative of the Observations Contained in the Essay on the Picturesque, by Sir Uvedale Price* (London: 1830), caption to Plate 76.

78 Price, *Essays on the Picturesque*, II, 312.

79 Price, *Essays on the Picturesque*, III, 281.

80 Price, *Essays on the Picturesque*, III, 316.

81 Society for Bettering the Condition and Improving the Comforts of the Poor, *To the English Cottager*, 1800.

82 In its combination of prescribed cavalry manoeuvres and its rhetoric of the natural allegiance of the yeomanry to the Loyalist cause, *Defense of Property* is prescient of the actual events of the Peterloo massacre of 1819.

83 Humphry Repton, *Fragments on the Theory and Practice of Landscape Gardening* (London: 1816), XXXVI.

84 Repton, *Landscape Gardening*, 603–4.

85 Ibid., 568.

86 Ibid., 472.

87 Stephen Daniels, *Humphry Repton: Landscape Gardening and the Geography of Georgian England* (New Haven: Yale University Press, 1999), 59–65.

88 Daniels cites Repton's sympathy with amputees on this point. Ibid., 65.

89 Letter, July 6, 1812, quoted in Lady Margaret Ishbel Frances Glyn Meade-Fetherstonhaugh and Oliver Warner, *Uppark and Its People* (London: Allen and Unwin, 1965).

90 Price, *Essays on the Picturesque*, II,171–369.

91 Ibid., 335–6.

92 Price, *Essays on the Picturesque*, III, 270–1.

93 Ibid., 301.

94 Ibid., 302.

95 Ibid., 328–9.

96 Br. 458. Panel, 73.5 × 51.5 cm Glasgow Art Gallery, late 1630s. A later version of 1655 hangs in the Louvre (Br. 457). Kenneth Craig argues that the painting is intended as an allegory of the crucifixion. Dutch kitchen paintings typically included biblical scenes partially obscured in the background and thus had the general meaning of warnings against gluttony and worldliness. A famous example is Pieter Aertsen's *Butcher's Shop* (1551 Uppsala University) which includes an ox on a gallows (viewed from the same angle as the Rembrandt) as part of an allegory about the Prodigal Son, which is itself taken to be an allegory of Christ's coming. Rembrandt reduces all of the figurative and spatial complexity of such paintings to the one monumental image of the ox and thus transcodes its genre with paintings of higher status. Kenneth M. Craig, 'Pieter Aertsen and the Meat Stall', *Oud Holland*, no. 96 (1982); Kenneth M. Craig, 'Rembrandt and the Slaughtered Ox', *Journal of the Warburg and Courtauld Institutes* XLVI (1983); Scott A. Sullivan, *The Dutch Gamepiece* (Montclair, New Jersey: Allanheld & Schram, Woodbridge Boydell Press, 1984).

97 Price, *Essays on the Picturesque*, III, 315–16.

98 Knight, *Principles of Taste*, 84–5.

99 It is possible that Price's choice of subject might have been coloured by the fact that butchers were themselves stock figures of English culture in this period and much lionized by William Hogarth for their independence and impatience with artificiality of manner, or French foppishness. Ben Rogers, *Beef and Liberty* (London: Chatto and Windus, 2003).

100 Reynolds quoted in Price, *Essays on the Picturesque*, III, 318.

101 Derrida, 'Economimesis', 22.

102 Jacques Derrida, 'Parergon', in *The Truth in Painting* (Chicago and London: University of Chicago Press, 1987), 2 and passim.

103 Sir Joshua Reynolds, *Discourses on Art*, ed. Robert R. Wark (New Haven and London: published for the Paul Mellon Centre for Studies in British Art (London) Limited by Yale University Press, 1975), I, 18.

104 Price, *Essays on the Picturesque*, III, 306.

105 Price, *Essays on the Picturesque*, I, 83–101.

106 Price, *Essays on the Picturesque*, I, 102. 'Of the three characters, two only are to any degree subject to the improver; to create the sublime is above our contracted powers, though we may sometimes heighten and at all times lower its effects by art. It is, therefore, on a proper attention to the beautiful and the picturesque, that the art of improving real landscapes must depend.'

107 Reynolds 'Letter' in William Gilpin, *Three Essays: On Picturesque Beauty: On Picturesque Travel: And on Sketching Landscape: To Which Is Added a Poem on Landscape Painting* (London: R. Blamire, 1792), 35–6.

108 Kant, *Critique of Judgement*, 92.

109 Wolfgang Herrmann, *The Theory of Claude Perrault*, Studies in Architecture; V, 12 (London: A. Zwemmer, 1973); Claude Perrault, *Ordonnance for the Five Kinds of Columns after the Method of the Ancients*, (Santa Monica, California: Getty Center for the History of Art and The Humanities, 1993); Joseph Rykwert, *The First Moderns: The Architects of the Eighteenth Century* (Cambridge, Massachussetts: MIT Press, 1980).

110 Walter John Hipple, *The Beautiful, the Sublime and the Picturesque in Eighteenth-Century British Aesthetic Theory* (Carbondale: Southern Illinois University Press, 1957), 204.

111 Price, *Essays on the Picturesque*, I, 207. 'Great wits are sure to madness near allied/ And thin partitions do their bounds divide.' John Dryden and Nahum Tate, *Absalom and Achitophel, 1681 the Second Part of Absalom and Achitophel, 1682*, Scolar Press Facsimile (Menston, England: Scolar Press, 1970), pt.1, 1.

112 Price, *Essays on the Picturesque*, I, 204, 207.
113 Ibid., 206–7. The picturesque woman, if not a gypsy, might well be French, representing an equally risky liaison in Price's time. She attracts the phrases 'une phsionomie de fantaise, and the well known expression of un certain je ne sais quoi; it is also common to say of a woman – que sans être belle elle piquante – a word, by the bye, that in many points answers very exactly to the picturesque.' Price, *Essays on the Picturesque*, I, 73.
114 Price, *Essays on the Picturesque*, I, 71 and 203–4.
115 Edmund Burke, *A Philosophical Enquiry into the Origins of Our Ideas of the Sublime and the Beautiful* (Oxford and New York: Oxford University Press, 1990), 39.
116 Price, *Essays on the Picturesque*, I, 189.
117 Virgil and R. D. Williams, *The Aeneid* (Basingstoke: Macmillan, 1972), 111, 658.
118 Georges Bataille, 'Formless', in *Visions of Excess: Selected Writings, 1927–1939*, ed. Allan Stoekl (Minneapolis: University of Minnesota Press, 1985), 31.
119 Price, *Essays on the Picturesque*, I, 189, 203.
120 Price, *Essays on the Picturesque*, III, 278.
121 Price, *Essays on the Picturesque*, I, 195–6.
122 A quarry from which the stone for housing has been cut, being ornamented as a thing of value rather than as a cost, has become well known as a motif of the picturesque, through Hussey's description of such a situation at Scotney Castle, Kent. Christopher Edward Clive Hussey, *The Picturesque: Studies in a Point of View* (London: Cass, 1967), 2–4. Scotney Castle was designed by Edward Hussey, Anthony Salvin and William Sawrey Gilpin, from 1835. Another excellent example is Belsay Castle, Northumberland, Charles Monck, begun 1807.
123 Michael Fried, 'Art and Objecthood', *Art Forum* 5, no. 10 (1967).
124 Michael Fried, *Art and Objecthood: Essays and Reviews* (Chicago: University of Chicago Press, 1998), 42.
125 Toni Ross, '"Art and Objecthood" Three Decades On', *Australian and New Zealand Journal of Art* 1, no. 1 (2000).
126 For a survey of the idea of monstrosity, which belongs to an older discourse than that of the aesthetic of disgust, Mark Dorrian, 'On the Monstrous and the Grotesque', *Word and Image* 16, no. 3 (2000).
127 Adorno writes of what he calls 'happenings' and the hybridization of the arts as an attempt by art to absorb its own negation. He thinks that by 'conspicuously and wilfully ceding to crude material' art's tactic is to sink to a level below 'living consciousness [. . .] a stratum of mute reference to what is beautiful'. Theodor Wiesengrund Adorno, Rolf Tiedeman and Gretel Adorno, *Aesthetic Theory*, trans. Robert Hullot-Kentor, vol. 88, *Theory and History of Literature* (London: The Athlone Press, 1997), 258.
128 Ibid., 259.
129 Ibid., 3.
130 Ibid., 258–9. See Lambert Zuidervaart's discussion of Adorno's concept of 'mana'. Lambert Zuidervaart, *Adorno's Aesthetic Theory: The Redemption of Illusion* (Cambridge, Massachusetts: MIT Press, 1991), 110.
131 Robert Smithson and Nancy Holt, *The Writings of Robert Smithson: Essays with Illustrations* (New York: New York University Press, 1979), 52–7. There is much more than I presently have space to discuss in the relation of the picturesque, minimalism and architecture. Much of the relation of the latter two, and indeed the concept of objecthood in architecture has been studied by Mark Linder – Mark Linder, *Nothing Less Than Literal: Architecture after Minimalism* (Cambridge, Massachusetts: MIT Press, 2004). And a little by myself in John Macarthur, 'The Look of the Object: Minimalism in Art and Architecture, Then and Now', *Architecture Theory Review* 7, no. 1 (2002).
132 Lucy R. Lippard, *Six Years: The Dematerialization of the Art Object from 1966 to 1972: A Cross-Reference Book of Information on Some Esthetic Boundaries* (London: Studio Vista, 1973).
133 Walter Benjamin, 'The Work of Art in the Age of Its Mechanical Reproduction', in *Illuminations*, ed. H. Arendt (New York: Schocken Books, 1968).
134 Repton, 'A Letter to Uvedale Price Esq.' in Price, *Essays on the Picturesque*, III, 20.
135 Ruskin, *The Works of John Ruskin*, VI, 19–20.
136 The scene Ruskin describes is very like the Samuel Prout print of Amiens published in 'Notes on Prout and Hunt'. Ruskin, *The Works of John Ruskin*, XIV, facing 392. Ruskin's family had collected Prout and John Ruskin had followed his work from childhood, believing Prout's importance lay in his bringing picturesque principles to urban scenes.
137 Ruskin, *The Works of John Ruskin*, VI, 20.
138 Ibid., 18–19.
139 Ibid.
140 Price, *Essays on the Picturesque*, II, 321–2. The other artists mentioned are most likely Ruysdael and Hobbema.
141 According to Charles Crammer. Charles A. Crammer, 'Alexander Cozens's New Method: The Blot and General Nature', *The Art Bulletin* 79, no. 1 (1997).
142 Ruskin, *The Works of John Ruskin*, XXII, Appendix 1, 493–507.
143 Ibid., 494.
144 Elizabeth Helsinger argues that Ruskin begins with beauty (and truth) as the only aesthetic category and has picturesqueness and the sublime

as merely issues of points of view. She thinks that he then changes his mind and comes to admit the sublime as a separate category through the work on the 'noble picturesque' and the grotesque. Elizabeth K. Helsinger, *Ruskin and the Art of the Beholder* (Cambridge, Massachusetts: Harvard University Press, 1982).

145 'The Lamp of Memory' in Ruskin, *The Works of John Ruskin*, VIII, 221–47.

146 Ruskin, *The Works of John Ruskin*, VI, 16.

147 Ibid.

148 Ruskin, *The Works of John Ruskin*, V, 205–6.

149 In the 'Lamp of Memory' the discussion of the lower picturesque attention to detail is very close to Price and Reynolds in that the problem with the architectural picturesque is compared with the problem of those sculptors who too accurately depict hair. Price makes the same complaint of Denner, a painter who he says errs by too accurate an attempt at detail. Price, *Essays on the Picturesque*, III, 317.

150 Again this is a fundamental picturesque theme recalling Repton's insistence on the necessity of ornamental dwellings to anchor the look in the scenic view. See for instance his discussion of the role of a decorative Woodsman's cottage in his design for Blaise Castle Estate. Repton, *Landscape Gardening*, 264–7.

151 Ruskin, *The Works of John Ruskin*, VIII, 223.

152 Ruskin, *The Works of John Ruskin*, VI, 21.

153 Ibid., 11.

154 Ibid.

155 Ibid., 14–15.

156 'Of Vulgarity', in Ruskin, *The Works of John Ruskin*, VII, 343–62.

157 Ibid., 347–8.

158 Ruskin's ignoble picturesque is clearly an avatar of his ignoble grotesque. While the Gothic is nobly grotesque through forcefulness, the grotesque Renaissance of Venice is sickly and sickening. Mark Dorrian describes the action of a metaphor of breath, which links the divine and the monstrous – 'the play of the sublime image of divine truth upon the agitated surface of the fallen soul that gives rise to the grotesque.' Mark Dorrian, 'The Breath on the Mirror: On Ruskin's Theory of the Grotesque', Chora: Intervals in the *Philosophy of Architecture* 4 (2004).

159 Ruskin, *The Works of John Ruskin*, VIII, 313.

160 Ruskin, *The Works of John Ruskin*, I, 17.

161 Ibid., 28.

162 Karen Burns, 'Topographies of Tourism: "Documentary" Photography and the Stones of Venice', *Assemblage: Critical Journal of Architecture and Design Culture* 32 (1997); Lindsay Smith, *Victorian Photography, Painting and Poetry: The Enigma of Visibility in Ruskin, Morris and the Pre-Raphaelites*, Cambridge Studies in Nineteenth-Century Literature and Culture (Cambridge: Cambridge University Press, 1995).

163 Menninghaus, *Disgust*, 127.

164 It is in a similar context that Menninghaus introduces Karl Rosenkranz *Ästhetik des Häßlichen (Aesthetics of the Ugly)* of 1853. Ibid., 126–7.

165 This definition of romanticism follows that of Walter Benjamin in Walter Benjamin, *The Origin of German Tragic Drama* (London: New Left Books, 1977).

166 Ruskin, *The Works of John Ruskin*, IV, 380.

167 Ruskin, *The Works of John Ruskin*, X, 193.

168 Ibid., 191.

169 Ibid., 190.

170 George Edmund Street, *Brick and Marble in the Middle Ages: Notes of a Tour in the North of Italy* (London: J. Murray, 1855).

171 Robert Kerr, *The English Gentleman's House: Or, How to Plan English Residences, from the Parsonage to the Palace; with Tables of Accommodation and Cost, and a Series of Selected Plans* (London: John Murray, 1864), 383–5.

172 Ibid., note, 383.

173 Both these quotes and much of my background to this section I take from Elaine Harwood, 'Butterfield and Brutalism', *AA Files*, no. 26 (1994).

174 Republished as John Summerson, 'William Butterfield: Or, the Glory of Ugliness', in *Heavenly Mansions: And Other Essays on Architecture* (London: Cresset, 1949). The Brutalist reception of this essay is described in Harwood, 'Butterfield and Brutalism.'

175 Summerson, 'William Butterfield', 167.

176 Ibid., 166.

177 The Editor, 'Exterior Furnishing or Sharawaggi: The Art of Making Urban Landscape', *The Architectural Review* 95 (1944), 6.

178 D. Whewell in David Cooper, ed., *A Companion to Aesthetics*, Blackwell Companions to Philosophy (Oxford: Blackwell, 1992), 417.

179 See Ivor de Wolfe, 'Townscape: A Plea for an English Visual Philosophy Founded on the True Rock of Sir Uvedale Price', *The Architectural Review* 106 (1949); Editor, 'Exterior Furnishing'; Nikolaus Pevsner, 'Price on Picturesque Planning', *The Architectural Review* 95 (1944); Nikolaus Pevsner, 'The Genesis of the Picturesque', *The Architectural Review* 96 (1944); Nikolaus Pevsner, 'The Picturesque in Architecture', *RIBA Journal* 55 (1947).

180 Peter Reyner Banham, 'The New Brutalism', *Architecture Review*, no. 118 (1955), 13.

181 Ibid., 15.

182 J. Dubuffet quoted in Germain Viatte, 'Primitivism and Art Brut', in *Aftermath: France 1945–54: New Images of Man*, ed. Germain Viatte, Association francaise d'action artistique, and Barbican Art Gallery (London: Trefoil Books, 1982), 74.

183 Gilles Deleuze, *Cinema 2: The Time Image*, trans. H. Tomlinson and R. Galeta (London: Athlone, 1989), 3.

4 Irregularity

1 Anon, 'A Programme for the City of London', *The Architectural Review* 97, no. 582, June (1945); Nikolaus Pevsner, 'Visual Planning and the City of London', *The Architectural Association Journal* LXI, no. 699 (1945); Nikolaus Pevsner, 'Visual Planning and the City of London', *The Architects' Journal* 102, no. 2655 (1945).

2 Yve-Alain Bois, 'A Picturesque Stroll around Clara-Clara', in *October: The First Decade*, ed. A. Michelson et al. (MIT Press, 1987); Peter Collins, *Changing Ideals in Modern Architecture* (London: Faber and Faber, 1965); Richard A. Etlin, *Frank Lloyd Wright and Le Corbusier: The Romantic Legacy* (Manchester: Manchester University Press, 1994).

3 Leon Battista Alberti, *On the Art of Building*, trans. J. Rykwert, N. Leach and R. Tavernor (Cambridge and London: MIT Press, 1988).

4 Hubert Damisch, *The Origin of Perspective* (Cambridge and London: MIT Press, 1994).

5 Robin Evans, 'Figures, Doors, Passages', in *Translations from Drawing to Building* (Cambridge: MIT Press, 1997).

6 Bill Hillier and Julienne Hanson argue that such a logic where spatial depth is taken to be socially significant continues to be the case in the built environment of the present day. Bill Hillier and Julienne Hanson, *The Social Logic of Space* (Cambridge, New York, Sydney: Cambridge University Press, 1984).

7 Norbert Elias, *The Civilizing Process* (Oxford: Blackwell, 1978).

8 Robin Middleton, 'Introduction', in *The Genius of Architecture; or, the Analogy of That Art with Our Sensations*, ed. Nicholas Le Camus de Mézières (Santa Monica: The Getty Center, 1992), 45.

9 G. E. Fussell, *The English Rural Labourer: His Home, Furniture, Clothing, and Food from Tudor to Victorian Times* (London: The Batchworth Press, 1949); J. L. Hammond and Barbara Hammond, *The Village Labourer, 1760–1832: A Study in the Government of England before the Reform Bill* (London: Longmans, Green, 1911).

10 Tony Evans and Candida Lycett Green, *English Cottages* (London: Weidenfeld & Nicolson, 1982), 9.

11 Richard Reid, *The Shell Book of Cottages* (London: Michael Joseph, 1977), 11, 14.

12 Nathaniel Kent, *Hints to Gentlemen of Landed Property; to Which Are Now First Added, Supplementary Hints* (London: Longman and Rees, 1799), 207.

13 The Hammonds' figures are 74,518 acres enclosed from 1700–1760, 1,691,193 acres enclosed from 1761–1844. Something like 20 per cent of the total acreage of England was enclosed during the eighteenth and nineteenth centuries. Hammond and Hammond, *The Village Labourer*.

14 K. D. M. Snell makes a point of tracing the increasingly seasonal pattern of labour that accompanied improved agricultural method, showing that this relates directly to the fall off in female employment. K. D. M. Snell, *Annals of the Labouring Poor: Social Change and Agrarian England, 1660–1900* (Cambridge and New York: Cambridge University Press, 1985), ch. 1.

15 E. P. Thompson in *The Making of the English Working Class* analyses the major organized resistances to government for self-conscious political and class character. His assessment is that none of the groups were likely to be able to sustain a rebellion but that the Pitt's counter-revolution in fear of these eventualities, with acts against combination, and an increased oppression of the poor, eventually created the conditions under which a new class consciousness could emerge. Fear of the anger of the poor must have been sustained by widespread rioting which was undertaken as a redress of injustice, if without overt political programme, against bread prices and sometimes acts of enclosure. These protests have been collected and analysed by Andrew Charlesworth. Andrew Charlesworth, *An Atlas of Rural Protest in Britain 1548–1900* (London and Canberra: Croom Helm, 1983). An example is Otmoor, which was finally enclosed in 1823 despite great popular resistance from 1811 into the 1830s; see Hammond and Hammond, *The Village Labourer*.

16 Under an Act of Charles II of 1662. For a summary of the legislative history see Hammond and Hammond, *The Village Labourer*, 112.

17 According to the rather romantic account in Peter Laslett's *The World We Have Lost*; Further Explored, 3rd edn (London: Methuen, 1983).

18 In a letter to Samuel Whitbread, 1807, described in Hammond and Hammond, *The Village Labourer*, 181.

19 A point well made by G. E. Fussell, who takes this as the prior condition of the picturesque style of park. Fussell, *The English Rural Labourer*, 44.

20 Kent, *Hints to Gentlemen*, 282.

21 Board of Agriculture, *Communications to the Board of Agriculture; on Subjects Relative to the Husbandry and Internal Improvement of the Country*, vol. 1 (London: Geo. Nicol, 1797), 198–242.

22 Ibid.

23 See for instance: Thomas A. Markus and Honor Mulholland, *Order in Space and Society: Architectural Form and Its Context in the Scottish Enlightenment* (Edinburgh: Mainstream, 1982). and Nikolaus Pevsner, *A History of Building Types*, A. W. Mellon Lectures in the Fine Arts; 19 (London: Thames and Hudson, 1976).

24 Robin Evans, *The Fabrication of Virtue: English Prison Architecture, 1750–1840* (Cambridge and New York: Cambridge University Press, 1982); Michel Foucault, *Discipline and Punish: The Birth of the Prison* (Harmondsworth: Penguin, 1979).

25 Robert Kerr, 'On the Problem of Providing Dwellings for the Poor in Towns, Delivered before the Royal Institute of British Architects, on Monday, 3rd December, 1866', *Papers Read at the Royal Institute of British Architects* XVII (1866).
26 Robin Evans in 'Rookeries and Model Dwellings', describes the debate and the importance to the Victorians of the three-roomed plan with its separation and containment of the contagion of criminality and illicit sexuality. Robin Evans, 'Rookeries and Model Dwellings', *Architectural Association Quarterly* 10, no. 1 (1978).
27 Marcia Pointon, 'Gainsborough and the Landscape of Retirement', *Art History* 2, no. 4 (1979), 451.
28 John Barrell, *The Dark Side of the Landscape: The Rural Poor in English Painting, 1730–1840* (Cambridge: Cambridge University Press, 1980).
29 Uvedale Tomkyns Price 1685–1765. Uvedale's father Robert was also an accomplished amateur artist. The Prices collected Dutch landscape painting of the kind which inspired Gainsborough and which Uvedale refers to frequently in *Essays on the Picturesque*. See Stephen Daniels and Charles Watkins, *The Picturesque Landscape: Visions of Georgian Herefordshire* (Nottingham: Department of Geography, University of Nottingham, 1994), 40; Beryl Hartley, 'Naturalism and Sketching, Robert Price at Foxley and on Tour', in *The Picturesque Landscape: Visions of Georgian Herefordshire*, ed. Stephen Daniels and Charles Watkins (Nottingham: Department of Geography, University of Nottingham, 1994).
30 John Thomas Smith, *Remarks on Rural Scenery with Twenty Etchings of Cottages from Nature* (London: 1797), 7.
31 Ibid., 8–9.
32 Alberti, *Art of Building*.
33 Uvedale Price, *Essays on the Picturesque: As Compared with the Sublime and the Beautiful and, on the Use of Studying Pictures for the Purpose of Improving Real Landscape*, 3 vols (London: J. Mawman, 1810), I, 50–1.
34 Ibid., 51.
35 Ibid.
36 Ibid., I, 53.
37 Ibid., 70.
38 Ibid., 89.
39 Ibid.
40 Ibid., I, 73
41 Price, *Essays on the Picturesque*, II, 235, 301.
42 Andrew Ballantyne, *Architecture, Landscape, and Liberty: Richard Payne Knight and the Picturesque* (Cambridge and New York: Cambridge University Press, 1997), 16.
43 Richard Payne Knight, *The Landscape, a Didactic Poem, in Three Books. Addressed to Uvedale Price, Esq.*, first edn (London: printed by W. Bulmer and Co. and sold by G. Nicol, 1794); Uvedale Price, *Essay on the Picturesque*, first edn (Hereford: 1794).
44 Richard Payne Knight, *An Analytical Inquiry into the Principles of Taste*, 4th edn (London: T. Payne and J. White, 1808), 227; Price, *Essay on the Picturesque*, II, 202. Neither author mentions the irregularity of Vanbrugh Castle. Price notes the architect's admirable 'massiness', and Knight his siting of Blenheim and Castle Howard.
45 Kerry Downes, *Vanbrugh, Studies in Architecture*, vol. 16, Studies in Architecture (London: A. Zwemmer, 1977), 93–100.
46 At Edgehill Warwickshire, 1746–7. David Watkin thinks that this must be considered the 'parent' of Downton. David Watkin, *The English Vision: The Picturesque in Architecture, Landscape, and Garden Design* (London: John Murray, 1982), 51.
47 Sir Joshua Reynolds, *Discourses on Art*, ed. Robert R. Wark (New Haven and London: Published for the Paul Mellon Centre for Studies in British Art (London) Limited by Yale University Press, 1975), Discourse XIII, 244.
48 Ibid., XIII, 243.
49 Ballantyne, *Architecture, Landscape, and Liberty*, 260–8.
50 Knight, *Principles of Taste*, 164.
51 Ibid., 167.
52 Ibid., 164.
53 Ballantyne, *Architecture, Landscape, and Liberty*, 255.
54 Ibid., 164.
55 Ibid., 275.
56 Knight, *Principles of Taste*, 223.
57 Ibid., 225–6.
58 Price, *Essays on the Picturesque*, II, 268–9. Price carried out this idea when he commissioned a seaside house for himself at Aberystwyth from John Nash in 1797. He wrote of the commission in a letter to Sir George Beaumont (18 March 1798): 'he had a mind to build me a larger house indeed, but a square bit of architecture. I told him however, that I must have, not only some of the windows but some of the rooms turned to particular points . . .'. John Summerson, *The Life and Work of John Nash, Architect* (London: Allen & Unwin, 1980), 21. What Price neglects to mention is the house was not irregular, but triangular.
59 Repton, 'Red Book for Luscombe', 1799, quoted in Summerson, *John Nash*, 38.
60 Humphry Repton, *The Landscape Gardening and Landscape Architecture of the Late Humphry Repton Esq.*, ed. John Claudius Loudon (London: 1840), 500.
61 Ibid., 501–2.
62 Jill Franklin, *The Gentleman's Country House and Its Plan, 1835–1914* (London and Boston: Routledge & Kegan Paul, 1981).
63 In 1798 he began a 'castle' for himself at East Cowes on the Isle of Wight, which is similar to Luscombe.
64 Knight, *Principles of Taste*, 224–5.

65 Price, *Essays on the Picturesque*, I, 55.
66 Price, *Essays on the Picturesque*, III, 284–5.
67 Price himself was closely involved in the agricultural as well as the scenic improvement of his estate, Foxley in Herefordshire, to an extent that is surprising from the few rather nonchalant remarks about the improvement of villages in the *Essays on the Picturesque*. His improvements were based around a strategy drawn up for him by Nathaniel Kent in 1774 when Price was 24. Daniels and Watkins, *The Picturesque Landscape*.
68 Michael McMordie first pointed out the existence and significance of this corpus to me, and I thank him. An essential tool in researching these books is John Archer, *The Literature of British Domestic Architecture 1715–1842* (Cambridge, Massachussetts: MIT Press, 1989). This is a breathtakingly thorough bibliography and also provides an authorative synopsis and contextualization of the books. Archer lists 360 books, most of several editions, published on domestic architecture from 1715–1842. McMordie, who researched the books specifically dealing with the picturesque and hence mostly cottages, lists 94 between 1790 and 1835. Michael McMordie, 'Picturesque Pattern Books and Pre-Victorian Designers', *Architectural History, Journal of the Society of Architectural Historians of Great Britain*, no. 18 (1975); Michael McMordie, 'Pre-Victorian Origins of Modern Architectural Theory' (Doctoral Thesis, University of Edinburgh, 1972). I have examined about 120 of the books.
69 Paul Sandby (British, 1731–1809) named and popularized 'aquatint' in Britain.
70 J. Wyatt, H. Holland, G. Dance and S. P. Cockerell founded the Architectural Club in 1791. The most important organization before the Institute of British Architects was probably the Architectural Society founded in 1831, according to Barrington Kaye. Barrington Kaye, *The Development of the Architectural Profession in Britain: A Sociological Study* (London: G. Allen & Unwin, 1960).
71 John Plaw, *Sketches for Country Houses, Villas, and Rural Dwellings . . . Also Some Designs for Cottages* (London: J. Taylor, 1800), 4.
72 William Fuller Pocock, *Architectural Designs for Rustic Cottages, Picturesque Dwellings, Villas &C.* (London: 1807), 5–6.
73 James Malton, *An Essay on British Cottage Architecture: Being an Attempt to Perpetuate on Principle, That Peculiar Mode of Building Which Was Originally the Work of Chance* (London: 1798), 2.
74 Ibid., 4.
75 Ibid., 9, 4. This plea is undoubtedly intended to exercise the sentiments widely aroused by Oliver Goldsmith. Oliver Goldsmith, *The Deserted Village: A Poem* (London: W. Griffin and N. Douglas, 1770).
76 Malton, *British Cottage Architecture*, 5.
77 Ibid., 19.
78 Plaw, *Sketches for Country Houses*, 3. Plaw's earlier book is *Ferme Ornée; or Rural Improvements.*
79 Richard Elsam, *An Essay on Rural Architecture . . . Being an Attempt, Also, to Refute, by Analogy, . . . Mr James Malton's Essay, . . .* (London: Taylor's Architectural Library, 1803), 5.
80 Ibid., 6.
81 Ibid., 4.
82 Richard Elsam, *A Brief Treatise on Prisons* (London: J. Taylor, 1818). This was published two years after *Peasantry*. The discourse of separation that originates in Howard and the prisons of Wm. Blackburn is very evident in both works. John Howard built reformed cottages on his estate Cardington, Bedfordshire, after 1756, according to Joseph Burke, *English Art 1740–1800* (Oxford: Clarendon, 1976), 377.
83 Richard Elsam, *Hints for Improving the Condition of the Peasantry, . . . Designs for Cottages* (London: R. Ackerman [Gregg reprint 1971], 1816), 21, vii.
84 Ibid., 21.
85 Ibid., 25.
86 In this it is similar to a house by John Nash, Cronkhill, of 1802.
87 Joseph Michael Gandy, *Designs for Cottages, Cottage Farms, and Other Rural Buildings* (London: John Harding, 1805), iv.
88 Ibid., ix.
89 Being committed to regularity of building did not mean disavowal of the picturesque concept of landscape. Repton, in his first book, is clearly nervous about irregularity in building, at least partly because he proposed to reintroduce formal gardens between the house and the landscaped park. He quotes Lord Kames: 'Nature, indeed, in organized bodies comprehended under one view, studies regularity; which, for the same reason, ought to be studied in architecture; but in large objects, which cannot be surveyed but in parts, and by succession, regularity and uniformity would be useless properties, because they cannot be discovered by the eye. Nature, therefore, in her large works, neglects these properties; and, in copying nature, the artist ought to neglect them'. Lord Kames, *Elements of Criticism* in Repton, *Landscape Gardening*, 87.
90 D. Laing, *Hints for Dwellings: Consisting of Original Designs for Cottages, Farm-Houses, Villas, and Plain and Ornamental . . . Town Houses* (London: J. Taylor, [Gregg, repub. 1972], 1800), vi.
91 John Buonarotti Papworth, *Rural Residences, Consisting of a Series of Designs for Cottages, Decorated Cottages, Small Villas, and Other Ornamental Buildings* (London: 1818), 54.
92 Tony Bennett, *The Birth of the Museum: History, Theory, Politics* (London and New York: Routledge, 1995).

93 Robert G. Wetten, *Designs for Villas in the Italian Style of Architecture* (London: 1830). See also T. F. Hunt, *Architettura Campestre: Displayed in Lodges, Gardeners' Houses, and Other Buildings: In the Modern Italian Style.* (London: Longman, Rees, Orme, Brown and Green, 1827). Both are propositions for a modern Italian Style. Wetten, like Parker, emphasizes that he has considered expense and not included anything too magnificent, in case the use of a classically based style will deprive him of the villa license. It should. The highest class of villa resembles the Paris Opera, and even the medium-sized Design VI has caryatids.
94 Repton, *Landscape Gardening*, 455.
95 COMFORT 6.a. A state of physical and material well-being, with freedom from pain and trouble, and satisfaction of bodily needs; the condition of being comfortable (see COMFORTABLE 10). (OED Online.)
96 Pocock, *Architectural Designs for Rustic Cottages*, 8.
97 Malton's essay is based on his reading of Johann Georg Zimmermann, *Solitude Considered, with Respect to Its Influence Upon the Mind and Heart* (London: 1791).
98 James Malton, *A Collection of Designs for Rural Retreats, as Villas, Principally in the Gothic and Castle Styles of Architecture* (London: J. and T. Carpenter, 1802), vii, viii, ix.
99 Ian P. Watt, *The Rise of the Novel: Studies in Defoe, Richardson and Fielding* (Harmondsworth, Middlesex: Penguin Books, 1963).
100 John Buonarotti Papworth, *Hints on Ornamental Gardening . . . Designs for Garden Buildings* (London: R. Ackermann, 1823), 20.
101 R. Lugar, *Plans and Views of Buildings, Executed in England and Scotland in the Castellated and Other Styles* (London: J. Taylor, 1811; reprint, new extended edition of 1811 original), 11–12.
102 Repton, *Landscape Gardening*, 460–1.
103 Robin Evans, 'Developed Surface', in *Translations from Drawing to Building* (Cambridge: MIT Press, 1997).
104 Repton, *Landscape Gardening*, 513–19. One of Repton's 'Fragments', as he called his later essays, presents 'A ground plan, explained to a Lady' and this shows in plan an elaborated version of the ideal presented in the 'Modern Living Room'. The Plan that appears to be for a particular but unnamed house shows a suite of rooms wrapping an existing building. The old dining room gives out onto an enfilade of ten garden rooms which are: anteroom, breakfast room, tribune for books of prints, library or living room, tribune for music books, lobby to prevent damp, orangery, flower passage, conservatory and vinery, and aviary. Repton, *Landscape Gardening*, 513–19.
105 The OED (online) gives the first usage at 1825.
106 Evans, 'Developed Surface.'
107 Stephen Daniels has shown how much Repton's work was addressed to ladies and was part of a broader negotiation of polite behaviour between the sexes. Stephen Daniels, 'Gothic Gallantry: Humphry Repton, Lord Byron, and the Sexual Politics of Landscape Gardening', in *Bourgeois and Aristocratic Cultural Encounters in Garden Art, 1550–1850* (Washington: Dumbarton Oaks Research Library and Collection, 2002).
108 J. C. Loudon, *An Encyclopaedia of Cottage, Farm and Villa Architecture and Furniture* (London: Longman, Brown, Green, Longmans and Roberts, 1833), 2.
109 Ibid., 8.
110 Ibid., 1105.
111 Ibid., 8–20.
112 Ibid., 9. Loudon is very interested in water closets that were relatively novel in his time. He describes a mechanism which he claims to have seen in the British Museum for controlling the filling and emptying of the flushing cistern by attaching a string to the toilet door. He also seems quite convinced about the necessity for sexual differentiation with toilets, mentioning it again in Design XLI for 'Six cottages grouped together, with a view to economy in building them'. J. C. Loudon, *An Encyclopaedia of Gardening* (London: 1822), 147. 'Privy. In the yard there ought unquestionably be two privies, one for each sex; and these might, at very little expense be rendered water-closets.' Loudon, *An Encyclopaedia of Gardening*, 150.
113 Loudon, *Encyclopaedia of Cottage Architecture*, 1105.
114 Ibid., 1.
115 Malton, *British Cottage Architecture*, 27.
116 Robert Lugar, *Architectural Sketches for Cottages, Rural Dwellings, and Villas, in the Grecian . . . Etc* (London: T. Bensley and J. Taylor, 1805), 5.
117 Loudon, *Encyclopaedia of Cottage Architecture*, 1112–14.
118 Ibid., 1115.
119 Nigel Temple, *John Nash and the Village Picturesque* (Gloucester: Allen Sutton, 1979).
120 Repton, *Landscape Gardening*, 421–2. Humphry thought that his son suffered prejudice over his deafness. He studied Gothic architecture and produced a study of Tudor chimneys.
121 Stephen Daniels, *Humphry Repton: Landscape Gardening and the Geography of Georgian England* (New Haven: Yale University Press, 1999), 185–7.
122 Steven Brindle, 'Robinson, Peter Frederick (1776–1858)', in *Oxford Dictionary of National Biography*, edited by H. C. G. Matthew and Brian Harrison, Oxford University Press, http://80-www.oxforddnb.com.ezproxy.library.uq.edu.au/view/article/23862 (accessed January 26, 2005); M. H. Port, 'Goodwin, Francis (1784–1835),' in *Oxford Dictionary of National Biography*, edited by H. C. G. Matthew and Brian Harrison, Oxford University Press, http://80-www.oxforddnb.com.

ezproxy.library.uq.edu.au/view/article/10990 (accessed January 26, 2005).

123 Jill Allibone, *Anthony Salvin: Pioneer of the Gothic Revival* (Cambridge: Lutterworth Press, 1988), 29.

124 Elizabeth Manwaring, *Italian Landscape in Eighteenth Century England* (New York: Oxford University Press, 1925).

125 Lugar, *Architectural Sketches for Cottages*, Design XXVIII.

126 Papworth, *Rural Residences*, plate 17, 69–72.

127 For instance the Frank Thomas House, Oak Park Chicago, of 1901.

128 A similar interest in the vernacular simplified classical occurred in France and there are similarities between the stylistic interests of the British architects with Pierre-Charles-Joseph Normand's *Recueil Varié* of 1823, and François Léonard Seheult's *Maisons à Rome sur les Bords du Tibre (en haut) et près du Sainte-Marie du Trastévère* of 1811, the latter supposed to have been drawn from actual buildings as in Parker's book. The French architects are, however, rigourously symmetrical. Georges Gromort, *Small Structures: French Architecture of the Early Nineteenth Century* (New York: Van Nostrand Reinhold, 1986).

129 Summerson, *John Nash.*

130 Julien-David le Roy, *Les Ruines Des Plus Beaux Monuments De La Grèce* (Paris: 1758); James Stuart and Nicholas Revett, *The Antiquities of Athens* (London: Priestley & Weale, 1825 [first published 1762]).

131 Thomas Rickman, *An Attempt to Discriminate the Styles of English Architecture, from the Conquest to the Reformation* . . . (London: 1819).

132 William Chambers, *A Treatise on the Decorative Part of Civil Architecture . . . Fourth Edition, to Which Are Added Copious Notes, and an Essay on the Principles of Design in Architecture by John B. Papworth*, 4th edn (London: 1826).

133 Ibid., 42.

134 James Thomson, *Retreats: A Series of Designs, Consisting of Plans and Elevations for Cottages, Villas and Ornamental Buildings* (London: 1827), 14–15.

135 Alexander (Greek) Thomson, 1815–75. As far as I can see the two Thomsons are not related. Caledonia Road Church 1857, St Vincent St Church 1859.

136 Quoting A. W. N. Pugin from Benjamin Ferry, ed., *Recollections of A. Welby Pugin, and His Father, Augustus Pugin; with Notices of Their Works* (Edward Stanford, 1861). Also in Anon, 'Anthology: Pugin on the Picturesque', *The Architectural Review* 98, no. 586 (1945): lv.

137 Robert Kerr, *The English Gentleman's House: Or, How to Plan English Residences, from the Parsonage to the Palace; with Tables of Accommodation and Cost, and a Series of Selected Plans* (London: John Murray, 1864), 360.

138 Ibid., 371.

139 Ibid.

140 Ibid., 395.

141 Nikolaus Pevsner, 'The Picturesque in Architecture', *RIBA Journal* 55 (1947).

142 Nikolaus Pevsner, 'C 20 Picturesque', *The Architectural Review* 115, no. 688 (1954), 228–9.

143 'When a building, or other object, has been once viewed from its proper point, the foot should never travel to it by the same path which the eye has travelled over before. Lose the object, and draw nigh obliquely.' William Shenstone, 'Unconnected Thoughts on Gardening' in *The Works in Prose and Verse of William Shenstone Esq. In Two Volumes* (Edinburgh, 1764), 98.

144 Malton, *Designs for Rural Retreats*, 24.

145 Joseph Michael Gandy, *The Rural Architect; Consisting of Various Designs for Country Buildings, Accompanied with Ground Plans, Estimates and Descriptions* (London: John Harding, 1806), plate XXV, 'An Overseer's Cottage'.

146 Marc-Antoine Laugier, *An Essay on the Study and Practice of Architecture. Explaining the True Principles of the Science: Illustrated with Figures, Elegantly Engraved, . . . To Which Are Added, Directions for the Embellishment of Cities and the Laying out of Gardens* (London: Stanley Crowder and Henry Woodgate, 1756), 233–4.

147 David Watkin and Sir John Soane's Museum, *Sir John Soane: Enlightenment Thought and the Royal Academy Lectures*, Cambridge Studies in the History of Architecture (Cambridge and New York: Cambridge University Press, 1996), 366–7.

148 At Rushton in Northamptonshire. John Summerson, *Architecture in Britain: 1530 to 1830*, ed. Nikolaus Pevsner, The Pelican History of Art (London: Penguin, 1953), 41–2.

149 Malcolm Airs, 'Thorpe, John (1564/5–1655)', in *Oxford Dictionary of National Biography*, edited by H. C. G. Matthew and Brian Harrison, Oxford University Press, http://www.oxforddnb.com/view/article/27378 (accessed June 1, 2005). Jacques Androuet du Cerceau, *Livre d'architecture . . . contenant les plans & dessaings de cinquante bastimens tous differens*. . ., Paris, 1559.

150 Watkin and Museum, *Sir John Soane*, 335, plate 76.

151 Price in a letter to Sir George Beaumont, 18 March 1798, cited in Summerson, *John Nash*, 21.

152 D. Laing, *Plans, Elevations and Sections of Buildings Public and Private, Executed in Various Parts of England, &C. Including the New Custom-House, London* . . . (London: J. Taylor, 1818), plate 52.

153 The aesthetic valuation of the disgusting is the issue in my Chapter 3. But briefly here I could represent the link of the aesthetically valuable and the demanding with S. Alexander's typical statement of the issue: 'Some artists find their very triumphs in making the ugly or unattractive

aesthetically beautiful. Shakespeare's earlier manner, as in *A Midsummer Night's Dream*, delighted in easy beauty, and his later manner in the difficult beauty of many passages, say of Winter's Tale or Coriolanus.' Samuel Alexander, *Beauty and Other Forms of Value* (London: Macmillan, 1933), 164.

154 Charles Augustus Busby, *A Series of Designs for Villas and Country Houses. Adapted with Economy to the Comforts and Elegancies of Modern Life. With Plans and Explanations to Each* (London: 1808), 12–13.

155 Malton, *Designs for Rural Retreats*, plate 26.

156 The villa's sweeping concave sides suggest a comparison with a much better building that Malton may have known from prints. Carlo Borromini's church of S. Ivo della Sapienza is planned on intersecting equilateral triangles making up the figure of the Star of David.

157 Malton, *Designs for Rural Retreats*, 33.

158 Le Corbusier and Willy Boesiger, *Oeuvre Complete* (Zurich: Editions d'architecture Erlenbach, 1946), 60.

159 Le Corbusier, *Towards a New Architecture*, trans. Frederick Etchells (New York: Dover, 1931), 5.

160 Beatriz Colomina, *Privacy and Publicity: Modern Architecture as Mass Media* (Cambridge, Massachusetts and London: MIT Press, 1994), 312.

161 Walter Benjamin, 'Erfahrung Und Armut', in *Gesammelte Schriften* (Frankfurt: Suhrkamp Verlag, 1972); Walter Benjamin, 'On Some Motifs in Baudelaire', in *Illuminations*, ed. H. Arendt (New York: Schocken Books, 1968); Walter Benjamin, 'The Work of Art in the Age of Its Mechanical Reproduction', in *Illuminations*, ed. H. Arendt (New York: Schocken Books, 1968).

162 Le Corbusier, *Precisions: On the Present State of Architecture and City Planning, With . . . [Other Essays]* (Cambridge and London: MIT Press, 1991), 136.

163 Etlin, *Frank Lloyd Wright and Le Corbusier*. Etlin gives the picturesque the same role in the development of Frank Lloyd Wright, and this makes the concept so general as to weaken what he has to say about Le Corbusier.

164 John Pennethorne, *The Elements and Mathematical Principles of the Greek Architects and Artists, Recovered by an Analysis and Study of the Remaining Works of Architecture Designed and Erected in the Age of Pericles* (London: 1844).

165 Arthur Cates and Rev. Geoffrey Tyack, 'Pennethorne, John (1808–1888)', in *Oxford Dictionary of National Biography*, edited by H. C. G. Matthew and Brian Harrison, Oxford University Press, http://www.oxforddnb.com/view/article/21870 (accessed February 1, 2005).

166 Etlin, *Frank Lloyd Wright and Le Corbusier*.

167 H. Allen Brooks, *Le Corbusier's Formative Years: Charles-Edouard Jeanneret at La Chaux-De-Fonds* (Chicago and London: University of Chicago Press, 1997); Etlin, *Frank Lloyd Wright and Le Corbusier*, 106–12. Christof Schnoor has recently made a thorough study of the manuscript and determined Le Corbusier's sources to be: Paul Schultze-Naumburg, Kulturarbeiten. Band 4. Der Stadtebau, Munich: Callwey, 1906, 11; Theodor Fischer, Stadterweiterungsfragen, Stuttgart: DVA, 1903; Joseph August Lux, Der Stadtebau und die Grundpfeiler der heimischen Bauweise, Dresden: Kuhtmann, 1908; Albert Erich Brinckmann, Platz und Monument, Berlin: Wasmuth, 1908. Christoph Schnoor, 'La Construction Des Villes: Charles-Edouard Jeannerets Erstes Städtebauliches Traktat Von 1910/11' (Doctoral Thesis, Technischen Universität Berlin, 2003); Christoph Schnoor, 'Overcoming Limits: Le Corbusier's Early Treatise "La Construction Des Villes"' (paper presented at *Limits: Proceedings of the 21st Annual Conference of the Society of Architectural Historians, Australia and New Zealand*, Melbourne, 2004).

168 Schnoor, 'Overcoming Limits'.

169 Colin Rowe, 'The Mathematics of the Ideal Villa: Palladio and Le Corbusier Compared', *The Architectural Review* 101, no. 603 (1947).

170 Alan Colquhoun, *Essays in Architectural Criticism: Modern Architecture and Historical Change*, Oppositions Books (Cambridge, Massachusetts, and London: MIT Press, 1981); Alan Colquhoun, *Modernity and the Classical Tradition: Architectural Essays 1980–1987* (Cambridge, Massachusetts and London: MIT Press, 1989); Michael Dennis, *Court and Garden: From the French Hotel to the City of Modern Architecture* (Cambridge, Massachusetts and London: MIT Press, 1986).

171 Dennis, *Court and Garden*, 202.

172 Antony Moulis, 'Drawing Experience: Le Corbusier's Spiral Museum Projects' (Doctoral Thesis, The University of Queensland, 2002).

173 Michael Fried, 'Art and Objecthood', *Art Forum* 5, no. 10 (1967).

174 OED Online.

175 Richard Serra quoted in Bois, 'A Picturesque Stroll', 344.

176 Ibid., 349.

177 Ibid., 363.

178 Ibid., 368.

179 Mark Jarzombek provides a stiff critique of this slippage, which he finds first in early twentieth-century aesthetics and then repeated with deleterious effects in the American academies of architecture. Mark Jarzombek, 'De-Scribing the Language of Looking: Wölfflin and the History of Aesthetic Experientialism', *Assemblage*, no. 23 (1994); Mark Jarzombek, *The Psychologizing of Modernity: Art, Architecture, and History* (Cambridge: Cambridge University Press, 2000).

180 Bois, 'A Picturesque Stroll', 367.

181 Colin Rowe, 'The Mathematics of the Ideal Villa', in *The Mathematics of the Ideal Villa, and Other Essays* (Cambridge, Massachusetts: MIT Press, 1976), 4.

182 Bois, 'A Picturesque Stroll', 356.
183 Ibid.
184 Ibid., 370.
185 Ibid., 359.
186 Robert Morris, 'Notes on Sculpture', in *Minimal Art: A Critical Anthology*, ed. Gregory Battcock (New York: E. P. Dutton & Co., 1968), 228.
187 Rosalind Krauss, 'The Grid, the /Cloud/, and the Detail', in *The Presence of Mies*, ed. Detlef Mertins (New York: Princeton Architectural Press, 1994).
188 Hermann Muthesius and Stanford Anderson, *Style-Architecture and Building-Art: Transformations of Architecture in the Nineteenth Century and Its Present Condition* (Santa Monica, California: Getty Center for the History of Art and the Humanities; Distributed by the University of Chicago Press, 1994).

5 Appropriation

1 OED Online.
2 Humphry Repton, *The Landscape Gardening and Landscape Architecture of the Late Humphry Repton Esq.*, ed. John Claudius Loudon (London: 1840), 601.
3 Sir Henry Wotton, *The Elements of Architecture* (London: 1624), 4.
4 John Dixon Hunt, '"Lordship of the Feet": Towards a Poetics of Movement in the Garden', in *Landscape Design and the Experience of Motion*, ed. M. Conan, Dumbarton Oak Colloquium on the History of Landscape Architecture (Washington DC: Dumbarton Oaks Research Library and Collection, 2003).
5 William Shenstone, 'Unconnected Thoughts on Gardening' in *The Works in Prose and Verse of William Shenstone Esq. In Two Volumes* (Edinburgh, 1764), 94–110.
6 Thomas Whately, *Observations on Modern Gardening* (London: 1770), 1.
7 According to John Dixon Hunt, the text of Rousham is Edmund Spenser's *The Fairie Queene.* John Dixon Hunt, *Gardens and the Picturesque: Studies in the History of Landscape Architecture* (Cambridge, Massachusetts: MIT Press, 1992), 86. Hunt describes the emblematic garden as does Ronald Paulson. Ronald Paulson, *Emblem and Expression: Meaning in English Art of the Eighteenth Century* (London: Thames and Hudson, 1975).
8 Repton, *Landscape Gardening*, 533.
9 Wotton, *The Elements*, 4.
10 Repton, *Landscape Gardening*, 53.
11 Ibid., 97.
12 Ibid., 225.
13 Ibid., footnote, 226.
14 Ibid., 328.
15 Ibid., 39.
16 Ibid., 84.
17 Ibid., 225.
18 William Gilpin, *A Dialogue Upon the Gardens of the Right Honourable the Lord Viscount Cobham at Stowe in Buckinghamshire*, vol. 176 (Los Angeles: Augustan Reprint Society WA Clark Memorial Library, UCLA, 1748/1976), 45.
19 Ibid., 23.
20 Repton, *Landscape Gardening*, 602.
21 Ibid., 31.
22 Humphry Repton, *Fragments on the Theory and Practice of Landscape Gardening* (London: 1816), 568–70.
23 Ibid.
24 Repton, *Landscape Gardening*, 473–5. The example is Oulton, near Leeds, on the estate of John Blayds, Red Book 1810. The background landscape is that of Temple Newsam, landscaped by Brown.
25 Ibid.
26 Ibid., 602–4
27 Ibid., 603.
28 Ibid., 603–4.
29 Uvedale Price, *Essays on the Picturesque: As Compared with the Sublime and the Beautiful and, on the Use of Studying Pictures for the Purpose of Improving Real Landscape*, 3 vols (London: J. Mawman, 1810), II, 312.
30 Repton, *Landscape Gardening*, 603–4.
31 Ibid., 604.
32 OED Online.
33 Repton, *Landscape Gardening*, fig. 47, p. 151.
34 Whateley, *Observations on Modern Gardening*, 148.
35 John Barrell, 'The Public Prospect and the Private View: The Politics of Taste in Eighteenth Century Britain', in *Projecting the Landscape*, ed. J. C. Eade (Canberra: Humanties Research Centre, Australian National University, 1987).
36 Repton, *Landscape Gardening*, 194.
37 My thanks to Sir Joshua and Lady Rowley for showing me the Book and permitting me to quote from it. Humphry Repton, Tendring Hall (Suffolk) manuscript 1791 for Sir William Rowley, unpaginated, in the collection of Sir Joshua and Lady Rowley.
38 Soane published his design in *Plans, Elevations, and Sections of Buildings executed in the counties of Norfolk and Suffolk &c.* (plates xviii–xxi). The house has since been destroyed.
39 *Tendring Red Book*, unpaginated.
40 *Tendring Red Book*, unpaginated.
41 *Tendring Red Book*, unpaginated.
42 Nigel Temple, *John Nash and the Village Picturesque* (Gloucester: Allen Sutton, 1979).
43 Price, *Essays on the Picturesque*, III, 18–19.
44 Ibid., 128–34.
45 Ibid., 130.
46 Ibid., 132.
47 George Mason, *An Essay on Design in Gardening. First Published in mdcclxviii. Now Greatly Augmented. Also a Revisal of Several Later*

Publications on the Same Subject (London: 1795); Allen S. Weiss, *Mirrors of Infinity: The French Formal Garden and 17th-Century Metaphysics* (New York: Princeton Architectural Press, 1995), 15.

48 In this section I rely on the work of Louis Marin. Louis Marin, *Portrait of the King* (Minneapolis: University of Minnesota Press, 1988); Louis Marin, *Utopics: Spatial Play* (New Jersey: Macmillan Humanites, 1984).

49 Horatio Walpole, 'On Modern Gardening', in *Anecdotes of Painting* (London: 1762–4).

50 Stephen Copley and Peter Garside, eds, *The Politics of the Picturesque: Literature, Landscape and Aesthetics since 1770* (Cambridge: Cambridge University Press, 1994), 6.

51 W. J. Thomas Mitchell, 'Imperial Landscape', in *Landscape and Power* (Chicago: University of Chicago Press, 1994), 29.

52 David Hansen et al., *John Glover and the Colonial Picturesque* (Hobart, Tasmania: Tasmanian Museum and Art Gallery, Art Exhibitions Australia Limited, 2003).

53 Robert Dingley, 'Glover, John (1767–1849)', in *Oxford Dictionary of National Biography*, edited by H. C. G. Matthew and Brian Harrison, Oxford University Press, http://www.oxforddnb.com/view/article/10827 (accessed January 19, 2006); Simon Fenwick, 'Smith, John (1749–1831)', in *Oxford Dictionary of National Biography*, edited by H. C. G. Matthew and Brian Harrison, Oxford University Press, http://www.oxforddnb.com/view/article/25851 (accessed January 19, 2006).

54 This and the following sections owe much to the research of Mathew Aitchison who is writing his doctorate under my direction. Apart from unpicking the sequence of events I am grateful to Aitchison for his analysis and opinions about the historical interpretation which has assisted me here and in a paper which we wrote jointly. John Macarthur and Mathew Aitchison, 'Ivor De Wolfe's Picturesque, or, Who and What Was Townscape?' (paper presented at the *Limits: Proceedings of the 21st Annual Conference of the Society of Architectural Historians, Australia and New Zealand*, Melbourne, 2004). Aitchison has since broadened out and updated this research in Mathew Aitchison, 'Visual Planning and the Picturesque: Sir Nikolaus Pevsner and Townscape Revisited' (paper presented at the *Limits: Proceedings of the 21st Annual Conference of the Society of Architectural Historians, Australia and New Zealand*, Melbourne, 2004).

55 Nikolaus Pevsner, 'Conclusions', in *The Picturesque Garden and Its Influence Outside the British Isles*, ed. Nikolaus Pevsner (Washington DC: Dumbarton Oaks, Trustees for Harvard University, 1974).

56 The Pevsner manuscript is now held at the Getty Research Library along with his papers. Aitchison explains the extent of the manuscript and its relation to Townscape in Aitchison, 'Visual Planning'.

57 Nikolaus Pevsner, 'Heritage of Compromise: A Note on Sir Joshua Reynolds Who Died One Hundred and Fifty Years Ago', *The Architectural Review* 92 (1942); Nikolaus Pevsner, 'Price on Picturesque Planning', *The Architectural Review* 95 (1944); Nikolaus Pevsner, 'The Genesis of the Picturesque', *The Architectural Review* 96 (1944).

58 Pevsner MS transcribed by Aitchison, 'Visual Planning'.

59 Nikolaus Pevsner, *The Englishness of English Art: An Expanded and Annotated Version of the Reith Lectures Broadcast in October and November 1955* (Harmondsworth: Penguin Books, 1976), 163–80.

60 Nikolaus Pevsner, 'C 20 Picturesque', *The Architectural Review* 115, no. 688 (1954).

61 Peter Reyner Banham, 'The New Brutalism', *Architecture Review*, 118 (1955); Reyner Banham, 'Revenge of the Picturesque: English Architectural Polemics, 1945–1965', in *Concerning Architecture: Essays on Architectural Writers and Writing Presented to Nikolas Pevsner*, ed. John Summerson (London: Allen Lane, The Penguin Press, 1968).

62 David Watkin, *Morality and Architecture: The Development of a Theme in Architectural History and Theory from the Gothic Revival to the Modern Movement* (Oxford: Clarendon Press, 1977); David Watkin, 'Sir Nikolaus Pevsner: A Study In "Historicism"', *Apollo* 136, no. 367 (1992). Given Watkin's own expertise, it is strange that he ignores the picturesque aspects of Pevsner's work in the *AR*. He makes Pevsner into the kind of 'Bauhausian' against which the AR's Townscape was directed. This elision is strange considering Watkin wrote a book on the picturesque and is considered an expert in the field – as we point out, Pevsner is a key figure of his historiography.

63 The Editor, 'Exterior Furnishing or Sharawaggi: The Art of Making Urban Landscape', *The Architectural Review* 95 (1944): 6–7.

64 Ibid., 3.

65 Anon, *The Architectural Review.* 100, no. 599, April (1946): 275.

66 The Editor, 'Exterior Furnishing or Sharawaggi: The Art of Making Urban Landscape', *The Architectural Review* 95 (1944), 3.

67 Ibid., 6.

68 Ibid., 5.

69 For example: John Betjeman, 'The Seeing Eye or How to Like Everything', *The Architectural Review* 86 (1939).

70 Peter L. Laurence, 'Contradictions and Complexities: Jane Jacob's and Robert Venturi's Complexity Theories', *Journal of Architectural Education* 59, February (2006).

71 Gordon Cullen, 'Townscape Casebook', *The Architectural Review* 106 (1949).

72 The Editor, 'Exterior Furnishing or Sharawaggi:

The Art of Making Urban Landscape', *The Architectural Review*. 95 (1944).

73 Ibid., 5.

74 Ivor de Wolfe, 'Townscape: A Plea for an English Visual Philosophy Founded on the True Rock of Sir Uvedale Price', *The Architectural Review*. 106 (1949), 361.

75 The Editor and Gordon Cullen, 'Westminster Regained: Proposals for the Replanning of the Westminster Precinct.', *The Architectural Review*. 102, no. 611 (1947), 159–70.

76 Gordon Cullen, 'The Midlands Experiment', *Architecture Review*, no. 116 (1954).

77 Repton, *Landscape Gardening*.

78 Gordon Cullen, *Townscape* (London: Architectural Press, 1961), 196.

79 John Ruskin, *The Library Edition: The Works of John Ruskin*, ed. E. T. Cook and Alexander Wedderburn (London: George Allen, 1903–12), V, 205–6.

80 Heinrich Wölfflin, *Principles of Art History: The Problem of the Development of Style in Later Art*, trans. M. D. Hottinger (New York: Dover, 1950); Heinrick Wölfflin, *Classic Art: An Introduction to the Italian Renaissance* (London: Phaidon, 1952); Wilhelm Worringer, *Form in Gothic* (London: G. P. Putnam's Sons, 1927).

81 Mark Jarzombek, 'De-Scribing the Language of Looking: Wölfflin and the History of Aesthetic Experientialism', *Assemblage*, 23 (1994): 65.

82 Price, *Essays on the Picturesque*, II, 312. See discussion in Chapter 3.

83 Richard Payne Knight, *An Analytical Inquiry into the Principles of Taste*, 4th edn (London: T. Payne and J. White, 1808), 320. Hussey describes Richard Payne Knight's project thus: 'picturesque qualities, Knight maintained, were the abstract emotive qualities that alone had aesthetic value. All other kinds of beauty were associative – with sex, prosperity, wealth, content, and so on – and were non-aesthetic.' Christopher Edward Clive Hussey, *The Picturesque: Studies in a Point of View* (London: Cass, 1967), 17.

84 Pevsner first visited England to conduct research in 1930. He emigrated in 1933.

85 Brian Harrison, 'Pevsner, Sir Nikolaus Bernhard Leon (1902–1983)', in *Oxford Dictionary of National Biography*, edited by H. C. G. Matthew and Brian Harrison, Oxford University Press, http://www.oxforddnb.com/view/article/21870 (accessed February 1, 2005).

86 Gilly's essays and a catalogue of his library with an excellent account of his interest in the picturesque by Fritz Neumeyer are available as Friedrich Gilly, *Friedrich Gilly: Essays on Architecture, 1796–1799*, Texts and Documents (Santa Monica, California: Getty Center for the History of Art and the Humanities, Chicago, distributed by the University of Chicago Press, 1994).

87 Christian Cajus Lorenz Hirschfeld's *Theorie der Gartenkunst* (1779–1785) (reprinted Hildesheim: Olms Verlag, 2003).

88 Gilly, *Friedrich Gilly: Essays on Architecture, 1796–1799*. Footnote on page 143. Gilly writes with reference to the combination of formal elements in the English garden 'It is a true pleasure to hear what a young English author has to say of this study of grand effects in a work recently translated under the title *Über den guten Geschmack bei ländlichen Kunst- und Garten-Anlagen* (Leipzig, 1798).' This volume is a translation of Uvedale Price's first *Essay on the Picturesque* 1794 without the author being named. Thanks to Mathew Aitchison for making this connection.

89 Later Pückler-Muskau greatly popularized the landscaping style of Repton, whose son John Adey had had unsuccessful commissions in Germany in the 1820s. J. C. Loudon toured Germany three times. On the Reptons see Manfred Uhlitz, 'Humphry Repton's Einfluß Auf Dei Gartenkünstlerishen Ideen Des Fürsten Pücher-Muskau' (Freie University, 1988).

90 Nikolaus Pevsner, 'A Pioneer of Town-Planning (Book Review)', *The Architectural Review* 100, no. 600 (1946), 86; Rudolf Wittkower, 'Camillo Sitte's Art of Building Cities in an American Translation', *Town Planning Review* 19 (1946–7).

91 Pevsner, 'A Pioneer', 186.

92 Pevsner, *The Englishness*, plates.

93 Frederick Gibberd, *Town Design*, 2nd edn (London: Architectural Press, 1955).

94 Nikolaus Pevsner, *Europäische Architecture: Von Den Anfängen Bis Zur Gegenwart* (Munich: Prestel-Verlag, 1967).

95 Aitchison, 'Visual Planning'.

96 Editor, 'Exterior Furnishing', 8.

97 Ivor de Wolfe, 'Townscape: A Plea for an English Visual Philosophy Founded on the True Rock of Sir Uvedale Price', Ibid., 106 (1949): 860.

98 Nikolaus Pevsner, 'The Picturesque in Architecture', *RIBA Journal* 55 (1947).

99 Pevsner, 'C20 Picturesque.'

100 Ibid.: 228–9.

101 Pevsner, 'On Picturesque Planning'; Price, *Essays on the Picturesque*, II, 312, III, 284–5.

102 Pevsner, 'Picturesque in Architecture.'

103 Wim Denslagen, *Architectural Restoration in Western Europe: Controversy and Continuity* (Amsterdam: Architectura and Natura Press, 1994), 34–55.

104 George R. Collins and Christiane Crasemann Collins, *Camillo Sitte: The Birth of Modern City Planning, with a Translation of the 1889 Austrian Edition of His City Planning According to Artistic Principles* (New York: Rizzoli, 1986), 166.

105 John Piper, 'Pleasing Decay', *Architecture Review* (1947): 93.

106 Ibid.

107 George R. Collins and Christiane Crasemann Collins, *Camillo Sitte: The Birth of Modern City*

Planning, with a Translation of the 1889 Austrian Edition of His City Planning According to Artistic Principles (New York: Rizzoli, 1986), 246. This same section of Sitte is quoted as an anthologized document in The Editor, 'Anthology. Indoor-Outoor Living [Camillo Sitte: The Art of Building Cities. Chapter X. Modern Limitations on Art in City Planning. Reinhold, New York, 1945', *The Architectural Review* 111, no. 664, April (1952), 275.

108 Editor, 'Exterior Furnishing', 6.

109 The Editor, 'The First Half Century', *The Architectural Review* 101, no. 601 (1947): 31–2.

110 Editor, 'Exterior Furnishing', 5.

111 de Wolfe, 'Townscape', 362, 358.

112 Ibid., *The Architectural Review* 106 (1949): 358.

113 Ibid., 362.

114 Ibid., 361.

115 Ibid., 358.

116 Ibid., 362.

117 Ibid., 355–56.

118 Ibid., 362.

119 Ivor de Wofle, *Civilia: The End of Sub Urban Man: A Challenge to Semidetsia* (London: Architectural Press, 1971), 7.

120 Ibid., 30, 26.

121 Ibid., 21.

122 Ibid., 10.

123 Editor, 'Exterior Furnishing', 3.

124 de Wolfe, *Civilia*, 91.

125 Reyner Banham, 'De Wolfe the Author?' (Letter to the Editor), *The Architectural Review* (1975).

126 Mark Linder, *Nothing Less Than Literal: Architecture after Minimalism* (Cambridge, Massachusetts: MIT Press, 2004), 33.

127 Colin Rowe and Fred Koetter, 'Collage City', *The Architectural Review* 158, no. 952 (1975), 75.

128 Colin Rowe and Fred Koetter, *Collage City* (Cambridge, Massachusetts: MIT Press, 1978), 98.

129 Ibid., 122.

130 Ibid., 97.

131 Ibid., 36.

132 Ibid., 34.

133 Ibid., 90.

134 Jakobson uses this distinction to define the poetic function of language in Roman Jakobson, 'Linguistics and Poetics', in *Language in Literature* (Cambridge: The Belknap Press of Harvard University Press, 1987). He uses the same distinction to describe the literary tropes of metaphor and metonymy. See Roman Jakobson, 'Two Aspects of Language', in the same volume. Advocates for the adoption of a parallel distinction include Diana Agrest and Françoise Choay. Diana Agrest, 'Towards a Theory of Production of Sense in the Built Environment', in *On Streets*, ed. Stanford Anderson (Cambridge, Massachusetts: MIT Press, 1978); Françoise Choay, 'Semiology and Urbanism', in *Meaning in Architecture*, ed. Charles Jencks and George Baird (London: Barrie & Rockliff the Cresset Press, 1969). For the architectural semiotics of the time see *Meaning in Architecture* and especially the Choay essay: Choay, 'Semiology and Urbanism.' In 1971 Choay edited an issue of *l'Architecture d'Aujourd'hui* which included Françoise Choay, Roland Barthes and Michel Butor, 'Semiologie Et Urbanisme', *l'Architecture d'Aujourd'hui*, no. 153 December–January (1970–1).

135 William Ellis, 'Type and Context in Urbanism: Colin Rowe's Contextualism', *Oppositions* 18 (1979), 9.

136 Ibid., 7.

137 Rowe and Koetter, *Collage City*, 14.

138 Clement Greenberg, *Art and Culture: Critical Essays* (Boston: Beacon Press, 1961).

139 Yve-Alain Bois, Centre Georges Pompidou and Rosalind E. Krauss, eds, *Formless: A User's Guide* (New York: Zone Books, 1997), 97.

140 Ibid., 108.

141 Ibid., 90.

142 Yve-Alain Bois, 'A Picturesque Stroll around Clara-Clara', in *October: The First Decade*, ed. A. Michelson et al. (Cambridge, Massachusetts: MIT Press, 1987).

143 Leo Steinberg, *Other Criteria: Confrontations with Twentieth-Century Art* (New York: Oxford University Press, 1972).

144 Ibid., 88.

145 Ibid., 90.

146 Matisse as quoted by George Gerster in the best of the 'from the air' genre Georg Gerster, *Grand Design: The Earth from Above* (Los Angeles: Knapp Press, 1988). Gerster does not give, and I have been unable to find, a source for Matisse's remark.

147 Malevich and other painters' relation to aircraft and aerial views is discussed in Richard Wohl, *A Passion for Wings: Aviation and the Western Imagination 1908–1918* (New Haven and London: Yale University Press, 1994).

148 Anthony Vidler has also shown how Le Corbusier's use of the aerial photograph in arguments about the rationalization of cities fed a counter use by the Situationists, who thought aerial photographs provided evidence of the impure and unplanned city of events. Anthony Vidler, 'Photourbanism: Planning the City from above and Below', in *A Companion to the City*, ed. Gary Bridge and Sophie Watson (Oxford: Blackwell, 2000).

149 Captain Gordon H. G. Holt, 'Architecture and Aerial Photography', *Architecture Review* 45, January (1919), 4–9.

150 Ibid., 5.

151 Marin, *Portrait of the King*; Marin, *Utopics*.

152 Nadar was the pseudonym of Gaspard-Félix Tournachon, 1820–1910, who took out a patent on using aerial photography for map-making in 1855.

153 On the issue of this work in Steichen's oeuvre see Allan Sekula, 'The Instrumental Image: Steichen at War', *Art Forum* XIV, no. 4 (1975).
154 Rowe and Koetter, *Collage City*, 149.
155 Price, *Essays on the Picturesque*, II, 144.
156 See the ideas of Slavoj Zizek in his chapter 'The King is a Thing' in Slavoj Zizek, *For They Know Not What They Do: Enjoyment as a Political Factor*, 2nd edn (London and New York: Verso, 2002). These are in turn reflections on Hegel and on Ernst Hartwig Kantorowicz. See Ernst Hartwig Kantorowicz, *The King's Two Bodies: A Study of Mediaeval Political Theology* (Princeton, New Jersey: Princeton University Press, 1957).
157 Rem Koolhaas et al., 'Bigness, or the Problem of Large', in *Small, Medium, Large, Extra-Large* (Rotterdam: 010 Publishers, 1995).
158 Rem Koolhaas, 'Generic City', in *Small, Medium, Large, Extra-Large*, ed. Rem Koolhaas et al. (Rotterdam: 010 Publishers, 1995).
159 Ibid., 1250.
160 Kate Orff, 'Landscape', in *Great Leap Forward*, ed. Rem Koolhaas et al. (Koln and Cambridge, Massachusetts: Taschen and Harvard Design School, 2001), 390.
161 Ibid., note 67, p. 416.

6 Movement

1 Michel Conan, *Landscape Design and the Experience of Motion*, vol. 24, Dumbarton Oak Colloquium on the History of Landscape Architecture (Washington DC: Dumbarton Oaks Research Library and Collection, 2003), 12–13.
2 John Dixon Hunt, '"Lordship of the Feet": Towards a Poetics of Movement in the Garden', in *Landscape Design and the Experience of Motion*, ed. M. Conan, Dumbarton Oak Colloquium on the History of Landscape Architecture (Washington DC: Dumbarton Oaks Research Library and Collection, 2003).
3 Robert Adam and James Adam, *Works in Architecture of Robert and James Adam*, 3 vols (London: 1773–1882), I, 2. The passage on movement was first a part of an unpublished essay on architectural theory by James Adam drafted in November 1772, according to David Watkin. David Watkin and Sir John Soane's Museum, *Sir John Soane: Enlightenment Thought and the Royal Academy Lectures*, Cambridge Studies in the History of Architecture (Cambridge and New York: Cambridge University Press, 1996), 28.
4 A. A. Tait, 'Adam, Robert (1728–1792).' In *Oxford Dictionary of National Biography: From the earliest times to the year 2000*, edited by H. C. G. Matthew and Brian Howard, Oxford University Press (accessed February 1, 2005).
5 Sandby, Lecture 6, cited in Watkin and Museum, *Sir John Soane*, 50.
6 Caroline van Eck, *Organicism in Nineteenth Century Architecture: An Enquiry into Its Theoretical and Philosophical Background* (Amsterdam: Architectura & Natura, 1994), 80.
7 Sir Joshua Reynolds, *Discourses on Art*, ed. Robert R. Wark (New Haven and London: Published for the Paul Mellon Centre for Studies in British Art (London) Limited by Yale University Press, 1975), XIII, 243.
8 Ibid., 244.
9 Ibid., 241.
10 Uvedale Price, *Essays on the Picturesque: As Compared with the Sublime and the Beautiful and, on the Use of Studying Pictures for the Purpose of Improving Real Landscape*, 3 vols (London: J. Mawman, 1810), II, 292.
11 Ibid., 212–13.
12 Ibid., 227.
13 Ibid., 301.
14 Ibid., 235.
15 Ibid., 123.
16 Ibid., 298.
17 Joshua Reynolds and Harry Mount, *A Journey to Flanders and Holland (Art, Patrons, and Public)* (Cambridge and New York: Cambridge University Press, 1996), 60.
18 Price, *Essays on the Picturesque*, II, 298.
19 William Hogarth and Ronald Paulson, *The Analysis of Beauty* (New Haven, Connecticut: Published for the Paul Mellon Centre for Britsh Art by Yale University Press, 1997), 29.
20 Ibid., lii.
21 David Bindman, 'Hogarth (1697–1764)', in *Oxford Dictionary of National Biography: From the Earliest Times to the Year 2000*, ed. H. C. G. Matthew and Brian Howard (Oxford: Oxford University Press, 2004).
22 Price, *Essays on the Picturesque*, II, 234.
23 Walter John Hipple, *The Beautiful, the Sublime and the Picturesque in Eighteenth-Century British Aesthetic Theory* (Carbondale: Southern Illinois University Press, 1957), 261; Richard Payne Knight, *An Analytical Inquiry into the Principles of Taste*, 4th edn (London: T. Payne and J. White, 1808), 150.
24 Heinrich Wölfflin, *Renaissance and Baroque*, trans. Kathrin Simon (Ithaca, New York: Cornell University Press, 1966), 38.
25 Ibid., 29.
26 Price, *Essays on the Picturesque*, I, 51.
27 Wölfflin, *Renaissance and Baroque*, 32.
28 Ibid., 44.
29 Price, *Essays on the Picturesque*, II, 204–5.
30 Ibid., 205.
31 Wölfflin, *Renaissance and Baroque*, 46.
32 Ibid., 58.
33 An excellent discussion of this body of thought and Wölfflin's place in it is the Introduction to Harry Francis Mallgrave and Eleftherios Ikonomou, *Empathy, Form and Space: Problems in German*

Aesthetics 1873–1893 (Santa Monica: Getty Center for the Arts and Humanities, 1994).
34 Anon and Uvedale Price, *Über Den Guten Geschmack Bei Ländlichen Kunst- Und Garten-Anlagen* (Leipzig: 1798).
35 1754 published by Christian Friedrich Voss. Discussed by Ronald Paulson in Hogarth and Paulson, *Analysis of Beauty*, xlv.
36 Joan Goldhammer Hart, 'Heinrich Wölfflin: An Intellectual Biography' (PhD, University of California Berkeley, 1981), 342.
37 Heinrich Wölfflin, *Principles of Art History: The Problem of the Development of Style in Later Art*, trans. M. D. Hottinger (New York: Dover, 1950), 26.
38 Heinrich Wölfflin, *Kunstgeschichtliche Grundbegriffe: Das Problem Der Stilentwickelung in Der Neueren Kunst* (Basel: Schwabe & Co., 1963), 41.
39 The distinction between 'picturesque' and 'painterly' does lead to some odd sentences in the translation of *Principles*, which is what led me to compare editions. Lacking German myself I was grateful for the assistance of Mark Jarzombek and Mathew Aitchison.
40 Herbert Read, 'Introduction', in *Classic Art: An Introduction to the Italian Renaissance*, ed. Heinrich Wölfflin (London: Phaidon, 1952), vi.
41 OED quoting *Times Literary Supplement* 16th June 441/1, 1932.
42 Hart, 'Heinrich Wölfflin', 154–62.
43 Ibid., 158.
44 Wölfflin, *Principles of Art History*, 26–7. The 'picturesque' which vanishes is '*pittorescke*' whereas the previous words are '*malerisch*'.
45 Wölfflin, *Kunstgeschichtliche Grundbegriffe: Das Problem Der Stilentwickelung in Der Neueren Kunst*, 42. The difference in this case seems to be that '*pittorescke*' is preferred for the description of genre subjects.
46 Price, *Essays on the Picturesque*, III, 238–9.
47 Wölfflin, *Principles of Art History*, 26.
48 Wölfflin, *Kunstgeschichtliche Grundbegriffe: Das Problem Der Stilentwickelung in Der Neueren Kunst*, 39–43; Wölfflin, *Principles of Art History*, 23–7.
49 Here and on the next page, he clearly means people moving in the scene and not the moving observer.
50 Wölfflin, *Principles of Art History*, 23–4.
51 Immanuel Kant, *Kant's Critique of Aesthetic Judgement*, trans. James Creed Meredith (Oxford: Clarendon Press, 1911), 41.
52 Wölfflin, *Principles of Art History*, 25.
53 Price, *Essays on the Picturesque*, II, 277.
54 Scott only refers to Wölfflin once in the body text. Geoffrey Scott, *The Architecture of Humanism: A Study in the History of Taste*, 2nd edn (London: Constable, 1924), 225.
55 Richard M. Dunn, 'Scott, Geoffrey (1884–1929)', in *Oxford Dictionary of National Biography*, edited by H.C.G. Matthew and Brian Harrison, Oxford University Press, http://www.oxforddnb.com/view/article/21870 (accessed January 25, 2006).
56 Scott, *Architecture of Humanism*, 227.
57 Ibid., 82. This idea is supported by Ernst Gombrich and Thomas Puttfarken as discussed in Chapter 2. E. H. Gombrich, 'The Renaissance Theory of Art and the Rise of Landscape', in *Norm and Form* (London: Phaidon, 1966); Thomas Puttfarken, *The Discovery of Pictorial Composition: Theories of Visual Order in Painting 1400–1800* (New Haven, Connecticut and London: Yale University Press, 2000).
58 Scott, *Architecture of Humanism*, 85–6.
59 Ibid., 81.
60 Schmarsow quoted in Mallgrave and Ikonomou, *Empathy, Form and Space*, 64.
61 Schmarsow quoted in ibid., 291.
62 Sigfried Giedion, *Space, Time and Architecture: The Growth of a New Tradition* (Cambridge, Massachusetts: Harvard University Press, 1967), 118–19.
63 Ibid., 529.
64 Paul Frankl, *Principles of Architectural History: The Four Phases of Architectural Style, 1420–1900*, trans. James F. O'Gorman (Cambridge, Massachusetts: MIT Press, 1968). (Paul Frankl, *Entwichlungsphasen de neueren Baukunst*, Leipzig, 1914.)
65 Mallgrave and Ikonomou, *Empathy, Form and Space*, 64.
66 Walter Benjamin, 'The Work of Art in the Age of Its Mechanical Reproduction', in *Illuminations*, ed. H. Arendt (New York: Schocken Books, 1968).
67 Tom Gunning, 'The Cinema of Attraction: Early Film, Its Spectator and the Avant-Garde', *Wide Angle*, no. 8 (1986).
68 www.billviola.com
69 Mallgrave and Ikonomou, *Empathy, Form and Space*, passim.
70 Heinrich Wölfflin, 'Prolegomena to a Psychology of Architecture', in *Empathy, Form and Space: Problems in German Aesthetics 1873–1893*, ed. Harry Francis Mallgrave and Eleftherios Ikonomou (Santa Monica: Getty Center for the Arts and Humanities, 1994), 159.
71 Mallgrave and Ikonomou, *Empathy, Form and Space*, 43.
72 Ibid.
73 Wölfflin, 'Pyschology of Architecture', 169.
74 Reynolds, *Discourses on Art*, 7.
75 Ibid., 241.
76 Ibid., 238.
77 Ibid., 240.
78 That Benjamin was there I have learned from Thomas Levin. Thomas Y. Levin, 'Walter Benjamin and the Theory of Art History: An Introduction To "Rigorous Study of Art History"', *October*, no. 47 (1988). Martin Warnke

tells us that Wölfflin lectured from the final text in Berlin in December. Benjamin wrote from Munich to Fritz Radt of his impressions of Wölfflin in November and December of that year. Martin Warnke, 'On Heinrich Wölfflin', *Representations* 27 (1989).

79 Walter Benjamin 'To Herbert Belmore', August 12, 1912, in Walter Benjamin, Gershom Scholem and Theodor Wiesengrund Adorno, *The Correspondence of Walter Benjamin, 1910–1940* (Chicago: University of Chicago Press, 1994).

80 According to John McCole, *Walter Benjamin and the Antimonies of Tradition* (Ithaca and London: Cornell University Press, 1993). See also Levin, 'Walter Benjamin and the Theory of Art History.'

81 Walter Benjamin, letters to Fritz Radt dated 'Munich, Nov. 21, 1915' and 'Munich, Dec. 4, 1915', cited in Levin, 'Walter Benjamin and the Theory of Art History', 79. Cited in full by Gershom Scholem, 'Walter Benjamin Und Felix Noeggerath', in *Walter Benjamin Und Sein Engel*, ed. Gershom Scholem (Frankfurt: M. Suhrkamp, 1983).

82 Benjamin quoted in Levin, 'Walter Benjamin and the Theory of Art History', 79.

83 Benjamin, 'The Work of Art', 216.

84 Ibid., 217.

85 Ibid.

86 Wölfflin, *Principles of Art History*, 21.

87 Price, *Essays on the Picturesque*, I, 71. This paragraph carries an illustrative footnote which is the anecdote of the wrinkly ancient lady which I quote in 'Disgust'.

88 Walter Benjamin, 'Curriculum Vitae III', in *Selected Writings*, ed. Michael W. Jennings and Marcus Paul Bullock (Cambridge, Massachusetts: Belknap Press, 1996); Walter Benjamin, 'On Language as Such and the Language of Man', in *Selected Writings*, ed. Michael W. Jennings and Marcus Paul Bullock (Cambridge, Massachusetts: Belknap Press, 1996).

89 Something of this shift in method, together with a more balanced account of Wölfflin can be found in the later essay 'The Rigorous Study of Art History'. Walter Benjamin, 'The Rigorous Study of Art History', in *Selected Writings*, ed. Michael W. Jennings and Marcus Paul Bullock (Cambridge, Massachusetts: Belknap Press, 1996).

90 Benjamin, 'The Work of Art', 240.

91 Benjamin, 'Vigorous Study.'

92 Ibid., 670.

93 Chapter 2 pp. 25–7.

94 Wölfflin, *Principles of Art History*, 21.

95 Walter Benjamin, 'On the Mimetic Faculty', in *Reflections: Essays, Aphorisms, Autobiographical Writings* (New York: Harcourt Brace Jovanovich, 1978), 333.

96 Theodor Wiesengrund Adorno, Rolf Tiedeman and Gretel Adorno, *Aesthetic Theory*, trans. Robert Hullot-Kentor, vol. 88, Theory and History of Literature (London: The Athlone Press, 1997). This paragraph also draws on Shierry Weber Nicholsen, *Exact Imagination, Late Work: On Adorno's Aesthetics* (Cambridge, Massachusetts: MIT Press, 1997).

97 Henri Bergson, *Matter and Memory* (New York: Zone Books, 1991), 55–6. Here I also draw on Gilles Deleuze's discussion in Gilles Deleuze, *Cinema I: The Movement Image*, trans. H. Tomlinson and B. Habberjam (London: Athlone Press, 1986), 87–9.

98 Deleuze, *Cinema I*, 87–8.

99 Bergson, *Matter and Memory*, 197–8.

100 Ibid., 218.

101 Hogarth and Paulson, *Analysis of Beauty*, 104.

102 Ibid., 104–5.

103 Samuel Weber, *Theatricality as Medium* (New York: Fordham University Press, 2004). My original idea for this chapter came as I was reading Wölfflin while attending seminars by Professor Weber at the Queensland University of Technology in May 1997. Professor Weber was kind enough to discuss my ill-formed ideas with me and I am grateful for his advice.

104 Walter Benjamin, 'What Is Epic Theatre?', in *Illuminations* (New York: Harcourt, Brace and World, 1955), 147.

105 Weber, *Theatricality as Medium*, 44.

106 Ibid., 46.

107 Modified translation of Benjamin's 'What is Epic Theatre?' in ibid.

Index

Page numbers in *italics* denotes illustration